Save the World on Your Own Time

Save the World
ON YOUR OWN TIME

Stanley Fish

OXFORD
UNIVERSITY PRESS

2008

OXFORD

UNIVERSITY PRESS

Oxford University Press, Inc., publishes works that further
Oxford University's objective of excellence
in research, scholarship, and education.

Oxford New York
Auckland Cape Town Dar es Salaam Hong Kong Karachi
Kuala Lumpur Madrid Melbourne Mexico City Nairobi
New Delhi Shanghai Taipei Toronto

With offices in
Argentina Austria Brazil Chile Czech Republic France Greece
Guatemala Hungary Italy Japan Poland Portugal Singapore
South Korea Switzerland Thailand Turkey Ukraine Vietnam

Published by Oxford University Press, Inc.
198 Madison Avenue, New York, New York 10016

www.oup.com

Oxford is a registered trademark of Oxford University Press

Previous versions of certain portions of this book appeared in
different form in *Change, Harper's Magazine*, the *Chicago Tribune*,
the *Chronicle of Higher Education*, and the *New York Times*.

Library of Congress Cataloging-in-Publication Data
Fish, Stanley Eugene.
Save the world on your own time / Stanley Fish.
p. cm.
Includes bibliographical references and index.
ISBN 978-0-19-536902-1
1. College teachers—United States—Political activity.
2. Education, Higher—Aims and objectives—United States.
3. Education, Higher—Political aspects—United States.   I. Title.
LB2331.72.F57 2008
378.1'2—dc22   2008008146

1 3 5 7 9 8 6 4 2

Printed in the United States of America
on acid-free paper

To the memory of my mother,
Ida Fish

Acknowledgments

My greatest debt is to Cybele Tom of Oxford University Press, who received a medley of disparate essays—some too long, some too short, all too repetitive—and in a remarkably short time transformed an unformed mass into something that actually had a shape. The work of revising and refining that shape took a bit more time, but it would not have been possible were it not for Cybele's initial creative act. I am grateful to my agent Melissa Flashman for finding Cybele and for believing in a project that others sometimes doubted. Without the help of Mary Olszewska, who organized my life and kept track of all its loose ends, none of this would have been put together in the first place. These three did the work so that I could get the credit. Thank you.

Contents

Save the World on Your Own Time

Introduction

Not long ago, there was a time when I was responsible for a college with close to 30 departments and units, a budget of between 50 and 55 million dollars, 400 tenure-track faculty members, 700 staff, 10,000 undergraduate students, 2,000 graduate students, and 17 buildings. On any given day, I had to deal with disciplinary proceedings, tenure and promotion cases, faculty searches, chair searches, enrollment problems, fundraising, community outreach, alumni relations, public relations, curriculum reform, counteroffers, technology failures, space allocation, information systems, chair meetings, advisory committee meetings, deans council meetings, meetings with the provost, student complaints, faculty complaints, parent complaints, and taxpayer complaints. Office hours were 8:30 a.m. to whenever and often extended into the evenings and weekends. Vacations were few and far between. The pressure never relaxed.

When I left the job after slightly more than five years, I felt that I had all the time (well, not quite all) in the world at my disposal, and for a while, spent it by trying to improve everyone I met, whether or not those I ministered to welcomed my efforts.

I took my opportunities wherever I found them. While I still lived in Chicago, but after I stepped down as dean, the building next door to mine was bought by a developer. For a long time, no development occurred, and the lawn and bushes were allowed to grow wild. The developer, however, had made the mistake of putting his telephone number on an overlarge sign, and as a reward he received a series of dyspeptic phone calls from me accusing him of being a bad neighbor, an irresponsible landlord, and an all-around no-goodnik.

During the same period, I would go into a store or stand in a ticket line and was often greeted by someone who asked, "And how are you today, young man?" That is my least-favorite salutation, and I quickly delivered a lecture and, I trust, a bit of improvement: "When you call someone who is obviously not young 'young man,' what you are doing is calling attention to his age and making him feel even older than he is; don't do it again!"

I delivered an even longer lecture to the blameless fast-food workers who routinely handed me a bagel along with a small container of cream cheese and a plastic knife that couldn't cut butter. I said, "Look, if I wanted to put my own bagel together, I would have bought the ingredients and taken them home; when I go to a restaurant I expect service; I don't expect to be asked to do your job; and besides there's not enough cream cheese here to cover the bagel's surface; what's the matter with you guys?"

But those were just my weekend activities. Although I was no longer a dean, I couldn't shake the habit of being at the office every day, all day. Because I had nothing particular to do, I roamed the halls looking for things that were wrong, and I found them.

Stray pieces of furniture you couldn't give away sat (or sprawled) in front of an office door. I stuck my head in and informed the occupant (why did he or she listen to me?) that the offending items must be removed by the end of the day.

Continuing down the halls, I found the panels separating two elevators festooned with announcements of lectures that took place two years ago. I proceeded to rip the leaflets down. Halfway through I decided that no one should be posting anything there anyway; so I removed every announcement, no matter how current, and, for good measure, I tore away the surface the announcements adhered to and threw all the thumbtacks and push-pins into the trash.

I noticed that someone had left a small carton of books, intended no doubt for impecunious graduate students who might have made good use of them. I didn't care; into the trash they went, too.

Next, I went into the new cafe in the main administration building and saw that the rug on the floor was full of crumbs and looked as if it hadn't been vacuumed in days. No one knew whose job it was, and I took it as my job to find out. I returned to my office and made phone calls until I found someone who answered her phone, although in a short time she wished she hadn't.

But then it was time to go to class (I was still teaching), where, in an enclosed space, my students received the full force of my reforming zeal. I told them that I hadn't the slightest interest in whatever opinions they might have and didn't want to hear any. I told them that while they may have been taught that the purpose of writing is to express oneself, the selves they had were not worth expressing, and that it would be good if they actually learned something. I told them that on the basis of their performance so far they should sue their previous teachers for malpractice. I told them that anyone who says "I know it, but I can't explain it" would flunk the course.

After an hour and a half they escaped, except for one of them, who came to my office for further instruction. Although it was the end of the third week, she was still not quite sure about the structure of the basic English sentence. (This, of course, was a reflection on me, not her.) I took her through the subject and predicate slots and she seemed to understand who or what an actor is and the relationship of the actor to the action performed, but she couldn't quite get the concept of the object of the action.

We were working with a sentence she had composed, "I threw the book into the garbage." I asked her, "In that sentence what is the relationship between 'threw' and 'book'?" She didn't know. I tried again: "What is the impact on the object of the action?" She didn't understand the question.

I decided that an illustration might do the trick; so I picked up a book on my desk and threw it. It hit a shelf of books a few feet away. She said nothing for a few seconds and then asked in a voice calmer than mine would have been, "Can I drop this course?" "Yes," I answered (hoping to escape prosecution), and she left—the one person in the entire week who managed to get away.

—⁂—

What is this all about? I wondered. What's driving me to do these things? I got part of the answer by looking up obsessive-compulsive disorder on the Internet and running down the list of symptoms. (Checking to see whether you have OCD is a form of OCD.) I found the following matches: fear of dirt; a need to have things just so; preoccupation with rules and schedules; rigidity; inflexibility; concern with order and symmetry; and saving containers when they are no longer needed. A perfect score.

And then it occurred to me that those are the very characteristics that make a dean effective: an obsessive need "to have things just so," a need to have things that are not right, put right.

What could I do aside from harassing perfectly innocent people who would have had every right to have me committed? Write this book was the answer. Although I was no longer in charge of a liberal arts college, I could satisfy my need to put the world in order by telling anyone who would listen how it should be done.

The first job, I decided, was to define the task. No serious reflection about an activity can get off the ground until the activity is characterized in a way that distinguishes it from all other activities. It is only when you know what the job is that you can know if you are really doing it, rather than doing some other job you were neither trained nor paid for.

It is when academics either don't know or have forgotten exactly what it is they are supposed to do that trouble begins, and criticisms of the academic enterprise multiply. These days, everyone, whether speaking from the left or the right, says the same thing—colleges and universities are in a sorry state, and ideology is the problem. One group finds ideology in the efforts of activists like David Horowitz, who wishes to monitor and alter the political make-up of the faculty, especially in the humanities and social sciences; while the other group finds ideology in the inability or unwillingness (these are two different arguments) of liberal faculty members to refrain from imposing their political views on students.

There's a lot of huffing and puffing on either side, and while I'm not writing to say, "a plague on both your houses," I am writing with the intention of carefully parsing the terms central to the controversy. Not because I hope to solve problems, but because I hope to dis-solve them, to suggest

that the problems pretty much go away when you understand
and act on a simple imperative—do your job—which comes
along with two corollary imperatives—don't do somebody
else's job and don't let someone else do your job.

So let us begin with a simple question. What exactly is
the job of higher education and what is it that those who
teach in colleges and universities are trained and paid to do?
The two parts of the question have an obvious logical relationship: before you can speak sensibly about the scope and
limits of a task, you have to know exactly what it is, what
distinguishes it from other tasks. I put it that way because it
is part of my argument that the coherence of tasks depends
on their being distinctive. Think of it in consumer terms;
you need something to be done, and you look in a phone
book or search the Internet until you come upon a description of services that matches your need. What you want is a
specialist, someone with the right training and credentials,
and you might be suspicious if someone told you that he or
she could do just about anything. To be sure, there are jacks
of all trades, people who claim that they can do just about
anything, and while that claim may prove out occasionally,
more often than not you will feel most comfortable when
you find a person or a company with a skill set that is reassuringly narrow: "this is what we do; we don't do those
other things; but if this particular thing is what you want
done, we're the people to turn to."

This narrow sense of vocation is shunned by many teaching in the academy today, and it was not popular in the
1960s when I was a young faculty member at the University
of California at Berkeley. In the wake of the Free Speech
Movement a faculty union had been formed and I had
declined to join it. Some members of the steering committee asked me why, and I asked them to tell me about
the union's agenda. They answered that the union would

(1) work to change America's foreign policy by fighting militarism, (2) demand that automobiles be banned from the campus and that parking structures be torn down, and (3) speak out strongly in favor of student rights. In response I said (1) that if I were interested in influencing government policy I would vote for certain candidates and contribute to their campaigns, (2) that I loved automobiles and wanted even more places to park mine, and (3) that I didn't see the point of paying dues to an organization dedicated to the interests of a group of which I was not a member. How about improvements in faculty salaries, better funding for the library, and a reduction in teaching load?

You, sir, I was admonished, do not belong in a university.

No, they didn't know what a university is and a lot of people still don't.

ONE

The Task of Higher Education

Pick up the mission statement of almost any college or
university, and you will find claims and ambitions that
will lead you to think that it is the job of an institution of
higher learning to cure every ill the world has ever known:
not only illiteracy and cultural ignorance, which are at least
in the ball-park, but poverty, war, racism, gender bias, bad
character, discrimination, intolerance, environmental pollution, rampant capitalism, American imperialism, and the
hegemony of Wal-Mart; and of course the list could be
much longer.

Wesleyan University starts well by pledging to "culti-
vate a campus environment where students think critically, participate in constructive dialogue and engage in
meaningful contemplation" (although I'm not sure what
meaningful contemplation is); but then we read of the
intention to "foster awareness, respect, and appreciation
for a diversity of experiences, interests, beliefs and identities." Awareness is okay; it's important to know what's
out there. But why should students be taught to "respect"

a diversity of interests, beliefs, and identities in advance of assessing them and taking their measure? The missing word here is "evaluate." That's what intellectual work is all about, the evaluation, not the celebration, of interests, beliefs, and identities; after all, interests can be base, beliefs can be wrong, and identities are often irrelevant to an inquiry.

Yale College's statement also starts well by promising to seek students "of all backgrounds" and "to educate them through mental discipline," but then mental discipline turns out to be instrumental to something even more valuable, the development of students'"moral, civic and creative capacities to the fullest." I'm all for moral, civic, and creative capacities, but I'm not sure that there is much I or anyone else could do as a teacher to develop them. Moral capacities (or their absence) have no relationship whatsoever to the reading of novels, or the running of statistical programs, or the execution of laboratory procedures, all of which can produce certain skills, but not moral states. Civic capacities—which mean, I suppose, the capacities that go along with responsible citizenship—won't be acquired simply because you have learned about the basic structures of American government or read the Federalist Papers (both good things to do). You could ace all your political science and public policy courses and still drop out and go live in the woods or become the Unabomber. And as for creative capacities, there are courses in creative writing in liberal arts colleges, and colleges of fine arts offer instruction in painting, sculpture, pottery, photography, drafting, and the playing of a variety of musical instruments. But even when such courses are housed in liberal arts venues, they belong more to the world of professional instruction—if you want to make something, here's how to do it—than to the world of academic interrogation. The discipline of Art History belongs to that world;

creating art does not. (I know this sounds circular—courses in creativity don't fit my definition of academic, so I deny them the label, but bear with me.)

Michigan State's statement promises everything. The university, it announces, will produce "an effective and productive citizen" who "contributes to society intellectually, through analytical abilities and in the insightful use of knowledge; socially, through an understanding and appreciation of the world and for individual group beliefs and traditions; ethically, through sensitivity and faithfulness to examined values; and politically through the use of reason in affairs of state." Aside from its ungrammaticalness ("understanding...for" is not an English construction), this ambitious mouthful confuses a hoped-for effect—graduates who perform admirably as citizens—with what can actually be taught. Analytical abilities can be taught as can knowledge, but "insightful use" is a matter of character, and character cannot be taught, at least not by Ph.D.'s in English or Chemistry. I don't know what "an appreciation of the world" means, and "individual group beliefs and traditions" is a pathetic and incoherent attempt to sit on the fence of at least three issues. As for examining values, that *is* a proper task for the academy, but ensuring "faithfulness" to values is not. How could such fidelity be measured, and who would be qualified to measure it? And one hopes of course that those charged with the management of our political destiny employ "reason" when conducting affairs of state, but whether they do won't depend on their having taken courses in symbolic logic.

So what is it that institutions of higher learning are supposed to do? My answer is simple. College and university teachers can (legitimately) do two things: (1) introduce students to bodies of knowledge and traditions of inquiry that had not previously been part of their experience; and

(2) equip those same students with the analytical skills—of argument, statistical modeling, laboratory procedure—that will enable them to move confidently within those traditions and to engage in independent research after a course is over. If you think about it, that's a lot to ask. It's at least a full-time job and it wouldn't seem to leave much room for taking on a bunch of other jobs.

I'm not saying that there is no connection at all between the successful practice of ethical, social, and political virtues and the courses of instruction listed in the college catalogue; it's always possible that something you come across or something a teacher says may strike a cord that sets you on a life path you might not otherwise have chosen. But these are contingent effects, and as contingent effects they cannot be designed and shouldn't be aimed at. (It's not a good use of your time to aim at results you have only a random chance of producing.)

What can be designed are courses that introduce students to a demarcated field, reading lists that reflect the current state of disciplinary knowledge, exams or experiments that test the ability of students to extend what they have studied to novel fact situations, and in-class exercises that provoke students to construct and solve problems on their own. The designing of these (and related) structures and devices makes sense in the context of an aim that is specific to the pedagogical task—the aim of passing on knowledge and conferring skills.

Anyone who asks for more has enlisted in the "we-are-going-to-save-the world" army along with Derek Bok, the former president of Harvard and the author of *Our Underachieving Colleges.* Here is a partial list of the things Bok believes colleges and universities should be trying to achieve: "help develop such virtues as racial tolerance, honesty and social responsibility"; "prepare...students to be active, knowledgeable citizens in a democracy"; "nurture...good moral character." He notes that "college catalogues regularly announce an intention to go beyond intellectual pursuits to nurture such behavioral traits," but laments that some professors (I am one he cites) believe that the only proper ends of the university are those that involve " 'the mastery of intellectual and scholarly skills.' "

My response is that the limited, focused nature of this latter aim—it has one target, not many or all—is what makes it at least potentially achievable. Teachers can, by virtue of their training and expertise, present complex materials in ways that make them accessible to novices. Teachers can also put students in possession of the analytical tools employed by up-to-date researchers in the field. But teachers cannot, except for a serendipity that by definition cannot be counted on, fashion moral character, or inculcate respect for others, or produce citizens of a certain temper. Or, rather, they cannot do these things unless they abandon the responsibilities that belong to them by contract in order to take up responsibilities that belong properly to others. But if they do that, they will be practicing without a license and in all likelihood doing a bad job at a job they shouldn't be doing at all. When that happens—and unfortunately it does happen—everyone loses. The students lose because they're not getting what they paid for (it will be said that they are getting more, but in fact they are getting less). The university loses because its resources have been appropriated for a nonacademic purpose. Higher education loses, because it is precisely when teachers offer themselves as moralists, therapists, political counselors, and agents of global change rather than as pedagogues that those who are on the lookout for ways to discredit higher education (often as a preliminary to taking it over) see their chance.

Does this mean that questions of value and discussion of current issues must be banished from the classroom? Not at all. No question, issue, or topic is off limits to classroom discussion so long as it is the object of academic rather than political or ideological attention. To many this will seem a difficult, if not impossible, distinction, but in fact, as I will argue in the following chapters, it is an easy one.

I should acknowledge up front that mine is a minority view and that any number of objections to it have appeared in the literature. There is the objection that what I urge is out of step both with history and with the best of current thinking. My argument, says Mark D. Gearen, president of Hobart and William Smith Colleges, "belies a rich history and deep tradition of civic responsibility within American Higher Education," a tradition, he adds, that is "articulated nearly universally in the mission statements of colleges and universities across the country" (Letter to the *New York Times*, May 24, 2004). In support of his position, President Gearen cites the 900 college and university executive officers who say, collectively, that "higher education has an unprecedented opportunity to influence the democratic knowledge, dispositions, and habits of the heart that graduates carry with them into the public sphere" ("Presidents' Declaration on the Civic Responsibility of Higher Education"). Nine hundred to one seems pretty conclusive, even if you add to my side worthies like Aristotle, Kant, Cardinal Newman, Max Weber, Learned Hand, Harry Kalven, John Hope Franklin, and Jacques Derrida. But we're not taking votes here; the merits or defects of my thesis should themselves be established by academic means, that is, by argument, and it is my argument—presented in the chapters of this book—that I am right and the nine hundred are wrong.

Chapter 2, "Do Your Job," lays out the general thesis: the academy's dignity and integrity depend on its being able to identify the task it properly performs. Thus my three-part mantra: do your job, don't try to do someone else's job, and don't let anyone else do your job.

Chapter 3, "Administrative Interlude," discusses the job of administrators separately because the work of administrators is often underappreciated and scorned. It is crucial that administrators understand what their role is in higher education, and I would argue, it is equally important that faculty understand what administrators make possible for them.

Chapter 4, "Don't Try to Do Someone Else's Job," insists that academics resist the temptation to take on extra-academic tasks, no matter how noble they may be. I'll clarify the doctrines of academic freedom and free speech, which are often understood (wrongly) to require (or allow) professors to step across the line I wish to draw between academic activity and partisan political activity. My deflationary definition of academic freedom is narrowly professional rather than philosophical, and its narrowness, I contend, enables it to provide clear answers to questions (about Holocaust Denial, Intelligent Design, polemical classroom rants) blurred by more ambitious definitions.

Chapter 5, "Don't Let Anyone Else Do Your Job," responds to the neoconservative attack on the academy and especially to the charge that left-leaning teachers are corrupting our youth by preaching relativism, atheism, and a disdain for truth. Neoconservatives want an academy where their politics are given a proportional representation (they call it balance or intellectual diversity) in the selection of texts and faculty members. I want an academy inflected by no one's politics, but by the nitty-gritty obligations of teaching and research.

Chapter 6 talks about the dangerous attempts by the government to withdraw funds from public education and exert more control over what it is no longer paying for. Chapter 7 revisits the basic issues.

The topics considered and arguments waged in these chapters vary, but everything follows from the wish to define academic work precisely and narrowly in opposition to those who would expand it to include everything under the sun and a few things above it. I take my text from a provost at the University of Wisconsin, Madison, who, in response to students demanding that the university declare a position on the then impending invasion of Iraq, said, "The University of Wisconsin does not have a foreign policy." Nor, I would add, does it have a domestic policy, or an environmental policy, or an economic policy, or any policy except an educational policy. The dangers inherent in a more expansive notion of what colleges and universities should be doing were dramatically illustrated in April 2006 when a major association of British higher education professors voted to boycott Israeli universities and refuse to do business with Israeli academics until they publicly disavowed the policies and practices of their government. The surrender of the academic enterprise to political considerations could not be more blatant. It might be thought that the practices I inveigh against in the following pages—announcing one's political allegiances in class, poking fun at the administration in power, railing against capitalism, giving the writing course over to discussions of various forms of discrimination—are, at least in comparison, less toxic and therefore less culpable. But as far as I am concerned they are the fruit of the same poisoned tree.

TWO

Do Your Job

So back to the basic question. What exactly is the job of someone who teaches in a college or a university? My answer is simple and follows from legal theorist Ernest Weinrib's account of what is required if an activity is to have its own proper shape. It must present itself "as a *this* and not a *that.*"

A THIS...

As I have already said, the job of someone who teaches in a college or a university is to (1) introduce students to bodies of knowledge and traditions of inquiry they didn't know much about before; and (2) equip those same students with the analytical skills that will enable them to move confidently within those traditions and to engage in independent research should they choose to do so.

Job performance should be assessed on the basis of academic virtue, not virtue in general. Teachers should show up for their classes, prepare lesson plans, teach what has been advertised, be current in the literature of the field, promptly correct assignments and papers, hold regular office hours, and give academic (not political or moral) advice. Researchers should not falsify their credentials, or make things up, or fudge the evidence, or ignore data that tells against their preferred conclusions. Those who publish should acknowledge predecessors and contributors, provide citations to their sources, and strive always to give an accurate account of the materials they present.

That's it, there's nothing else, and nothing more. But this is no small list of professional obligations, and faculty members who are faithful to its imperatives will have little time to look around for causes and agendas to champion.

...AND NOT A THAT

A faculty committee report submitted long ago to the president of the University of Chicago declares that the university exists "only for the limited...purposes of teaching and research" and reasons that "since the university is a community only for those limited and distinctive purposes, it is a community which cannot take collective action on the issues of the day without endangering the conditions for its existence and effectiveness" (Kalven Committee Report on the University's Role in Political and Social Action, November 11, 1967). Of course it can and should take collective (and individual) action on those issues relevant to the educational mission—the integrity of scholarship, the evil of plagiarism, and the value of a liberal education. Indeed failure to pronounce early and often on these matters would constitute a dereliction of duty. But neither the university as a collective nor its faculty as individuals should advocate personal, political, moral, or any other kind of views except academic views.

My point is not that academics should refrain from being political in an absolute sense—that is impossible—but that they should engage in the politics appropriate to the enterprise they signed onto. That means arguing about (and voting on) things like curriculum, department leadership, the direction of research, the content and manner of teaching—everything that is relevant to the responsibilities we take on when we accept a paycheck.

The distinction I am insisting on—between what a university properly stands for and what is, at most, tangential to its core activities—can be illustrated by the debate about free speech zones on campuses. Some activists on both the left and the right protest such zones and argue that the entire university should be a free speech zone, one large Hyde Park corner, for after all isn't the university primarily a place for the unfettered expression of ideas? The answer is no. The university is primarily a place for teaching and research. The unfettered expression of ideas is a cornerstone of liberal democracy; it is a prime political value. It is not, however, an academic value, and if we come to regard it as our primary responsibility, we will default on the responsibilities assigned us and come to be what no one pays us to be—political agents engaged in political advocacy.

The only advocacy that should go on in the classroom is the advocacy of what James Murphy has identified as the intellectual virtues, "thoroughness, perseverance, intellectual honesty," all components of the cardinal academic virtue of being "conscientious in the pursuit of truth" ("Good Students and Good Citizens," *New York Times*, September 15, 2002). A recent Harris Poll revealed that in the public's eye teachers are the professionals most likely to tell the truth; and this means, I think, that telling the truth is what the public expects us to be doing. If you're not in the pursuit-of-truth business, you should not be in the university.

I have been accused (by educational philosophers Elizabeth Kiss and Peter Euben) of ignoring "the vast and varied terrain of general undergraduate education, professional and vocational education, residential life, and extracurricular activity on America's college and university campuses." Yes, I ignore these activities, and the reason I do is captured in the word "extracurricular," that is, to the side of the curriculum. The core of a college or university experience should be the academic study of the questions posed by the various disciplines, but that core is surrounded by offices of housing, transportation, recreation, financial aid, advising, counseling, student services, and much more. Even though these activities support and in some instances make possible what goes on in the classroom and the laboratory, they are not academic. Therefore those who engage in them, either on the student side or the staff side, should not receive academic credit for doing so. I have no objection to internship programs, community outreach, peer tutoring, service learning, etc., as long as they are not thought of as satisfying graduation or grade requirements.

The exceptions one might think of do not weaken my point, but make it clearer: a student who returns from an internship experience and writes an academic paper (as opposed to a day-by-day journal or a "what-I-did-on-my-summer-vacation" essay) analyzing and generalizing on her experience, should get credit for it; and a student in a school of education who teaches in an inner city school under faculty supervision should certainly get credit for that; it is part of her academic training.

But what about professional schools and professional training? Kiss and Euben observe correctly that the "core mission" of professional education, as it is usually understood, inescapably involves influencing "students' behavior beyond [the] classroom" by putting them in possession of

skills they are expected to apply directly in a specific line
of work. If this is, in fact, what transpires in a particular
professional school—if students are taught methods and
techniques in the absence of any inquiry into their sources,
validity, and philosophical underpinnings—that professional
school is not the location of any intellectual activity and is
"academic" only in the sense that it is physically housed in
a university.

The question "is it academic or is it job training?" is endlessly debated in the world of law schools, where there is an
inverse relationship between hands-on training (of the kind
apprentices used to receive before there were law schools)
and prestige. The more highly ranked the law school, the
less its students will be put in touch with the nitty-gritty
of actual practice and the more versed they will be in the
arcana of interpretive theory, moral philosophy, Coasean
economics, and even literary criticism. It is commonplace
for graduates of top-ten law schools to report that the law
school experience left them unprepared to deal with the
tasks and problems they encountered as working lawyers. In
response, a law school faculty might reply—and by so replying reinforce the distinction I have been insisting on—"We
are intellectuals, not mechanics; what we do is teach you
how to think about the things we think about, and what we
prepare you for is life as a law professor; that's our job. The
rest you get elsewhere."

DRAWING THE LINE: ACADEMICIZING

There are many objections to this severe account of what
academics should and shouldn't do, but one is almost always
raised—how do you draw the line? Even if your intentions
are good, how do you refrain from inadvertently raising
inappropriate issues in the classroom? I call this the objection

of impossibility, which takes two forms. One form says that teachers come to the classroom as fully developed beings who have undergone certain courses of instruction, joined political parties, embraced or refused religious allegiances, pledged themselves to various causes, and been persuaded to the truth of any number of moral or ideological propositions. In short, teachers believe something, indeed many things, and wouldn't it be impossible for them to detach themselves from these formative beliefs and perform in a purely academic manner? Wouldn't the judgments they offered and the conclusions they reached be influenced, if not largely determined, by the commitments I say they should set aside?

This objection contrives to turn the unavailability of purity—which I certainly acknowledge—into the impossibility of making distinctions between contexts and the behaviors appropriate to them. Even if it is the case that whatever we do is shaped to some extent by what we've done in the past, that past is filtered through the conventional differences by which we typically organize our daily lives. We understand, for example, that proper behavior at the opera differs from proper behavior at a ball game, and we understand too that proper behavior at the family dinner table differs from proper behavior at a corporate lunch. It would be possible to trace our actions in all of these contexts back to decisions made and allegiances formed long ago, but those actions would still be distinguishable from one another by the usual measures that mark off one social context from another. The fact that we bring a signature style, fashioned over many years, to whatever we do does not mean that we are always doing the same thing. We are perfectly capable of acting in accordance with the norms that belong to our present sphere of activity, even if our "take" on those norms is inflected somewhat by norms we affirm elsewhere.

But is it so easy to compartmentalize one's beliefs and commitments? Yes it is. In fact, we do it all the time when we refrain, for example, from inserting our religious beliefs or our private obsessions into every situation or conversation no matter what its content. Those who cannot or will not so refrain are shunned by their neighbors and made the object of satires by authors like Swift and Dickens. Setting aside the convictions that impel us in our political lives in order to take up the task of teaching (itself anchored by convictions, but ones specific to its performance) is not at all impossible, and if we fail to do it, it is not because we could not help ourselves, but because we have made a deliberate choice to be unprofessional.

The second form of the impossibility objection asserts that there can be no distinction between politics and the academy because everything is political. It is the objection that in many courses, especially courses given at a law school or by political science departments, the materials being studied are fraught with political, social, ethical, moral, and religious implications. How can those materials be taught at all without crossing the line I have drawn? Should they be excluded or allowed in only if they have first been edited so that the substantive parts are cut out? Not at all. I am not urging a restriction on content—any ideology, agenda, even crusade is an appropriate object of study. Rather I am urging a restriction on *what is done with the content* when it is brought into the classroom. If an idea or a policy is presented as a candidate for allegiance—aided by the instructor, students are to decide where they stand on the matter—then the classroom has been appropriated for partisan purposes. But if an idea or a policy is subjected to a certain kind of interrogation—what is its history? how has it changed over time? who are its prominent proponents? what are the arguments for and against it? with what other policies is it usually packaged?—then its partisan thrust will have been blunted, for it will have become an object of analysis rather than an object of affection.

In the fall of 2004, my freshman students and I analyzed a speech of John Kerry's and found it confused, contradictory, inchoate, and weak. Six weeks later I went out and voted for John Kerry. What I was doing in class was subjecting Kerry's arguments to an academic interrogation. Do they hang together? Are they coherent? Do they respond to the issues? Are they likely to be persuasive? He flunked. But when I stepped into the ballot box, I was asking another set of questions: Does Kerry represent or speak for interests close to mine? Whom would he bring into his administration? What are likely to be his foreign policy initiatives? How does he stand on the environment? The answers I gave to the first set of *academic* questions had no relationship whatsoever to the answers I gave to the second set of *political* questions. Whether it is a person or a policy, it makes perfect sense to approve it in one venue and disapprove it in another, and vice versa. You could decide that despite the lack of skill with which a policy was defended (an academic conclusion), it was nevertheless the right policy for the country (a political decision). In the classroom, you can probe the policy's history; you can explore its philosophical lineage; you can examine its implications and likely consequences, but you can't urge it on your students. Everything depends on keeping these two judgments, and the activities that generate them, separate.

Again, this is not to say that academic work touches on none of the issues central to politics, ethics, civics, and economics; it is just that when those issues arise in an academic context, they should be discussed in academic terms; that is, they should be the objects of analysis, comparison, historical placement, etc.; the arguments put forward in relation to them should be dissected and assessed *as* arguments and not as preliminaries to action on the part of those doing the assessing. The action one takes (or should take) at the conclusion of an academic discussion is the action of rendering an *academic* verdict as in "that argument makes sense," "there's a hole in the reasoning here," "the author does (or does not) realize her intention," "in this debate, X has the better of Y," "the case is still not proven." These and similar judgments are judgments on craftsmanship and coherence—they respond to questions like "is it well made?" and "does it hang together?" The judgment of whether a policy is the right one for the country is not appropriate in the classroom, where you are (or should be) more interested in the structure and history of ideas than in recommending them (or dis-recommending them) to your students. To be sure, the ideas will be the same whether you are dissecting them or recommending them; but dissecting them is what you are supposed to do if you are paid to be an academic. Recommending them is what you do when you are a parent, or a political activist, or an op-ed columnist, all things you may be when the school day ends, but not things you should be on the university's or state's dime.

It might be objected that while it may be easy to remain within academic bounds when the debate is about the right interpretation of *Paradise Lost*, the line between the academic and the political has been blurred before the discussion begins when the subject is ethics and students are arguing, for example, about whether stem cell research is a good or bad idea.

But students shouldn't be arguing about whether stem cell research is a good or bad idea. They should be studying the arguments various parties have made about stem cell research. Even in a class focused on ethical questions, the distinction I would enforce holds. Analyzing ethical issues is one thing; deciding them is another, and only the first is an appropriate academic activity. Again, I do not mean to exclude political topics from the classroom, but to insist that when political topics are introduced, they not be taught politically, that is, with a view to either affirming or rejecting a particular political position.

The name I give to this process whereby politically explosive issues are made into subjects of intellectual inquiry is "academicizing." *To academicize a topic is to detach it from the context of its real world urgency, where there is a vote to be taken or an agenda to be embraced, and insert it into a context of academic urgency, where there is an account to be offered or an analysis to be performed.*

Take, for example, a question that was much debated in newspapers and on talk shows during the second term of George W. Bush's presidency: is George W. Bush the worst president in our history? How could you academicize *that* question? Simple. Turn the question itself into an object of study. You might begin by inquiring into the American fascination, even obsession, with ranking. We rank everything: restaurants, movies, athletes, cities, national parks, automobiles, hotels, vacation spots, spas, beers, tennis racquets, golf clubs, novels, appliances, computers, cameras, malls, and of course colleges and universities. What's that all about? Is it because Americans are upwardly mobile and require tangible evidence of the heights to which they have or have not risen? Is it because in the absence of a fixed class structure we need some way to measure where we belong? After you've discussed the significance of ranking in American life, you can return to the ranking of presidents and pose some historical questions: When were the first rankings and what was the announced reason for making them? What kind of shift has there been in the rankings over the years? Whose stock has gone up and whose down and why? Do presidents themselves ever comment on their position in the ranking? What kinds of things do they say? The more this line of inquiry is pursued, the less the question "Is George W. Bush in fact the worst president in our history?" will be fore-grounded. The urgency of that question—which is political—will have been replaced by the urgency to understand a phenomenon. The question will have been academicized. Consider as another example the Terry Schiavo tragedy. How can this event in our national history be taught without taking sides on the issues it raises? Again, simple: discuss it as a contemporary instance of a tension that has structured American political thought from the founders to John Rawls—the tension between substantive justice, justice rooted in a strong sense of absolute right and wrong, and procedural justice, justice tied to formal rules that stipulate the steps to be taken and the persons authorized to take them. On one side were those who asked the question: what is the morally right thing to do about Terry Schiavo? On the other side there were those who asked the question: who is legally entitled to make the relevant decisions independently of whether or not we think those decisions morally justified? Once these two positions are identified, their sources can be located in the work of Locke, Kant, Mill, Isaiah Berlin, and others, and the relationship between those sources and the Schiavo incident can become the focus of analysis. As this is happening—as the subject is being academicized—there will be less and less pressure in the class to come down on one side or the other and more and more pressure to describe accurately and fully the historical and philosophical antecedents of both sides. A political imperative will have been replaced by an academic one. There is no topic, how-ever politically charged, that will resist academicization. Not only is it possible to depoliticize issues that have obvious political content; it is easy.

But is it a good idea? The objection of impossibility often arrives in tandem with the objection of unworthiness. It says that even if it is possible to set aside one's political convictions when conducting a class, it would be unworthy to do so because it would be a dereliction of one's duty as a human being concerned with the well-being of the world. After all, the complaint goes, the times cry out for sane, informed voices and here are you urging the most educated and cosmopolitan segment of our population to remain silent.

Actually I am urging professors to remain silent on important political issues only when they are engaged in teaching. After hours, on their own time, when they write letters to the editor or speak at campus rallies, they can be as vocal as they like about anything and everything. That distinction is not likely to satisfy a critic like Ben Wallace, who complained on huffingtonpost.com (in response to a *New York Times* op-ed) that "under Fish's rule, a faculty member in the South in the 1950's could not embrace and urge the idea that segregation is wrong and that students should act to remedy the situation." That's right. In the 1950s the legal and moral status of segregation was a live political question working its way through legislatures and courts, which were (and are) the proper venues for adjudicating the issue. Faculty members were free to air their views in public forums and many did, but those who used the classroom as a soapbox were co-opting a space intended for other purposes. Today the situation is quite different. Segregation, at least the nonvoluntary kind, is no longer a live issue; it has been settled and there is no possibility at all of reviving it. Consequently it would now be entirely appropriate to discuss it in a classroom and even appropriate for a professor to declare (as some have declared of slavery) that it really wasn't so bad. The professor who said that would no doubt be challenged, but the challenge would be to an assessment of an historical event, not to a policy recommendation in the present. In the case of segregation there is no need to insist that the topic be academicized; history has already academicized it, which means that, in the truest sense of the word, it is now academic.

How do you know whether or not you are really academicizing? Just apply a simple test: am I asking my students to produce or assess an account of a vexed political issue, or am I asking my students to pronounce on the issue? Some cases are easy. The writing instructor who appended to his syllabus on Palestinian poetics the admonition "Conservative students should seek instruction elsewhere" was obviously defaulting on his academic responsibilities. So are those professors who skip a class in order to participate in a political rally; even if their students are not encouraged to attend the rally, a message is being sent, and it is the wrong message.

Some teachers announce their political allegiances up front and believe by doing so they inoculate their students against the danger of indoctrination. But the political affiliations of a teacher will be irrelevant if political questions are analyzed rather than decided in the classroom. Coming clean about your own partisan preferences might seem a way of avoiding politics, but it sends the message that in this class political judgments will be part of what's going on, and again that is the wrong message.

(It might seem that I have violated my own strictures when I acknowledged a few pages ago that I voted for John Kerry at the end of 2004. Am I not announcing my political allegiances? No, because I offered the anecdote as an example, not as a piece of political persuasion. I was reporting on a political act, but I was not performing one.)

The wrong message can be sent by institutions as well as by those they employ. The basic test of any action contemplated by a university should take the form of a simple question:

has the decision to do this (or not do this) been reached on educational grounds? Let's suppose the issue is whether or not a university should fund a program of intercollegiate athletics. Some will say "yes" and argue that athletics contributes to the academic mission; others will say "no" and argue that it doesn't. If the question is decided in the affirmative, all other questions—should we have football? should we sell sweatshirts? should we have a marching band?—are business questions and should be decided in business terms, not in terms of global equity. Once the university has committed itself to an athletic program it has also committed itself to making it as profitable as possible, if only because the profits, if there are any, will be turned into scholarships for student athletes and others.

The same reasoning applies to investment strategies. It is the obligation of the investment managers to secure the best possible return; it is not their obligation to secure political or social or economic justice. They may wish to do those things as private citizens or as members of an investment club, but as university officers their duty is to grow the endowment by any legal means available. The argument holds also for those in charge of maintenance and facilities. The goal should be to employ the best workers at the lowest possible wages. The goal should not be to redress economic disparities by unilaterally paying more than the market demands.

When a university sets wages, it sets wages, period (sometimes a cigar is just a cigar). The action has its own internal-to-the-enterprise shape, and while one could always abstract away from the enterprise to some larger context in which the specificity of actions performed within it disappears and everything one does is "taking a stand," it is hard to see that anything is gained except a certain fuzziness of reference. The logic—the logic of the slogan "everything is political"—is too capacious, for it amounts to saying that whenever anyone does anything, he or she is coming down on one side or another of a political controversy and "taking a stand." But there is a difference between a self-consciously political act (such as the one my wife performs when she refuses to purchase goods manufactured by companies engaged in or benefitting from research on animals) and an act performed with no political intention at all, although it, inevitably, has a political effect (at least by some very generous definition of what goes into the political). Universities can pay wages with two intentions: (1) to secure workers, whether faculty or staff, who do the job that is required and do it well and (2) to improve the lot of the laboring class. The first intention has nothing to do with politics and everything to do with the size of the labor pool, the law of supply and demand, current practices in the industry, etc. The second intention has everything to do with politics— the university is saying, "here we declare our position on one of the great issues of the day"—and it is not an intention appropriate to an educational institution.

Nor is it appropriate for universities to divest their funds because they morally disapprove of countries or companies. The University of California at Berkeley periodically debates the wisdom or morality of accepting tobacco money. What's wrong with tobacco money? One simple answer was given by Stanton Glantz, a professor of cardiology at the University of California, San Francisco, when he declared, "The tobacco companies are crooks."

His judgment was apparently backed up by a ruling in a Washington, D.C., district court. Judge Gladys Kessler asserted that the defendants, a number of tobacco companies, had (among other things) deceived the American people about the dangers of smoking and "distorted the truth about low-tar and light cigarettes . . . in order to achieve their goal—to make money." But a district court ruling is hardly definitive, and the companies are working on an appeal that will challenge both the facts in the decision and the jurisdiction of the court. Even if Judge Kessler's ruling is affirmed, it will establish not that the tobacco companies are crooks, but that in the course of marketing a legal product they engaged in misleading advertising and other questionable business practices.

If universities must distance themselves from any entity that has been accused of being ethically challenged, there will be a very long list of people, companies, and industries they will have to renounce as business partners: brokerage firms, pharmaceutical firms, online-gambling companies, oil companies, automobile manufacturers, real-estate developers, cosmetic companies, fast-food restaurants, Hewlett-Packard, Microsoft, Wal-Mart, Target, Martha Stewart, Richard Grasso, and George Steinbrenner. And if you're going to spurn companies involved with Sudan, what about North Korea, Iran, Syria, China, Columbia, the Dominican Republic, Venezuela, Argentina, Russia, Israel, and (in the eyes of many left-leaning academics) the United States? These lists are hardly exhaustive and growing daily. Taking only from the pure will prove to be an expensive proposition (even Walt Disney won't survive the cut) and time consuming too, as the university becomes an extension of Human Rights Watch.

But it's the principle of the thing, isn't it? "There are some things one needs to do based on principle," declared California regent Norman Pattiz. To my mind that's just the trouble—universities acting indiscriminately on principle. I'm not saying that universities should be unprincipled, but that the principles they adhere to and enforce should be the principles appropriate to their mission and not principles that belong to other enterprises. And by mission, I don't mean the overblown, grandiose claim to cure all ills and make the world better found in university mission statements, but the educational and pedagogical mission, the mission of teaching and research.

But what about truth? Isn't it the case that universities "are supposed to be about truth and not about fraud," as Professor Glantz insisted? Same answer: there are many things to be true or false about, and not all of them fall within the university's sphere. It is up to courts to determine whether the tobacco companies have acted fraudulently and to levy penalties if it is found that they have. The truths the university is pledged to establish and protect are truths about matters under academic study: Is string theory a powerful analytic tool or a fiction? Is Satan the hero of *Paradise Lost*? Do the voting patterns of senior citizens vary regionally? And those truths are unrelated to and unaffected by the truths, whatever they may be, about the business practices of tobacco companies.

But if you take their money, aren't you endorsing their ethics and in effect becoming a partner in their crimes? No. If you take their money, you're taking their money. That's all. The crimes they may have committed will be dealt with elsewhere, and as long as the funds have not been impounded and are in fact legally the possession of those who offer them, the act of accepting them signifies nothing more than appreciation of the gift and the intention to put it to good academic use.

So are there no circumstances in which a university should decline funds offered to it, except the circumstance of money legally (not morally) dirty? Yes, there is one— when the funds come with strings attached, when the donor says these are the conclusions I want you to reach, or these are the faculty I want you to hire, or these are the subjects I want you to teach or stop teaching. Every university already has a rule against accepting donations so encumbered, and it is a matter of record that tobacco companies abide by this restriction and do not expect (although they may hope) that their contributions will produce results friendly to their cause.

In fact there is only one funding source that attempts to exert control over what the university does with the money it receives, and that is the state legislatures and (in the case of private universities) the boards of trustees that are notorious for threatening to withdraw financial support unless the university gives the right courses and promotes or fires the right professors. That, as I will argue later, is the real danger to university integrity—not corporations skirting the edge of illegality or cozying up to repressive regimes, but the very people who are supposedly looking out for the enterprise and are instead trying to bend it to their purposes.

Sometimes the danger to institutional integrity comes from academics themselves when they try to bend the university to a political purpose. This is what happened at Southern Methodist University when it became clear that the campus was the likely location of the George W. Bush Presidential Library. (It's now a done deal.) Immediately, alumni and some faculty began to say things like, "I find it patently offensive for the Board [of SMU] to consider such an affront to justice given the Bush record," and "Do we want SMU to benefit from a legacy of massive violence?" and "Why on earth would you want anything with that man's name stamped on it?" A group of Methodist ministers, including some bishops, set up a Web site that asked members of the church and other concerned citizens to sign a petition indicating their disapproval of the proposed library. Two theology professors associated with the university complained in the student newspaper of "the secrecy of the Bush administration and its virtual refusal to engage with those holding contrary opinions" (could there be a more blatant

instance of the pot calling the kettle black?) and asked, rhe-
torically, "what does it mean ethically to say that regardless
of an administration's record and its consequences, it makes
no difference when considering a bid for the library?"

What it means is that the question of the ethics of the Bush
administration—does it condone torture? does it invade the
privacy of American citizens? does it sacrifice the environment to the interests of the oil and gas industry?—is independent of the question, is it a good thing for there to be a
public repository of the records of a national administration
for the purposes of research and education? Once that question is answered in the affirmative—and any other answer is
almost inconceivable—the ethical performance (along with
the political, military, and economic performance) of the
administration becomes a matter of study rather than something you are either affirming or rejecting. Historians do
not require that men and women whose lives and works
they chronicle be admirable; the requirement is that they
be significant, and that is a requirement every president, of
whatever party or reputation, meets by definition.

Some members of the SMU Perkins School of Theology
announced, self-righteously, "We count ourselves among
those who would regret to see SMU enshrine attitudes and
actions widely deemed as ethically egregious." But SMU
would not be "enshrining" any attitudes or actions by housing the library; rather it would be helping to assure that a set
of historical attitudes and actions will be subject to scholarly
analysis. "Ethically egregious" may or may not be the judgment history delivers on the Bush presidency, but the fact
that some members of the SMU community have made that
judgment (as others have at times made it of the Clinton,
Reagan, Carter, Ford, Nixon, Truman, Eisenhower, and
Roosevelt presidencies) was not a reason for them to say no
to the library unless they believed (wrongly) that it is the job

of a university to impose a moral litmus test on the materials it lets into its archives or classrooms.

That is exactly what many of the protestors did believe, and they cited as evidence SMU's Code of Ethics, which celebrates the "Pursuit of truth, Integrity in work, Respect for persons, Responsible use of resources, and Accountability." After all, one protestor declared, "Institutions of education are all about values." Yes they are, but the values they are about are academic values, not values in general. A university is pledged to determining the truth about the texts its faculty studies. It is not pledged to confining itself to texts of whose truthfulness it is convinced. A university is pledged to respect the persons of its employees, which means that it evaluates everyone by the same set of nondiscriminatory standards. It does not mean that it restricts the object of its academic attention to people and groups that do not discriminate. A university is pledged to use its resources—money, equipment, labor—responsibly, but neither the responsibility nor irresponsibility of those entities it chooses to study is something it is pledged to consider. Those who think that by insisting on a moral yardstick, the university protects its integrity have it all wrong; the university forsakes its integrity when it takes upon itself the task of making judgments that belong properly to the electorate and to history. A university's obligation is to choose things worthy of study, not to study only things that it finds worthy.

WHAT'S LEFT?

But wouldn't a university uninvolved in the great issues of the day be a place without passion, where classrooms were bereft of lively discussion and debate?

Definitely not. While the urgency of the political question will fade in the classroom I have imagined, it will have become a far livelier classroom as a result. In the class-rooms I have in mind, passions run high as students argue about whether the religion clause of the First Amend-ment, properly interpreted, forbids student-organized prayers at football games, or whether the Rawlsian notion of constructing a regime of rights from behind a "veil of ignorance" makes sense, or whether the anthropological study of a culture inevitability undermines its integrity. I have seen students discussing these and similar matters if not close to coming to blows then very close to jump-ing up and down and pumping their fists. These students are far from apathetic or detached, but what they are attached to (this again is the crucial difference) is the *truth* of the position to which they have been persuaded, and while that truth, strongly held, might lead at some later time to a decision to go out and work for a candidate or a policy, deciding *that* is not what is going on in the classroom.

By invoking the criterion of truth, I've already answered the objection that an academicized classroom—a class-room where political and moral agendas are analyzed, not embraced—would be value-free and relativistic. If anything is a value, truth is, and the implicit (and sometimes explicit) assumption in the classroom as I envision it is that truth, and the seeking of truth, must always be defended. To be sure, truth is not the only value and there are others that should be defended in the contexts to which they are central; but truth is a pre-eminent *academic* value, and adherence to it is exactly the opposite of moral relativism. You will never hear in any of my classes the some-people-say-X-but-others-say-Y-and-who's-to-judge dance. What I strive to deter-mine, together with my students, is which of the competing accounts of a matter (an academic not a political matter) is the right one and which are wrong. "Right" and "wrong" are not in the lexicon of moral relativism, and the students who deliver them as judgments do so with a commitment as great as any they might have to a burning social issue. Students who are asked to compare the models of heroism on display in the *Iliad*, the *Aeneid*, and Wordsworth's *Prelude*, or to chart the changes in the legal understanding of what the founders meant when they enjoined Congress from establishing a religion, will engage in discussions that are at least as animated as any they might have in the dorm room about some pressing issue of the day. It is only if you forget that academic questions have histories, and that those histories have investments, and that those investments are often cross- and interdisciplinary that you could make the mistake of thinking that confining yourself to them and resisting the lure of supposedly "larger" questions would make for an experience without spirit and energy.

Not only is the genuinely academic classroom full of passion and commitment; it is more interesting than the alternative. The really dull classroom would be the one in which a bunch of nineteen- or twenty-year-olds debate assisted suicide, physician-prescribed marijuana, or the war in Iraq in response to the question "What do you think?" Sure, lots of students would say things, but what they would say would be completely predictable—a mini-version of what you hear on the Sunday talk shows—in short, a rehearsing of opinions. Meanwhile the genuine excitement of an academic discussion where you have a chance of learning something, as opposed to just blurting out uninformed opinions, will have been lost. What teacher and student are jointly after is knowledge, and the question should never be "What do you think?" (unless you're a social scientist conducting a survey designed to capture public opinion). The question should be "What is the truth?" and the answer must stand up against challenges involving (among other things) the quality and quantity of evidence, the cogency of arguments, the soundness of conclusions, and so forth. At the (temporary) end of the process, both students and teachers will have learned something they didn't know before (you always know what your opinions are; that's why it's so easy to have them) and they will have learned it by exercising their cognitive capacities in ways that leave them exhilarated and not merely self-satisfied. Opinion-sharing sessions are like junk food: they fill you up with starch and leave you feeling both sated and hungry. A sustained inquiry into the truth of a matter is an almost athletic experience; it may exhaust you, but it also improves you.

A RADICAL PROPOSITION: TEACH WRITING IN WRITING CLASSES

Improvement of a particular skill is supposedly the point of composition classes, but in no area of the curriculum has the lure of supposedly larger questions proven stronger. More often than not anthologies of provocative readings take center stage and the actual teaching of writing is shunted to the sidelines. Once ideas are allowed to be the chief currency in a composition course, the very point of the course is forgotten. That is why I say to my students on the first day of class, "We don't do content in this class. By that I mean we are not interested in ideas—yours, mine, or anyone else's. We don't have an anthology of readings. We don't discuss current events. We don't exchange views on hot-button issues. We don't tell each other what we think about anything—except about how prepositions or participles or relative pronouns function." The reason my students and I don't do any of these things is that once you begin talking about ideas, the focus is shifted from the linguistic forms that make the organization of content possible to this or that piece of content, usually some recycled set of pros and cons about abortion, affirmative action, welfare reform, the death penalty, free speech, and so forth. At that moment, the task of understanding and mastering language will have been replaced by the dubious pleasure of reproducing the well-worn and terminally dull arguments one hears or sees on every radio and TV talk show.

Students who take so-called courses in writing where such topics are the staples of discussion may believe, as their instructors surely do, that they are learning how to marshal arguments in ways that will improve their compositional skills. In fact, they will be learning nothing they couldn't have learned better by sitting around in a dorm room or a coffee shop. They will certainly not be learning anything about how language works; and without a knowledge of how language works they will be unable either to spot the formal breakdown of someone else's language or to prevent the formal breakdown of their own.

In my classes, the temptation of content is felt only fleetingly; for as soon as students bend to the task of understanding the structure of language—a task with a content deeper than any they have been asked to forgo—they become completely absorbed in it and spontaneously enact the discipline I have imposed.

What exactly is that discipline? On the first day of my freshman writing class I give the students this assignment: you will be divided into groups and by the end of the semester each group will be expected to have created its own language, complete with a syntax, a lexicon, a text, rules for translating the text and strategies for teaching your language to fellow students. The language you create cannot be English or a slightly coded version of English, but it must be capable of indicating the distinctions—between tense, number, manner, mood, agency, and the like—that English enables us to make.

You can imagine the reaction of students who think that "syntax" is something cigarette smokers pay, guess that "lexicon" is the name of a rebel tribe inhabiting a galaxy far away, and haven't the slightest idea of what words like "tense," "manner" and "mood" mean. They think I'm crazy. Yet fourteen weeks later—and this happens every time— each group has produced a language of incredible sophistication and precision.

How is this near miracle accomplished? The short answer is that in the course of the semester the students come to understand a single proposition: a sentence is a structure of logical relationships. In its bare form, this proposition is hardly edifying, which is why I immediately supplement it with a simple exercise. "Here," I say, "are five words randomly chosen; turn them into a sentence." (The first time I did this the words were coffee, should, book, garbage, and quickly.) In no time at all I am presented with twenty sentences, all perfectly coherent and all quite different. Then comes the hard part. "What is it," I ask, "that you did? What did it take to turn a random list of words into a sentence?" A lot of fumbling and stumbling and false starts follow, but finally someone says, "I put the words into a relationship with one another."

Once the notion of relationship is on the table, the next question almost asks itself: what exactly are the relationships? And working with the sentences they have created the students quickly realize two things: first, that the possible relationships form a limited set; and second, that it all comes down to an interaction of some kind between actors, the actions they perform, and the objects of those actions.

The next step (and this one takes weeks) is to explore the devices by which English indicates and distinguishes between the various components of these interactions. If in every sentence someone is doing something to someone or something else, how does English allow you to tell who is the doer and who (or what) is the doee; and how do you know whether there is one doer or many; and what tells you that the doer is doing what he or she does in this way and at this time rather than another?

Notice that these are not questions about how a particular sentence works, but questions about how any sentence works, and the answers will point to something very general and abstract. They will point, in fact, to the forms that, while they are themselves without content, are necessary to the conveying of any content whatsoever, at least in English.

Once the students tumble to this point, they are more than halfway to understanding the semester-long task: they can now construct a language whose forms do the same work English does, but do it differently.

In English, for example, most plurals are formed by adding an "s" to nouns. Is that the only way to indicate the difference between singular and plural? Obviously not. But the language you create, I tell them, must have some regular and abstract way of conveying that distinction; and so it is with all the other distinctions—between time, manner, spatial relationships, relationships of hierarchy and subordination, relationships of equivalence and difference—languages permit you to signal.

In the languages my students devise, the requisite distinctions are signaled by any number of formal devices—word order, word endings, prefixes, suffixes, numbers, brackets, fonts, colors, you name it. Exactly how they do it is not the point; the point is that they know what it is they are trying to do; the moment they know that, they have succeeded, even if much of the detailed work remains to be done.

I recall the representative of one group asking me, "Is it all right if we use the same root form for adjectives and adverbs, but distinguish between them by their order in the sentence?" I could barely disguise my elation. If the students could formulate a question like that one, they had already learned the lesson I was trying to teach them.

It is a lesson that bears repeating. Just listen to *National Public Radio* for fifteen minutes or read a section of the *New York Times* and you will be able to start your own collection of howlers, from the (now ubiquitous) confusion of "disinterested" and "uninterested" (which sometimes takes the form of a parallel confusion of "disinvite" and "uninvite," the latter not an English verb form); to the disastrous and often comical substitution of "enervate" for "energize"; to the attribution of reticence to persons who are merely reluctant; to participles with no subjects or too many; to errors of pomposity ("between you and I," dubbed by a former colleague the "Cornell nominative"); to pronouns without referents or as many referents as there are nouns in the previous five sentences; to singular subjects with plural verbs (and the reverse); to dependent clauses attached to nothing; to mismatched tenses attached to the same action; to logical redundancies like, "The reason is because..." (I'm afraid I've been guilty of that one myself); not to mention inelegant repetitions and errors of diction made by people who seem to be writing a language they first encountered yesterday.

It seems that the art of speaking and writing precisely and with attention to grammatical form is less and less practiced. And I cannot claim that by writing this book, I will revive it. But I can offer some precepts that might at least improve the teaching of writing in our colleges and universities. All composition courses should teach grammar and rhetoric and nothing else. No composition course should have a theme, especially not one the instructor is interested in. Ideas should be introduced not for their own sake, but for the sake of the syntactical and rhetorical points they help illustrate, and once they serve this purpose, they should be sent away. Content should be avoided like the plague it is, except for the deep and inexhaustible content that will reveal itself once the dynamics of language are regarded not as secondary, mechanical aids to thought, but as thought itself. If content takes over, what won't get done is the teaching of writing, something the world really needs and something an academic with the appropriate training can actually do. But he or she won't ever get around to doing it if the class is given over to multiculturalism or racial injustice or globalization or reproductive rights or third-world novels or any of the other "topics," which, as worthy of study as they might be, take up all the air space and energy in the room and leave the students full of banal opinions but without the ability to use prepositions or write a clean English sentence.

The irony is that if you limit yourself to matters of composition and ask the students to confront the workings of language at the smallest level, you will have instructed them in something far deeper than all the hot-button issues that are initially so exciting and quickly become so boring.

How exactly would that instruction occur? What are its methods? A full answer would require a book of its own, but I can offer a small example of the process in action. One day I was talking with a law student who, although he had turned thirty-one the day before, didn't yet have a firm grasp of what a sentence is. I gave him my standard mantra—a sentence is a structure of logical relationships—but that didn't help. What did help—and usually helps, I find—is a return to basics so basic that it is almost an insult.

I asked him to write a simple three-word English sentence. He replied immediately: "Jane baked cookies." Give me a few more with the same structure, I said. He readily complied, but one of his examples was, "Tim drinks excessively." The next forty minutes were spent getting him to see why this sentence was not like the others (a kind of *Sesame Street* exercise), but he couldn't do that until he was able to see and describe the structure of sentences like, "Jane baked cookies."

I pointed to "baked" and asked him what function the word played. He first tried to tell me what the word meant. No, I said, the word's meaning is not relevant to an understanding of its function (meaning is always the enemy of writing instruction); I want to know what the word does, what role it plays in the structure that makes the sentence a sentence and not just a list of words. He fumbled about for a while and finally said that "baked" named the action in the sentence. Right, I replied, now tell me what comes along with an action. Someone performing it, he answered. And in the sentence, who or what is performing the action? "Jane," he said happily. Great! Now tell me what function the word "cookies" plays. Progress immediately stalled.

For a long time he just couldn't get it. He said something like, " 'Cookies' tells what the sentence is about." No, I said, that's content and we're not interested in content here (content is always the enemy of writing instruction); what I want to know is what structural relationship links "cookies" to the other parts of the sentence. More confusion. I tried another tack. What information does "cookies" provide? What question, posed implicitly by another of the sentence's components, does it answer? It took a while, but that worked. It answers the question, "What was baked?" he offered. Yes, I said, you've almost got it. Now explain in abstract terms that would be descriptive of any sentence with this structure, no matter what its content or meaning, the structural logic that links a word like "baked," a word that names an action, to a word like "cookies." More fumbling, but then he said "cookies" is what is acted upon. It was only then that I told him that in the traditional terminology of grammar, the thing acted upon is called the object. Had I given him the term earlier, he would have nodded, but he wouldn't have understood a thing. Now, he had at least the beginning of an understanding of how sentences are constructed and what work a sentence does; it organizes relationships between actors, actions, and things acted upon.

We still had to deal with "Tim drinks excessively," but at least there was something to build on. Does "excessively" name what is acted upon by the action "drinks"? No, he replied. What, then, does it do? A relapse into content: it tells what's happening. That's what "drinks" does, I reminded him. What information, in relation to "drinks" as a word with a specific function, does "excessively" provide? It was coming more quickly now. It tells us in what way he drinks, he said. Yes, the function of "excessively," and of any other word occupying the same structural slot, is to tell you something about the manner in which an action is performed. Oh, he said, an adjective. No, an adverb, I replied, but the term is less important than your understanding of the structural role. Does that mean, he asked, that the adverbial role can be played by more than one word, by many words? Now we were rolling.

I drove home the point of the lesson so far by asking him two simple questions. How many sentences, with different contents, are there that display the structures actor-action-acted upon or actor-action-manner of action? An infinite number, he replied. How many forms of the two structures are there? Only one, he said. Now you know, I told him, that form comes first, content second. If you grasp the abstract structural form of sentences like these, you can produce millions of them; you can organize any content whatsoever by imposing on it the logic of these forms.

The next exercise was considerably more sophisticated, but he completed it more quickly. Write a sentence that begins with the phrase "even though." No problem at all. He produced a bunch of them, including, "Even though I stayed up all night, I wasn't tired." How many "even though" sentences exist out there? I asked. He knew the drill: an infinite number. And how many forms? One. Now came the hard part. Describe that form without reference to any particular content. Describe, that is, the structure of every "even though" sentence ever written.

He quickly saw that the answer lay in the relationship between the two clauses (which he called "phrases"), but he had a hard time saying what the relationship was. He came up with the idea of contradiction but agreed that contradiction was too strong. He thought about it some and settled on a word he was familiar with as a law student. The second clause, he said, is a rebuttal of the first. Almost there. What does it rebut? It rebuts, he replied, what you would expect to follow from the first clause. You mean, I said (offering more help than I should have, but the afternoon was disappearing), that the second clause undoes in some way the expectation produced by the first. He acknowledged that this is what he meant.

What if the sentence read, "Even though I stayed up all night, I was tired." Oh, he replied, that wouldn't be a good "even though" sentence because the second part would say exactly what you would have expected it to say. How about if the sentence were just, "I stayed up all night; I wasn't tired." What would the difference be? He got it immediately. You wouldn't know from the beginning that the expectation produced by the first part is going to be disappointed. Isn't a sentence that begins with "notwithstanding" somewhat like an "even though" sentence? he wondered. You bet! End of the second lesson, except for my pointing out to him that while he always knew how to generate "even though" sentences and was capable of identifying misuses of the form, he now was able to describe the form and under-stand precisely how it works.

My assumption in all of this was that this analytical alert-ness to form, this ability to recognize forms and know when they are properly or improperly deployed, would translate into a greater alertness to the operations of form in his own writing. That assumption has not yet been tested empirically, but it should be noted that none of the more substantive, content-based approaches to the task seem to teach writ-ing at all. We've now had decades of composition courses in which students do little but exchange their ill-informed views, and student writing has only gotten worse. Doesn't it make sense to think that if you are trying to teach them how to use linguistic forms, linguistic forms are what you should be teaching?

This discussion of the teaching of writing might seem to be a digression from my main task of identifying appropriate and inappropriate forms of pedagogical behavior. But in fact, the present state of composition studies is the clearest example of the surrender of academic imperatives to the imperatives of politics. Those instructors who turn their courses over to discussions of oppression and the evils of neoliberalism say things like "teaching grammatical rules is a form of social indoctrination," and "notions of correctness are devices by means of which the powers that be extend their illegitimate hegemony." In classrooms where these are the mantras, the subordination of academic work to the work of ideology is complete before the first lesson has been taught.

BLURRING THE LINE

If you're doing academic rather than political work, you are, as I've said repeatedly, producing accounts and descrip-tions, rather than urging courses of action or taking a stand on some great question of the day. But hewing to the line I have drawn between analysis and advocacy is no guarantee that those who read or hear you will recognize and appreciate what you are doing. Someone who finds the distinction either opaque or false may well receive your disinterested analyses as if they were recommendations. You may be just expounding and defending academic views, but you will be heard as doing something more sinister. This is what happened to me in 2002, when I was accused of promoting terrorists' views and even of being a kind of terrorist myself. The accusation was made by another academic, a man named John Carey. Carey is a professor at Oxford and in September of 2002 he published a piece in the London *Times Literary Supplement* entitled "A Work in Praise of Terrorism? September 11 and *Samson Agonistes*." Carey described me (or rather my views) as "monstrous" and wondered why, unlike most people with "common humanity," I failed to condemn "mass murder."

Why would anyone say such things about an English teacher? What was my crime? Well, it turns out that my crime was that I had published a reading of John Milton's poetic drama *Samson Agonistes*, a retelling of the story of the biblical Samson who pulled down the supporting pillars of a Philistine temple, thereby killing, along with himself, thousands of men, women, and children he had never met. What drew Carey's ire is that in my reading of the play I declare Samson's act to be praiseworthy because he performed it in the conviction, or at least the hope, that it was what God wanted him to do. No, Carey protested, that can't be what Milton intended us to understand, for if it were, he would not be a great poet, but a murderous bigot, and anyone who, like Stanley Fish, says otherwise must himself be an apologist for murderous bigots and an advocate of violence to boot.

Now Carey can only come to this conclusion because he thinks that by offering an interpretive account of Samson's act, I endorse its morality and endorse by analogy other acts of religiously inspired violence, including the acts perpetrated by those who brought down the World Trade Towers. Were this so, I would be a very bad boy indeed, but in fact I endorse nothing except the correctness of my reading. I don't say, "religiously inspired violence is good"; I say that religiously inspired violence is what's going on in *Samson Agonistes*, and I say too that Milton does not encourage us to condemn it. That's a debatable reading, but it is a reading and not the declaration of my personal moral position. The proper response to my reading on the part of someone who disagrees with it would be first to say that it is wrong, and then to give reasons and cite evidence in support of that judgment. It is not a proper response to call me names and accuse me of besmirching the reputation of a great poet, as if a poet could only be great if he displayed sentiments approved of by John Carey. Neither I nor Milton should be attacked on the basis of the policies we are recommending, for neither of us is recommending any policies. He's writing a poem. I'm interpreting one.

Carey's mistake is the one that is the target of my argument on every page of this book. He confuses an academic argument with the practice of politics and conflates the writing of a poem with the publishing of a manifesto. Thus he declares that if Fish is right and *Samson Agonistes* does in fact condone religiously inspired violence, the play should be "withdrawn from schools and colleges, and indeed banned more generally as an incitement to terrorism." Neither *Samson Agonistes* nor I condone anything, and the only thing the play incites is reading, and along with reading a reflective stance toward the issues it dramatizes. "Reflective" is the key word, because it names both what poets do—reflect on matters like the relationship between political action and religious commitment—and what interpreters do in return—trace out the shape of reflection as it poses problems and teases them out to their edges. The exploration of problems, not their solution, and certainly not a program of political action, is what poetry offers. And if we take up that offer, our reward is not a recipe for dealing with the next crisis in our lives but a deepened understanding of the questions and moral conundrums the poet presents for our contemplation. Poems don't ask you to do anything except read them and be responsive to the intricacies of their unfolding.

If Milton's poetry is to be withdrawn from the schools, it should not be because its message is dangerous—having a message is not the business it's in—but because it fails to perform the business of poetry, the business of providing oases of reflection amid the urgencies that press in on us when we are being citizens, parents, politicians, soldiers, entrepreneurs, lawyers, doctors, engineers, etc.

WHAT'S THE USE?

I have gone on at such length about poetry and what is appropriate to it because poetry is the liberal arts activity par excellence. Indeed, when liberal arts education is doing its job properly, it is just like poetry because, like poetry, it makes no claims to efficacy beyond the confines of its performance. A good liberal arts course is not good because it tells you what to do when you next step into the ballot box or negotiate a contract. A good liberal arts course is good because it introduces you to questions you did not know how to ask and provides you with the skills necessary to answer them, at least provisionally. And what do you do with the answers you arrive at? What do you do with the habits of thought that have become yours after four or more years of discussing the mind/body problem, or the structure of DNA, or Firmat's theorem, or the causes of World War I? Beats me! As far as I can tell those habits of thought and the liberal arts education that provides them don't enable you to do anything, and, even worse, neither do they prevent you from doing anything.

The view I am offering of higher education is properly called deflationary; it takes the air out of some inflated balloons. It denies to teaching the moral and philosophical pretensions that lead practitioners to envision themselves as agents of change or as the designers of a "transformative experience," a phrase I intensely dislike. I acknowledge a sense in which education can be transformative. A good course may transform a student who knew little about the material in the beginning into a student who knows something about it at the end. That's about all the transformation you should or could count on. Although the debates about what goes on in our colleges and universities are often conducted as if large moral, philosophical, and even theological matters are at stake, what is really at stake, more often than not, is a matter of administrative judgment with respect to professional behavior and job performance. Teaching is a job, and what it requires is not a superior sensibility or a purity of heart and intention—excellent teachers can be absolutely terrible human beings, and exemplary human beings can be terrible teachers—but mastery of a craft. Teachers who prefer grandiose claims and ambitions to that craft are the ones who diminish it and render it unworthy.

A convenient summary of the grandiose claims often made for teaching can be found in an issue of the journal *Liberal Education*. Here are some sentences from that issue:

- A classroom that teaches the virtues of critical analysis and respectful debate can go at least some way to form citizens for a more deliberative democracy.
- A liberal arts college or university that helps young people to learn to speak in their own voices and to respect the voices of others will have done a great deal to produce thoughtful and potentially creative world citizens.
- The aims of a strong liberal education include...shaping ethical judgment and a capacity for insight and concern for others.
- Contemporary liberal education must look beyond the classroom to the challenges of the community, the complexities of the workplace, and the major issues in the world.
- Students need to be equipped for living in a world where moral decisions must be made.

To which I respond, no, no, no, no, and no. A classroom that teaches critical analysis (sometimes called "critical thinking," a phrase without content) will produce students who can do critical analysis; and those students, no matter how skillfully analytical they have become, will not by virtue of that skill be inclined to "respect the voices of others." Learning how to perform in the game of argument is no guarantee either of the quality or of the morality of the arguments you go on to make. Bad arguments, bad decisions, bad actions are as available to the members of Phi Beta Kappa as they are available to the members of street gangs. And moreover, as I said earlier, respecting the voices of others is not even a good idea. You shouldn't respect the voices of others simply because they *are* others (that's the mistake of doctrinaire multiculturalism); you should respect the voices of those others whose arguments and recommendations you find coherent and persuasive.

And as for ethical judgment in general, no doubt everything you encounter helps to shape it, but reading novels by Henry James is not a special key to achieving it; and indeed—and there are many examples of this in the world— readers of Henry James or Sylvia Plath or Toni Morrison can be as vile and as cruel and as treacherous as anyone else. And if students "need to be equipped for living in a world where moral decisions must be made," they'd better seek the equipment elsewhere, perhaps from their parents, or their churches, or their synagogues, or their mosques. Nor can I agree that "contemporary liberal education must look beyond the classroom to the challenges of the community"; for it is only one short step from this imperative to the asser- tion that what goes on in the liberal arts classroom is merely preliminary to what lies beyond it, one short step to the judgment that what goes on in the liberal arts classroom acquires its value from what happens elsewhere; and then it is no step at all to conclude that what goes on in the lib- eral arts classroom can only be *justified* by an extracurricular payoff.

And here we come to the heart of the matter, the justifi- cation of liberal education. You know the questions: Will it benefit the economy? Will it fashion an informed citizenry? Will it advance the cause of justice? Will it advance anything? Once again the answer is no, no, no, and no. At some level of course, everything we ultimately do has some relationship to the education we have received. But if liberal arts educa- tion is doing *its* job and not the job assigned to some other institution, it will not have as its aim the bringing about of particular effects in the world. Particular effects may follow, but if they do, it will be as the unintended consequences of an enterprise which, if it is to remain true to itself, must be entirely self-referential, must be stuck on itself, must have no answer whatsoever to the question, "what good is it?" In a wonderful essay titled "What Plato Would Allow" (*Nomos* XXXVII, 1995), political theorist Jeremy Waldron muses about the appropriate response to someone who asks of philosophers, "What's the point of your work?" or "What difference is it going to make?" He replies (and I agree completely with him) that "we are not really doing...philosophy, and thus paradoxically...we are probably not really being of much use, unless we are largely at a loss as to how to answer that question."

Daniel Cottom comes to the same conclusion in his book *Why Education Is Useless*. His argument is that the accusation of inutility should be affirmatively embraced. "We should have done with the attempt to declare that education is useful," if only because "declarations of its usefulness prove to be beneath contempt." Cottom and I, however, part company on a crucial point. Whereas I reject justifying academic work because to do so means to deny it its own value—the value that leads people to take it up in the first place—Cottom turns the difficulty of justification into a positive virtue and therefore into a back-door form of justification. What he does is romanticize the inutility of academic work and celebrate it as a necessary counterweight to everything that is wrong with modern life. "We ought to celebrate the uselessness at the core of higher education and we should do so by seeing in the institutionalization of this uselessness a standing cultural commitment against the tyranny of stupidity in any form: the market, technocracy, the state, even the people." There is more than a whiff of academic exceptionalism here, the seductive and self-enhancing idea that professors are rarified creatures who, by virtue of their immersion in the library and the laboratory, are immune to the temptations and vulgarities to which lesser mortals fall. But it is no part of my intention to glorify or politicize the inutility of academic work. I just want to say that inutility is a fact about it, and a defining, not a limiting, fact. An unconcern with any usefulness to the world is the key to its distinctiveness, and this unconcern is displayed not in a spirit of renunciation (priesthood is not the goal here), but in a spirit of independence and the marking of territory.

An activity whose value is internal to its performance will have unpredictable and unintended effects in the world outside the classroom. But precisely because they are unpredictable and unintended, it is a mistake to base one's teaching on the hope of achieving them. On more than one occasion I have had an experience many professors will recognize. A student you haven't seen in years rushes up to you and says, "Oh, Professor, I think so often of that class in 1985 (or was it 1885?) when you said X and I was led by what you said to see Y and began on that very day to travel the path that has now taken me to success in profession Z. I can't thank you enough!"

You, however, are appalled, because you can't imagine yourself ever saying X (in fact you remember spending the entire semester saying anti-X) and you would never want anyone to exit from your class having learned Y (a lesson you have been preaching against for twenty years) and you believe that everyone would be better off if profession Z disappeared from the face of the earth. What, you might ask, did I do wrong?

The correct answer is quite likely, "nothing." It is the question that is wrong because it assumes that we are responsible for the effects of our teaching, whereas, in fact, we are responsible only for its appropriate performance. That is, we are responsible for the selection of texts, the preparation of a syllabus, the sequence of assignments and exams, the framing and grading of a term paper, and so on.

If by the end of a semester you have given your students an overview of the subject (as defined by the course's title and description in the catalogue) and introduced them to the latest developments in the field and pointed them in the directions they might follow should they wish to inquire further, then you have done your job. What they subsequently do with what you have done is their business and not anything you should be either held to account for or praised for. (Charlton Heston once said to Lawrence Olivier, "I've finally learned to ignore the bad reviews." "Fine," Olivier replied, "now learn to ignore the good ones.")

The question of what you are responsible for is also the question of what you should aim for, and what you should aim for is what you *can* aim for—that is, what you can reasonably set out to do as opposed to what is simply not within your power to do.

You can reasonably set out to put your students in possession of a set of materials and equip them with a set of skills (interpretive, computational, laboratory, archival), and even perhaps (although this one is really iffy) instill in them the same love of the subject that inspires your pedagogical efforts. You won't always succeed in accomplishing these things—even with the best of intentions and lesson plans there will always be inattentive or distracted students, frequently absent students, unprepared students, and on-another-planet students—but at least you will have a fighting chance given the fact that you've got them locked in a room with you for a few hours every week for four months.

You have little chance (and that entirely a matter of serendipity), however, of determining what they will make of what you have offered them once the room is unlocked for the last time and they escape first into the space of someone else's obsession and then into the space of the wide, wide world.

And you have no chance at all (short of a discipleship that is itself suspect and dangerous) of determining what their behavior and values will be in those aspects of their lives that are not, in the strict sense of the word, academic. You might just make them into good researchers. You can't make them into good people, and you shouldn't try.

Of course, somewhere down the line the answer a student once gave to an academic question may factor into the moral response he or she gives in a real-life crisis; but down the line is a long distance away, and meanwhile both faculty members and students will do well to remember the point of the enterprise they are *now* a part of.

Earlier I said that the liberal arts are like poetry because they make no claim to benefits beyond the pleasure of engaging in them. They are also like virtue because they are their own reward. That is, the reward is here and now, not some intangible benefit—wisdom, grace, gravitas—you will reap later. If you are committed to an enterprise and have internalized its values, you don't spend much time asking questions like "what is this good for?" You have already answered that question by sticking with the job: it's good because it's what you like to do.

THREE

Administrative Interlude

But you can't do it in a vacuum. And although academics would be reluctant to admit it, the conditions that make what they do possible are established and maintained by administrators. When I was a dean, the question I was most often asked by faculty members was, "Why do administrators make so much more money than we do?" The answer I gave was simple: administrators work harder, they have more work to do, and they actually do it.

At the end of my tenure as dean, I spoke to some administrators who had been on the job for a short enough time to be able still to remember what it was like to be a faculty member and what thoughts they had then about the work they did now. One said that she had come to realize how narcissistic academics are: an academic, she mused, is focused entirely on the intellectual stock market and watches its rises and falls with an anxious and self-regarding eye. As an academic, you're trying to get ahead; as an administrator, you're trying "to make things happen for other people"; you're "not advancing your own profile, but advancing the institution, and you're more service oriented." A second new administrator reported that he finds faculty members "unbelievably parochial, selfish, and self-indulgent." They believe that their time is their own even when someone else is paying for it. They say things like "I don't get paid for the summer." They believe that they deserve everything and that if they are ever denied anything, it could only be because an evil administrator has committed a great injustice. Although they are employees of the university (and in public universities, of the state), they consider themselves independent contractors engaged fitfully in free-lance piecework. They have no idea of how comfortable a life they lead.

Neither, said a third administrator recently up from the ranks, do they have any idea of how the university operates. They seem proud of their parochialism and boast of their inability to access the many systems that hold the enterprise together. Ignorance of these matters is not a failing, but a badge of honor. Their first response to budget crises is to call for a cut in the administration, although, were the administrators to disappear, they wouldn't be able to put one foot in front of the other.

Although it would shock faculty members to hear it said, administration is an intellectual task, for it requires the ability to solve problems across a range of contexts without ever losing sight of the larger vision in which those contexts live and move and have their being. Here's a typical scenario. In one year in my time in the dean's office, the campus took a hit of about 10 percent, many millions of dollars. At that moment the college's revenues (95 percent state dollars) totaled about fifty-three million, forty-eight of which was earmarked for salaries. That left five million for everything else: operating expenses, new programs, new hires, additional instruction, etc. Obviously, a 10 or 12 percent additional cut would have left us unable either to pay the salaries already on the books or to provide the instruction mandated by the same folks who would be mandating the cut. (Political officials keep making statements about "fat" and scraping the "bottom of the barrel"; but they are either ignorant or dishonest or both; there is no fat and the barrel was scraped clean some time ago.)

What makes the problems administrators face more complicated and intractable than the problems faculty members face is the difficulty of getting a handle on them. Since budget figures constitute a moving target, they cannot be used to determine what wiggle room, if any, a dean or a provost might have when thinking about searches that have been authorized but not yet concluded. Should they be cancelled by an administration that would then display fiscal prudence in a climate that will applaud it but probably not reward it, or should the searches be allowed to continue with the risk that the administrators will be thought irresponsible? Should an administrator use what little he or she has to strengthen departments already strong? Or should the administrator shore up weak departments on the reasoning that this may be their last chance for a while to get any help? Eventually, an administration will move to something like a resolution, and then spend the next three years watching the results that will indicate whether the right people were disappointed (no matter what you do, somebody—often nearly everybody—will be unhappy).

To be sure, not all situations administrators face are that momentous or dramatic, but almost all of them involve problems of coordination that require calculations of incredible delicacy made in relation to numerous (and sometimes potentially conflicting) institutional goals and obligations. To whom shall we assign space, that most precious of academic commodities? How shall we adjudicate between the need for more offices, more labs, more homes for interdisciplinary work, more student and faculty lounges? If space becomes available in a remote building, should we provide relief to a space-poor department by sending some of its members to that outpost, or would that relief be the cause of even greater ills (loss of community, divided government, etc.)? An alternative might be to relocate the entire department, but if we did that, would we risk losing the benefits (casual but productive conversations, access to each other's seminars and lectures, opportunities for team teaching) proximity brings?

Another set of issues administrators face lies at the intersection of the professional and the personal. A complaint is made by a faculty member against his or her chair. The matter is not so grave as to constitute a grievance within the university guidelines, but is serious enough to threaten the internal health of the department. Do you speak to each of the parties separately and set yourself up as a judge of conflicting evidence, or do you call them both in and practice therapy without a license? Should you be attentive to the human dimension of the situation and worry about who is feeling pain about what, or should you be responsive only to the needs of the institution and settle for a truce that leaves everyone's hostile emotions in place? ("You guys may continue to hate each other, but you must agree to act with professional courtesy, even if you do so with gritted teeth.") Should you regard the present situation as a closed system or should you inquire into the prior behavior of the combatants with a view to determining whether one of them is a "bad egg" always looking for trouble? Or should you decide that to do any of these things would be to do too much and simply inform the chair about the disgruntled colleague and say, in effect, you deal with it, it's your job. (Unfortunately, if you opt for this strategy and let the cup pass, it will end up on your desk anyway.)

My point, I trust, is obvious: in the course of making a decision, an administrator must perform a complex act of taking into account any number of goals (short and long range), constituencies, interests, opportunities, costs, dangers; and at every point in a somewhat abstract calculation he or she must keep constantly in mind the forces and resources that must be marshaled (if they in fact can be) if the course of action decided upon is to be implemented in a way that leaves intact one's ability to deal flexibly with the next situation, and the next, and the next. This is what I meant when I said earlier that administration is an intellectual task: it requires the capacity to sift through mounds of data while at the same time continually relating what the data reveal to the general principles and aspirations of the enterprise.

So when faculty members ask what are administrators needed for anyway, the answer should be obvious: to develop, put in place, and, yes, administer the policies and procedures that enable those who scorn them to do the work they consider so much more valuable than the work of administration. If it weren't for administrators, there would be no class schedules and therefore no classes to teach, no admissions office and therefore no students to dazzle, no facilities management and therefore no laboratories to work in, no tenure process and therefore no security of employment, no budget officers and therefore no funds for equipment, travel, lectures, and teaching awards.

ADVICE

If the administrative task is so complex and varied in its demands, how is anyone ever to learn how to do it? Mostly it's on-the-job training, but there are a few precepts that might be helpful.

Whenever a shoddy practice is allowed to continue even for a day, when an office is unresponsive, or a faculty member irresponsible, or a maintenance crew slipshod, or an elevator broken, or a phone system inefficient, everyone's morale suffers even if no one is conscious of it, and it is your job as an administrator to pursue the problem and insist that it be fixed even when it is located in a sphere over which you have no authority. Not only should you fight every battle, you should look for battles to fight, for what Conrad called the "flabby devil" is always settling into some corner of your world and you must always be ready to root him out.

The conventional wisdom says, "Keep your eye on the big picture." Don't sweat the details, delegate, and don't try to take care of everything.

Wrong.

If the pressure to do things right does not emanate from your office, it will not emanate from anywhere. If a department is not answering its phone, go to the office and find out why. If a class is not being met regularly, call in the instructor. If a light bulb has not been replaced in a few days, bug building and grounds. If old furniture clutters the halls, have it removed. If a classroom's walls are peeling, arrange to have it painted. If lectures are ill attended, do everything you can to get the people out, including coercing them. If the bookstore is inadequate, agitate. If there are no places on campus to sit down, figure out ways to put in some seating on the cheap. Do everything you can every day.

This, of course, is a recipe for burnout, but burning out is what administrators are supposed to do. That is why the shelf-life of administrators is about as short as the careers of NFL running backs, and for the same reason: they take too many hits.

FOUR

Don't Try to Do
Someone Else's Job

Some of the hits taken by administrators will be delivered by those faculty members who have forgotten (or never knew) what their job is and spend time trying to form their students' character or turn them into exemplary citizens.

I can't speak for every academic, but I am not trained to do these things, although I am aware of people who are: preachers, therapists, social workers, political activists, professional gurus, inspirational speakers. Teachers, as I have said repeatedly, teach materials and confer skills, and therefore don't or shouldn't do a lot of other things—like produce active citizens, inculcate the virtue of tolerance, redress injustices, and bring about political change. Of course a teacher might produce some of these effects—or their opposites—along the way, but they will be, or should be, contingent and not what is aimed at. The question that administrators often ask, "What practices provide students with the knowledge and commitments to be socially responsible citizens?" is not a bad question, but the answers to it should not be the content of a college or university course. No doubt, the practices of responsible citizenship and moral behavior should be encouraged in our young adults, but it's not the business of the university to do so, except when the morality in question is the morality that penalizes cheating, plagiarizing, and shoddy teaching. Once we cross the line that separates academic work from these other kinds, we are guilty both of practicing without a license and of defaulting on our professional responsibilities.

But isn't it our responsibility both as teachers and as citizens to instill democratic values in our students? Derek Bok thinks so and invokes studies that claim to demonstrate a cause and effect relationship between a college education and an active participation in the country's political life: "researchers have shown that college graduates are much more active civically and politically than those who have not attended college" (*Our Underachieving Colleges*). But this statistic proves nothing except what everyone knows: college graduates have more access to influential circles than do those without a college education. It does not prove that the inclination to participate in political life is produced by the *content* of a course or set of courses; a college degree may be a ticket of entry to the corridors of power; it does not follow, however, that the experience of earning it particularly fits one to walk those corridors successfully.

Even if there were a definite correlation between education and an active citizenry, that would not be a reason for teaching with the aim of fostering civic participation. Civic participation is a political rather than an academic goal. In a critique of my position, Elizabeth Kiss and Peter Euben ask, "Does a commitment to nurture core democratic principles on campus—to encourage and on occasion even to *force* students to engage as respectful equals with people of other races, cultures, religions, and ideologies—amount to an unjustifiable form of indoctrination?" The answer is "yes." Respecting those of other cultures, religions, and ideologies is a particular model of ethical behavior, but it would not be the preferred model of some libertarians, free-market economists, orthodox Jews, Amish, fundamentalist Christians, and members of the Aryan Nation, all of whom, the last time I looked, are American citizens and many of whom are college students. A university administration may believe with Kiss and Euben that "principles of equality and respect" form the core of democratic life, but if it pressures students to accept those principles as theirs, it is using the power it has to impose a moral vision on those who do not share it, and that is indoctrination if anything is. (It should go without saying that such an accusation would not apply to avowedly sectarian universities; indoctrination in a certain direction is quite properly their business.) As long as respect for the culture, religion, and ideology of the other is a contested ethic rather than a universal one, a university that requires it or attempts to inculcate it is engaged not in educational but in partisan behavior.

Bok is certainly aware that discussions of value harbor the danger of partisan indoctrination but believes that there is "a way of promoting certain values that does not amount to unacceptable indoctrination." But how does one tell the difference between acceptable and unacceptable indoctrination? The answer, it turns out, is that indoctrination is acceptable when it is performed in the service of the values favored by whomever is doing the indoctrinating. Bok's list of preferred values is a plausible one. He tells us that he favors honesty, the keeping of promises, and "more understanding of different races, backgrounds, and religions," goals, he says, "with which no reasonable person is likely to disagree." This is the oldest move in the liberal playbook—stigmatize in advance values antithetical to those liberalism professes and then dare anyone to disagree on pain of being declared unreasonable. (John Locke did it first in the *Letter Concerning Toleration*, 1689.) Bok attempts to blunt the coercive implications of what he urges by leaving room for student disagreement: "a student should always be free to question principles of behavior...no matter how correct they may seem." But rather than removing indoctrination from the classroom, this turns the classroom into a theater of competing indoctrinations. Permitting students to plump for the values they prefer as a counterweight to the values preferred by their professor sends the message that affirming (or rejecting) values is the business we are in, and that, as I've already said, is the wrong message. Preferring (or dispreferring) values on the part of anyone, teacher or student, is just not a proper academic activity.

Paul Street, an urban researcher in Chicago, complains that by conceiving the academic task so narrowly, I turn professors into "good Germans, content to leave policy to those who are 'qualified' to conduct state affairs—people like George W. Bush and Donald Rumsfeld." Street's statement displays everything that is wrong about confusing teaching and political advocacy. Without bothering to argue the case, he assumes that George W. Bush and Donald Rumsfeld are today's fascist-militarists, and that it should be the business of every right-thinking (meaning left-thinking) academic to teach and write about the evil of their policies so that the emergence of a new Third Reich can be nipped in the bud.

Admittedly, many Americans and most academics in the humanities and social sciences share Street's political views, but does that mean that the educational experience of our students (many of whom hold opposing views) should be guided by them? Should the evil and perfidy of the Bush administration be the baseline assumption in the light of which history, literature, political theory, philosophy, and social science are taught? I think not (nor do I think that the virtue of the Bush administration should be the baseline assumption). In a classroom, the gathering of evidence on the way to reaching a conclusion is the prime academic activity. In Street's classroom, that activity would have been abandoned from the get-go; for him, the evidence is already in and the conclusion—a partisan conclusion—has been reached in advance.

Later in the piece Street identifies himself as "a former academic" who left the academy and now spends his time leading teach-ins and doing other politically oriented community work. He was right to leave; it was not his kind of thing. He was wrong to urge those who remain to perform in the classroom as he now does outside of it. Street can stand for all of those '60s activists who transferred their disappointed hopes for political revolution to higher education and the classroom. An entire generation has grown up believing that, as a provost at Brooklyn College put it, "Teaching is a political act." Only bad teaching is a political act.

Nor is teaching a political act in the milder sense of preparing students to assume their roles as citizens in a democratic society. Those who think that the fashioning of democratic citizens is an important educational goal are likely also to think that the business of education should be conducted in a democratic manner. They reason that because we live in a democratic society, the institutions we inhabit—and especially our institutions of higher education—should embody democratic principles.

But one need only recall the principles of democracy in order to see how poorly they fit the needs of an educational institution. Take the key principle of equality, for example. Under it, individual citizens have equal rights independently of differences in their intelligence, level of accomplishment, or age: seniority is a category of the census rather than the basis of privilege; anyone can say anything he or she likes (as long as it is not an incitement to violence, libel, or treason), and the state will levy no penalties even if what is said is unpopular or idiosyncratic in the extreme. Contrast that with what happens in college universities where the one man, one vote rule applies only if you've earned tenure, and seniority confers both privilege and power, and what you say or write can lead to your being denied promotion if your senior colleagues don't like it, and a thousand other things that come to mind the moment one starts to think of ways in which what goes on in the world of the academy is anything but democratic. It is not that there is a deliberate intention to be *un*democratic; it's just that being democratic rather than facilitating college business will often be seen to frustrate it by setting up obstacles in its way. While democratic governance is absolutely essential in a state dedicated to the idea that the people have the last word and the powerless can always vote out the powerful, democratic governance has a questionable relevance in a college or university where deans and provosts and presidents have the last word and can only be removed by someone above them in the hierarchy.

It is a question finally of what business we are in, and we are in the education business, not the democracy business. Democracy, we must remember, is a political not an educational project. It is a response to a problem formulated in the seventeenth century by the founders of Enlightenment Liberalism. The problem is that in any modern nation-state, citizens are committed to a bewildering array of belief systems, or as John Rawls calls them, "comprehensive doctrines." These are so disparate and so opposed to one another that if they are given their full sway in the public sphere, the result will be conflict, endless strife, and, eventually, civil war. The solution? Regard all citizens as free and equal political agents endowed with rights independently of what they happen to believe or who they happen to be, men, women, black, white, rich, poor, successful, or unsuccessful. The rights accorded every citizen are checks against abuses of power, and the most important check is provided by the ballot box, which allows the citizenry periodically to throw the rascals out.

The question is, what has this to do with scholarship and teaching, and the answer is, absolutely nothing. It is not the case that members of the academy are regarded as equal citizens despite differences in length of service, professional performance, research accomplishments, pedagogical effectiveness, etc. It is just these differences that make for *un*equal treatment, again not because administrators and promotion committees are being undemocratic, but because assessment and evaluation, not democracy, define their professional obligations. Moreover, evaluation and assessment are not tasks that can be distributed evenly across the population, both because those who are being evaluated cannot assume the role of judges in their own case, and because some in the population—students, staff, janitorial workers—lack the credentials that would make their evaluations meaningful and relevant. Even though certain elements of democratic procedures and principles may prove useful in an academic setting—note that "useful" is an administrative, not a moral, notion—democracy is not *generally* appropriate as a standard and benchmark in academic life.

ACADEMIC FREEDOM

But what about the doctrine of academic freedom? Isn't it a quintessentially democratic idea and isn't it essential to the enterprise of higher education? Most faculty members certainly think so, for whenever they get into trouble for something they've said or want cover for something they're about to say or do, academic freedom is the first phrase on their lips. But more often than not, it is a phrase wrongly invoked in situations where it does not apply. Consider the following example. In May 2003, journalist Chris Hedges was invited by President Paul Pribbenow to give the commencement speech at Rockford College. He spoke about Iraq and said among other things that the United States was an occupying force, and that "we will pay for this." Three minutes into his speech someone pulled the plug on the microphone; President Pribbenow spoke to the crowd and invoked academic freedom. Audience members shouted out protests. One of the soon-to-be graduates sitting on the stage got up and left. Hedges resumed speaking but cut his speech short and later said that he was surprised and saddened. "I had seen that in Belgrade, but I wasn't expecting to see it here."

What, then, are the First Amendment and academic freedom issues here? Exactly zero. Everyone did what he or she did freely. Pribbenow was free to invite Hedges. Hedges was free to say anything he liked, and even if Pribbenow had asked him to speak on a particular topic or avoid others, he would have been free to say no and decline the gig. The audience members were free to protest. The college would have been free to remove the protestors from the room, but there was no obligation to do so in the name of protecting the speaker's First Amendment rights. The soon-to-be graduate was free to leave the stage.

One might ask whether all these people *ought* to have done what they freely did, but that would be a question not of academic freedom but of appropriateness and judgment. Judgment was what President Pribbenow failed to exercise. He said that he wanted commencement "to be more than a pop speech," but could he not have anticipated that someone would have said what one member of the audience did say? "The day belongs to the students. It doesn't belong to a political view"? (Note that this doesn't mean that it was unconstitutional to give the platform over to a political view; it was just unwise.) Hedges said that this was not the first college at which he had given such a speech, but had he ever given one at a commencement? A commencement is a particular kind of occasion; it is, quite precisely, a ceremony, a formal rite of passage where etiquette and ritual are more important, and more appropriate, than profundity. Inviting controversial speakers to campus is certainly a good idea, but inviting controversial speakers to give a commencement address may not be. Pribbenow is reported to have decided that from now on he will seek speakers who would address matters important to people graduating from college. In short he will seek commencement speakers who will give a commencement speech. In the end, a lot of heat but little light; not many lessons learned—except the lesson that administrators should think things through before issuing invitations—and certainly no lesson about free speech or academic freedom.

Nor was either free speech or academic freedom the issue when the administration of Nova Southeastern University in Davie, Florida, invited author Salman Rushdie to be the commencement speaker at the Farquhar College of Arts and Sciences in 2006. Some student members of the International Muslim Association protested the invitation, presumably because they agreed with those who regarded Rushdie's 1988 novel *The Satanic Verses* as a blasphemy against Islam and the prophet Muhammad. Graduating senior Fahreen Paravez decided not to attend. "I was looking forward to my graduation," she said, but "when I found out that Salman Rushdie would be the speaker, I was appalled." Taken aback by the protest, NSU officials defended themselves by denying any malign intention—"Choosing Rushdie was not meant to insult anyone," said spokesperson Dean Don Rosenblum—and by pointing out that as a speaker Rushdie "fits well with NSU's yearlong study of Good and Evil." Apparently neither Rosenblum nor anyone else saw the tension between these two defenses: if Good and Evil is the theme, Rushdie must represent the former (you're not going to invite evil to be your speaker) and those who condemned him (and issued a fatwa against him) the latter; and if, as the protest indicated, there were graduating seniors who aligned themselves with the Ayotollah Khomeini and against Rushdie, they were sure to be insulted. It was not to the point to declare, as Rosenblum did, that Rushdie is "an outspoken advocate of freedom of expression, which is a critical core value of the university." To invoke freedom of expression as a core value is to elevate it above any and all of the sentiments that might be expressed; expression itself, rather than its content, becomes the cornerstone of your theology. But it is not, presumably, the cornerstone of the Muslim students' theology, and what they heard when the mantra of free speech was preached at them was another statement by the university that their beliefs—especially those that would lead to labeling some expressions blasphemous—are wrong.

The university tried to wriggle out of this one by turning the occasion into an educational experience. Professor Eileen Smith said, "I have great hopes that [Rushdie's] visit will inspire dialogue and a respectful, but lively, exchange of intellectual ideas." That sounds like what goes on, or should go on, in a classroom, but a graduation ceremony is not a class. The students do not come prepared to exchange intellectual ideas. They come prepared to be entertained, congratulated, and sent out into the world. They've already had four years of serious inquiry, and if that has been insufficient, 20 minutes more isn't going to be of much help. This day is reserved for lighter pleasures, and it is a commencement speaker's job to provide them. Rushdie's visit was trumpeted (in the college's announcement) as the "capstone" to a series of public lectures and classroom discussions of "tolerance, acceptance and social justice." One assumes that in the class-rooms and at the public lectures vigorous participation was encouraged, and those who disagreed with the teacher or speaker could make their disagreement known in a context that had a place for it. But graduation speeches are not usu-ally followed by question and answer periods or by a panel made up of persons representing opposing views. A gradu-ation speech is a take it or leave it proposition and those who prefer to leave it must either walk out or resolve to stay home. Fahreen Parvez had it exactly right when she said, "If he were there for any other event, that would have been fine, because that's optional; but having him at graduation, it's not appropriate because that's for the families and the students." When you're the proud parent of a graduating son or daugh-ter, the last thing you want to hear is something that will make you think. You want to hear something that will make you feel good. Professor Smith asserted that "the choice of Rushdie as speaker inspires questions, invites challenges and embodies larger issues." That's exactly the problem.

One year later, in 2007, it was the president of Columbia University, Lee Bollinger, who was seduced by the lure of larger issues. At the conclusion of his remarks to those assem-bled to hear and question President Mahmoud Ahmadinejad of Iran, Bollinger declared, "I am only a professor, who is also a university president, and today I feel all the weight of the modern civilized world yearning to express...revulsion at what you stand for."

By using the word "also" to introduce the fact of his administrative identity, Bollinger seemed to be saying, "I am a professor first and a university president second." But as everyone knows or should know, while university presidents may "also" be faculty members, both their obligations and their rights flow from their positions as administrators.

The obligation of a senior administrator is to conduct himself or herself in such a way as always to bring honor and credit to the institution he or she serves. Just what this general imperative requires will vary with the particular situations an administrator encounters, but at the very least we could say that an administrator who brings attention of an unwelcome kind to a university is probably not focusing on the job. He or she may be doing some other job—speaking truth to power, standing up for free speech, protesting against various forms of injustice—and those jobs may be well worth doing, but they belong to someone else.

So when President Bollinger said on another occasion, "I have free speech too," he was of course correct. He is free, like a faculty member, to say what he thinks about any issue when he is not in the classroom and bound by academic protocols; but unlike a faculty member, anything he says, even in extracurricular contexts, can be held against him by his employers. University administrators serve at will; and while, like other citizens, they enjoy freedom of speech, they do not enjoy immunity, as faculty members generally do, from the consequences—including possible dismissal— brought on by their having spoken freely.

Another way to put this is to say that when it comes to the activities of senior administrators, concepts like freedom of speech and academic freedom are not to the point. What is to the point are academic judgment and performance; those are the standards in relation to which Bollinger's performance should be assessed.

Now, it may be that he was speaking to constituencies within the university that were unhappy with some of his earlier actions in the ongoing controversy about the teaching practices of the Department of Middle East Asian Languages and Cultures. So, there may have been internal reasons—reasons not fully known to me and other commentators from the outside—that could account for his decision to take center stage and aggressively attack the Iranian president before he spoke.

Even so, as a general rule, what an administrator should do when a controversial speaker comes to campus is lower the stakes and minimize the importance of the occasion. Not minimize the importance of the issues, but minimize the role of the university, which is not a player on the world stage but (at most) a location where questions of international significance can be raised in an academic manner.

Bollinger was correct when he said in his remarks that it is appropriate "for the university to conduct such an event," but it is not appropriate for the university to be a front-and-center protagonist in the event. When Bollinger hurled his challenges at Ahmadinejad, he was saying explicitly, "here's where I stand on these issues," and therefore saying implicitly, "here's where Columbia University stands."

But Columbia does not, or at least should not, stand anywhere on the vexed issues of the day, and neither should its chief executive, at least publicly. After it was all over, Bollinger was applauded by some faculty members and students who are pro-Israel, and criticized by others who see Israel as the oppressor of the Palestinian people and lament the influence of what has been called the Israeli lobby. It would have been better if neither constituency were pleased or distressed by what he said, which means that it would have been better if he had said nothing, at least nothing substantive enough to amount to a position.

But how could Bollinger have managed to say nothing of substance once the invitation to Ahmadinejad had been extended (by a dean) and the predictable explosion of publicity had generated enormous expectations? Easy. Don't play to the expectations; instead, damp them down by turning the occasion into an academic rather than a political one. Bollinger could have begun by saying what was undoubtedly true, that the university had received many communications from faculty, students, and members of the public, all of whom posed questions they would have liked to put to the Iranian president. He could have said that he had selected a number of the most frequently asked questions and then posed them in a way that distanced him from their emotional force. "How would you reply to the contention that...?" "Many are worried that...." "Some have seen a contradiction between...." Exactly the same topics would have been brought up—Holocaust denial, nuclear proliferation, terrorism, Iraq—but in a spirit of inquiry rather than personal outrage. He could have presented himself as someone who was delivering the mail rather than as someone who was making the news.

It could be objected that if Bollinger had conducted himself in this manner, a great opportunity to stand up for what is right and say things that needed to be said would have been missed. But that is the kind of opportunity a university administrator would do well to miss. Leave the geopolitical pronouncements to the politicians whose job it is to make them and follow them up with actions. Remember always what a university is for—the transmission of knowledge and the conferring of analytical skills—and resist the temptation to inflate the importance of what goes on in its precincts. And don't think that everything that comes your way is a matter of free speech and academic freedom. These grand abstractions are invoked by academics at the slightest pretext, but in most situations in which administrators are required to act, they will only get in the way of seeing clearly what is and is not at stake.

The typical discussion of academic freedom will include a lot of talk about the value of unpopular ideas, the primacy of freedom, the nature of truth, and FDR's Four Freedoms. It is a phrase that *seems* resonant with large, philosophical implications, but it is really a narrow, modest thing: it is the freedom to do one's academic job without interference from external constituencies like legislators, boards of trustees, donors, and even parents. It is best thought of as a matter of guild protectionism, the name given to the desire of academics—and it is a desire hardly unique to them—to go about their business in ways defined by the nature and history of *their* enterprise rather than by some external constituency. Academic freedom, correctly (and modestly) understood, is not a challenge to the imperative always to academicize; it is the *name* of that imperative; it is the freedom to be an academic, which is, by definition, *not* the freedom to be anything and everything else. It doesn't mean don't interfere with me *whatever* I do—that would be a freedom no society that wished to remain a society could countenance—just don't interfere with me as I'm doing my job, so long as, in doing it, I am not breaking any laws.

In saying this I am merely rephrasing the American Association of University Professor's 1915 Declaration of Principles on Academic Freedom. After defining academic freedom as "freedom of inquiry and research, freedom of teaching within the university or college, and freedom of extramural utterance," the declaration adds that the claim to academic freedom can be asserted only by "those who carry on their work in the temper of the scientific inquirer" and never by those who would use it "for uncritical and intemperate partisanship." That statement is informed by the fear that external interests are always trying to take control of the academy. It used to be the church, the authors of the statement declare, but now it is "barbarous trustees" who constitute the danger. Whatever the danger, vigilance and resistance are necessary, and the first thing to be done, the statement goes on to say, is to make sure that our own house is clean and that we're doing the job we're supposed to do.

In short, one exercises academic freedom when determining for oneself (within the limits prescribed by departmental regulations and graduation requirements) what texts, assignments, and exam questions will best serve an academic purpose; one violates academic freedom by deciding to set aside academic purposes for others thought to be more noble or urgent.

Of course one is free to prefer other purposes to the purposes appropriate to the academy, but one is not free to employ the academy's machinery and resources in the service of those other purposes. If what you really want to do is preach, or organize political rallies, or work for world peace, or minister to the poor and homeless, or counsel troubled youths, you should either engage in those activities after hours and on weekends, or, if part-time is not enough time, you should resign from the academy, as Paul Street did, and take up work that speaks directly to the problems you feel compelled to address. Do not, however, hi-jack the academic enterprise and then justify what you've done by invoking academic freedom. The moment a teacher tries to promote a political or social agenda, mold the character of students, produce civic virtue, or institute a regime of tolerance, he or she has stepped away from the immanent rationality of the enterprise and performed an action in relation to which there is no academic freedom protection because there's nothing academic going on.

The limited freedom academics do enjoy follows from the task they perform. That task—extending the boundaries of received knowledge—does not have a pre-established goal; the open-endedness of intellectual inquiry demands a degree of flexibility not granted to the practitioners of other professions, who must be responsive to the customer, or to the bottom line, or to the electorate, or to the global economy. (That's why there's no such thing as "corporate manager freedom," or "shoe salesman freedom," or "dermatologist freedom.") If you think of academic freedom in this way—as a logical extension of a particular task and not as a free-standing value—you will be able to defend it both from those who see it as an unwarranted indulgence of pampered professors and from those pampered professors who would extend it into a general principle that allows them to say and do, or not do, whatever they like. To those who regard academic freedom as an unwarranted indulgence you can say, no, it's not an indulgence, it's a necessary condition for engaging in this enterprise, and if you want this enterprise to flourish, you must grant it; and to those professors who turn freedom into license by using the classroom as a partisan pulpit, or by teaching materials unrelated to the course description, or by coming to class unprepared or not at all, you can say, "look, it's freedom to do the job, not freedom to change it or shirk it."

FREE SPEECH

But isn't academic freedom a subset of the overarching category of freedom of speech, a freedom accorded to all citizens by the Constitution?

Yes, of course professors have the right to say what they like *as citizens* (subject to the usual restrictions on libel, treason, and incitements to violence), but in their professional capacities the freedom they might claim is defined and limited by the nature of the task they are performing. My so-called free-speech rights will be very different depending, for example, on whether I am a fan at a baseball game or a nurse in an operating room. In the first context, my free-speech rights are pretty broad; I can yell any number of things, even abusive profane things, without being silenced, or arrested, or thrown out of the stadium. In the context of the operating room, however, my free-speech rights barely exist at all; if I decide, in the middle of a procedure, to advocate for a higher salary or better working conditions for nurses, I will have no First Amendment defense when I am hauled out of the room and later fired. The reason is that I would have been fired not because of the content of what I said, but because my words, whatever their content, were uttered in a setting that rendered them inappropriate and even dangerous.

Academic situations fall somewhere in between the baseball stadium and the medical operating theater. In the context of the academy, where free speech is generally highly valued, you will have more or less free-speech rights depending on what you're doing and where you're doing it. If I am a student, and I begin to say something, and the teacher cuts me off and says that my point is beside the point he or she wishes to pursue, I have no free-speech recourse. On the other side, as an instructor I can conduct my class in any manner I like—lecture, discussion, group presentations— and I can assign whatever readings I judge to be relevant to the course's topic. Those are pedagogical choices, and I cannot be penalized for making them.

But if I harass students, or call them names, or make fun of their ethnicity, or if I use class time to rehearse my personal political views or attempt to win students over to them, I might well find myself in a disciplinary hearing, either because I am abusing my pedagogical authority or because I am turning the scene of instruction into a scene of indoctrination. What you are free to say in some venues you are not free to say in all venues, and your lack of freedom is not a First Amendment matter; it is a matter, rather, of the appropriateness or inappropriateness of certain kinds of speech relative to certain contexts of employment or social interaction.

Take the case of Ward Churchill. Churchill was a professor at the University of Colorado at Boulder, and he became famous, or rather infamous, because of an essay he wrote several years ago in which he went so far as to say that those who died in the September 11 attack on the World Trade Center were part of the military-industrialist machine that had produced the policies that had produced the hatred that eventually produced the terrible events of that day. When Churchill's remarks (which had appeared in an obscure journal) were unearthed and then publicized by Bill O'Reilly and other conservative commentators, legislators and ordinary citizens called for him to be fired. The argument for his dismissal was made on Chris Matthews's *Hardball*, by Kevin Lundberg, a state representative, who said that Churchill should be "held accountable" to "a common sense of values shared by the culture." Only in that way could he exhibit "professional integrity." But the reverse is true. If Churchill were to limit his conclusions to those already reached by the culture, he would throw his professional integrity out the window.

The fact that a large number of the officials and citizens of Colorado hated what Ward Churchill said is interesting sociologically. It is an answer to the (rather curious) question: what does Colorado think of Ward Churchill? But both the question and the answer (or any answer) have nothing to do with the question of his employment unless we want to go in the direction (symbolized for many by the old Soviet Union) of an academy whose research results are known in advance because they will always support the policies and reigning values of the state.

To its credit, the university's administration made the right call. Chancellor Philip DiStefano declared that "Professor

Churchill has the constitutional right to express his personal views." But DiStefano muddied the waters of the point he had just made when he added, "His essay on 9/11 has outraged and appalled us and the general public." This is at once confused and self-serving. One knows what DiStefano is up to: he is wrapping himself in the flag and mantra of strong First Amendment doctrine, that is, "I despise what you say, but I will defend to the death your right to say it." But it is not the job of a senior administrator either to approve or to disapprove of what a faculty member writes in a nonuniversity publication. It is his job to make the jurisdictional boundaries clear, to say something like "Mr. Churchill's remarks to the general public about matters of general political concern do not fall under the scope of the university's jurisdiction. He is of course free to make them, although one should not assume that in doing so he speaks for the university." Notice that this would stop short of either disavowing or embracing Churchill's remarks. The university can protect the integrity of its enterprise only if it disengages entirely from the landscape of political debate, if it says, in effect, we do academic, not political, business here. Simply by throwing in the egregious "has . . . appalled us," DiStefano has the university coming down on one side of a political question, and he also creates a First Amendment issue where there was none before.

DiStefano's statement may come back to haunt the university now that Churchill has been dismissed after a committee of scholars found him guilty of plagiarism and misrepresentation of his credentials. An appeal is in process, and one argument being made by Churchill's defenders is that the decision to scrutinize his record so closely was politically motivated, even if the ostensible reasons for firing him were appropriately pedagogical. It would not surprise me were Churchill's attorneys to cite what DiStefano said as evidence that he was being discriminated against because of the content of his constitutionally protected speech. After all, it could be argued, doesn't the fact that the chancellor of the university declared himself "appalled" by Churchill's ideas suggest that he had been disciplined because he holds those ideas?

In 2006, Kevin Barrett, a lecturer at the University of Wisconsin at Madison, took his place alongside Churchill as a college teacher whose views on 9/11 led politicians and ordinary citizens to demand that he be fired.

Mr. Barrett, who had a one-semester contract to teach a course titled "Islam: Religion and Culture," acknowledged on a radio talk show that he shared with students his conviction that the destruction of the World Trade Center was an inside job perpetrated by the American government. The predictable uproar ensued, and the equally predictable battle lines were drawn between those who disagree about what the doctrine of academic freedom does and does not allow.

Mr. Barrett's critics argued that academic freedom has limits and should not be invoked to justify the dissemination of lies and fantasies. Mr. Barrett's supporters (most of whom were not partisans of his conspiracy theory) insisted that it is the very point of an academic institution to entertain all points of view, however unpopular. This was the position taken by the university's provost, Patrick Farrell, when he ruled that Mr. Barrett would be retained: "We cannot allow political pressure from critics of unpopular ideas to inhibit the free exchange of ideas."

Both sides got it wrong. Each assumed that academic freedom is about ideas; one side thought that no idea should be ruled out in advance, while the other wanted to draw the line at propositions (like the denial of the Holocaust or the flatness of the world) considered by almost everyone to be crazy or dangerous.

But in fact, academic freedom has nothing to do with the expression of ideas. It is not a subset of the general freedom of Americans to say anything they like. Rather, academic freedom is the freedom of academics to *study* anything they like; the freedom, that is, to subject any body of material, however unpromising it might seem, to academic interrogation and analysis, to what I have called academicization. Any idea can be brought into a classroom if the point is to inquire into its structure, history, influence, etc. But no idea belongs in the classroom if the point of introducing it is to recruit students for or against a political agenda.

It is a matter of record that Mr. Barrett has a political agenda. He is a member of a group calling itself Scholars for 9/11 Truth, an organization with the declared aim of persuading Americans that the Bush administration "not only permitted 9/11 to happen but may even have orchestrated these events." The question is not, did he introduce his students to this account of the events of September 11, 2001? The question is, did he proselytize for it? Provost Farrell didn't quite see it that way, because he was too hung up on questions of content and balance. He thought that the important thing was to ensure a diversity of views in the classroom, and so he was reassured when Mr. Barrett promised to surround his "unconventional" ideas and "personal opinions" with readings "representing a variety of viewpoints."

But the number of viewpoints Mr. Barrett presented to his students was not the measure of his responsibility. There is, in fact, no academic requirement to include more than one view of an academic issue, although it is often pedagogically useful to do so. The true requirement is that no matter how many (or few) views are presented to the students, they should be offered as objects of analysis rather than as candidates for allegiance.

Thus the question Provost Farrell should have put to Mr. Barrett was not "Do you hold these views?" (he can hold any views he likes), or "Do you proclaim them in public?" (he has that right no less than the rest of us), or even "Do you surround them with the views of others?"

Rather, the question should have been: "Do you separate yourself from your partisan identity when you are in the employ of the citizens of Wisconsin and teach subject matter—whatever it is—rather than urge political action?" If the answer had been yes, allowing Mr. Barrett to remain in the classroom would have been warranted. If the answer had been no (or if a yes answer was followed by classroom behavior that contradicted it), he should have been shown the door. Not because he would have been teaching the "wrong" things, but because he would have abandoned teaching for indoctrination.

In neither the Churchill nor the Barrett case, then, is freedom of speech the real issue. But the temptation to view any issue as implicating one's free-speech rights is apparently irresistible. Indeed, the modern American version of crying wolf is crying First Amendment. If you want to burn a cross on a black family's lawn, or buy an election by contributing millions to a candidate, or vilify Jerry Falwell and his mother in a scurrilous "parody," and someone or some government agency tries to stop you, just yell "First Amendment rights" and you will stand a good chance of getting to do what you want to do. Frederick Schauer, a First Amendment scholar at Harvard University's Kennedy School, names this strategy "First Amendment opportunism."

Take the case of the editors of college newspapers who will always cry First Amendment when something they've published turns out to be the cause of outrage and controversy. In recent years, the offending piece or editorial or advertisement usually involves (what is at least perceived to be) an attack on Jews. A few years back, the *Daily Illini*, an independent student newspaper at the University of Illinois at Urbana-Champaign, printed a letter from a resident of Seattle with no university affiliation. The letter ran under the headline "Jews Manipulate America" and argued that because their true allegiance is to the state of Israel, the president should "separate Jews from all government advisory positions"; otherwise, the writer warned, "the Jews might face another Holocaust."

When the predictable firestorm of outrage erupted, the newspaper's editor responded by declaring, first, that "we are committed to giving all people a voice"; second, that, given this commitment, "we print the opinions of others with whom we do not agree"; third, that to do otherwise would involve the newspaper in the dangerous acts of "silencing" and "self-censorship"; and, fourth, that "what is hate speech to one member of a society is free speech to another."

Wrong four times.

I'll bet the *Daily Illini* is not committed to giving all people a voice—the KKK? man-boy love? advocates of slavery? would-be Unabombers? Nor do I believe that the editors sift through submissions looking for the ones they disagree with and then print those. No doubt they apply some principles of selection, asking questions like is it relevant, or is it timely, or does it get the facts right, or does it present a coherent argument? That is, they exercise judgment, which is quite a different thing from silencing or self-censorship. No one is silenced because a single outlet declines to publish him; silencing occurs when that outlet (or any other) is forbidden by the state to publish him on pain of legal sanction; and that is also what censorship is.

As for self-censoring, if it is anything, it is what we all do whenever we decide it would be better not to say something or cut a sentence that went just a little bit too far or leave a manuscript in the bottom drawer because it is not yet ready. Self-censorship, in short, is not a crime or a moral failing; it is a responsibility.

And, finally, whatever the merits of the argument by which all assertions are relativized—your hate speech is my free speech—this incident has nothing to do with either hate speech or free speech and everything to do with whether the editors are discharging or defaulting on their obligations when they foist them off on an inapplicable doctrine, saying in effect, "The First Amendment made us do it."

To be sure, the First Amendment protects unpopular as well as popular speech. But what it protects unpopular speech *from* is abridgement by the government of its free expression; it does not protect unpopular speech from being rejected by a newspaper, and it confers no positive obligation to give your pages over to unpopular speech, or popular speech, or any speech. There is no First Amendment issue here, just an issue of editorial judgment and the consequences of exercising it. You can print or say anything you like; but if the heat comes, it's yours, not the Constitution's.

In these controversies, student editors are sometimes portrayed, or portray themselves, as First Amendment heroes who bravely risk criticism and censure in order to uphold a cherished American value. But they are not heroes; they are merely confused and, in terms of their understanding of the doctrine they invoke, rather hapless.

Not as hapless, however, as the Harvard English department, which made a collective fool of itself three times when, in 2003, it invited, disinvited, and then reinvited poet Tom Paulin to be the Morris Gray Lecturer. Again the flash point was anti-Semitism. In his poetry and in public comments, Paulin had said that Israel had no right to exist, that settlers on the West Bank "should be shot dead," and that Israeli police and military forces were the equivalent of the

Nazi SS. When these and other statements came to light shortly before Paulin was to give his lecture, the department voted to rescind the invitation. When the inevitable cry of "censorship, censorship" was heard in the land, the department flip-flopped again, and a professor-spokesperson declared, "This was a clear affirmation that the department stood strongly by the First Amendment."

It was of course nothing of the kind; it was a transparent effort of a bunch that had already put its foot in its mouth twice to wriggle out of trouble and regain the moral high ground by striking the pose of First Amendment defender. But, in fact, the department and its members were not First Amendment defenders (a religion they converted to a little late), but serial bunglers.

What should they have done? Well, it depends on what they wanted to do. If they wanted to invite this particular poet because they admired his poetry, they had a perfect right to do so. If they were aware ahead of time of Paulin's public pronouncements, they could have chosen either to say something by way of explanation or to remain silent and let the event speak for itself; either course of action would have been at once defensible and productive of risk. If they knew nothing of Paulin's anti-Israel sentiments (difficult to believe of a gang of world-class researchers) but found out about them after the fact, they might have said, "Ooops, never mind" or toughed it out, again alternatives not without risk.

But at each stage, whatever they did or didn't do would have had no relationship whatsoever to any First Amendment right—Paulin had no right to be invited—or obligation—there was no obligation either to invite or to disinvite him, and certainly no obligation to reinvite him, unless you count the obligations imposed on yourself by a succession of ill-thought-through decisions. Whatever the successes or failures here, they were once again failures of judgment, not doctrine.

A failure of judgment was also at the heart of the Larry Summers saga, which ended with his resignation as the president of Harvard. Summers got into trouble when he speculated at an academic conference that the underrepresentation of women in the sciences might have a genetic basis.

The offended academic left saw Summers's remarks as an affront to its causes and as the latest chapter in the sad history of gender discrimination. The right (both inside and outside the academy) regarded the entire hullabaloo as an instance of political correctness run amok at the expense of Summers's First Amendment rights. And pundits on both sides thought that something deep about the nature of a university was at stake here. Brian McGrory, a *Boston Globe* columnist, achieved a new high in fatuousness, even in this rather dreary context, when he observed portentously, "I've always assumed that the strength of the academy is its ability to encourage difficult questions."

Well, that may be the strength of the academy, but it is not the strength sought by search committees when they interview candidates for senior administrative positions. No search committee asks, "Can we count on you to rile things up? Can we look forward to days of hostile press coverage? Can you give us a list of the constituencies you intend to offend?" Search committees do ask, "What is your experience with budgets?" and "What are your views on the place of intercollegiate athletics?" and "What will be your strategy for recruiting a world-class faculty?" and "How will you create a climate attractive to donors?"

Summers offered serial apologies for his comments but accompanied them with a defense that took them back. I was, he said, just being provocative. But being provocative is not in the job description. If straight-talking, with no concern for the fall-out that may follow, is what you like to do, you may not be cut out to be a university administrator. Not every virtue (if straight-talking is a virtue, and I have my doubts) is pertinent to every practice, and it is surely part of your responsibility to know what virtues are appropriate to the position you hold.

Stanley Kurtz opined in the *National Review* that Summers's critics had "turned him into a free-speech martyr," but that piece of alchemy could have been performed only if he had been prevented from speaking or punished by some state authority for the content of his words. In fact, he spoke freely, and if he suffered the consequences, they are not consequences from which the First Amendment protected him.

The First Amendment says that, in most circumstances, you can't be stopped from saying something and that, in many (but not all) circumstances, the content of what you say cannot be a reason for imprisoning you or firing you. But that doesn't mean that you get a free pass; you are not exempt from criticism; you are not exempt from public ridicule; you are not exempt from being voted out of your country club; and if what you have said causes enough of a ruckus, you are not exempt from being removed from your position, so long as the reason given for your removal is that your words have created conditions such that you can no longer do your job and not that somebody up there doesn't like their content. There is a big difference between "I don't like what that guy said, and I'm going to fire him" and "I don't like the effects brought about by what he said, and I'm going to fire him." The first raises constitutional issues (at least in some contexts); the second doesn't. It's just a judgment on job performance. The content of what Summers said was irrelevant to the only question that should been asked: is he discharging the duties and obligations of his office in a way that protects the reputation of the university and fosters its academic, political, and financial health? The Harvard Corporation asked that question, answered it in the negative, and came to a conclusion that had nothing whatsoever to do with Summers's free-speech rights.

The distinction between academic issues and free-speech issues seems to be a difficult one for both academics and those who criticize them. In 1997, the State University of New York at New Paltz sponsored a conference called "Revolting Behavior: The Challenges of Women's Sexual Freedom." Some called it borderline pornography and others celebrated it as an exercise in free speech. But what was interesting and depressing about the controversy was that both sides were indulging in the usual forms of bad faith, which they disguised by invoking sonorous abstractions.

Then governor George E. Pataki and the trustees who were egging him on displayed bad faith when they declared that the issue is scholarship and academic standards. No, the issue for them was that the scholarship represented in the conference's panels was scholarship they didn't like, in part because it didn't resemble the scholarship they encountered when they attended college a generation or two ago.

They didn't remember (and neither do I) any professor of theirs talking about body parts, excretory functions, the sex trade, dildos, bisexuality, transvestism, and lesbian pornography on the way to explicating Shakespeare or analyzing the political strategies of Queen Elizabeth I. But like it or not, that is the kind of talk and research being engaged in by many professors today.

Arguing against what is new in intellectual circles is of course a respectable and necessary activity, but it is, or should be, an activity reserved for people who have read the relevant texts and are informed about the history and traditions of the disciplines. Governor Pataki and his political appointees were not those people.

Things weren't much better on the other side. If the critics of the New Paltz conference missed the mark (because they didn't know what the mark was and were not really interested in it anyway), the conference's defenders had their own way of obscuring what was really at stake.

To hear them talk, what was at stake was the abstract notion of free speech rather than the academic quality of what had actually been spoken. If it's speech and it takes place on a campus, they seemed to say, then it should be allowed to go on no matter what its content.

The trouble with this line of reasoning is that it short-circuits the consideration of the educational question—the question of what subjects and modes of instruction are educationally appropriate—and gives administrators reluctant to make decisions an all-purpose rationale for doing little and explaining nothing.

When SUNY trustee Candace de Russy complained that the conference "had absolutely nothing to do with the college's undergraduate mission," the college president, Roger W. Bowen, should have replied either, "Yes it does, and here's why," or, "You're right, and I made a mistake." Instead he went on about academic freedom and then added, as if to assure everyone that he knew trash when he saw it, that he "personally found several of their planned panel topics offensive."

"Offensive" is a word that allows Bowen to make a judgment and withdraw from it at the same time. He used it to avoid the real question: not whether the panels were offensive or inoffensive—neither quality is a reason for putting a panel on—but whether they were plausibly related to some sound educational purpose.

President Bowen was doing just what Governor Pataki did, but with an ACLU twist. Mr. Pataki said, I don't like it and therefore it doesn't belong on the campus. President Bowen said, I don't like it and therefore it does belong on the campus. The governor was trying to make campus life dance to the tune of his personal convictions. The college president was running away from his stated personal convictions—even those that relate to his office—in his eagerness to stand up for the First Amendment. One man was trying to do the other's job; the other had forgotten what his job is.

Both men were spouting the rhetoric demanded by their political situations, playing to constituencies—conservative Republicans and First Amendment zealots, respectively— that had very little stake in what actually happens at New Paltz and soon moved on to some other hot spot in the ongoing culture wars.

Meanwhile the news media, as usual, rode the story's extremes, and talk show panelists got to spend a couple of weeks hurling sound bites at one another—you say no tax dollars for whips, I say the First Amendment first, last, and always.

But that's not what it was really about. What it was really about was responsibility and the making of distinctions— distinctions about what a governor is supposed to do and what a college president is supposed to do, and the responsibility of one to keep his hands off the educational process and the responsibility of the other to be hands-on and not confuse genuine judgment with the invocation of some magic phrases.

BENEFITS AND REWARDS

Those magic phrases—academic freedom and free speech— are what provide an alibi for professors who cannot tell the difference between a soapbox and a teacher's podium. It seems that every other day there is a report in the newspaper about teachers who inveigh against George Bush, or call

Israel the new Third Reich, or ridicule the claims and practices of organized religion, or champion the claims and practices of organized religion. These reports almost always provoke outrage and lead to demands by citizens and legislators that the offenders be removed from the classroom and taken off the payroll. Faculty associations and liberal watchdog groups (most of the activities found objectionable emanate from the left) respond by invoking academic freedom and free speech, and pretty soon the debate—predictable and dreary—becomes one about the nature of academic expression and the extent to which it does and does not have limits.

But this can of worms need never be opened if academics begin with the understanding that they are first and foremost academics and not wise men, gurus, and saviors, and that the only obligation to which they must be faithful is the obligation to present the material in the syllabus and introduce students to state-of-the-art methods of analysis. A teacher who understands this to be his obligation will never even be tempted to cross the line between pedagogy and activism. If everyone followed me in the resolve always to academicize, there would be no point to monitoring the political affiliation of faculty members, for that affiliation, whatever it might be, would not (except in the most attenuated way) be generating the analyses, descriptions, and data entries that serve as the basis of study and publication.

The advantage of this way of thinking about the issue is that it outflanks the sloganeering and posturing both sides indulge in: on the one hand, faculty members who shout "academic freedom" and mean by it an instructor's right to say or advocate anything at all with impunity; on the other hand, state legislators who shout "not on our dime" and mean by it that they can tell academics how to do their jobs.

FIVE

Don't Let Anyone Else Do Your Job

Of course, there's no shortage of people who will step in to do your job if you default on it. The corporate world looks to the university for its workforce. Parents want the university to pick up the baton they may have dropped. Students demand that the university support the political cause of the moment. Conservatives believe that the university should refurbish and preserve the traditions of the past. Liberals and progressives would like to see those same traditions dismantled and replaced by what they take to be better ones. Alumni wonder why the athletics teams aren't winning more. Politicians and trustees wonder why the professors aren't teaching more. Whether it is state legislators who want a say in hiring and course content, or donors who want to tell colleges how to spend the funds they provide, or parents who are disturbed when Dick and Jane bring home books about cross-dressing and gender change, or corporations that want new departments opened and others closed, or activist faculty who urge the administration to declare a position on the war in Iraq, there is no end of interests intent on deflecting the university from its search for truth and setting it on another path.

Each of these lobbies has its point, but it is not the university's point, which is, as I have said over and over again, to produce and disseminate (through teaching and publication) academic knowledge and to train those who will take up that task in the future.

But can the university defend the autonomy it claims (or should claim) from public pressures? Is that claim even coherent? Mark Taylor would say no. In a key sentence in the final chapter of his book *The Moment of Complexity* (2001), Taylor declares that "the university is not autonomous but is a thoroughly parasitic institution, which continually depends on the generosity of the host so many academics claim to reject." He continues: "The critical activities of the humanities, arts, and sciences are only possible if they are supported by the very economic interests their criticism so often calls into question." The standard rhetoric of the academy may be anti-market, but the "university and the people employed in it have always been *thoroughly* implicated in a market system."

As a description of the university's inevitable involvement with, and dependence on, the forces and investments of the larger society, this seems to me exactly right. But the prescriptive conclusion that Taylor draws from this description seems to me to be exactly wrong: let's stop pretending, he says, that we can operate in a splendid (but fictional) isolation from everything that enables us; let's accept the fact that we are in, and of, the market and "find new ways to turn market forces to [our] own advantage"; let's go beyond the kind of critical analysis that does little more than "promote organizations and institutions whose obsolescence is undeniable."

But if we are worried about obsolescence and the loss of relevance, the surest way to court both is to become so attuned to the interests and investments of other enterprises—the market, global politics, the information revolution—that we are finally indistinguishable from them. If there is nothing that sets us apart, if there is nothing distinctive about our task or the criteria for accomplishing it, if there is nothing that marks our work as ours and not everyone's, there will be no *particular* reason to support us by giving us a room (or a franchise) of our own. We will be exactly what Taylor suggests we are—a wholly owned (and disposable) subsidiary of something larger. Distinctiveness is a prerequisite both of our survival and of our flourishing. Without it we haven't got a prayer.

Taylor might reply that any distinctiveness we might claim would be illusory in light of the academy's radical dependence on others for financial support. No autonomy, no distinctiveness, no independent project. To argue in this way is to make what I call the "network" mistake—the mistake of thinking that because an entity or a practice has a form only in a network of relations, it is incoherent to speak of its properties, or of the boundaries that separate and distinguish it from other nodal points in the network. Since identity is network-dependent, the reasoning goes, nothing can be spoken of and examined as if it were freestanding and discrete.

The trouble with that reasoning is that it operates at a level of generality so high that you can't see the trees for the forest.

Yes, everything is finally interconnected and has a diacritical rather than a substantive existence (and is therefore, in some sense, not identical with itself), but it doesn't follow that there is nothing distinctive to say about "it," any more than it would follow that because the heart and lungs and the spinal cord are what they are by virtue of the system of which they are components, they perform no isolable functions, display no special characteristics, obey no special laws, and cannot be studied in their own right.

No one would say that about the parts of the body; nor should it be said of the university, which, despite the fact that the conditions of its possibility are exterior to it, does have an internal reality to which you must be attentive if you would hope to make observations that are relevant and (perhaps) helpful.

Indeed, if you do not attend to the internal perspective of a practice, you will be in danger of missing what is most crucial to its performance and you will ask it to do things appropriately done within the precincts of other practices, or you will complain that it does badly or minimally what it should not be doing at all. That is a risk more than courted by some of those who responded indignantly to John J. Mearsheimer's declaration (April 1998) that the University of Chicago "is a remarkably amoral institution" that makes "little effort to provide [students] with moral guidance." By that Mearsheimer does not mean that the university is immoral and gives bad counsel or that individual faculty members lack strong moral views; rather he means that the university gives no counsel, and that it is the professional, and in some sense moral, obligation of faculty members to check their moral commitments at the door.

The professional obligation is moral because it holds faculty members to the *particular* morality of the institution, the morality that comes along with its immanent rationality, which is the rationality of truth seeking, to which one cannot be faithful if one does not "condemn cheating, academic fraud, and plagiarism," all actions "antithetical to the search for truth."

To be sure, that is not the whole of morality—there are legions of moral issues left unaddressed—but it is, or should be, the whole of academic morality. Mearsheimer concedes that an academic morality, narrowly construed, does not meet all of the moral "demands of our society," but, he says, universities are not the institutions equipped or authorized to meet those demands: "providing moral guidance is no longer in their job description. . . . Religious institutions and families are expected to provide their members with explicit advice about moral virtue, but universities are not."

For the most part, those who take issue with Mearsheimer's statements fall into the everything-is-interconnected error. They reason that no human activity is without a moral dimension and add that this is particularly true of the activity of teaching. "I wonder," asks one such critic who responded to Mearsheimer's essay, "how we can expect our students to engage seriously and honestly in higher education itself if we studiously avoid all concern with moral education?"

And another interlocutor points out that in the humanities, the concerns of moral education are the explicit content of key texts: "How does [Mearsheimer] suppose anyone manages to teach Aristotle's *Ethics*, the Gospel according to St. Matthew, the works of Plato, Kant, and William James. . . without engaging students in genuine inquiry about what is moral and ethical behavior, and on what kind of persons they should become?"

But the fact that moral concerns turn up in the texts students study doesn't mean that what the students are learning about is morality. They are learning about the ways in which poets, philosophers, and political theorists structure their inquiries and reflections. Those inquiries and reflections will often begin and end with moral questions, but what makes those authors worth studying is not the answers they happen to give to those questions—you can find Plato and James compelling without either affirming or rejecting the morality they seem to be urging—but the verbal, architectonic, or argumentative skills they display in the course of implementing the intention to write a poem, or a piece of philosophy, or a meditation on the nature of government.

The "genuine inquiry" in which students are (or should be) engaged is not an inquiry about what kind of person they should be but an inquiry about what kind of person Plato or Hobbes or Rawls or Milton thought they should be, and for what reasons, and with what poetic or philosophical force. The exam question is not, "If you were to find yourself in such and such a situation, what should you do?" The exam question is, "If you were to find yourself in such and such a situation, what would Plato, Hobbes, Rawls, and Kant tell you to do and what are the different assumptions and investments that would generate their different recommendations?"

You can answer that question in a good academic fashion—answer it, that is, as an academic question—without coming down on the side of any morality whatsoever, and no instructor should penalize you because you stick to the business at hand and decline the invitation—often proffered, but always to be declined—to make the educational experience everything in general and nothing in particular.

I know that my strictures against university involvement in political/moral matters can be read as an argument for passivity in the face of attacks on the academic enterprise. Elizabeth Kiss and Peter Euben assert that when I say "aim low," I mean "lay low." In fact I have repeatedly faulted senior administrators for laying low when it came time to defend their universities against funding cuts, legislative intrusions, and public pressures (as applied, for example, by newspaper editorials and radio talk shows). Indeed I have urged not passivity but an aggressive and proactive stance that would have administrators playing offense rather than defense. I have made the further point that universities argue from weakness when they say to a legislature, or to a state board of higher education, or to a congressional committee, "See, what we do does in fact contribute to the state's prosperity, or to the community's cultural life, or to the production of a skilled workforce." All these claims may be true (although I doubt it), but to make them the basis of your case is to justify your enterprise in someone else's terms and play *his* game, and that, I contend, is to be passive in the defense of the institution's core values. Better, I counsel, to stand up for those values—for intellectual analysis of questions that may never have a definitive or even a useful answer, for research conducted just because researchers find certain problems interesting, for wrestling with puzzles only five hundred people in the whole world are eager to solve—and when those values are dismissed or scorned, challenge the scorner to exhibit even the slightest knowledge of what really goes on in the classroom or the laboratory; and when he or she is unable to do so, ask, "Is that the way you run *your* business, by pronouncing on matters of which you are wholly ignorant?" Now this advice may not be good advice—although the defensive strategies currently employed by administrators don't seem to work—but it is certainly not advice to be passive or lay low. Rather, it is advice to put your best food forward, which means, I believe, to put your *own* foot forward, and not someone else's.

This is a lesson forgotten or never learned by those administrators who performed badly in the wake of September 11. An example is the president of the University of South Florida, who agreed to the dismissal of a professor for having appeared on a television show and answered questions about statements he had made thirteen years previously. The reason given by the university for its action was that the hostile response to the professor's appearance disrupted day-to-day business (this is the "heckler's veto" argument, firmly rejected by a succession of Supreme Court decisions), but the real reason was that the president, rather than being true to her obligation to defend the academic enterprise, had given it over to the very political forces from which she should have protected it. She became the agent of those forces, and by doing their job, she defaulted on her own. You don't stand up for that enterprise by publicly judging (or, for that matter, approving) the constitutionally protected speech of those who look to you to be the spokesperson for, and the guarantor of, the integrity of their professional labors. In this case, the professor in question was later deported by the State Department after an investigation. But the fact that the president's suspicions of him proved out in the end does not mean that she was right to act on them before he was accorded due process.

SHOULD UNIVERSITIES BE DEMOCRATIC?

"Due process" is a phrase in the lexicon of democracy, and my use of it might suggest that I am linking academic operations to democratic principles. But as I argued earlier, the question of how a democracy is to be administered and the question of how a university is to be governed are quite distinct, in part because university governance is a practical not a philosophical matter. That is to say, there is no *general* model of university governance. Each institution is differently situated with respect to its history, its mission, its size, the number and nature of its programs, its relationship to local, state, and national governments, its legal obligations and attendant dangers, its mechanisms of funding, and so on. Even something so apparently extraneous as the number of buildings and rooms on a campus can affect and perhaps undermine a grand proposal of governance reform. If revised regulations call for regular meetings and consultations but there are not enough spaces or hours in the day for either, the anticipated new utopia will quickly become the old dystopia, but even worse because expectations will have been provoked and then disappointed.

Nevertheless, while there may not be a general scheme of governance to which all should conform, there are general considerations that will be pertinent to any particular conversation. One might begin the conversation by clarifying some terms that are too often loosely employed. There is one term that rather than clarifying I would like to remove. That term is "stakeholder." Originally, the word referred to the third person who held the stakes—money, property, or some other good—for which two others were competing. But we now use the term in a much broader sense to mean all those who are (or might be) affected by an action taken by an organization or group.

Given a definition so capacious, who are the stakeholders in the world of higher education? Here is one answer offered in a white paper prepared for the ERIC Clearinghouse on Higher Education: "These stakeholders include higher education's associations, funding organizations, the U.S. Department of Education, related congressional committees, accrediting institutions, system-level offices, governors, state departments or boards of education, state legislatures, students, alumni, local community members, trustees, senior administrators, faculty leaders and presidents." The fact of a list as large as this one provokes protests on behalf of those who are not on it: staff, janitors, managers of student unions, community associations, professional sports teams, textbook publishers, book stores, vendors, caterers, neighborhood businesses, real estate developers, to name a few. Indeed, if the filter of inclusion is anyone who "might be affected," then there is no reason to exclude anyone, including newborn babies who certainly have a stake, albeit a long range one, in the enterprise.

Obviously a notion so diffuse will generate an equally diffuse model of governance, and it is no surprise that the authors (or are they stakeholders?) of the ERIC white paper end with this recommendation: "Perhaps a new governance model is in order for the university of the future—one that places the attitudes, values, and expectations of internal and external stakeholders at the center." In short, go out and ask everyone in sight how a university should be organized, and then build the answers, along with all the relevant "attitudes, values, and expectations," into a structure. Can anyone say "paralysis"? It has often been remarked that movement in a university is glacially slow, but glaciers will seem like rushing streams if no action can be taken that does not first satisfy the expectations of every so-called stakeholder.

It follows that the question of who are the stakeholders is an unprofitable one and is certainly not the right question to begin with. The right question is the one I've been asking on every page of this book. What's the nature of the academic enterprise? Once that question has been answered, the scope of its goals can be specified precisely, and it becomes possible to determine who should be given the responsibility for achieving them. The two answers often given to the question are: (1) We are a business. (2) We are in the business of democracy.

Much has been written about the inappositeness of thinking of the university as a business. Here is a representative statement by the Association of Governing Boards of Universities and Colleges:

> Nonprofit colleges and universities differ from businesses in many respects. They do not operate from a profit motive, and the "bottom lines" of colleges and universities are far more difficult to measure. They also differ from businesses in the sense that the processes of teaching, learning, and

research often are at least as important as "the product," as measured by the conferring of degrees or the publication of research results. And by virtue of their special mission and purpose in a pluralistic society, they have a tradition of participation in institutional governance that is less common in and less appropriate for business.

I find nothing here to disagree with, except, perhaps, for the gratuitous phrase "pluralistic society." I don't see that pluralism has anything to do with it. If, in fact, colleges and universities do have a core purpose, that purpose would have belonged to colleges and universities in the pre–World War II period when, while the society may have been pluralistic, the student population and the faculty certainly were not. I also am a bit bothered by the words "special mission." Every profession or practice has a special mission; if it did not, it would have no claim on our attention or support; if what it did were done elsewhere by others, there would be no reason for anyone to seek its services. I suspect that "special mission" carries a moral or even religious connotation: we are special because we live the life of the mind while others perform in less exalted ways. This form of academic smugness is always unattractive and spectacularly ineffective as a defense of the enterprise. Still, when all is said and done, the list of differences between the business world and the academic world offered here is pretty much on target. Higher education is just not in the same business as business.

There is nothing wrong, of course, with a university that is efficient, monitors its expenditures, and husbands its resources, so long as these and other bottom line strategies are understood to be in the service of a project they neither contain nor define. Things go wrong when the first question asked is "how much will it cost?" or "how much will it bring in?" rather than "what will it contribute?" or "how promising is it?"; for then decisions will be made without any reference to the reasons there are colleges and universities anyway. As Larry Gerber puts it in an essay in *Academe*: "advocates of a top-down management style who want to transform faculty from professionals into 'employees' and students into 'consumers' tend to see liberal education as a waste of time and resources, because they fail to see the immediate 'payoff' of the liberal and fine arts and because they are willing to allow the 'market' to determine what should and should not be taught." Once in place, Gerber continues, this market mentality spreads throughout the institution with unhappy results: "Encouraging students to view themselves primarily as consumers...too often results in pressures for lowering academic standards,...[since] student preferences to avoid courses with heavy reading assignments...may well result in administrative pressures on faculty to lower standards in order to maintain enrollments."

Gerber's antidote for these and other looming disasters is shared governance, which, he says, is more likely than the top-down corporate model of management "to foster the unimpeded pursuit and dissemination of knowledge that are necessary for the healthy development of society." But why should this be so? As long as the unimpeded pursuit of knowledge is acknowledged to be at the center of the university's mission, everyone in the chain of command, however it is configured, will have it in his or her mind to foster it. The values come first and if they are in place, they can be implemented by any organizational structure, although one can still argue about which organizational structure is best suited to the job.

Think, for example, about a department. Its structure might be autocratic, an old-fashioned head appointed for an indefinite term and responsible only to the dean, or it might be roughly egalitarian, the chair elected by the faculty and expected to carry out its wishes as they have been expressed in votes. There is much to be said about the advantages and disadvantages of these models, but good scholarship and good pedagogy can flourish or fail to flourish in either, and this remains true if we extrapolate from the department to the college and then to the university. The question of who does or does not participate in governance is logically independent of the question of whether the work being done is good or bad. Despite what Gerber would claim, the case for shared governance cannot rest on an intimate connection between its imperatives, which are philosophical and moral, and the imperatives of the academic project. What we do in the shop and how and by whom the shop is run are different matters. To conflate them is to turn an intellectual question—what is good scholarship and teaching?—into a political one—who shares in the power?

This is what Gerber does, and he does it because he makes the mistake—a natural and attractive one—of thinking that because we live in a democratic society, the institution we inhabit should embody democratic principles. The reasoning is that if democracy is good for the polity as a whole, it must be good for higher education. But what makes democracy work is an insistence on the priority of procedure over substance, or as Kant put it, the priority of the right over the good. Questions of the good are to be bracketed for the purposes of public life because to put them on the political table is to invite back the divisiveness the entire scheme is designed to outflank. In the words of legal philosopher Ronald Dworkin, the democratic liberal state is one that is, in its operations, "independent of any particular conception of the good life," which means, Thomas Nagel tells us, that in political deliberations "appeals to the truth" must be eschewed and we must learn to bracket our beliefs "whether moral, religious, or even historical and scientific" and regard them "simply as someone's beliefs rather than as truths."

However accurate this may be as a description of our civic duty, it does not describe our academic duty. An academic does not bracket or withdraw from his or her strong views about what is true; rather the task is to present, elaborate, and then defend those views by giving reasons and marshaling evidence. The task, in short, is not to be democratic, but to be rational. There may be times when the performance of rationality requires democratic process, but the two should not be identified. And it follows that if democratic imperatives are only instrumental and not central to academic purposes, the rationale for shared governance pretty much collapses; for in its strongest form, with its insistence that the franchise be extended as widely as possible, it is indistinguishable from representative democracy and therefore from the stakeholder model, in which, because everyone is in charge, no one is in charge. The question of who does and does not share in governance is not a philosophical one to be answered by some political theory; you answer it by identifying the task and surveying the resources and obstacles attendant upon it. Then you are in the position to figure out who should be given the responsibility for getting the job done, a matter not of grand moral pronouncements, but of good management.

Indeed, shared governance is not a style of management, but an impediment to management for reasons elaborated by John Lombardi, president of the University of Massachusetts at Amherst. "Universities for the most part do not have management; they have governance," which Lombardi defines as "the political process that balances the various competing interests of an institution through a complicated and lengthy process." Governance of the shared kind has the tendency to substitute process for action, and that, says Lombardi, means that action will be endlessly deferred.

> To improve, the university must have management. It must have direction. The institution must consult... must listen, and it must respond to... advice from its many constituencies, but it must nonetheless act, and often it must act without complete consensus.

The difference between management and shared governance is that management is by and large aware of its instrumental status—it does not define the job, but helps to get it done—while those who preach the gospel of shared governance tend to think of it as another name for the job, or, at the very least, as the model of organization that belongs naturally to the job. That is why advocates of shared governance are likely to be unimpressed when Lombardi complains that this politically inspired concept, when put into operation, prevents the organization from moving forward. Exactly right, the self-righteous faculty member will reply, and it's a good thing too, because the organization—meaning the senior administration from the office of the dean to the president to the board of trustees—is a structure of power, and it is one's positive duty to frustrate its working.

Here is still another way in which academic life differs from the life of business. In the business world, those at the top of the organizational hierarchy are regarded (not only by themselves but by others lower on the food chain) as the key players and as the ones best positioned and equipped to make the important decisions. In the academic world, by contrast, faculty members regard senior administrators with contempt, believing them to be either burnt-out scholars or failed scholars whose flame was never ignited in the first place. The organizational chart of a university may suggest that authority rests with the administrators, who, as the management class, set the standards to which faculty, the labor class, must conform. But faculty are reluctant to think of themselves as labor (hence the resistance to unionization) and are convinced—a conviction that seems to be issued to them along with the Ph.D.—that authority really rests with them and that the hierarchy announced in the organizational chart is a fiction they are in no way obliged to respect. I once explained this to someone who asked, "Well, if they think that, why don't they assume the positions in the hierarchy themselves?" The answer, of course, is that they would believe that any such grubbing after administrative power is beneath them; they, after all, inhabit the life of the mind, and because they inhabit the life of the mind, they have a right not to be coerced by bean-counters in three-piece suits and power dresses and certainly should not aspire to be like them.

This sense of entitlement—we are the real center of the enterprise; deans, provosts, and presidents only serve us—comes easily to those who assimilate the university to the model of democracy, a model in which power is assumed to be always corrupt and always in need of rebuke and check by those of purer heart and mind. If you are a dean or a provost, you might be understandably reluctant to share governance with a crew like that; for you would know that they would come to the task with a set of attitudes that, rather than facilitating the smooth running of the university's machinery, is likely to put a spanner in the works, and is likely to do so for what will seem to them to be *moral* reasons: we are doing no more than asserting our intellectual or academic freedom, which in some cases turns out to be not only freedom from external intrusions into the everyday business of workplace, but freedom from the everyday obligations of the work place. Why should I teach three days a week? Why should I teach this subject just because my chair told me to? Why must I post office hours and keep them? Why can't I hold class at my house or at the beach?

As someone who has been there, I have a great deal of sympathy with Harry Haynsworth, retired president and dean, William Mitchell College of Law, who, after fourteen years of wrestling with the appropriate division of governance responsibilities between the faculty and the administration, reported that "in recent years I have consciously tried to limit the number of issues that will ultimately come before the entire faculty for its approval." Haynsworth knows that he is out of step with conventional wisdom. "I have been told more than once that my views on faculty governance boundaries are much too narrow and not in accordance with the traditions of academia and the practices of most faculties." He continues to believe, however, that his "basic convictions are sound and are supported by respectable authority."

His convictions are also supported by what is practiced in most colleges and universities. In very few institutions is governance really shared, even when official documents declare that it is. Here, for example, is a sentence from the "Guidelines for Shared Governance" at the University of Arizona: "Students, classified staff and professional personnel should participate in the shared governance process where appropriate and in a fitting manner." And who gets to decide what is fitting and appropriate? The answer is given by another sentence: "The Task Force recommends that the President commits to and takes a leadership role in smoothing the way for shared governance at all levels." In the final document, approved by the faculty senate in April 2005, the true and sensible meaning of shared governance becomes clearer:

> the success of the University and the positive morale of the faculty and administration are dependent upon continued use of the collective intelligence of the university

community.... This requires extensive sharing of information and a shared understanding that faculty representatives
and administrators strive always for informed mutual support through shared governance dialogue.

"Shared governance dialogue" is a phrase I almost like
despite its clunkiness because it gets close to telling the
truth. What is, in fact, important to morale and therefore to
the success of the university is *talk* about shared governance,
for what really ought to be shared is information. Faculties are not distressed because they have too small a portion
of the administrative task—one provost told me recently,
"when they ask for money and governance I always give
them governance because they soon tire of using it"—but
because they only learn about administrative decisions after
they have been made. It is the withholding of information,
not of responsibility, that leaves faculty members feeling left
out, taken for granted, and generally disrespected. For some
reason, the hoarding of information is a reflex action on
the part of most administrations. The thinking may be to
control the situation by controlling the flow of information;
but the truth is that in the absence of information, rumor,
conspiracy theories, and ultimately real conspiracies rush in
to fill the space that would not even have been there if full
disclosure had been the policy. Tell them everything: share
every piece of information you have the moment you have
it, and they will be quite happy to leave the governance
to you, especially if as you distribute the information you
invite them to talk about the issues it raises. They get to feel
that they are a part of what is going on; you get the benefit
of hearing their views without having to promise that you
will act in accordance with them.

This is also the way to deal with students who always
want to have a say in everything. And while students may

be excused for wanting to play a role not properly theirs, administrators should know better and should always remember the differences between tasks and the capabilities necessary to perform them. I'm not saying don't consult with students. Consult with everyone, but don't confuse consulting with the sharing of the franchise. Student evaluation of teaching is bad enough (I lost that battle over forty years ago), but at least those forms are sometimes read with caution by those who know what they are and what they are not. No such caution, or knowledge, or competence attends the performance of students who are allowed by some misguided administration to vote or serve on search committees. They will influence the process according to their interests (what else would you expect them to do?), but their interests are short term and only obliquely related to the interests of those who will spend much of their lives in the institution.

If students should be kept to the side of academic business because they haven't the qualifications for the job, the same is true for trustees, donors, politicians, parents, and concerned members of the general public, all of whom have lots of ideas that should be politely listened to and then filed away under "not to the academic point." It's not that these people aren't smart; they're usually very smart in their own lines of work. It's just that most of the time the models and examples they urge on you presuppose conditions and criteria that have nothing to do with the conditions and criteria of the academy.

THE CULTURE WARS

Invoking criteria that are beside the point of the academic enterprise is what routinely happens in the culture wars, now in their third decade. Who is winning?

If victory for the right meant turning back or retarding the growth of programs like women's studies, African American studies, Chicano studies, Latino studies, cultural studies, gay and lesbian (and now transgender) studies, postmodern studies, and poststructuralist theory, then the left is winning big time, for these programs flourish (especially among the young) and are the source of much of the intellectual energy in the liberal arts.

But if the palm is to be awarded to the party that persuaded the American public to adopt its characterization of the academy, the right wins hands down, for it is now generally believed that our colleges and universities are hotbeds of radicalism and pedagogical irresponsibility where dollars are wasted, nonsense is propagated, students are indoctrinated, religion is disrespected, and patriotism is scorned.

In short, the left may have won the curricular battle, but the right won the public-relations war. The right did this in the old-fashioned way, by mastering the ancient art of rhetoric and spinning a vocabulary that, once established in the public mind, performed the work of argument all by itself. The master stroke, of course, was the appropriation from the left (where it had been used with a certain self-directed irony) of the phrase "political correctness," which in fairly short order became capitalized and transformed from an accusation to the name of a program supposedly being carried out by the very persons who were the accusation's object. That is, those who cried "political correctness" invented an entity about which they could then immediately complain. This was genius.

Now they're doing it again, this time by taking a phrase that seems positively benign and even progressive (in a fuzzy-left way) and employing it as the Trojan horse of a dark design. That phrase is "intellectual diversity," and the vehicle that is bringing it to the streets and coffee shops

of your home town is David Horowitz's Academic Bill of
Rights, which has been the basis of legislation introduced
in Congress, has stirred some interest in a number of state
legislatures, and has been the subject of editorials (both pro
and con) in leading newspapers.

Opponents of the Academic Bill of Rights contend that
despite disclaimers of any political intention and an explicit
rejection of quotas, the underlying agenda is the decidedly
political one of forcing colleges and universities to hire conservative professors in order to assure ideological balance.

Horowitz replies (in print and conversation) that he has no
desire to impose ideological criteria on the operations of the
academy; he does not favor, he tells me, legislation that would
have political bodies taking over the responsibility of making
curricular and hiring decisions. His hope, he insists, is that
colleges and universities will reform themselves, and he offers
the Academic Bill of Rights (which is the product of consul-
tation with academics of various persuasions) as a convenient
base-line template to which they might refer for guidance.

For the record, and as one of those with whom he has
consulted, I believe him, and I believe him, in part, because
much of the Academic Bill of Rights is as apolitical and
principled as he says it is. It begins by announcing that "the
central purposes of a University are the pursuit of truth,
the discovery of new knowledge through scholarship and
research, the study and reasoned criticism of intellectual
and cultural traditions . . . and the transmission of knowledge
and learning to a society at large." (I shall return to the clause
deleted by my ellipsis.)

The bill goes on to define academic freedom as the policy of "protecting the intellectual independence of professors, researchers and students in the pursuit of knowledge
and the expression of ideas from interference by legislators
or authorities within the institution itself."

In short, "no political, ideological or religious ortho-doxy will be imposed on professors." Nor shall a legislature "impose any orthodoxy through its control of the university budget," and "no faculty shall be hired or fired or denied promotion or tenure on the basis of his or her political or religious beliefs." The document ends by declaring that academic institutions "should maintain a posture of organizational neutrality with respect to the substantive disagreements that divide researchers on questions within, or outside, their fields of inquiry."

It's hard to see how anyone who believes (as I do) that academic work is distinctive in its aims and goals and that its distinctiveness must be protected from political pressures (either external or internal) could find anything to disagree with here. Everything follows from the statement that the pursuit of truth is a—I would say, *the*—central purpose of the university. For the serious embrace of that purpose precludes deciding what the truth is in advance, or ruling out certain accounts of the truth before they have been given a hearing, or making evaluations of those accounts turn on the known or suspected political affiliations of those who present them.

But it is precisely because the pursuit of truth is the cardinal value of the academy that the value (if it is one) of intellectual diversity should be rejected.

The notion first turns up, though not by name, in the clause I elided where Horowitz lists among the purposes of a university "the teaching and general development of students to help them become creative individuals and productive citizens of a pluralistic society."

Teaching, yes—it is my job, as I have said repeatedly, to introduce students to new materials and equip them with new skills; but I haven't the slightest idea of how to help students become creative individuals. And it is decidedly not my job to produce citizens for a pluralistic society or for any other. Citizen building is a legitimate democratic activity, but it is not an academic activity. To be sure, some of what happens in the classroom may play a part in the fashioning of a citizen, but that is neither something you can count on—there is no accounting for what a student will make of something you say or assign—nor something you should aim for. As admirable a goal as it may be, fashioning citizens for a pluralistic society has nothing to do with the pursuit of truth.

For Horowitz, the link between the two is to be found in the idea of pluralism: given the "unsettled character of all human knowledge" and the fact (which is a fact) "that there is no humanly accessible truth that is not in principle open to challenge," it follows, he thinks, that students being prepared to live in a pluralistic society should receive an education in pluralism; and it follows further, he says, that it is the obligation of teachers and administrators "to promote intellectual pluralism" and thereby "protect the principle of intellectual diversity."

But it is a mistake to go from the general assertion that no humanly accessible truth is invulnerable to challenge to the conclusion that therefore challenges must always be provided. That is to confuse a theory of truth with its pursuit and to exchange the goal of reaching it for a resolution to keep the question of it always open.

While questions of truth may be generally open, the truth of academic matters is not general but local; questions are posed and often they do have answers that can be established with certainty; and even if that certainty can theoretically be upset—one cannot rule out the future emergence of new evidence—that theoretical possibility carries with it no methodological obligation. That is, it does not mandate intellectual diversity, a condition that may attend some moments in the pursuit of truth when there is as yet no clear path, but not a condition one must actively seek or protect.

To put it simply, intellectual diversity is not a stand-alone academic value, no more than is free speech; either can be a help in the pursuit of truth, but neither should be identified with it; the (occasional) means should not be confused with the end.

Now if intellectual diversity is not an academic value, adherence to it as an end in itself will not further an academic goal; but it will further some goal, and that goal will be political. It will be part of an effort to alter the academy so that it becomes an extension of some partisan vision of the way the world should be.

Such an effort will not be a perversion of intellectual diversity; intellectual diversity as a prime academic goal is already a perversion, and its transformation into a political agenda, despite Horowitz's protestations and wishes to the contrary, is inevitable and assured. It is just a matter of which party seizes it and makes it its own.

For a while (ever since the *Bakke* decision), it was the left that flew the diversity banner and put it to work in the service of affirmative action, speech codes, hostile-environment regulations, minority hiring, and more. Now it is the right's turn, and Horowitz himself has mapped out the strategy and laid bare the motives:

> I encourage [students] to use the language that the left has deployed so effectively on behalf of its own agendas. Radical professors have created a "hostile learning" environment for conservative students. There is a lack of "intellectual diversity" on college faculties and in academic classrooms. The conservative viewpoint is "under-represented" in the curriculum and on its reading lists. The university should be an "inclusive" and intellectually "diverse" community. (April 2003)

It is obvious that for Horowitz these are debating points designed to hoist the left by its own petard; but the trouble with debating points is that they can't be kept in bounds. Someone is going to take them seriously and advocate actions that Horowitz would probably not endorse.

Someone is going to say, let's monitor those lefty professors and keep tabs on what they're saying; and while we're at it, let's withhold federal funds from programs that do not display "ideological balance"; and let's demand that academic institutions demonstrate a commitment to hiring conservatives; and let's make sure that the material our students read is pro-American and free of the taint of relativism; and let's publish the names of those who do not comply.

This is not a hypothetical list; it is a list of actions already being taken. In fact, it is a list one could pretty much glean from the Web site of Colorado state senator John K. Andrews Jr., a site on which the Academic Bill of Rights is invoked frequently.

Andrews, like everyone else doing the intellectual diversity dance, insists that he opposes "any sort of quotas, mandated hiring or litmus test"; but then he turns around and sends a letter to Colorado's universities asking them to explain how they promote "intellectual diversity." If he doesn't like the answers he gets, he promises to sponsor legislation to "ensure academic freedom."

Anne Neal, of the Lynne Cheney–inspired American Council of Trustees and Alumni, plays the same double game in a piece entitled "Intellectual Diversity Endangered." First she stands up for the value of academic freedom ("no more important value to the life of the mind"), but then she urges university trustees to see to it "that all faculty ... present points of view other than their own in a balanced way" (something you might want to do but shouldn't have to do), and to "insist that their institutions offer broad-based survey

courses," and "to monitor tenure decisions" for instances
of "political discrimination," and to "conduct intellectual
diversity reviews and to make the results public." In short,
she urges trustees to take over the university and conform its
operations to neoconservative imperatives.

The irony is that while intellectual diversity is urged as a
way of fighting the politicization of the university, it *is* the
politicization of the university, for it requires the faculty to
display the same proportion of Democrats and Republicans
as is found in the general population, which makes about as
much *academic* sense as requiring the same proportion in the
corporate boardroom or on the roster of the Boston Red
Sox would make economic or athletic sense.

As one example of the damage that can be done under
the banner of intellectual diversity, consider Florida House
Bill 837 introduced a couple of years ago by state representative Dennis Baxley. In that bill we read that students have
a right "to take reasoned exception to the data and views
offered in any course of study," that students have a right
to the introduction in a course of "a broad range of serious
scholarly opinion," and that "the fostering of a plurality of
serious scholarly methodologies and perspectives should be
a significant institutional purpose."

Sounds innocuous, but the bland words barely mask an
effort to take instruction out of the hands of instructors by
holding them to curricular quotas and threatening them
with student lawsuits if they fail to comply. First of all, students do not have any rights except the right to competent
instruction, and one part of being a competent instructor
is the ability (and responsibility) to make judicious—not
legislatively imposed—decisions about what materials and
approaches are to be taught. The decision to include or
exclude a particular approach should depend on the instructor's academic judgment and not on the need to display a

mandated balance by some measure that is never announced,
but is, we know, the measure of how many so-called conservative voices and approaches are represented. You shouldn't
be reduced to saying, I guess I'll have to look for one of
these because I don't have enough of them on the syllabus.
You should instead be asking is this text or methodology
really important and worth devoting precious class time to?

Should teachers really be forced to introduce a perspective just because it is out there and is supported by a group
of true believers? "Yes" would be the answer of representative Baxley, who when asked for an example of the kind of
professorial behavior that might lead to a grievance cited
the refusal of biology teachers to discuss Intelligent Design
when students raise questions about it. The overwhelming
professional and disciplinary consensus is that the theory of
Intelligent Design is not the answer to any scientific question and that therefore study of it should take place in cultural studies courses. The overriding of that professional
consensus proposed by Mr. Baxley is a naked example of the
political agenda that will always be found just below the surface of apparently benign slogans like intellectual diversity,
pluralism, and balance, all bad ideas because they substitute
political goals for academic ones.

—⚶—

It is more than a little ironic that these bad ideas—turned to
political advantage by the right—often have their home on
the left. When, for example, George W. Bush said that evo-
lution and Intelligent Design should be taught side by side
so that students "can understand what the debate is about,"
he probably didn't know that he was signing on to the wisdom of Gerald Graff, a professor of English at the University
of Illinois, Chicago, and founder of Teachers for a Democratic Culture, an organization dedicated to "combating

conservative misrepresentations" of what goes on in college classrooms. Graff and Intelligent Design are now a couple on the Internet even though he had never written a word on the subject until he wrote in protest against his having been "hijacked by the Christian Right." He has, however, written many words urging college instructors to "teach the conflicts" that typically grow up around an issue so that students will learn that knowledge is neither inertly given nor a matter of personal opinion ("I've got mine and you've got yours"), but is established in the crucible of controversy. Although Graff makes his case for teaching the controversies in a book titled *Beyond the Culture Wars* (he wants partisan posturing to be replaced by rational debate), the culture wars have now appropriated his thesis and made it into a weapon in the arsenal of the Intelligent Design warriors. From Bush on down to every foot soldier in the army, "teach the controversy" is the battle cry.

It is an effective one, for it takes the focus away from the scientific credibility of Intelligent Design—away from the question, "Why should it be taught in a biology class?"—and puts it instead on the more abstract issue of freedom and openness of inquiry. Rather than saying, "we're right and the other guys are wrong and here are the scientific reasons," they say things like "questions of right and wrong must always be left open," "every idea should at least get a hearing," "unpopular or minority views should be represented and not suppressed," and "what currently counts as knowledge should always be suspect because it will typically reflect the interests and preferences of those in power." This last bit is standard vulgar postmodernism of the kind one gets by reading a page or two of some French theorist, and what is interesting about its appearance in these debates is that those who mouth it don't believe it for a minute; it's just a matter of political tactics.

Philip E. Johnson, a leading Intelligent Design advocate, is quite forthright about this. "I'm no postmodernist," he declares in an interview, but "I've learned a lot" from reading them. What he's learned, he reports, is how to talk about "hidden assumptions" and "power relationships" and how to use those concepts to cast doubt on the authority of "science educators" and other purveyors of the reigning orthodoxy. My views, he says, "are considered outlandish in the academic world," but the strategy he borrows from the postmodernists—the strategy of claiming to have been marginalized by the powers-that-be—is, he boasts, "dead bang mainstream academia these days."

This is nothing if not clever, but it is also disingenuous and a bit dishonest because it involves hitching your wagon to a set of ideas you really despise. In an academy where talk of marginalization and hegemonic exclusion is routine, Johnson and his friends can use that talk (in which they have no real stake) to gain a hearing for ideas that have failed to make their way in the usual give-and-take of the academic debates Graff celebrates. While in Graff's book "teach the controversies" is a serious answer to a serious question—how can we make students aware of the underlying issues that structure academic discourse?—in the work of Johnson and other Intelligent Design proponents, "teach the controversies" is the answer to no question. Instead it is a wedge for prying open the doors of a world to which they have been denied access by gatekeepers—individual scientists, departments of biology, professional associations, editors of learned journals—who have found what they say unpersuasive and beside the scientific point. They say "teach the controversy," but they mean, "let us into the conversation even though the almost universal judgment of authoritative researchers is that we have nothing relevant to contribute."

They get away with this (or at least try to) by lowering the stakes in the guise of upping them. They appeal to a higher value—the value of fairness or the value of controversy as a moral good in and of itself—and thereby avoid questions about the qualifications necessary to be legitimate competitors in the intellectual arena. They insulate their arguments from detailed objections by attaching them to an abstract value, which is then piously affirmed. In the light of this value—fairness and/or free inquiry—their claims shed their specificity and become indistinguishable from the claims of their opponents. They ask, "In a democratic discussion, shouldn't every voice be heard?" rather than asking, "Which voices have earned (through the usual mechanisms of validation) the right to be heard?"

The same leveling effect is achieved when Intelligent Designers invoke a long view of history. Isn't it the case, they ask, that only a few decades ago it was evolutionary theory that was kept out of some classrooms in this country? That proved to be an error, they point out, and isn't it possible that someday the present policy of refusing to teach Intelligent Design in science classes will be thought to have been an error too? After all, haven't many once discredited theories and avenues of research been accepted by a later generation of scholars? And doesn't history show us that apparently settled wisdom is often kept in place by those whose careers are invested in it?

The answer to all these questions is "Yes," but the yes carries with it no methodological implications because the long view of history does not provide any answers to questions posed at a particular moment in time. All it does is tell you how some of those answers fared. The fact that some of them have not fared well does not tell you how to proceed with a new question (like "has evolutionary biology led to advances in understanding and research?") that arises in the present. "Expert judgment" as a category of validation is not discredited generally because it has occasionally turned out to be wrong. You have to go with the evidence you have, even if it is true that the evidence you have may be overtaken in the long run. It would not be a method at all—it would be a bizarre non sequitur—to say, "Given that we don't know now what might turn up in the distant future, let's systematically distrust everything that now appears to us to be sound and true."

Unfortunately (or fortunately for the Intelligent Design agenda), this is precisely what is said by some postmodernists and multiculturalists, and in saying it they are merely drawing out the implications of one strain of liberalism, the strain that finds its source in John Stuart Mill's insistence (in *On Liberty*) that knowledge should never be allowed to settle and congeal. This has also been the view of First Amendment doctrine, at least since *New York Times v. Sullivan* (1964), a case in which the values of truth and accuracy are subordinated to the supposedly greater value of "uninhibited, robust, and wide-open" discussion. In its opinion the Court blurs the distinction between true and false statements by recharacterizing the latter (in a footnote that cites Mill) as a "valuable contribution to the public debate," thus paving the way for those who, like the advocates of Intelligent Design, assert that their views deserve to be considered (and taught) even when—especially when—the vast majority of authorities in the field have declared them to be without scientific merit. It is an assertion that liberals by and large resist when the message asking for a place at the table is racist or sexist, but it is a logical consequence of liberalism's privileging of tolerance and multivocality over judgment.

Liberalism privileges tolerance because it is committed to fallibilism, the idea that our opinions about the world, derived as they are from the local, limited perspectives in which we necessarily live, are likely to be in error even when, again especially when, we are wholly committed to them. Because this mistake is natural to us, because the beliefs we acquire always seem to us to be perspicuous and indubitable, it is necessary, liberalism tells us, to put obstacles in the way of our assenting too easily to what are finally only our opinions.

By rooting itself in fallibilism, liberalism casts a prospective shadow on any determination of right and wrong and makes it difficult to justify the exclusion from the conversation of any point of view. A reasonable methodological caution—don't assume that your convictions are incapable of being proven wrong—is pressed until it becomes a metaphysical imperative—always assume that whatever "authoritative selection" has delivered is the result of a politically inspired act of exclusion. This transformation of a "check and balance" into a hermeneutics of suspicion was always implicit in liberalism's logic, but it achieves fully realized form in those versions of postmodernism and multiculturalism that preach the unavoidability of perspective, the inevitability of prejudice, and (therefore) the suspect status of any generally held view. (Postmodernism is liberalism taken seriously.) Whether or not conservative activists believe in this deconstruction of received authority (and by and large they don't), they are clever enough to appropriate it for their own purposes. If liberal polemicists can defend gay marriage by challenging the right of a church or a state to define what marriage is, why, the argument goes, can't Intelligent Design proponents demand equal time in the textbooks and the classroom by challenging the right of Ivy League professors or journal editors to say what science is?

Intelligent Designers are not the first denizens of the right to borrow arguments and strategies from the liberal and postmodern left. Holocaust deniers, to whom they are often compared (over 180,000 items on Google), were there before them. In the early '90s Holocaust denier Bradley Smith was able to place a series of ads (actually mini-essays) in college student newspapers in part because he presented his ideas under the heading "The Holocaust Controversy: The Case for Open Debate." Not the case for why there was no campaign to exterminate the Jews, not the case for why Hitler was innocent of any genocidal thoughts, not the case for why Holocaust-promoting Jews are just trying to drum up "financial support for Jewish causes" (all things asserted in the body of the ad), but the case for open debate, and how could anyone, and especially academics, be against that? Ours is not a "radical point of view," Smith asserts. We are just acting on premises that "were worked out some time ago during a little something called the Enlightenment." All we're saying, insists Mark Weber, another prominent denier, is, "Let's hear both sides." Don't "Americans have the right to judge the important issues for themselves?"

Proponents of Intelligent Design are rightly outraged when their efforts are linked to the efforts of Holocaust deniers, for there is no *moral* equivalence between the two projects. One, after all, is in the business of whitewashing genocide, while the other is in the business of giving to God the credit for having created the wonders of the physical world. (I know that Intelligent Design literature stays away from the word "God," but no one, in or out of the movement, thinks that the answer to the question "designed by whom?" is anything but God.) There is however an equivalence of strategy that makes the linking of the two inevitable: in both cases issues that have been settled in the relevant institutional precincts—departments of History and Biology, scientific journals, etc.—are reopened and finessed by reframing them as abstract philosophical questions: instead of "What is the evidence for the Holocaust having occurred and is it persuasive?" ask "Isn't debate something that should not be foreclosed?" Instead of "What data in the world of observation and experiment can be cited in support of Intelligent Design?" ask "Shouldn't explanatory accounts, even those disdained by mainstream researchers, be given equal time in our classrooms?" Intelligent Designers and Holocaust deniers, despite the differences between them, play the same shell game; they both say look *here*, in the highest reaches of speculation about inquiry in general, and not *there*, in the places where the particular, nitty-gritty work of empirical inquiry is actually being done. They both contrive to deflect criticism by moving immediately to a perspective so broad and all-inclusive that all claims are legitimized not because they have proven out in the competition of ideas but simply because someone is asserting them. When any claim has a right to be heard and taught just because it is one, judgment falls by the wayside and is replaced by the imperative to let a hundred (or a million) flowers bloom.

There's a word for this, and it's relativism. Polemicists on the right regularly lambaste left intellectuals for promoting relativism and its attendant bad practices—relaxing or abandoning standards, letting into the curriculum any idea no matter how outlandish so long as some constituency is attached to it, trashing received wisdom by impugning the motives of those who have established it, setting aside evidence that is inconvenient and putting in its place grand theories supported by nothing but the partisan beliefs and desires of the theorizers. Whether or not this is true of the right's targets, it is certainly true of the right itself, which turns relativist whenever its members invoke the mantras of "teach the controversies" or "keep the debate open" not out of a commitment to scrupulous scholarship (although that will be what is asserted) but in an effort to accomplish by misdirection and displacement what they could not accomplish by evidence and argument.

But didn't they learn it from the cultural left? And isn't the cultural left in part responsible for the flourishing of agendas it despises? This is certainly the view of historians like Deborah Lipstadt, who declares (in *Denying the Holocaust*) that the postmodern deconstruction of established authority "created an atmosphere of permissiveness toward the questioning of historical events and made it hard...to assert that there is anything 'off limits' for this skeptical approach." Science writer Joe Kaplinsky makes the same point when he observes that when creationists (by whatever name) call into question the motives of mainstream researchers, they have been taught to do so by left radicals "who pioneered the idea that...claims to expertise generally were little more than an excuse to assert power by marginalizing the voice of the victim." In short, once the corrosive skepticism of postmodern thought is let loose, nothing is safe from its leveling force.

Yes and no. Yes, it is the case that postmodern thought (as the logical extension of liberal thought) delegitimates the claim of any account to be exhaustive, complete, and invulnerable to challenge. The reasoning (a version of fallibilism) is that because accounts emerge in the course of history and come to us in vocabularies that belong to a particular moment in the adventure of inquiry, it is always possible, and perhaps even probable, that in time new vocabularies will replace the old ones and bring with them new, and newly authoritative, accounts.

So far so good. The mistake, and it is one made by some postmodern thinkers and seized upon by their neoconservative opponents, is to go from this perfectly ordinary description of how knowledge is established, tested, and sometimes dislodged—this, after all, *is* the scientific method—to the extraordinary and unearned conclusion that nothing that has been established as knowledge is to be trusted. The essence of the mistake is to think that the inevitable and blameless historicity of all accounts relativizes them with respect to measures like accuracy, trustworthiness, validity, and legitimacy. But postmodern thought places all accounts on an equal footing only in the sense that it renders them equally historical—equally the products of human judgment—which means that none of them is the result of a direct, unmediated encounter with reality as it exists apart from any human, temporally bounded vocabulary whatsoever. That said, however, all the important differences remain, the differences that arise from the different projects of inquiry in relation to which the different vocabularies have been developed. Sociology, political science, anthropology, literary criticism, the law, science, theology—all these areas of investigation have their own particular histories that include procedures and tests for assessing the worth and value of proposed contributions to the enterprise. These procedures and tests are typically specific to the project to whose urgencies they are a response. Literary critics want to find out what a poem means. Political scientists want to find out what motivates voters. Lawyers and legal theorists worry about how to determine whether or not a proposed statute is constitutional. Scientists hazard and test hypotheses in an effort to lay bare the structures of the material world. There is of course some commerce between these enterprises—they are not hermetically sealed islands—but the decorums and accepted routines of one cannot easily be transferred to another.

A doctrinaire postmodernist might respond by saying that the lines between disciplines have themselves been drawn in history by fallible men and women. They are a product of human judgment and therefore can always be redrawn. Yes, but you don't redraw a line simply by saying that it is possible to redraw it. The actual work of marshaling evidence and making arguments in support of a newly drawn line must still be done, and postmodernism has nothing to contribute to that work. Postmodernism is a general and abstract description of the way knowledge is established and challenged. It tells us that any establishing or challenging of knowledge is a historical rather than a transcendent event. But postmodernism is not itself decisive in either effort. It is neither a challenge to nor an affirmation of any conclusion historically situated agents have reached because it itself has no historical content. That is, one cannot rehearse the tenets of postmodernism and then adduce a "therefore" that is directed at some matter of fact. Nothing you might say in response to questions like "what is your theory of truth?" or "is there a reality independent of cultural perspectives?" will have the slightest influence on how you proceed when you are asked to produce an interpretation of a poem, or write an account of an historical event, or replicate the results of a laboratory experiment. You can be persuaded by postmodern arguments on the very general level of their usual assertion—everything is mediated, everything comes to us under a description, the stipulation of fact is always perspective-specific—and you can still hold firmly to judgments of truth, accuracy, correctness, and error as they are made in the precincts of some particular realm of inquiry.

Both the left and the right (for different reasons) have a stake in believing that postmodern thought has consequences, either good or bad. The left wants to believe that postmodernism undermines or calls into question all settled structures of knowledge and authority. The right takes left-postmodernists at their word because it wants to believe that those who rehearse postmodern arguments are the sworn enemies of the good and the true. But postmodern thought is without consequences for anything. It troubles no present arrangement of things. It is not the answer to any locally posed question. It will not direct you to strike out in either this or that direction as you begin your investigation. It will not authorize or stand in the way of any agenda. Outside the rarified precincts in which it competes with other high-level philosophical theses, postmodern thought does no real work at all. It does, however, do rhetorical and political work. That is, it can be employed either as a resource, or as an accusation, or as a diversion by someone who is looking to score points.

That is why postmodernism and deconstruction are so often invoked as "scare words" by neoconservative polemicists who believe that by attacking them, they are attacking an agenda embraced by the intellectual left. But neither postmodernism nor deconstruction is an agenda; they are epistemological arguments.

The argument, basically, is that the structures of intelligibility in which we more or less unselfconsciously live—the coherences that seem to present themselves naturally to us as we look at and move about in the world—are not natural at all, are not the result of the world's pre-existing patterns of meaning imprinting themselves on our perception, but are constructed. They are not constructed by anyone in particular (this is not a conspiracy theory), but by traditions of inquiry, practice, and rhetoric that in time acquire enough traction and perdurability to become components in our storehouse of common sense. Once this state has been achieved (again by no one in particular), an idea or a behavior or an agenda that might have earlier been seen as new or odd or even bizarre becomes part of the landscape, becomes naturalized, becomes what we think *within* rather than what we think *about*, and it takes a special effort (which in the ordinary course of things few will make) to return us to the moment when something now in the category of "the taken for granted" or "what goes without saying" was seen as strange, unassimilated, and a candidate for possible rejection. That special effort is sometimes called simply "critique" and sometimes called "deconstruction" (although it was certainly available to human beings long before deconstruction was a concept), a word that has nothing to do with destruction (a mistake commonly made), but with the activity of showing how a part of our experience that seems given and inevitable was, in fact, constructed by human agents. Deconstruction undoes, at least analytically, that act of construction and lays bare (or at least that is the claim) its origins in history. (I should add that this is only one strain of deconstructionist thought.)

An example might help, and I turn to what might seem an unlikely source, the comedian Bob Newhart. When he came up in the '50s, Newhart was a standup comic whose prop was a telephone. He would appear on stage with the telephone and take a phone call from some historical personage with whom he would then engage in conversation; you knew what his interlocutor was saying because Newhart would repeat it, often in a tone of incredulity, before responding. In one of his more famous routines he is a functionary in the government of Queen Elizabeth I talking to Sir Walter Raleigh, who has for some time been in the New World conducting an expedition funded by the Crown. What he wants to find out is whether the government is getting anything for its money. Accordingly, he asks Raleigh if he has discovered the passage to India or at least some gold, and when the answer is "no" to both, he explodes in exasperation, "Don't you have *anything* for us, Walter?" Raleigh's reply is delivered in piecemeal to the audience as Newhart's character finds himself unable to believe any of it. "What's that, Walter, you've discovered a leaf? It grows in the ground? You pick it, you roll it up, and—am I hearing this right, Walter?—you put it in your mouth and LIGHT IT ON FIRE!!?"

What Newhart is doing, obviously, is zeroing in on a practice—the smoking of cigarettes—that was in the 1950s when he performed the routine so familiar a part of the American landscape that no one (except for a few medical researchers) ever thought much about it or contested its right to exist; and by means of his theatricalized (and anachronistic) telephone conversation, he is taking us back imaginatively to the world as it was before that practice became so habitual as to be nearly invisible. He is, in short, deconstructing it, showing that it is not natural, did not come with the moon and the stars, and, in a formulation dear to early practitioners of deconstruction, could have been otherwise, indeed, could have not been at all.

The example allows me to make several points. First, this act of deconstruction was performed before anyone had uttered the word deconstruction (although the early twentieth-century Russian Formalists employed a similar technique they called "defamiliarization," probably a better term), which tells us that whatever it is, deconstruction is not an arcane academic practice, but a practice engaged in by anyone who for some reason is struck by the oddity of a piece of behavior accepted uncritically by society.

My second point is that Newhart's routine would not be effective today, in the twenty-first century, because the practice that is its object no longer has the naturalized status it once enjoyed. You might say that smoking has been deconstructed in the past thirty years by the very culture of which it was once an integral and barely remarked part. (Remember everyone in *Casablanca, The Maltese Falcon, Gentlemen's Agreement,* and *The Best Years of Our Lives* puffing away merrily?) It is sometimes charged (by Lipstadt, for example) that deconstruction is the enemy of history and of historical fact (and thereby guilty of undermining the academic endeavor). But the reverse is true: deconstruction is an investigation into the way facts have been historically produced, the way they have passed from the state of hypotheses or strange new assertions to the stage of being so ordinary and undoubted and here-to-stay that no one thinks to pay them any particular attention, and the conditions that might lead to their regaining the status of the anomalous and the deviant.

My third point is that deconstruction or critique is not politically inflected. As a technique for uncovering occluded and forgotten assumptions, it is available both to the left and to the right. To be sure, this is not its public face; for in the public mind, deconstruction is associated with the left and with radical nihilism. This was the case in spades in the days following September 11, 2001. Who would have thought in those first few minutes, hours, days that what we now call 9/11 was to become an event in the culture wars? Now years later, nothing could be clearer, though it was only on September 22, 2001, that the first sign appeared, in a *New York Times* opinion piece written by Edward Rothstein and entitled "Attacks on U.S. Challenge the Perspectives of Postmodern True Believers." A few days later (on September 27), Julia Keller wrote a smaller piece in the *Chicago Tribune*; her title: "After the Attack, Postmodernism Loses Its Glib Grip." In the September 24 issue of *Time*, Roger Rosenblatt announced "the end of the age of irony" and predicted that "the good folks in charge of America's intellectual life" would now have to change their tune and no longer say that "nothing was real" or that "nothing was to be believed in or taken seriously." And on October 1, John Leo, in a piece entitled "Campus Hand-Wringing Is Not a Pretty Sight," blamed just about everything on the "very dangerous ideas" that have captured our "campus culture"; to wit, "radical cultural relativism, nonjudgmentalism, and a postmodern conviction that there are no moral norms or truths worth defending."

Well, that certainly sounds bad—no truths, no knowledge, no reality, no morality, no judgments, no objectivity—and if postmodernists are saying that, they are not so much dangerous as silly. Postmodernists, however, say no such thing, and what they do say, if it is understood at all, is unlikely to provoke either the anger or the alarm of our modern Paul Reveres. Most of the time, it is not understood. Rothstein tells us (without benefit of any citations) that "postmodernists challenge assertions that truth and ethical judgment have any objective validity." Well, it depends on what you mean by "objective." If you mean a standard of validity and value that is independent of any historically emergent and therefore revisable system of thought and practice, then it is true that many postmodernists would deny that any such standard is or could ever be available. But if by "objective" one means a standard of validity and value that is backed up by the tried-and-true procedures and protocols of a well-developed practice or discipline—history, physics, economics, psychology, etc.—then such standards are all around us, and we make use of them all the time without any metaphysical anxiety.

As Richard Rorty, one of Rothstein's targets, was fond of saying, "Objectivity is the kind of thing we do around here." That is, objectivity is just another name for trying to get something right in a particular area of inquiry. Historians draw conclusions about the meaning of events, astronomers present models of planetary movements, psychologists offer accounts of the reading process, consumers make decisions about which product is best, parents choose schools for their children—all of these things and many more are done with varying degrees of confidence, and in no case is the confidence rooted in a philosophical account (positive or skeptical) of objectivity. Rather, the researcher begins in some context of practice, with its received authorities, sacred texts, exemplary achievements, and generally accepted benchmarks, and from within the perspective (and not within the perspective of a general theory) of that context—thick, interpersonal, densely elaborated—judges something to be true or inaccurate, reasonable or irrational, and so on.

It seems, then, that the unavailability of an absolutely objective vantage point, of a god's eye view, doesn't take anything away from us. If, as postmodernists sometimes assert, objective standards of a publicly verifiable kind are unavailable, they are so only in the sense that they have always been unavailable (this is not, in other words, a condition postmodernism has caused), and we have always managed to get along without them, doing a great many things despite the fact that we might be unable to shore them up in accordance with the most rigorous philosophical demands.

Now, I would not be misunderstood. I am not saying that there are no universal values or no truths independent of particular perspectives. I am saying that whatever universal values and independent truths there may be (and I believe in both), they are not acknowledged by everyone and no mechanism exists that would result in their universal acceptance. When I offer a reading of a poem or pronounce on a case in First Amendment law, I do so with no epistemological reservations. I regard my reading as true—not provisionally true, or true for my reference group only, but true. But I am just as certain that I may very well be unable to persuade others, no less educated or credentialed than I, of the truth so perspicuous to me. And here is a point that is often missed, the independence from each other of two assertions thought to be contradictory: (1) I believe X to be true and (2) I believe that there is no mechanism, procedure, calculus, test, by which the truth of X can be necessarily demonstrated to any sane person who has come to a different conclusion (not that such a demonstration can never be successful, only that its success is contingent and not necessary). In order to assert something and mean it without qualification, I of course have to believe that it is true, but I don't have to believe that I could demonstrate its truth to all rational persons. (Persuasion is a contingent matter.) The claim that something is universal and the acknowledgment that I couldn't necessarily prove it are logically independent of each other. The second does not undermine the first.

Once again, then, a postmodern argument turns out to be without any deleterious consequences (it is also without any positive consequences), and it certainly does not stand in the way of condemning those who have proven themselves to be our enemies in words and deeds. Nor should this be surprising, for, after all, as I have noted, postmodernism is a series of arguments, not a way of life or a recipe for action. Your belief or disbelief in postmodern tenets is independent of your beliefs and commitments in any other area of your life. You may believe that objectivity of an absolute kind is possible or you may believe that it is not, but when you have to decide whether a particular thing is true or false, neither belief will hinder or help you. What will help you are archives, exemplary achievements, revered authorities, official bodies of evidence, relevant analogies, suggestive metaphors—all available to all persons independently of their philosophical convictions, or of the fact that they do or do not have any.

If postmodernism does not have the metaphysical con-sequences claimed for it by its detractors, neither can it have the consequence of promoting unpatriotic behavior, an accusation made by William Bennett, former secretary of education, in his book *Why We Fight: Moral Clarity and the War on Terrorism* (2002). In this book we learn that the problems not only of the current moment but of the last forty years stem from the cultural ascendancy of those "who are unpatriotic" but who, unfortunately, are also "the most influential among us." The phrase "among us" is a nice illus-tration of the double game Bennett plays throughout the book. On one reading, "the diversity mongers [and] multi-culturalists," mistaken though they may be in their views, are part of "us"; that is, they are citizens, participating with the rest of us in the back and forth of deliberative democracy. On another reading, however, these cultural relativists are "among us" as a fifth column might be among us, servants of an alien power who prosecute their subversive agenda under the false colors of citizenship. That the second is the reading Bennett finally intends (though he wants to get moral credit for the first) is made clear when he charges these peddlers of "relativism" with unpatriotism, and in that instant defines a patriot as someone who has the same views he has.

This also turns out to be Bennett's definition of honesty and truth-telling. As the remedy for what he and his allies see as the moral enervation of the country, Bennett urges "the reinstatement of a thorough and honest study of our history," where by "honest" he means a study of history that tells the same story he and his friends would tell if they were in control of the nation's history departments. Unfortunately (at least as he sees it), history departments are full of people like Columbia's Eric Foner, who drew Bennett's ire for wondering which is worse, "the horror that engulfed New York City or the apocalyptic rhetoric emanating daily from the White House." Bennett calls this sentiment "atrocious rot." Maybe it is, maybe it isn't, but even if it were atrocious rot, it could be honest atrocious rot; that is, it could be Foner's honest attempt, as a citizen and historian, to take the truthful measure of what the events of September 11 and their aftermath mean. But in Bennett's view, Foner and all the other "Foners of the United States" are not merely mistaken (which is how we usually characterize those on the opposite side of us in what John Milton called the "wars of truth"); they are "insidious," they are engaged in "violent misrepresentation," they practice "distortion," they "sow widespread and debilitating confusion," they "weaken the country's resolve," they exhibit "failures of character," they drown out "legitimate patriots," they display a "despicable nature," they abandon "the honest search for truth."

This long list of hit-and-run accusations is directed at those who would give different answers than Bennett would to questions still being honestly debated seven years later. It is one thing to believe that someone has gotten something wrong; it is quite another to believe that the someone you think to be wrong is by virtue of that error unpatriotic, devoted to lies, and downright evil.

There is a tension in Bennett's book—one common to jeremiads on the right—between his frequent assertions that our cultural condition couldn't be worse and his equally frequent assertions that the vast majority of Americans thinks as he does. How can the enemy at once be so small in number and so disastrously effective? The answer is to be found in the fact that this small band controls our colleges and universities, and the result is the "utter failure of our institutions of higher learning," a failure the product of which is a generation of college students ignorant of our history and imbued with the virus of "cultural and moral relativism." In the pages of the *Wall Street Journal*, the *Washington Times*, the *American Enterprise*, and other venues, alarms are sounded because, according to surveys, 85 percent to 97 percent of faculty members in the humanities and social sciences departments of our most prestigious universities identify themselves as left of center.

If these figures are correct (and I believe they are), they raise at least three questions: How has this happened? What does it mean for hiring and instruction in our universities? And what, if anything, should be done about it?

To the first question, those who report the survey results and proclaim "the shame of America's one-party campuses" have a simple answer: it's a vast left-wing conspiracy, part of "a gigantic social machine working to push society to the left," according to Robert Locke of FrontPageMagazine.com.

To the second question, Locke and his colleagues give essentially the same answer: colleges and universities conspire by offering "academic employment to liberals only." But if you know how the hiring process works, this accusation makes no sense. Departments are required by law to advertise a position and consider all applications. Applicants are asked to provide transcripts, writing samples, and recommendations from senior scholars.

On the basis of these materials, a search committee selects three or four finalists who are brought to campus and questioned closely about their teaching and research interests. No inquiry into an applicant's political allegiances is made or allowed. As a dean, I interviewed more than three hundred job seekers, and although I found out a lot about their research and teaching agendas, I couldn't have told you anything about their political agendas if my life depended on it.

It's not just that universities don't set out to hire only liberals; it's that they couldn't implement that resolve even if they had it. You can't apply a political test if you know nothing about the politics of those in your pool.

But so what? someone might reply. No matter how they got there, liberals are in the classroom, where, laments Walter Williams in the *Washington Times*, they now teach America's sons and daughters "that the Founders of the United States were fascists," that literature "written by 'dead white men' is a tool of exploitation," and that "one person's vision of reality is just as valid as another's."

But this inference from politics to pedagogy holds only if it is assumed that once you know how someone voted in the last election you also will know what and how they teach. And that assumption does not hold. The fact that someone voted Democratic or Republican in an election will tell you nothing about his or her position on the questions that are an academic's stock in trade, questions such as: Is the ability to use language hard-wired? Was the Civil War an economic struggle? Do voters respond negatively to negative advertising? Someone on either side of these or a thousand other questions could have voted Republican, or Democratic, or Libertarian, or Green, or may not have voted at all. There is no necessary or even likely correlation between the political views of a faculty member and the views he or she may have on a disputed issue in an academic field.

In 2000 I was a registered Democrat and voted for Gore. In 2000 I also completed a book portraying the English poet John Milton as a conservative, hard-core Christian authoritarian. I am not a conservative hard-core Christian, but I believe Milton was one, and it is the truth about Milton that I'm trying to get at when I write and teach. My understanding of what that truth is has nothing whatsoever to do with the way I voted, and I could change my mind about Milton and still remain a Democrat or I could become a Republican and have exactly the views about Milton I have now. Of course there always will be some faculty members who are political liberals and who also have been persuaded by postmodern arguments, but this coincidence of political and intellectual commitments is just that—coincidental—and by no means certain.

So the twin bases of the neoconservative complaint collapse: the fact of a predominantly liberal faculty says nothing necessarily about what the faculty teaches, and the faculty is not the product of some giant leftist social machine. But the question remains, what is it the product of?

The answer is a history too complicated to tell here, but it would include the GI Bill of Rights, which gave people like me—children of working-class immigrants—the opportunity to attend college and enter the professorate, bringing with them the largely union politics they grew up in. It also would include the waves of feminist, black, Hispanic, and gay activism that brought hitherto underrepresented and therefore politically active ethnic populations into the academy. The '60s "radicals" who transferred the idealism of their political hopes to the idealism of a transformative theory of education make up another element of the answer.

These were not planned events and patterns; they just occurred, and when the dust settled, the academy—or at least the liberal arts side of it—had become the home of many people who thought of themselves as progressive and on the left.

This brings us finally to the third question: what should be done about it?

Since "it" is not the result of Machiavellian design and does not entail the dire consequences feared by our modern Cassandras and Chicken Littles, there doesn't seem to be a real need to do anything. And we certainly should not do what the neoconservatives urge us to do—insist on "an approximate equality in the numbers of left-of-center and right-of-center faculty" (Robert Locke).

Ideological or political balance, I say once again, is not a legitimate goal for an academic institution any more than it would be for a corporate boardroom (where, I suspect, the relevant statistics would be more cheering to the conservative heart), and in both cases the reason is the same: that's not the business they're in.

Corporations are in the business of expanding markets and turning profits. Universities are in the business of producing and disseminating knowledge. The issue for both will not be what your politics are, but whether you know what you're doing and are doing it well.

Still, it might be argued that even if the liberal faculty is an accident of history and that faculty's teaching does not exist in a causal relationship with its politics, it would be a good thing if there were more conservatives in the mix. That might be a reasonable social goal, but the trick would be to achieve it. Because it cannot legitimately be the goal of a university to enforce a political balance in its faculty, the strategies employed must come from the supply side.

I can think of two.

The Heritage Foundation, the American Enterprise Institute, or other well-funded, highly organized outfits on the right might send waves of recruiters to the nation's high schools, where they would seek out bright, ambitious young conservatives and urge them to consider a career teaching French poetry or the economics of the Weimar Republic.

The second strategy is more likely to work and is one I heartily endorse: the same organizations could lobby for an increase in academic entry salaries from the current $50,000 to $60,000 range to something in the range of $150,000 to infinity.

Add to that a few perks like condos in Aspen, company yachts, junkets to Tahiti, and personal research budgets in the high six figures and put it all into a package with the academic equivalent of stock options, and I'll bet that in a very short time the political profile of the professorate will look satisfyingly different to those who now complain about a faculty that tilts to the left.

I doubt that those on the right will take up my suggestions, if only because complaining is what they like to do, and in 2007, they were doing it in a film called *Indoctrinate U*, directed by Evan Coyne Maloney. You may think that universities are places where ideas are explored and evaluated in a spirit of objective inquiry. But in fact, Maloney tells us, they are places of indoctrination where a left-leaning faculty teaches every subject, including chemistry and horticulture, through the prism of race, class, and gender; where minorities and women are taught that they are victims of oppression; where admissions policies are racially gerrymandered; where identity-based programs reproduce the patterns of segregation that the left supposedly abhors; where students and faculty who speak against the prevailing orthodoxy are ostracized, disciplined, and subjected to sensitivity training; where conservative speakers like Ward Connerly are shouted down; where radical speakers like Ward Churchill are welcomed; where speech codes mandate speech that offends no one; where the faculty preaches diversity but is itself starkly homogeneous with respect to political affiliation; where professors regularly use the classroom as a platform for their political views; where students parrot back the views they know their instructors to hold; where course reading lists are heavy on radical texts and light on texts celebrating the Western tradition; where the American flag is held in suspicion; where military recruiting personnel are either treated rudely or barred from campus; where the default assumption is that anything the United States and Israel do is evil.

This is a large bill of particulars, but hardly a new one; Alan Bloom, Dinesh D'Souza, Roger Kimball, Charles Sykes, Lynne Cheney, Alan Kors, Anne Neal, and David Horowitz, among others, precede Maloney—and while each of the complaints is presented as equally weighty, some are more significant than others and a few are red herrings.

The question of who gets to speak on campus is one of them. Speakers are typically invited to campus by departments and by elected student committees charged with the responsibility of distributing student fees. One group decides what work in the discipline is important and cutting-edge; the other decides more on the basis of popularity and notoriety. Neither is particularly interested in balance; nor should they be.

Balance requires that you ask the question, "Did every constituency get its turn or its share?" But to ask that question is to replace judgment with the criterion of proportional representation, and in the academy that is almost always a bad idea.

As for the clannishness of students who hang out only with those of their own race and ethnicity, that is certainly worrisome, and it is likely that the strong marking of identity in admissions policies, course descriptions, and race- or gender-based centers contributes to it. But to call it segregation is to fudge the distinction between forced separation and a separation voluntarily chosen (even if it is a separation you lament). Maloney does exactly this when he reports on racially skewed admissions practices while his screen shows grainy-imaged footage of the pre–*Brown v. Board of Education* days. They're the same, he's saying. No they're not.

Then there's the matter of speech codes. This is a fake issue. Every speech code that has been tested in the courts has been struck down, often on the very grounds—you can't criminalize offensiveness—invoked by Maloney. Even though there are such codes on the books of some universities, attempts to enforce them will never hold up. Students don't have to worry about speech codes. The universities that have them do, a point made by *Indoctrinate U* when Maloney tells the story of how Cal Poly was taken to the cleaners when it tried to discipline a student for putting up a poster with the word "plantation" in it.

Another red herring is the accusation that there is too little patriotism on campus. Maloney interviews a bus driver who was forced by a university to remove an American flag because it might make foreign students uncomfortable. Removing a flag from a university bus may be an act the wisdom of which might be questioned, but the question would go to the university's competence, not its patriotism. (There is a difference between being stupid and being disloyal.) Universities by definition are neither patriotic nor unpatriotic; striking political stances in either direction is not the business they are properly in.

Still, when all the red herrings and nonissues have been checked off, there remain some serious questions. Why, Maloney asks, should "schools pay people to operate offices and programs that are blatantly political in nature?" (He has in mind offices and programs like Women's Studies, Gay and Lesbian Studies, African American Studies, Chicano Studies.)

The answer to that question is to pose two others: (1) Are there in fact programs with those names that are more political than academic? (2) Do programs with those names have to be more political than academic?

The answer to the first question is yes, to the second no. It is certainly the case that many of these programs gained a place in the academy through political activism, but that doesn't mean that once they are in place political activism need be, or should be, the content of their activities. Race, gender, and class are serious topics and as such worthy of serious study. There are more than enough legitimate academic projects to keep an ethnic or gender studies department going for decades—the recovery of lost texts, the history of economic struggle and success, the relationship of race, ethnicity, and gender to medical research. And there is no reason in principle that such investigations must begin or end in accusations against capitalism, the white male Protestant establishment, and the U.S. government.

But some of them do. Some of these programs forget what the prupose of a university is and continue to think of themselves as extensions of a political agenda. And students who take courses in those programs may well feel the pressure of that agenda. When that happens, an administration should step in and stop it. And if it doesn't, it deserves every criticism this documentary levels.

How many such programs are there? Maloney strongly implies that they are all like that but offers little evidence except the anecdotal evidence of the dozen or so people he interviews. In other places in his documentary he offers as evidence the familiar (and, as I have acknowledged, accurate) statistics indicating that in many departments 75 percent to 95 percent of the faculty self-identifies as left of center. Noting that Stanford's Diversity Office advertises itself as promoting difference, Maloney guesses that "it isn't doing such a great job," given that in the humanities Democrats outnumber Republicans 144 to 10. He quotes a student who declares, "The university totally ignores that diversity of thought means political diversity."

No it doesn't. Political diversity means that in terms of its partisan affiliations, a university faculty should look like America and display the same balance of Democrats and Republicans as can be found in the country's voting rolls. But this requirement of proportional political representation makes sense only if ballot box performance predicts and tracks classroom performance. And, as I have already pointed out, it does not. In many social science departments, there is a split right down the middle between partisans of quantitative methods (techniques like statistical modeling) and partisans of qualitative methods (inquiries rooted in philosophy and theory). But, as the statistics Maloney cites show, 90 percent of those on either side of this divide will be registered Democrats. What this means is that knowing the political registration of a faculty member tells you nothing necessarily about the way in which he or she teaches. (Academic commitments and partisan commitments are independent variables.)

Still, "necessarily" is an important qualifier, and as *Indoctrinate U* makes clear, there are those who do not distinguish between academic and partisan politics and allow the latter to inflect the former, often in the name of social justice. Once again, the question is how many of them are there? Anne Neal, president of the conservative watch-dog group the American Council of Trustees and Alumni, asks that question on camera and answers it by reporting that in a survey of students a "significant percentage... complained that politics was being introduced in the classroom" and 42 percent "said their book lists were one-sided."

Here, again, we have the part that should be taken seriously and the red-herring or fake-issue part. Book lists take their shape from the instructor's judgment that a particular text is important to the area of inquiry. There is no reason— at least no pedagogical reason—to demand that a book list contain representatives of every approach out there. But we should take seriously the part about professors who use the classroom as a stage for their political views. Maloney speculates that perhaps one out of seven performs in this way. I would put the number much lower, perhaps one out of twenty-five. But one out of ten thousand would be one too many.

Academics often bridle at the picture of their activities presented by Maloney, and other conservative critics and accuse them of grossly caricaturing and exaggerating what goes on in the classroom. Maybe so, but so long as there are those who confuse advocacy with teaching, and so long as faculty colleagues and university administrators look the other way, the academy invites the criticism it receives in this documentary. In 1915, the American Association of University Professors warned that if we didn't clean up our own shop, external constituencies, with motives more political than educational, would step in and do it for us. Now they're doing it in the movies and it's our own fault.

SIX

Higher Education
under Attack

So I return in the end to my one-note song: if academics did only the job they are trained and paid to do—introduce students to disciplinary materials and equip them with the necessary analytic skills—criticism of the kind Maloney mounts would have no object, and the various watch-dog groups headed by David Horowitz, Daniel Pipes, and others would have to close shop. But even if this day were to arrive, the academy would not be home free because there would still be the problem I have alluded to but not fully addressed—the problem of money. Who is going to pay for the purified academic enterprise I celebrate in these pages? The unhappy fact is that the more my fellow academics obey the imperative always to academicize, the less they will have a claim to a skeptical public's support.

How do you sell to legislators, governors, trustees, donors, newspapers, etc., an academy that marches to its own drummer, an academy that asks of the subjects that petition for entry only that they be interesting, an academy unconcerned with the public yield of its activities, an academy that puts at the center of its operations the asking of questions for their own sake? How, that is, do you justify the enterprise? As I have already pointed out, you can't, in part because the demand for justification never comes from the inside. The person who asks you to justify what you do is not saying, "tell me why *you* value the activity," but "convince me that *I* should," and if you respond in the spirit of that request, you will have exchanged your values for those of your inquisitor. It may seem paradoxical to say so, but any justification of the academy is always a denigration of it. The only honest thing to do when someone from the outside asks, "what use is this venture anyway?" is to answer "none whatsoever," if by "use" is meant (as it always will be) of use to those with no investment in the obsessions internal to the profession. That answer will surely sound strangely in the ears of donors and those who remember that many public universities were established (by the Morrill and Hatch Acts) with a declared expectation of what they would do for the state. Nevertheless, it is the only answer that respects and preserves the academy's autonomy.

This is not the answer that will by itself reverse the trend of the past forty years, which have seen revenues systematically withdrawn from public education. In January of 2002, Mark Yudof, then president of the University of Minnesota, wrote an essay for the *Chronicle of Higher Education* titled, "Is the Public Research University Dead?" Now, six years later, the most optimistic answer one could give is "Not yet."

The key word in Yudof's title is "public," which has traditionally been short for "state supported." There's both the rub and the question: in an era of declining state support, when is it no longer accurate to designate an institution "public"?

George M. Dennison, president of the University of Montana at Missoula, recalls that in the '60s and '70s the usual assumption was "that the public should pay from 70 percent to 80 percent of the cost of higher education." Now the figure is more likely to be 25 percent (if you're lucky), and in some states the figure is 10 and headed downward. Only ten years ago, Dennison reports, the ratio of state-appropriated funds to tuition dollars in his state was 3 to 1. Now it is 2 to 1 in the other direction: "$1 of state appropriations for every $2 of tuition and fees."

The university's expenditures, Dennison says, have increased markedly, in part because of a large increase in the number of students it is asked to serve; but "fully 98 percent of the increased funding has come from tuition and fees and private support, not from the state."

The story is the same everywhere, despite what some irresponsible politicians sometimes say. Even in those states where the raw sums expended on higher education have been rising, the percentage of the budget devoted to higher education—the figure that means something because it reflects general changes in the cost of doing business and providing services—is declining.

In Wisconsin and other states the level of state support has been more than halved in the past fifteen years. The dilemma was summed up by Katharine C. Lyall, retired chancellor of the University of Wisconsin system: "They want high access, low tuition, top quality, and no tax increases to pay for it."

The result, as Yudof puts it, is a breaking of the compact negotiated long ago by state governments and public research universities: "In return for financial support from taxpayers, universities agreed to keep tuition low and provide access for students from a broad range of economic backgrounds, train graduate and professional students, promote arts and culture, help solve problems in the community, and perform groundbreaking research."

That's a tall order and, up to now, the universities have pretty much been doing their part—giving educational opportunities to millions who would have otherwise been denied them—but in recent years they have been largely abandoned by their partners. Nevertheless, universities are regularly told to make do with what they have, tighten their belts, become more efficient, eliminate frills, teach more, and pay less.

The result is predictable, and you can read about it in your daily newspaper: the very legislators who have withdrawn the money now turn around and berate universities for not providing what they are unwilling to pay for. "It's outrageous," said Richard S. Jarvis, then chancellor of the Oregon University System, "that the state should become a minority partner in educating its undergraduates."

In 2003, Republican representatives John A. Boehner (later to become majority leader of his party) and Howard McKeon issued a report that, if taken seriously, would have the effect of accelerating the decline Jarvis laments. The spirit presiding over this report is not the spirit of academic autonomy, but the spirit of consumer capitalism. Entitled the "College Cost Crisis," the report asserts that higher education costs are "skyrocketing" and the reason is "wasteful spending" by colleges and universities.

It is certainly true that college costs are rising. The first question is, are the increases disproportionate to increases in other sectors—housing, transportation, food, travel, entertainment, books, medical care, prescription drugs? (The answer is "No.") And second, do colleges and universities charge more because they have to pay more for the goods and services necessary to their operation? Had they bothered to ask, McKeon and Boehner would have found that the answer to the second question is a very big "Yes."

Utility costs are way up, insurance costs (especially for university medical centers) have more than doubled, and the tab for constructing new buildings and renovating or maintaining old ones is out of sight. New security costs have been mandated (but not funded) in the wake of September 11. The cost of information systems—barely on the horizon in the '70s, the report's favored decade and a time when student registration was still being done manually in the gym— is now astronomical. The cost of materials and equipment, especially for the new technologies that come with the new sciences (nano technology, neuroscience, bio-everything) developed in the past three decades is soaring. And of course the cost of putting faculty members in the classrooms is higher than it used to be, especially in the increasing number of areas (like computer science, finance, management, engineering) where higher education has to compete for personnel with the corporate sector.

Not only have the costs of these materials and services escalated, but universities are forced to buy more of them because the number of students they are asked to accommodate has grown and continues to grow. Because Boehner and McKeon take no account at all of any of these changes in the real costs of doing business—changes the universities did not impose, but changes they must live with—the statistics they invoke with such a flourish are meaningless, or, rather, they are meaningful only within the bizarre and ignorant assumption that everything in the world of higher education is the same as it was in 1970 except for the price of the entry ticket.

If the methodology of the report is shoddy, the assumptions that drive it are even worse. One assumption is that colleges and universities should be responsive to what Americans believe, as in "Americans believe wasteful spending by college and university management is the No. 1 reason for skyrocketing college costs." But if what Americans believe is false (as it is in this instance), colleges and universities, rather than taking that falsehood seriously and conforming their actions to it, should labor to remove it; they should engage in education, not pandering.

To be sure, the study of what Americans believe is something that advertisers, vendors, and politicians are right to be interested in, and it can even be a proper academic subject, but it should not be what drives the academy's actions. It is entirely appropriate for General Motors, despite the number of people who (like me) are fans of Oldsmobile, to cease producing that automobile because its public image—what Americans believe about it—translates into poor sales. It is not appropriate for a university, an academic not a mercantile enterprise, to decide that because classics, history, German, French, American literature, anthropology, political science, and philosophy (among others) are little valued by many Americans and bring in little, if any, revenues, they should be eliminated.

Yet that is exactly what would happen (and in some places is already happening) if the second large assumption informing the Boehner-McKeon report—the assumption that colleges and universities should run their shops as if they were businesses—were taken to heart.

This too, according to the report, is something Americans believe: "Americans believe institutions of higher learning are not accountable enough to parents, students, and taxpayers—the consumers of higher education." But parents, students, and taxpayers are consumers of higher education only in the sense that they pay for it if they want it; they are not consumers in the sense that the operations of higher education should reflect either their desires or their judgments.

When I go to buy a new suit I know in advance what I want and need—something for work, something for leisure, something for a wedding—and I visit various vendors in order to compare products and prices. By definition, however, the recipients of higher education do not know in advance what they need. If they did, they wouldn't need it, and what they often want, at least at the outset, is an education that will tax their energies as little as possible. Should educators give it to them? Absolutely not. Should curricular matters—questions of what subjects should be studied, what courses should be required, how large classes should be—be settled by surveying student preferences or polling their parents or asking Representatives Boehner and McKeon? No, again.

If colleges and universities are to be "accountable" to anyone or anything, it should be to the academic values—dedicated and responsible teaching, rigorous and honest research—without which higher education would be little different from the bottom-line enterprise its critics would have it become.

By the evidence of this report—not the evidence in the report; there's precious little of that—Boehner and McKeon wouldn't recognize an academic value if it ran over them. Indeed the word "academic" scarcely appears in what they write (if they wrote it), and perhaps this is how it should be, given a performance as slipshod and superficial as theirs is.

"Slipshod" and "superficial" are words not strong enough to describe the Web site the legislators set up as a "resource" addendum to their report. The centerpiece of the Web site—College Cost Central: A Resource for Parents, Students, & Taxpayers Fed Up with the High Costs of Higher Education—is a list of twelve yes/no questions to which those same parents, students, and taxpayers are asked to respond. Only three of the questions are real. The others are designed to elicit—no coerce—responses that can then be used to support the conclusions McKeon and Boehner have reached in advance of doing any research at all. Here, for example, is question 1: "Can colleges and universities be doing more to control their spending and avoid large tuition hikes that hurt parents and students?" Although this has the form of a question, its core content is four unsubstantiated assertions: (1) colleges and universities do not control their spending; (2) uncontrolled spending is the sole cause of tuition hikes; (3) those hikes are large (in relation to what norms or practices is never specified); and (4) they hurt parents and students. The real question then is, "do you think that colleges and universities should stop doing these horrible things?" and of course anyone who understands it that way (and what other way is there to understand it?) will answer "yes" and thus provide Boehner and McKeon with one more piece of "evidence" with which to convict higher education of multiple offenses.

If a question doesn't coerce, it imputes blame where there may not be any. Here is question 12: "Do you believe the construction of facilities at colleges and universities is contributing to the dramatic increases in the cost of higher education?" The suggestion is that a "yes" answer (to which the respondent is obviously directed) would mean that colleges and universities were doing something wrong. But what would it be? Constructing laboratories? dormitories? libraries? classroom buildings? Could an academic institution be doing its job and *not* be constructing facilities? What's the point of this question? No point really, accept to add one more (underdefined) item to the list of crimes of which colleges and universities are presumed guilty in this indictment masquerading as a survey.

It is not an indictment solely constructed by Boehner and McKeon, who are merely playing their part in a coordinated effort to commandeer higher education by discrediting it. If the public can be persuaded that institutions of higher education are fiscally and pedagogically irresponsible, the way will be open to a double agenda: strip colleges and universities of both federal and state support and then tie whatever funds are left to "performance" measures in the name of accountability and assessment. The folks who gave us the political correctness scare in the '90s (and that was one of the best PR campaigns ever mounted) are once again in high gear and their message is simple: higher education is too important to be left to the educators, who are wasting your money, teaching your children to be unpatriotic and irreligious (when they are teaching at all), and running a closed shop that is hostile to the values of mainstream America. It's a potent formula: less money, more controls, and controls by the right people; not pointy-headed professors or woolyheaded administrators, but hard-headed businessmen who will rein in the excesses (monetary and moral) to which people with too many advanced degrees are prone.

So much is clear and indisputable. What is not clear is the response of the academic community to this assault on its autonomy and professional integrity. Too often that response has been of the weak-kneed variety displayed by the Association of American Universities when then president Nils Hasselmo offered a mild criticism of Mr. McKeon's ideas and then said, "We look forward to working with Mr. McKeon." No, you should look forward to defeating Mr. McKeon and his ilk, and that won't be done by mealymouthed metooism. If the academic community does its usual thing and rolls over and plays dead, in time it will *be* dead.

But what is the alternative? One step would be to educate the general public, something I attempted on a small scale when I was dean and a parent, in the course of making a complaint, would say to me, "After all, as a taxpayer I pay your salary." I always responded by asking a question: what percentage of the university's operating costs do you guess are covered by public funds? Almost always, the answer was something on the order of 75 percent. When I said, no, the figure is just 25 percent and heading downward and added that in some states the figure has dipped below 10 percent, the reaction was usually one of surprise and dismay.

I followed up with another question: what percentage of the cost to educate a student do you guess is covered by tuition? Again, the parent was usually shocked by the answer: if you include not just classroom education but the cost of everything that must be in place for that education to occur—a library, laboratories, computer centers, building maintenance, utilities, safety patrols, and more—tuition covers only 26 percent. At this point in the conversation the unhappy parent began to see what public universities are facing these days: "You're telling me that state funds are being withdrawn at the same time expenses are exceeding tuition by a factor of four to one, and you're barred by law from raising tuition. How can you stay in business?"

A good question, but one more appropriately put to the people who are doing the damage, the state and federal officials who are supposedly in charge of ensuring the health and prosperity of higher education. It is they who must be made to confront the consequences of their actions.

Again, I tried to do my small part when I was a dean. In the course of several years, I said many nasty things about members of Congress, Illinois state representatives and senators, the governor of Illinois, the governor's budget director, and the governor-appointed Illinois Board of Higher Education. I called these people ignorant, misinformed, demagogic, and dishonest and repeatedly suggested that when it came to colleges and universities, either they didn't know what they were talking about or (and this is worse) they did know and were deliberately setting out to destroy public higher education.

In response they sent me nice notes, trekked across the state to visit me in my office, invited me to talk with their colleagues, bought my books (and actually read them), took me to lunch, and promised to arrange a dinner with the governor. (It never happened.)

What was going on here? Why did people of whom I had been unfailingly (and acerbically) critical respond by being unfailingly nice and even, on occasion, deferential?

I got the hint of an answer from the first state representative who came to see me. As she walked through the door, she said, "Well, I managed to find your office, so we all can't be as dumb as you say we are." Two things were obvious: she had certainly gotten the message. And it was the message— harsh, accusatory, scornful—that had gotten her to come.

The conclusion I drew from this and other interactions was not that public life is full of masochists looking for a chance to be beaten again, but that senior university administrators and lobbyists have been talking to legislators and governors (and, yes, trustees) in the wrong way.

That is, campus administrators have been diplomatic, respectful, conciliatory, reasonable, sometimes apologetic, and always defensive, and they would have done much better, I think, if they had been aggressive, blunt, mildly confrontational, and just a bit arrogant. When I talked to university officials and suggested that they go on the offensive when faced with budget cuts, threats of new control, baseless accusations of waste, etc., they demurred and said, "It wouldn't be good to irritate them."

Well, "irritate" is not quite what I had in mind. "Get their attention" is more in the right direction, "make them uncomfortable" would be better, and "cause them pain" would hit the mark. It was Ronald Reagan who figured out that a university system offers the perfect target for making political (and sometimes financial) hay because it is at once visible and populated by persons who, although (or because) they are the bearers of many advanced degrees, are unlikely to fight back. Or, if they do fight back, it will be with tools that are spectacularly ineffectual.

Those will be, not surprisingly, the tools of their trade—fact, reason, argument, theory, never anything ad hoc or ad hominem. So when, for the ten-thousandth time, the charge is made that faculty members only teach six or nine or twelve hours a week and spend the rest of their time doing pointless research or drinking lattes in a cafe, the university community will respond with mind-numbing statistics, with elaborate (and largely unpersuasive) accounts of how the state will ultimately benefit from a study of gender reversal in Shakespeare or from a mathematical proof that only five people in the world understand, and (although it doesn't follow at all) with a resolution to do better. And then next year or next month when the same things are said, it will have to be done all over again, and with as little effect.

In general, there are two things that won't work, and they are the only two things universities ever try.

First of all, it won't work to explain the academic world to nonacademics while standing on one foot. That is, you can't in a short time teach people to value activities they have never engaged in, or persuade them that if research into the ways and byways of Byzantine art is not supported, the world will be poorer. Remember, it takes four or more years to initiate students into the pleasures of the academic life, and in many cases the effort is not successful. Why should anyone think that the lessons could be taught and accepted in twenty minutes?

If telling our story in the hope that its terms will be adopted by those who have never lived it won't work, neither will the attempt to translate it into their terms by retelling it in the vocabulary of business or venture capitalism.

Colleges and universities surely must observe good business practices in the relevant areas (purchasing, service contracts, construction, maintenance), but colleges, as I have said earlier, are not businesses. They do not drop product lines that have lost market share. They do not dismiss employees who cease to be productive or run into a bad patch. They do not monitor every moment of every working day. They will wait years for a research program to pan out and won't consider it a breach of contract if it doesn't.

To be sure, sometimes a faculty project will pay off (with a patent, a large grant, a Nobel Prize), but more often it will not even pay its own way. If a bottom-line criterion is applied to the academy, 90 percent of what goes on will fail the test, and, therefore, defending the academy in bottom-line terms is a losing proposition, unless you want to reach the conclusion that most of what academics do should be abandoned.

But what's left? If explaining to our critics what we do won't work, and if redescribing the enterprise in the vocabulary of their vocations won't work either, what will work?

Well, maybe nothing. Maybe the academy will just have to learn to live (and perhaps die) in this brave new world where money is withdrawn from public higher education at the same time that ever more strict controls are imposed. But my experience suggests that it might just be worth a try to stand up for ourselves unapologetically, and to comport ourselves as if we were formidable adversaries rather than easy marks.

This would mean allowing no false statement by a public official to pass uncorrected and unrebuked. (Not only must the record be set straight; those who have gotten it wrong must be made to feel bad if only so that they will think twice before doing it again.) It would mean embracing the fact that few nonacademics understand what we do and why we do it, and turning it into a weapon. Instead of saying, "Let me tell you what we do so that you'll love us," or "Let me explain how your values are really our values too," say, "We do what we do, we've been doing it for a long time, it has its own history, and until you learn it or join it, your opinions are not worth listening to."

Instead of defending classics or French literature or sociology, ask those who think they need defending what they know about them, and if the answer is "not much" (on the model of "don't know much about the Middle Ages"), suggest, ever so politely, that they might want to go back to school. Instead of trying to justify your values (always a weak position), assume them and assume too your right to define and protect them. And when you are invited to explain, defend, or justify, just say no.

But again, will it work? It just might (I offer no guarantees), and for two reasons. First, it will be surprising, and, because surprising, disconcerting: legislators, governors, and trustees don't expect academics to hit back or (even better) hit first, and at the least you will have gotten them off balance. Second, they quite possibly will like it, will like being challenged rather than toadied to, will like being taken seriously enough to engage with, will like being party to a conversation of the kind that fills our days, will like, in short, being spoken to as if they were academics.

The attraction that bashing the academy has for politicians and others has a source in the anti-intellectualism that has always been a part of American life. It is our version of the no-nonsense empiricism and distrust of eloquence bequeathed to us by the British and refined into an art in the "a man's gotta do what a man's gotta do" spirit of Western expansion.

But that same anti-intellectualism has its flip side in an abiding fascination with those who devote themselves to what is called (I dislike the phrase, but it is sometimes useful) the life of the mind. Nonacademics either want to beat us up or have dinner with us. If we don't let them do the first—if we fight back with all we have and all we are—we'll have more chances to do the second; and a familiarity not rooted in contempt might in time pay off.

Will it happen? I doubt it. Once I found myself sitting in a doctor's waiting room, and sitting next to me was one of the university's lobbyists. We talked and commiserated about budgetary woes, new demands and restrictions, recycled misconceptions, and the like. As one of us (I forgot which) got called into the inner sanctum, I said, "The next time you go before some committee in the legislature, take me with you." He said, "Will you behave?"

Some people never learn.

SEVEN

A Conclusion and Two Voices
from the Other Side

In conclusion, let me summarize my argument and the entailments it implies. The grounding proposition is that both the coherence and the value of a task depend on its being distinctive. Beginning with that proposition, I ask: What is the distinctive task college and university professors are trained and paid to perform? What can they legitimately (as opposed to presumptuously) claim to be able to do? My answer is that college and university professors can introduce students to bodies of material new to them and equip those same students with the appropriate (to the discipline) analytical and research skills. From this professional competence follow both obligations and prohibitions. The obligations are the usual pedagogical ones—setting up a course, preparing a syllabus, devising exams, assigning papers or experiments, giving feedback, holding office hours, etc. The prohibitions are that an instructor should do neither less nor more.

Doing less would mean not showing up to class or showing up unprepared, not being alert to the newest approaches and models in the field, failing to give back papers or to comment on them in helpful ways, etc. Doing more would be to take on tasks that belong properly to other agents—to preachers, political leaders, therapists, and gurus. The lure of these other (some would say larger or more noble) tasks is that they enhance, or at least seem to enhance, the significance of what a teacher does. But in fact, I argue, agendas imported into the classroom from foreign venues do not enrich the pedagogical task, but overwhelm it and erode its constitutive distinctiveness. Once you start preaching or urging a political agenda or engaging your students in discussions designed to produce action in the world, you are surely doing something, but it is not academic, even if you give it that name.

You know you are being academic (rather than therapeutic or political or hortatory) when the questions raised in your classroom have the goal of achieving a more accurate description or of testing a thesis; you know that you are being (or trying to be) something else when the descriptions you put forward are really stepping stones to an ideological conclusion (even one so apparently innocuous as "we should respect the voices of others"). The academic enterprise excludes no topic from its purview, but it regards any and every topic as a basis for analysis rather than as a stimulus to some moral, political, or existential commitment. Not to practice politics, but to study it; not to proselytize for or against religious doctrines, but to describe them; not to affirm or reject affirmative action, but to explore its history and lay out the arguments that have been made for and against it.

My contention is that if every college or university instructor were to hew to this discipline—were to do his or her job and refrain from doing jobs that belong appropriately to others—those who want to do our jobs for us would have no traction or point of polemical entry because politics, or religion, or ethics would enter the classroom only as objects of analysis and not as candidates for approval or rejection. The culture wars, at least in the classroom, would be over. There would still be a basis for argument and correction. You could still say, I don't think your account is quite right for the following reasons. But the reasons would belong to the canons of argument and evidence and not to any political, religious, or ethical agenda.

The name I give to this academic categorical imperative is "academicizing." To academicize an issue is to detach it from those contexts where it poses a choice of what to do or how to live—shall I join the priesthood or join the army?—and insert it into an academic context where it invites a certain kind of interrogation. What is its history? Why has it been thought significant? What are the prevailing answers to the questions it raises? Where do those answers come from? The more these and related questions are posed, the less will students feel the urgency to bear personal witness in one direction or another.

But for many, that is just the problem. I acknowledged at the outset that mine is a minority position. Indeed, in some quarters it is a position regarded as so neolithic and retrograde that no one bothers even to argue against it. Mark Bracher, a professor at Kent State, begins a recent essay by declaring confidently, "Many literature teachers and scholars are committed to promoting social justice through both their teaching and their scholarship." Bracher spends no time discussing whether promoting social justice is an appropriate academic goal. He is just distressed that not very much has been done in the way of accomplishing it. "But despite this commitment of critical and pedagogical activity to political and ethical ends, there is little evidence that literary study has made much difference in the injustice that permeates our world." (To me, that's the good news.)

Injustice would be diminished, Bracher believes, if sympathy and compassion for others were increased. And that, he says, should be the work of the classroom: "If literary study could systematically help students overcome their indifference to the suffering that surrounds them, and experience compassion for the sufferers, it would make a significant contribution to social justice." But literary study could have this effect only if it were no longer literary study, that is, if the study of stylistic effects, genres, meters, verse forms, novels, romance, epic, the contest of interpretations—everything that belongs to literary study as something distinctive, something one could master, something one could teach—were made instrumental to an end not contemplated by those who either produce the literature or consume it. To be sure, some poets or novelists write with the purpose of expanding the sympathies of their readers, but what of those who do not? Either their works will be distorted when they are bent to a measure foreign to their intention, or they will not be taught because they are not useful to the *nonliterary* purpose of the course. Either way, the course will be a course in literary study only by name, and the students will be offered a character transplant when they signed on for something more modest, to wit, a course of instruction.

But who gave Mark Bracher (or any other teacher employed by a college or university) the authority first to decide what the world and his students need in the way of moral improvement, and second to turn his classroom into a social/ethical laboratory? Isn't that straight indoctrination? Bracher asks the same questions and answers that the objection is naïve because indoctrination is already occurring anyway. "As currently practiced, literary pedagogy ... contributes to the production of docile subjects for global capitalism through, for example, enforcing classroom punctuality, reliability, obedience, and subordination." The account of cause and effect here is more than a bit crude. Is it really the case that if you come to class, and, even worse, come to class on time, and, worse still, conform your behavior to the protocols of classroom discipline, you will become a capitalist toady? (If only the work of ideology were that easy.) But the specific example Bracher offers is less important than his general argument that because there is no avoiding imposing values in one direction or another, we might as well impose the values in the direction we prefer: "we should forthrightly acknowledge that it is our job to change our students' behaviors and turn our attention to the question of what behaviors we should try to change, and what means we should use to do so." In short, if we don't push our politics, the classroom will be taken over by someone else's. After all, isn't everything political?

I have addressed this question several times in the course of this book, but it cannot be answered too often, if only because the "everything-is-political" mantra is ritually invoked by those who do not respect (or believe in) the distinction between academic work and political work. If by "political" we mean the presence in a situation of competing visions of the good and the true, then of course everything is political, for no form of socially organized life—be it marriage, industry, church life, the military, in addition to politics per se—is free of ideological conflict, and even when conflicts are (temporarily) resolved, the shape of the resolution will at some level be political too. But the fact that politics marks every context of human action doesn't mean that it is legitimate to import the politics appropriate to one context into another which, while no less political, will be home to a quite different politics There are corporate politics, domestic politics, office politics, mail-room politics, and locker-room politics, in addition to partisan politics and academic politics, and each of these will have different contents which in turn will legitimate different forms of political behavior. (In partisan politics, ad hominem attacks are within the pale; in academic politics, they are not.)

The content of academic politics is, among other things, disagreement about what texts should be taught, what methodological approaches are legitimate, what courses should be required, and which reading of a poem is correct. The content of partisan politics is, among other things, disagreement about what alliances the country should form, which wars it should wage, what social goals it should mandate, and which party should be elected. In both arenas, the political agent is trying to persuade his or her fellows to a particular conclusion; but in one the goal of persuasion is the adoption of a policy or a change in the country's direction, while in the other the goal is to establish, by argument and evidence, the superiority of one analysis or description or procedure over its (intellectual) rivals. If I vote against a literary theorist and for a Shakespearian in a tenure meeting, my act can be described as political because I am aligning myself with one party rather than another in an academic debate about personnel and curriculum. If I vote for a candidate or donate money to a cause, my action is also political, but in an entirely different register. I am trying to change the world rather than to change the minds of my colleagues about the future direction of the discipline.

It may seem paradoxical to say so, but the truth of the assertion that the political is everywhere means that there is no overarching sense of the political, no politics that is just politics per se, no politics that seeps into everything; there are just particular instances of politics in particular conventional/social settings. "Everything is political" means that there is no situation free of political contestation, not that the form of political contestation you find over here will be exactly like the form of political contestation you find over there. Correctly understood, the "everything is political" slogan sends you back to the differences—between practices and disciplines—those who invoke it want to deny. Once you realize that while politics is everywhere, it isn't the same politics, the cash value of saying that everything is political disappears; for it won't get those who say it to where they want to get—to a justification for bringing the politics appropriate to one project (the project of trying to elect people or pass laws) into the precincts of another (the project of determining which account of an academic matter is correct). That justification would only be available if there were a general category of the political apart from any particular contexts of political action, if all politics were the same in a stronger sense than the sense given by the lexical fact that they can be referred to by the same word. The availability of the word "political" to refer to what goes on in different contexts is what tricks people into thinking that the boundaries between contexts are illusory and without constraining or distinguishing effect.

It is only because he believes in the chimera of a general politics filling all nooks and crannies that Bracher can think he's scored a point when he asks, "Don't we choose our texts, formulate our writing assignments and organize classroom activities with the aim of getting our students to respond in particular ways?" Isn't that political? Yes, we do, and yes it is, but if we are teaching rather than proselytizing—doing academic politics and not ballot box politics—the particular responses we hope to elicit are responses to an academic question (what is the structure of this argument? is this text unified? is this account of the event complete?) and not to the question of what we should do about the economy or the AIDS epidemic or the pollution of the environment. Bracher needs to conflate those questions so that he can pursue his partisan agenda with a good conscience, so that he can say that because everything is political (a claim that is both true and trivial), we teachers can do anything we like.

At one point Bracher claims—it is an incredible claim—that his agenda is "politically neutral" and "aims not to inculcate particular values" but to "provide students with more complete, empirically and clinically validated knowledge of the causes of certain behaviors" he finds distressing. But within two paragraphs, he identifies these malign causes with the "American ideology that emphasizes hyper-individualism, self-reliance and social Darwinism"; within a few sentences "American ideology" has become "conservative ideology"; and within a few pages George W. Bush has emerged as an example of the conservative thinking that teachers must expose and oppose. Later Bush appears in a list with Osama bin Laden and Saddam Hussein as figures "toward whom [students] may feel animosity" of the kind they certainly feel toward "murderers, rapists, child molesters, and other criminals." If this is political neutrality, I wonder what political advocacy looks like.

Bracher is self-aware enough to ask the obvious question: "what right do we have to impose our view...—our 'liberal' or 'progressive' ideology—on our students?" "We have the right," he answers, "because the evidence supports...our ideology." In short, we're correct, those other guys are on the wrong side, and while we don't want them turning students into apologists for global capitalism, it's perfectly okay—indeed obligatory and moral—for us to turn students into agents of left-progressive change. Any conservative parent, legislator, or donor reading Bracher's essay will have plenty of evidence to support the conviction that liberal professors have abandoned teaching for indoctrination. Of course for Bracher this would not be an accusation. In his view teaching *is* indoctrination and the only question is, will it be our indoctrination or theirs?

The desire to indoctrinate is not the only reason some will reject the imperative always to academicize. There is also the desire to inspire, to bring one's students not simply to a point of understanding a subject matter but to a level of moral illumination that will infuse every moment of their lives with a deep meaning. In a recent book subtitled *Why Our Colleges and Universities Have Given Up on the Meaning of Life*, Anthony Kronman complains that an "old idea that a program of higher education should be . . . organized around the questions of the ends of human life lost its appeal in favor of a new idea that a college or a university is . . . a gathering of academic specialists inspired by their commitment to scholarship as a vocation." The old idea, the idea of providing training in the general "art of living," placed no bounds on the ambitions of a teacher who wanted to lead students in a search for the meaning of life. The new idea, the idea of teachers and students joined in an effort to determine the truth of a disciplinary matter—the interpretation of a poem, the causes of an event, the origins of a virus—limits both the kinds of questions that can be asked and the answers that can be appropriately given. Kronman would have us break out of these limits ("What is needed is relief from the inhibitions of the research ideal"), but it is my view that those very limits, if they are honored, allow us to identify with precision the tasks we are equipped to perform—teach materials and confer skills—and protect us from the accusation that we have ventured into precincts (of politics, morality, ethics) not properly ours.

The promise Kronman holds out is glorious. Teachers and students who are put in touch with the deep and abiding concerns that animate the great works of literature, philosophy, and history might experience a "kind of immortality" and even enact "the idea of eternity in their lives." No such reward awaits the disciplinary worker who must be satisfied with particulars and the narrow goal of making an account, or a description, or an interpretation just a bit more adequate to its object. Nevertheless, I maintain, it is the very modesty of the academicizing enterprise—its forsaking of the grand vision to which Kronman would call us—that makes it coherent and intelligible.

When Kronman links education to the search for an answer to "the question of life's meaning," he enrolls himself in a venerable humanistic tradition that includes, among others, Cicero, John Milton, Philip Sidney, Matthew Arnold. This is an impressive list that could easily be enlarged tenfold, but I have my own roster of worthies to invoke. "It is absolutely essential," declares Kant, "that the learned community at the university...contain a faculty that is independent...one that having no commands to give, is free to evaluate everything." Cardinal Newman says the same thing in a formulation that anticipates everything I have written here: "The process of training, by which the intellect, instead of being formed or sacrificed to some particular or accidental purpose, some specific trade or profession...is disciplined for its own sake...is called Liberal Education." And Jacques Derrida provides a deeply philosophical justification of the austerity I have been urging. "Thinking, if it is to remain open to the possibility of thought...must not seek to be economic." That is, it must not rest on the hope of a "real world" payoff. Why? Because "it belongs...to an economy of waste," an economy whose currency purchases nothing beyond its own expenditure. Therefore, Derrida concludes,

"Beware of ends." Beware, that is, of doing something for a reward external to its own economy. Do it because it is its own reward and look for no pleasures beyond the pleasure of responsible, rigorous performance. In short, and for the last time, just do your job. The world of grand and ambitious ends will take care of itself, and if it doesn't, you can always save it on your own time.

Selected Bibliography

Academic Bill of Rights. Available at studentsforacademicfreedom.org.

Althouse, Ann. "Stanley Fish Takes on the Kevin Barret Controversy." Available at http://www.althouse.blogspot.com/2006/07/stanley-fish-takes-on-kevin-barrett.html.

American Association of University Professor's 1915 Declaration of Principles. Available at http://www.akronaaup.org/documents/AAUP1915.pdf.

Bennett, William. *Why We Fight: Moral Clarity and the War on Terrorism.* New York: Doubleday, 2002.

Boehner, John A., and Howard McKeon. "College Cost Crisis." Available at http://www.epi.elps.vt.edu/Perspectives/collegecostsrep.pdf.

Bok, Derek. *Our Underachieving Colleges.* Princeton, N.J.: Princeton University Press, 2006.

Bracher, Mark. "Teaching for Social Justice: Reeducating the Emotions through Literary Study." *JAC* 26 (2006): 464.

Carey, John. "A Work in Praise of Terrorism? September 11 and *Samson Agonistes.*" *Times Literary Supplement*, 6 Sept. 2002: 15–16.

Churchill, Ward. "The Ghosts of 9-1-1: Reflections on History, Justice and Roosting Chickens." Available at http://www.altpr.org.

Churchill, Ward. " 'Some People Push Back': On the Justice of Roosting Chickens." Available at http://www.ratical.org.

Cottom, Daniel. *Why Education Is Useless.* Philadelphia: University of Pennsylvania Press, 2003.

Dennison, George M. "State Funding Leads toward Privatization." Available at http://www.umt.edu/urelations/MainHall/1102/funding.htm.

Dworkin, Ronald. "Liberalism." In *Public and Private Morality*, edited by · Stuart Hampshire. New York: Cambridge University Press, 1978.

Gearen, Mark D. Letter to the *New York Times*, 24 May 2004.

Gerber, Larry. "Inextricably Linked: Shared Governance and Academic Freedom." *Academe* 87 (May–June 2001): 22–24.

Graff, Gerald. *Beyond the Culture Wars*. New York: W. W. Norton & Company, 1992.

Haynsworth, Harry J. "Faculty Governance: Reflections of a Retiring Dean." *University of Toledo Law Review* (fall 2003): 93–100.

Hinshaw, Wendy Wolters. "Teaching for Social Justice? Resituating Student Resistance." *JAC* 27 (2007): 222–34.

Horowitz, David. "The Campus Blacklist." Available at http://www.frontpagemag.com/articles/Read.aspx?GUID=18DCCD2C-275B-489E-B920-266043279A09.

Indoctrinate U. DVD. Directed by Evan Coyne Maloney. 2007.

Kant, Immanuel. "The Contest of Faculties." In *Kant: Political Writings*, edited by H. S. Reiss. Cambridge: Cambridge University Press, 1991.

Kaplinsky, Joe. "Creationism, Pluralism, and the Compromising of Science." *Spiked*, 1 March 2005. Available at http://www.spiked-online.com/Articles/0000000CA910.htm.

Keller, Julia. "After the Attack, Postmodernism Loses Its Glib Grip." *Chicago Tribune*, 27 Sept. 2001.

Kiss, Elizabeth, and Peter Euben, eds. *Debating Moral Education*. Durham, N.C.: Duke University Press, 2008.

Kronman, Anthony. *Education's End: Why Our Colleges and Universities Have Given Up on the Meaning of Life*. Binghamton, N.Y.: Vail-Ballou Press, 2007.

Lipstadt, Deborah. *Denying the Holocaust*. New York: Penguin Group, 1994.

Locke, John. *A Letter Concerning Toleration*, edited by John Horton and Susan Mendus. New York: Routledge, 1991.

Locke, Robert. "The Liberal University: Our Demands." Available at http://www.frontpagemag.com/Articles/Read.aspx?GUID=5630FDCD-32B9-4BB1-A01D-2C39006389CB.

Leo, John. "Campus Hand-Wringing Is Not a Pretty Sight." Available at http://www.johnleo.com.

Lombardi, John V. "University Improvement: The Permanent Challenge." Available at http://www.jvlone.com.

McGrory, Brian. "Chill Sets In at Harvard." *Boston Globe*, 21 Jan. 2005. Available at http://www.boston.com/news/local/articles/2005/01/21/chill_sets_in_at_harvard.

Mearsheimer, John. "The Aims of Education." *Philosophy and Literature* 22 (1998): 137–55.

Michigan State University Mission Statement. Available at http://president.msu.edu/mission.php.

Mill, John Stuart. *On Liberty*. New York: Penguin Books, 1974.

Murphy, James Bernard. "Good Students and Good Citizens." *New York Times*, 15 Sept. 2002.

Nagel, Thomas. "Moral Conflict and Political Legitimacy." *Philosophy and Public Affairs* 16 (1987): 215–40.

Neal, Anne. "Intellectual Diversity Endangered." Available at http://www.cfif.org/htdocs/freedomline/current/guest_commentary/student_right_to_learn.htm.

Newman, John Henry. *The Idea of a University*. London: Longmans, Green and Co., 1893.

Rothstein, Edward. "Attacks on U.S. Challenge the Perspectives of Postmodern True Believers." *New York Times*, 22 Sept. 2001, late edition, A17.

Selingo, Jeffrey. "The Disappearing State in Public Higher Education." *Chronicle of Higher Education* 49 (2003).

Street, Paul. "A Farewell Message from Stanley Fish: 'Good Professors Do What They're Told.'" Available at http://www.punksinscience.org.

Taylor, Mark. *The Moment of Complexity*. Chicago: University of Chicago Press, 2001.

United States v. Philip Morris. United States District Court for the District of Columbia, Civil Action No. 99–2496 (GK), 2006.

University of Arizona Guidelines for Shared Governance. Available at http://w3fp.arizona.edu/senate/ShGovExtending.html.

Waldron, Jeremy. "What Plato Would Allow?" *Nomos* XXXVII, 1995.

Weinrib, Ernest J. "Legal Formalism: On the Immanent Rationality of Law." *Yale Law Journal* 97 (1988).

Weslyan University Mission Statement. Available at http://www.wesleyan.edu/deans/mission.html.

Yale College Mission Statement. Available at http://www.yale.edu/accred/standards/s1.html.

Yudof, Mark. "Point of View: Is the Public Research University Dead?" *Chronicle of Higher Education*, 11 Jan. 2002.

Index

The Coronation

The Coronation

A Fandorin Mystery

~

BORIS AKUNIN

TRANSLATED FROM THE RUSSIAN

BY ANDREW BROMFIELD

The Mysterious Press
New York

First published in Great Britain in 2009
by Weidenfeld & Nicolson.

First published in Russian as *Koronaciya* by
Zakharov Publishers, Moscow, Russia in 2000 and in Italian
as *Incoronazione* Edizioni Frassinelli, Milan, Italy in 2004.

Published simultaneously in Canada
Printed in the United States of America

First Grove Atlantic hardcover edition: February 2019

Library of Congress Cataloging-in-Publication data available for this title.

ISBN 978-0-8021-2781-5
eISBN 978-0-8021-4615-1

The Mysterious Press
an imprint of Grove Atlantic
154 West 14th Street
New York, NY 10011

Distributed by Publishers Group West

groveatlantic.com

19 20 21 22   10 9 8 7 6 5 4 3 2 1

20 May

He died in front of my very eyes, this strange and disagreeable gentleman.

It all happened so quickly, so very quickly.

The very instant the shots roared out, he was flung back against the cable.

He dropped his little revolver, clutched at the shaky handrail and froze on the spot, with his head thrown back. I caught a momentary glimpse of a white face, bisected by a black strip of moustache, before it disappeared behind the black mantle.

'Erast Petrovich!' I shouted, calling him by his given name and patronymic for the first time.

Or did I only mean to shout?

The precarious decking swayed beneath his feet. His head suddenly bobbed forward as if from a powerful jolt, his body began slumping, chest forward, over the cable, then swung round grotesquely – and the next instant it was already hurtling down, down, down.

The precious casket fell from my hands, struck a rock and split open. There was a flash of blinding sparks from the multi-coloured facets of the diamonds, sapphires and emeralds, but I did not even glance at these incalculable riches as they scattered into the grass.

From the ravine there came the soft crunch of an impact, and I gasped. The black bundle went tumbling down the steep slope, gathering speed along the way and only ceasing its nauseous whirling motion at the very edge of the stream. It dropped one lifeless hand into the water and lay there, face down in the gravel.

I had not liked this man. Perhaps I had even hated him. In any case, I had wanted him to disappear from our lives once and for all. But I had not wished for his death.

His trade was risk, he toyed with danger constantly, but somehow I had never thought he could be killed. He had seemed immortal to me.

I do not know how long I stood there like that, gazing stiffly down. It cannot have been very long. But time seemed to rupture, to split apart, and I fell into the rent – back into the old, serene life that had ended abruptly exactly two weeks earlier.

Yes, that was a Monday too, the sixth of May.

6 May

We arrived in the ancient capital of the Russian state in the morning. Owing to the imminent coronation festivities, the Nikolai I Station was congested with traffic and our train was sent off via a transfer line to the Brest Station, which seemed to me a rather ill-judged decision, to say the least, on the part of the local authorities. I can only assume that a certain coolness in relations between His Highness Georgii Alexandrovich and His Highness Simeon Alexandrovich, the governor-general of Moscow, must have played some part in it. I can think of no other way to explain the humiliating half-hour wait on the points at the marshalling yard and the subsequent diversion of our special express train from the main station to a secondary one.

And we were not met on the platform by Simeon Alexandrovich himself, as protocol, tradition, family connection and, ultimately, simple respect for an elder brother should have required, but only by a member of the reception committee, a minister of the imperial court who, incidentally, immediately departed for the Nikolai I station to receive the Prince of Prussia. But since when has the heir to the Prussian throne been accorded more attention in Moscow than the uncle of His Majesty, the admiral-general of the Russian fleet and the second most senior of the grand dukes of the imperial family? Georgii Alexandrovich did not show it, but I think he felt no less indignant than I did at such a clear affront.

It was a good thing at least that Her Highness, the Grand

Duchess Ekaterina Ioannovna, had stayed in St Petersburg – she is so zealous about the subtle points of ritual and maintaining the dignity of the royal family. The epidemic of measles that had laid low the four middle sons – Alexei Georgievich, Sergei Georgievich, Dmitry Georgievich and Konstantin Georgievich – prevented Her Highness, an exemplary and loving mother, from taking part in the coronation, the supreme event in the life of the state and the imperial family. There were, it is true, venomous tongues who claimed that Her Highness's absence at the celebrations in Moscow was to be explained less by maternal love than by a reluctance to play the part of a mere extra at the triumph of the young tsarina. There was also mention of last year's incident at the Christmas Ball, when the new empress suggested that the ladies of the royal family should establish a handicraft society, and that each of the grand duchesses should knit a warm cap for the little orphans at the Mariinsky Orphanage. Perhaps Ekaterina Ioannovna's reaction to this proposal was a little too severe. It is even quite possible that since then relations between Her Highness and Her Majesty had not been entirely good. However, no provocation was intended by My Lady's not coming to the coronation, I can vouch for that. Whatever Ekaterina Ioannovna's feelings towards Her Majesty may be, under no circumstances would she ever presume to neglect her dynastic duty without a very serious reason. Her Highness's sons really were ill.

That was sad of course but, as the common people say, every cloud has a silver lining, for the entire grand ducal court remained behind in St Petersburg with her, which significantly simplified the highly complex task facing me in connection with the temporary removal to the old capital. The court ladies were very upset that they would not see the festivities in Moscow and expressed their discontent – naturally, without transgressing the bounds of etiquette – but Ekaterina Ioannovna remained adamant: according to ceremonial procedure, a lesser court must remain where the majority of members of the grand ducal family

4

are located, and the majority of the Georgieviches, as our branch of the imperial house is unofficially known, had stayed in St Petersburg.

Four members of the family made the journey to the coronation: Georgii Alexandrovich himself, his eldest and youngest sons and his only daughter, Xenia Georgievna.

As I have already said, I was only too pleased by the absence of the ladies and gentlemen of the court. The court steward, Prince Metitsky, and the manager of the court office, Privy Counsellor von Born, would only have hindered me in doing my job by sticking their noses into matters entirely beyond their comprehension. A good butler does not need nannies and overseers to help him cope with his responsibilities. And as for the ladies-in-waiting and maids of honour, I simply would not have known where to accommodate them, so wretchedly inadequate was the residence allocated by the coronation committee to the Green Court – as our household is known, from the colour of the grand duchess's train. However, we will come to the matter of the residence later.

The removal from St Petersburg went smoothly. The train consisted of three carriages: the members of the royal family travelled in the first, the servants in the second, and all the necessary utensils and the luggage were transported in the third, so that I was constantly obliged to move from one carriage to another.

Immediately after our departure, His Highness Georgii Alexandrovich sat down to drink cognac with His Highness Pavel Georgievich and Gentleman of the Bedchamber Endlung. His Highness was pleased to drink eleven glasses, after which he felt tired and rested all the way to Moscow. Before he fell asleep, when he was already in his 'cabin', as he referred to his compartment, His Highness told me a little about a voyage to Sweden that had taken place twenty years earlier and made a great impression on him. The fact is, although Georgii Alexandrovich holds the rank of admiral-general, he has only ever been to sea on one occasion. The memories that he retains of this journey are most unpleasant, and he frequently refers to the French minister Colbert, who never sailed on a ship and yet transformed his country into a great maritime power. I have heard the story about the Swedish voyage many times, quite often enough to know it off by heart. The most dangerous part in it is the description of the storm off the coast of Gotland. Following the words 'And then the captain yells out, "All hands to the pumps"', His Highness is wont to roll his eyes up and swing his fist down hard onto the table. The same thing happened on this occasion, but there was no damage to the tablecloth and the tableware, since I had taken the timely measure of holding down the carafe and the glass.

When His Highness was quite worn out and began to lose the power of speech, I gave the sign to his valet to undress him and put him to bed, while I went to call on Pavel Georgievich and Lieutenant Endlung. As young men in the very pink of health, they were much less tired after the cognac. You might say, in fact, that they were not tired at all, so it was necessary to keep an eye on them, especially bearing in mind the particular temperament of the gentleman of the bedchamber.

Oh my, that Endlung! I ought not to say so, but Ekaterina Ioannovna made a great mistake when she decided that this gentleman was a worthy mentor for her eldest son. The lieutenant, of course, is a handsome brute, with a clear gaze, a fresh complexion, a neat parting in his golden hair and an almost childishly pink bloom to his cheeks – a perfect angel. Respectful and fawning with older ladies, he can listen with an air of the greatest interest to talk of the preacher Ioann Kronshtatsky or a greyhound's distemper. Yes, it is hardly surprising that Ekaterina Ioannovna's heart warmed to Endlung. Such an agreeable and – most important – serious young man, nothing like those good-for-nothing cadets from the Naval Corps or those scapegraces from the Guards

Company. A fine mentor she found for Pavel Georgievich's guardian on his first long voyage! A guardian of whom I have seen more than enough.

In the very first port, Varna, Endlung dolled himself up like a peacock in a white suit with a scarlet waistcoat, a cravat studded with stars and a massive Panama hat, and set out for a house of ill-repute, taking His Highness, still a boy at the time, along with him. I tried to intervene, but the lieutenant told me, 'I promised Ekaterina Ioannovna that I would not take my eyes off His Highness. Where I go, he goes.'

I said to him, 'No, Lieutenant, Her Highness said, where *he* goes, *you* must go!' But Endlung said, 'That, Afanasii Stepanovich, is hair-splitting. The important thing is that we shall be as inseparable as the Ajaxes.' And so he dragged the young midshipman round every den of iniquity as far as Gibraltar. But from Gibraltar back to Kronstadt both the lieutenant and midshipman behaved very quietly and didn't even go ashore, although they went running to the doctor four times a day for irrigation treatments. What kind of mentor is that? His Highness has changed in the company of this Endlung – he is quite a different person. I have even hinted this to Georgii Alexandrovich, but he simply brushed it off, saying, 'Never mind, that kind of experience can only be good for my Pauly, and Endlung may be a bit of a booby, but he is a good, open-hearted comrade; he won't cause any serious harm.' But in my view this is letting the goat into the garden, to use an expression from the common folk. I can see right through that Endlung – of course I can, since he is so very open. Thanks to his friendship with Pavel Georgievich, he has even been awarded a monogram for his shoulder straps, and now he has been made a gentleman of the bedchamber, which is quite unheard of – such an honourable title for a mere lieutenant!

Left alone together, the two young men had started a game of bezique for forfeits. When I glanced into the compartment, Pavel Georgievich called to me: 'Sit down, Afanasii. Have a game of American roulette with us. If you lose, I'll make you shave off those damn precious sideburns of yours.'

I thanked him and refused, saying that I was extremely busy, although I didn't have anything in particular to do. That would have been the last straw, to play His Highness at American roulette. And Pavel Georgievich knew himself that I would make a hopeless partner in the game – he was simply joking. In recent months he has developed a dismaying habit of bantering with me, and all thanks to Endlung – this is his influence. Endlung himself, it is true, has recently stopped taunting me, but Pavel Georgievich persists in the habit. Never mind. His Highness may do as he pleases; I have no complaints.

For example, just now he told me with an absolutely straight face: 'You know, Afanasii, that phenomenal growth on your face is provoking the envy of certain highly influential individuals. For instance, the day before yesterday at the ball, when you were standing by the door, looking so grand with your gold-plated mace and sideburns jutting out on both sides, all the ladies had eyes for no one but you, and no one even glanced at cousin Nicky, even though he is the emperor. You really, really must shave them off, or at the very least trim them.'

In actual fact, my 'phenomenal growth' is a perfectly ordinary full moustache with sideburns – sumptuous perhaps but by no means excessive, and at all events maintained in perfectly decent order. My father wore the same whiskers, and my grandfather before him, so I had no intention of either shaving them or trimming them.

'Skip it, Pauly,' Endlung intervened on my behalf. 'Stop tormenting Afanasii Stepanovich. Come on, play. It's your turn.'

I can see that I shall have to explain the relationship between the lieutenant and myself. There is a story to it.

On the very first day of the voyage on the corvette *Mstislav*, immediately after we left Sebastopol, Endlung ambushed me on deck, put his hand on my shoulder, looked at me with his eyes totally blank after all the wine he had drunk at the send-off party and said: 'Well, Afon, my little flunkey soul, those mops of yours are looking a bit wild. Is it the breeze that has swept them out like that? (My sideburns had indeed been tousled somewhat by the fresh sea wind – later I would be obliged to shorten them a little for the duration of the voyage.) Will you do something for me, as a personal favour? Run round to that skinflint of a steward and say that His Highness orders him to send a bottle of rum – to help prevent seasickness.'

All the time we were travelling to Sebastopol in the train, Endlung had teased me and mocked me in the presence of His Highness, but I had tolerated it, waiting for an opportunity to clarify matters face to face. Now the opportunity had presented itself.

I delicately removed the lieutenant's hand (at that time he was not yet a gentleman of the bedchamber) with my finger and thumb and said politely: 'Mr Endlung, if you have been visited by the fancy to define my soul, then it would be more accurate to refer to it, not as the soul of a "flunkey", but that of a "house-master", since for long and irreproachable service at His Highness's court I have been awarded that title, which is a rank of the ninth level, corresponding to that of titular counsellor, staff captain in the army or *lieutenant* in the fleet.' (I deliberately emphasised the latter title.)

Endlung exclaimed: 'Lieutenants don't wait on tables!'

And I said to him: 'One *waits* on tables in restaurants, sir, but in the royal family one *serves*, each performing his duty as honourably as he can.'

After that incident Endlung became as smooth as silk with me: he spoke politely, told no more jokes at my expense, addressed me by my name and patronymic and always spoke politely.

I must say that for a man in my position the question of degrees of politeness is particularly complicated, since we court servants have a quite distinctive status. It is hard to explain why it is insulting to be called by your first name by some people, and insulting to be addressed formally by others. But the latter are the only people that I can serve, if you take my meaning.

Let me try to explain. I can only tolerate being called by my first name by individuals of the royal family. Indeed, I do not tolerate it, but regard it as a privilege and a special distinction. I would simply be mortified if Georgii Alexandrovich, Her Highness or one of their children, even the very youngest, suddenly addressed me formally by my first name and patronymic. Two years ago I had a disagreement with Ekaterina Ioannovna concerning a maid who was unjustly accused of frivolous behaviour. I demonstrated firmness and stood my ground, and the grand duchess took offence and addressed me in strictly formal terms for an entire week. I suffered greatly, lost weight and could not sleep at night. And then we clarified matters. With her typical magnanimity, Ekaterina Ioannovna acknowledged her error. I also apologised and was allowed to kiss her hand, and she kissed me on the forehead.

But I digress.

The card players were being served by the junior footman Lipps, a novice whom I had brought with me especially to get a good look at him and see what he was worth. He had previously served at the Estonian estate of Count Beckendorf and had been recommended to me by His Excellency's house steward, an old acquaintance of mine. He seems like quite an efficient young lad and doesn't talk a lot, but it takes a while to recognise a good servant, unlike a bad one. In a new post everyone makes a great effort to do his best; you have to wait six months or a year, or even two, to know for certain. I observed how Lipps poured coffee, how deftly he changed a soiled napkin, how he stood in his position – that is very, very important. He stood correctly, without shifting from one foot to the other or turning his head. I decided he could probably be allowed to serve guests at small receptions.

The game was proceeding normally. First Endlung lost, and Pavel Georgievich rode along the corridor on his back. Then

Fortune turned her face away from His Highness and the lieutenant demanded that the grand duke must run to the lavatory, completely undressed, and bring back a glass of water.

While Pavel Georgievich was giggling and taking his clothes off, I quietly slipped out through the door, called the valet, told him that none of the servants must look into the grand duke's saloon and took a cape from the duty compartment. When His Highness skipped out into the corridor, peering around and covering himself with his hand, I tried to throw this long item of clothing over him, but Pavel Georgievich indignantly refused, saying that a promise is a promise, and he ran to the lavatory and then back again, laughing very much all the time.

It was a good thing that Madamoiselle Declique did not glance out to see what all the laughter was about. Fortunately, despite the late hour, His Highness Mikhail Georgievich had not gone to bed yet – he was pleased to jump up and down on a chair and then swung on a curtain for a long time. The youngest of the grand dukes is usually asleep at half past eight, but this time Mademoiselle had felt it possible to indulge him, saying that His Highness was too excited by the journey and would not fall asleep anyway.

In our Green Court the children are not raised strictly, unlike in the Blue Court of the Kirilloviches, where they maintain the family traditions of the Emperor Nikolai Pavlovich. There boys are raised like soldiers: from the age of seven they learn campaign discipline, are toughened by sluicing with cold water and put to sleep in folding camp beds. But Georgii Alexandrovich is regarded as a liberal in the imperial family. He raises his sons leniently in the French manner and, in the opinion of his relatives, he has completely spoiled his only daughter, his favourite.

Her Highness, thank God, did not come out of her compartment either and did not witness Pavel Georgievich's prank. Ever since St Petersburg she had locked herself away with a book, and I even know which one it was: *The Kreutzer Sonata*, a work by Count Tolstoy. I have read it, in case there might be talk about it among us butlers, simply in order not to appear a complete dunce. In my opinion it makes extremely boring reading and is quite inappropriate for a nineteen-year-old girl, especially a grand princess. In St Petersburg Ekaterina Ioannovna would never have allowed her daughter to read such smut and I can only think that the novel was smuggled into the baggage. The lady-in-waiting Baroness Stroganova must have provided it; it could not have been anyone else.

The two sailors did not quieten down until it was almost morning, following which even I allowed myself the luxury of dozing for a while because, to be quite honest, I was really rather tired after all the bustle and commotion before we left, and I anticipated that the first day in Moscow would not be easy.

The difficulties far exceeded all my expectations.

As it happens, in all the forty-six years of my life I have never been in the 'white stone capital' before, although I have travelled round the world quite extensively. The fact is, in our family Asiatic manners are not regarded favourably, and the only place in the whole of Russia acknowledged as being even slightly decent is St Petersburg. Our relations with the governor general of Moscow, Simeon Alexandrovich, are cool, and so we have no reason to spend time in the old capital. We usually even travel to Miskhor Grange in the Crimea by a roundabout route, via Minsk, since Georgii Alexandrovich likes to shoot a few bison in the Beloverzhsk forest reserve along the way. And I did not travel to the last coronation, thirteen years ago, since I held the position of assistant butler and was left to replace my superior at that time, the now-deceased Zakhar Trofimovich.

While we were travelling across the city from the station, I formed my first impression of Moscow. The city proved to be even less civilised than I had expected – absolutely no comparison with St Petersburg. The streets were narrow and absurdly twisted, the buildings were wretched, the public on the streets was slovenly and provincial. And this was when the city was making an almighty effort to preen its feathers on the eve of the arrival of the emperor himself: the facades of the buildings had been washed, the sheet metal of the roofs had been freshly painted, on Tverskaya Street (the main street of Moscow, a pale shadow of Nevsky Prospect) the tsar's monogram and two-headed eagles had been hung everywhere. I don't even know with what I can compare Moscow. It is the same kind of overgrown village as Salonica, which our yacht, the *Mstislav*, visited last year. Along the way we didn't see a single fountain, or a building with more than four storeys, or an equestrian statue – only the round-shouldered bronze Pushkin and, to judge from the colour of the metal, even that was a recent acquisition.

At Red Square, which was also quite a disappointment, our cavalcade divided into two. Their Highnesses set out, as befits members of the imperial family, to pay obeisance to the icon of the Virgin of Iversk and the holy relics in the Kremlin, while I and the servants went on to make ready our temporary Moscow residence.

Owing to the division of the court into two parts, I had to make do with an extremely modest number of servants. I had only been able to bring eight people with me from St Petersburg: His Highness's valet, Xenia Georgievna's maid, a junior footman (the aforementioned Lipps) for Pavel Georgievich and Endlung, a pantry man and his assistant, a 'white chef', and two coachmen for the English and Russian carriages. The intention was that I would serve tea and coffee myself – that is by way of being a tradition. At the risk of appearing immodest, I can say that in the entire court department there is no one who performs duties of this kind, which require not only great skill, but also talent, better than I do. After all, I did serve for five years as a coffee pourer with Their Majesties the deceased emperor and the present dowager empress.

Naturally, I could not count on being able to manage with only eight servants, and so I sent a special telegram requesting the Moscow Court Department to appoint a capable local man as my assistant and also to provide two postilions, a 'black chef' for the servants, a footman to serve the senior servants, two junior footmen for cleaning, a maid for Mademoiselle Declique and two doormen. I did not ask for more than that, since I realised perfectly well how scarce experienced servants would be in Moscow owing to the arrival of such a large number of exalted individuals. And I had no illusions concerning Moscow servants. Moscow is a city of empty palaces and decaying villas, and there is nothing worse than maintaining a staff of servants without anything for them to do. It makes people stupid, it spoils them. For instance, we have three large houses in which we live by turns (excluding the spring, which we spend abroad, because Ekaterina Ioannovna finds the period of Lent in Russia unbearably dull): during the winter the Family lives in its St Petersburg palace, during the summer in its villa at Tsarskoe Selo, during the autumn at the Miskhor Grange. Each of the houses has its own staff of servants, and I do not allow them to loaf about. Every time we move from one house to another, I leave behind an extremely long list of instructions, and I always manage to visit every now and then to check on things, and always without warning. Servants are like soldiers. You have to keep them busy all the time, or they will start drinking, playing cards and behaving improperly.

My Moscow assistant met us at the station, and while we were riding in the carriage he had time to explain some of the problems that awaited me. In the first place it turned out that my extremely moderate and rational request had not been met in full by the Court Department: they had only allocated one junior footman, they had not given us a chef for the servants, only a female cook, and the worse thing of all was that there was no maid for the governess. I was particularly displeased by this, because the position of governess is fundamentally ambivalent, lying as it does on the boundary line between service personnel and court staff; exceptional tact is required here in order to avoid offending and humiliating a person who is already constantly apprehensive for her own dignity.

'And that is still not the most deplorable thing, Mr Ziukin,' my Moscow assistant said with those distinctive broad Moscow 'a's when he noticed my dissatisfaction. 'The most lamentable thing of all is that instead of the Maly Nikolaevsky Palace in the Kremlin that was promised, you have been given the Small Hermitage in the Neskuchny Park as your residence.'

My assistant was called Kornei Selifanovich Somov, and at first glance I did not take to him at all: a rather unattractive, skinny fellow with protruding ears and a prominent Adam's apple. It was immediately obvious that the man had already reached the peak of his career and would not progress any further but remain stuck in the backwoods of Moscow until he retired.

'What sort of place is this Hermitage?' I asked with a frown.

'A beautiful house with a quite excellent view of the Moscow River and the city. It stands in a park close to the Alexandriisky Palace, which the emperor and empress will occupy immediately before the coronation, but . . .' Somov shrugged and spread his long arms '. . . it is dilapidated, cramped and it has a ghost.' He giggled but, seeing from my face that I was in no mood for jokes, he explained. 'The house was built in the middle of the last century. It used to belong to the Countess Chesmenskaya – the famous madwoman who was incredibly rich. You must have heard about her, Mr Ziukin. Some say that Pushkin based his Queen of Spades on her, and not the old Princess Golytsina at all.'

I do not like it when servants flaunt their erudition, and so I said nothing, but merely nodded.

Somov obviously did not understand the reason for my displeasure, for he continued in even more flamboyant style.

'The legend has it that during the reign of Alexander I, when everyone in society was playing the newfangled game of lotto, the countess played a game with the Devil himself and staked her own soul. The servants say that sometimes on moonless nights a white figure in a nightcap wanders down the corridor, rattling the counters for lotto in a little cloth bag.'

Somov giggled again, as if to make it clear that he, as an enlightened man, did not believe in such nonsense. But I took this news quite seriously, because every servant, especially if, like me, he happens to be a member of an old court dynasty, knows that ghosts and phantoms really do exist, and joking with them or about them is a foolish and irresponsible pastime. I asked if the ghost of the old countess did anything wicked apart from rattling the counters. Somov said no, that in almost a hundred years she had never been known to play any other tricks, and I was reassured. Very well, let her wander, that was not frightening. In our Fontanny Palace we have the ghost of Gentleman of the Bedchamber Zhikharev, a handsome Adonis and prospective favourite of Catherine the Great, who was poisoned by Prince Zubov. What is an old woman in a mob cap compared with him? Our otherworldly lodger behaves in the most indecent fashion: in the darkness he pinches the ladies and the servants, and he becomes especially rowdy on the eve of the feast of St John the Baptist. It is true, however, that he does not dare to touch the ladies of the royal family – after all he is a gentleman of the bedchamber. And then in the Anichkov Palace there is the ghost of a female student from the Smolny Institute who was supposedly seduced by Tsar Nikolai Pavlovich and afterwards took her own life. At night she oozes through the walls and drops cold tears on the faces of people who are asleep. It can hardly be pleasant to be woken by cold tears and confronted by a horror like that.

Anyway, Somov did not frighten me with his ghost. It was far worse that the house really did prove to be very cramped and lacking in many conveniences. That was hardly surprising – nothing in the property had been renovated since the Court Department bought it from the Counts Chesmensky half a century earlier.

I walked round the floors, calculating what needed to be done first. I must admit that Somov had coped rather well with the basic preparations: the covers had been removed from the furniture, everything was brilliantly clean, there were fresh flowers in the bedrooms and the grand piano in the large drawing room was correctly tuned.

The lighting was a great disappointment – there was not even gas, only antediluvian oil lamps. Ah, if only I had had just one week – I would have installed a small electric generator in the basement, laid the wires, and the palace would have looked quite different. Why did we need to skulk in the oil-lit twilight? It had been like that in the Fontanny Palace thirty years earlier. Now I would need a lamplighter to keep the lamps full of oil – they were English-made, with a twenty-four-hour clock mechanism.

On the subject of clocks, I counted nineteen table and wall clocks in the house, and they all told different times. I decided that I would wind the clocks myself – it is a job that requires punctuality and precision. One can always tell a good house kept in ideal order from the way that the clocks in different rooms all tell the same time. Any experienced butler will tell you that.

I discovered only one telephone apparatus, in the hallway, and immediately ordered another two lines to be laid: one to Georgii Alexandrovich's study and another to my room, since I would probably have to talk endlessly with the Alexandrovsky Palace, the governor general's residence and the Court Department.

But initially I had to decide which rooms to put people in, and that was a problem that really had me racking my brains.

There were only eighteen rooms on the two floors of the house. I simply cannot imagine how everyone would have been accommodated if the grand duchess and the other children and the entire court had been with us. Somov told me that the family of Grand Duke Nikolai Konstantinovich, including eight members of the royal family and a retinue of fourteen individuals, not counting servants, had been allocated a small mansion with fifteen rooms, so that the courtiers had been obliged to share a room between three or even four, and the servants had been accommodated over the stables. That was quite appalling, even though Nikolai Konstantinovich was two levels below Georgii Alexandrovich in seniority.

It was also inopportune that His Highness had invited his friend Lord Banville to the coronation. His Lordship was expected to arrive on the Berlin train early in the evening. The Englishman was unmarried, thank goodness, but I still had to allocate him two rooms: one for the lord himself and one for his butler. And God forbid that I should make any slips here. I know these English butlers: they are even more lordly than their masters. Especially Mr Smiley, who served His Lordship. Pompous and snobbish – I had had more than enough time to observe him the previous month in Nice.

And so I set aside the first floor for the royal household. The two rooms with windows facing towards the park and the tsar's palace were for Georgii Alexandrovich – they would be his bedroom and study. An armchair would go on the balcony, with a small table and a box of cigars, while a spyglass would be placed at the window that looked towards the Alexandriisky Palace, to make it more convenient for His Highness to observe the windows of his nephew the emperor. Xenia Georgievna would have the bright room with a view of the river, she would like that. The maid Liza would be beside her. I would put Pavel Georgievich in the mezzanine – he liked to be apart from the other members of the family, and there was a separate staircase leading up there, which was convenient for returning late. Endlung would be next to him, in the former closet. He was not such an important individual. Move in a bed, put a carpet on the floor and hang a bearskin on the wall, and no one would be able to tell that it was a closet. Little Mikhail Georgievich would have the spacious room with windows facing east – just right for a nursery. And beside it there was a very fine room for Mademoiselle Declique. I gave instructions to put a bunch of bluebells in there (they are her favourite flowers). I set aside the last room on the first floor as a small drawing room for peaceful leisure activities in the family circle, in case at least one evening might be left free during the bewildering days ahead.

The two largest rooms downstairs were naturally transformed into the main drawing room and the dining room; I prepared the two most decent bedrooms for the Englishmen, took one for myself (small but located in a strategically important position, under the stairs); and the rest of the servants had to be accommodated several to a room. *A la guerre comme à la guerre*, or, as we say in Russian, cramped but contented.

All in all, it turned out better than could have been expected.

Then began the troublesome business of unpacking the luggage: dresses, uniforms and suits, silver tableware, thousands of all sorts of small but absolutely essential items which make it possible to transform any shed into a decent and even comfortable refuge.

While the Moscow servants were carrying in the trunks and boxes, I observed each of them carefully to determine what each of them was worth and in which capacity he could be used to the greatest benefit. This is precisely the most important talent of any individual in command: the ability to determine the stronger and weaker sides of each of his subordinates, in order to exploit the former and leave the latter untouched. Long experience of managing a large staff of workers has taught me that there are few people in the world who are completely without talent and absolutely incapable. A use can be found for everyone. When someone in our club complains about the uselessness of a footman, a waiter or a maid, I think to myself, Ah my dear fellow, you are a bad butler. All of my servants become good ones in time. Everyone has to like his own work – that is the secret. A chef must enjoy cooking, a maid must enjoy creating order out of chaos, a groom must like horses and a gardener must like plants.

The supreme skill of the genuine butler is to have a thorough grasp of an individual, to understand what he likes, for, strangely enough, most people do not have the slightest idea of where their own inclinations lie and in what area they are gifted. Sometimes one has to try one thing and then another and then something else before one can get it right. And this is not simply a matter of work, although of course that is important. When a person does what he enjoys, he is contented and happy, and if all the servants in the house are at ease, cheerful and affable, this creates a quite special situation, or as they call it nowadays, *atmosphere*.

One must always encourage and reward one's subordinates – but in moderation, not simply for performing their duties conscientiously but for special diligence. It is essential to punish too, but only justly. At the same time, one must explain clearly for what exactly the punishment has been meted out and, naturally, it must under no circumstances be humiliating. Let me repeat: if a subordinate is failing to cope with his work, it is his superior who is to blame. I have forty-two people at the Fontanny Palace, fourteen in Tsarskoe Selo and another twenty-three in the Crimea. And they are all in the right positions, you can take my word for that. Pantaleimon Kuzmich, butler to His Highness the Grand Duke Mikhail Mikhailovich the senior, often used to say to me, 'You, Afanasii Stepanovich, are a genuine psychologist.' And he was not too proud to ask my advice in especially difficult cases. For instance, the year before last at the Gatchina Palace he found himself with a junior footman on his staff who was quite indescribably muddle-headed. Pantaleimon Kuzmich struggled and strained with him and then asked my advice. The lad was an absolute blockhead, he said, but he would be sorry to dismiss him. I took on the lad out of a desire to shine. He proved useless in the dining room and in the dressing room, and especially in the kitchen. In short, as the common people say, he was a tough nut. And then one day I saw him sitting in the courtyard, looking at the sun through a shard of glass. My curiosity was aroused. I stopped and observed him. He was toying with that piece of glass as if he had come by some priceless diamond, constantly breathing on it and wiping it on his sleeve. I was suddenly inspired. I set him to clean the windows of the house – and what do you think? My windows began to shine like pure mountain crystal. And there was no need to chase the lad – from morning until evening he polished one window pane after another. Now he's the finest window cleaner in the whole of St Petersburg and butlers line up to borrow him from Pantaleimon Kuzmich. That is what happens when a person finds his vocation.

No sooner had I wound the clocks in the house and the servants carried in the last hatbox from the last carriage, than the English guests arrived, and I discovered that there was another unpleasant surprise in store for me.

It turned out that Lord Banville had brought a friend with him, a certain Mr Carr.

I remembered His Lordship very well from Nice – he had not changed in the least: a smooth parting midway between his temples, a monocle, a cane, a cigar in his teeth, a ring with a large diamond on his index finger. And dressed impeccably, as always, a fine specimen of an English gentleman, wearing a black dinner jacket, perfectly ironed (and he had just come from the train!), a black waistcoat and a brilliantly white stiffly starched collar. On jumping down from the footboard, he threw his head back and laughed loudly like a horse neighing, which gave the maid Liza, who was hovering nearby, a great fright, but did not surprise me in the least: I was aware that His Lordship was an inveterate horseman who spent half his life in the stables, understood the language of horses and was almost able to communicate in it himself. At least, that was what I had been told by Georgii Alexandrovich, who had made Lord Banville's acquaintance at the races in Nice.

When he finished neighing, His Lordship held out his hand to help another gentleman out of the carriage and introduced him as his dear friend Mr Carr. This gentleman was a completely different specimen, of a kind that one is rather unlikely to encounter in our parts: hair of a remarkable straw-yellow colour, straight on top and wavy at the sides, which, one would imagine, never happens in nature. A smooth white face with a neat round mole like a velvet beauty spot on one cheek. The shirt worn by His Lordship's friend was not white but light blue – I had never seen one like it before. A light greyish-blue frock coat, an azure waistcoat with gold speckles and an absolutely blue carnation in the buttonhole. I was particularly struck by his unusually narrow boots with mother-of-pearl buttons and lemon-yellow gaiters. Stepping down gingerly onto the cobblestones, this strange man stretched elegantly and a capricious, affected smile appeared on his delicate doll-like face. Mr Carr's gaze fell on the doorman Trofimov, who was on duty on the porch. I had previously had occasion to note that Trofimov was quite hopelessly stupid and unfitted for any kind of employment except minding doors, but he looked impressive: a full *sazhen* in height, broad in the shoulder, with round eyes and a thick black beard. The Englishman approached Trofimov, who stood there as still as a stone idol, as he was supposed to do, and looked up at him, then for some reason tugged on his beard and said something in English in a high-pitched, melodic voice.

Lord Banville's inclinations had become quite clear in Nice, and Ekaterina Ioannovna, an individual of the very strictest principles, had refused to have anything to do with him, but Georgii Alexandrovich, being a broad-minded man (and also, let us note in passing, only too well acquainted with gentlemen of this kind from his circle of society acquaintances), found the English lord's predilection for effeminate grooms and rosy-cheeked footmen amusing. 'Excellent company, an outstanding sportsman and a true gentleman,' was what he told me in explaining why he had presumed to invite Banville to Moscow – after it had become clear that Ekaterina Ioannovna was not coming to the coronation.

The unpleasant surprise that I felt was not due to His Lordship's having brought his latest flame with him – after all, Mr Carr appeared to be a man of good society. The cause of my dismay was simpler than that: where was I to accommodate another guest? Even if they spent the night together, in order to observe the proprieties I would have to give the second Englishman a separate bedroom. I thought for a moment, and the solution came to me almost immediately: move the Moscow servants, with the exception of Somov, into the attic above the stables. That would free two rooms, one of which I would give to the Englishman and the other to the grand duke's chef, Maître Duval, who was feeling very aggrieved.

'Where is Mr Smiley?' I asked Lord Banville in French, since there were certain things that I had to explain to his butler.

Like most of the alumni of the Court Department, I was taught French and German from my childhood, but not English. In recent years the court has become quite significantly anglicised, and more and more often I have had reason to regret this shortcoming in my education, but formerly English had been regarded as an inelegant language and not essential for our service.

'He resigned,' His Lordship replied in French with a vague gesture of his hand. 'My new butler, Freyby, is there in the carriage. Reading a book.'

I went over to the carriage. The servants were deftly unloading the baggage and a fleshy-faced gentleman with a very haughty air was sitting on the velvet seat with his legs crossed. He was bald, with thick eyebrows and a neatly trimmed beard – in short, he didn't look anything like an English butler, or any sort of butler at all. Through the open door I saw the book that Mr Freyby was holding in his hands – it had a word in thick golden letters on the cover: 'Trollope'. I did not know what this English word meant.

'Soyez le bienvenu!' I greeted him with a polite bow.

His calm blue eyes gazed at me through his gold-rimmed spectacles. But he didn't answer.

'Herzlich Willkommen!' I said, trying German, but the Englishman's gaze remained politely neutral.

'You must be the butler Ziukin?' he said in a pleasant baritone voice. The sounds were quite incomprehensible to me.

I shrugged and spread my hands.

Then, with an expression of obvious regret, Mr Freyby put his book into the vast pocket of his frock coat and took out another book, much smaller than the first. He leafed through it and then pronounced several comprehensible words, one after the other.

'Vy ... dolzhny ... byt ... batler Ziukin?'

Ah, that's an English–Russian dictionary, I guessed, and mentally commended his foresight. If I had known that Mr Smiley, who could, at a pinch, make himself understood in French, was no longer in His Lordship's service and had been replaced by a new butler, I would also have equipped myself with a lexicon. After all, this Englishman and I would have to solve no small number of complex and delicate problems together.

As if he had been listening to my thoughts, Mr Freyby took another small volume, identical in appearance to the English–Russian dictionary, out of his other pocket. He handed it to me.

I took it and read the title on the cover: *Russian–English Dictionary with a reading of English words*.

The Englishman leafed through his own manual, found the word he needed and explained: 'A present ...'

I opened the small volume he had given me and saw that it was arranged in an artful and intelligent manner: all the English words were written in Russian letters and the stress was marked. I tried out the lexicon immediately. I wanted to ask which baggage belonged to whom. This came out as: 'Where ... whose ... baggage?'

And he understood me perfectly well!

He gestured casually to summon a footman who was carrying a heavy suitcase on his shoulder, and pointed one finger at a yellow label, on which it said 'Banville'. On looking more closely, I observed that there were labels stuck on all the items of baggage, some of them yellow with His Lordship's name, others blue with the inscription 'Carr' and still others red with the inscription 'Freyby'. Very rational, I thought; I shall have to adopt the same method.

Evidently considering the problem satisfactorily resolved, Mr Freyby extracted his large tome from his pocket and paid no more attention to me, and I thought that English butlers were of course all very fine and knew their business well, but there was still something that they could learn from us Russian servants. To be precise – cordiality. They simply serve their masters, but we love ours too. How can you serve a man if you do not feel love for him? Without that it is all mere mechanics, as if we were not living people, but machines. Of course, they do say that English butlers do not serve the master but the house – rather like cats, who become attached less to the person than to the walls around him. If that is so, then that kind of attachment is not to my taste. And Mr Freyby seemed somehow very strange to me. But then, I reasoned, a master like that is bound to have odd servants. And it is no bad thing that *mon collègue anglais* is, as the simple folk say, a bit on the queer side – he will get under my feet less.

There was too little time to contrive a proper lunch, and so I ordered the table to be laid for Their Highnesses' arrival in casual style, *à la pique-nique* – with the small silver service, on simple Meissen tableware and without any hot dishes at all. The food was ordered by telephone from Snyder's Delicatessen: pâté of snipe, asparagus and truffle pies, small fish pies, galantine, fish, smoked chicken and fruit for dessert. Never mind. After all, I could hope that by the evening Maître Duval would have familiarised himself with the kitchen and supper would be more *comme il faut*. Of course, I knew that in the evening Georgii Alexandrovich and Pavel Georgievich would be with His Imperial Majesty, who was expected at half past five in the afternoon and would go straight from the station to the Petrovsky Palace. The arrival of the emperor had deliberately been set for the sixth of May because that was His Majesty's birthday. From lunchtime the bells of Moscow – of which there are countless numbers – began pealing. The prayers for His Imperial Majesty and all the royal family to be granted good health and long life had begun. I made a mental note not to forget to have the canopy with the initial N set over the porch of the main entrance. If the sovereign should happen to visit, such a sign of attention from his family would be most appropriate.

Shortly after four Georgii Alexandrovich and Pavel Georgievich put on their dress uniforms and left for the station. Xenia Georgievna began sorting through the books in the small dining room, which in the Chesmenskys' time had apparently been used as a library. Lord Banville and Mr Carr locked themselves in His Lordship's room and asked not to be disturbed again today, and Mr Freyby and I, left to our own devices, sat down to have a bite to eat.

We were served by a junior footman by the name of Zemlyanoi, one of the Moscow contingent. Uncouth and rather awkward, but very willing. He gaped at me with wide-open eyes – no doubt he had heard of Afanasii Ziukin before. I must confess that it was flattering.

Soon Mademoiselle Declique joined us, having put her young ward down for his after-lunch *repos*. She had already taken lunch with Their Highnesses, but what kind of meal can one have, sitting beside Mikhail Georgievich? His Highness is possessed of an extremely restless temperament and is constantly getting up to some kind of mischief: he will either start throwing his bread about, or climb under the table so that one has to drag him back out. In short, Mademoiselle was glad to take coffee with us and she did justice to Filippov's admirable honey cakes.

Mademoiselle's presence was most opportune, since she knew English and managed the responsibilities of an interpreter perfectly.

In order to make a start on the conversation, I asked the Englishman: 'Have you been working as a butler for a long time?'

He answered with a very short word, and Mademoiselle translated: 'Yes.'

'There is no need for you to be concerned; the things have

26

been unpacked and no difficulties arose,' I said with a distinct hint of reproach, since Mr Freyby had taken no part at all in the unpacking, having sat in the carriage with his book to the very end of this important procedure.

'I know,' was the answer.

My curiosity was aroused – the Englishman's phlegmatic manner seemed to convey either a quite amazing indolence that exceeded all conceivable bounds, or the supreme chic of the butler's artistry. After all, he had not stirred a finger, and yet the things had been unloaded, unpacked, hung, and they were all in the right place!

'Have you looked into His Lordship's and Mr Carr's accommodation yet?' I asked, knowing perfectly well that since the moment he arrived Mr Freyby had not set foot outside his own room.

'No need,' he replied in English, and Mademoiselle translated equally succinctly into French: '*Pas besoin.*'

In the time that Mademoiselle had spent in our house I had been able to study her, and I could tell from the gleam in her eyes that she found the Englishman intriguing. Naturally, she knew how to control her curiosity, as a first-class governess accustomed to working in the finest houses of Europe should (before us, for instance, she had educated the son of the King of Portugal and had brought the most excellent references with her from Lisbon). But the Gallic temperament would sometimes break through, and when Mademoiselle Declique felt enthusiastic, amused or angry about something, bright little sparks lit up in her eyes. I would not have hired an individual with such a dangerous peculiarity as a servant, because those little sparks are a sure sign that still waters run deep, as the common folk say. But governesses, maids and tutors are not my concern – they come under the competence of the court steward, Metlitsky – and so I was able to admire the aforementioned sparks without the slightest anxiety.

And on this occasion Mademoiselle, dissatisfied with the

modest role of interpreter, could not resist asking (first in English and then, for me, in French): 'But how do you know that everything is in good order?'

At this point Mr Freyby uttered his first rather long phrase: 'I can see that Mr Ziukin knows his job. And in Berlin, where the things were packed, they were packed by a man who also knows his job.'

As if rewarding himself for the exhausting effort of producing such an extensive utterance, the butler took out a pipe and lit it, after first gesturing to ask the lady's permission. And I realised that I was apparently dealing with an absolutely exceptional butler, such as I had never encountered before in all my thirty years of service.

Shortly after six Xenia Georgievna declared that she was bored of being stuck inside and we – Her Highness, Mikhail Georgievich, Mademoiselle Declique and I – set out for a drive. I ordered the closed carriage to be brought, because the day had turned out overcast and windy, and after lunch a fine drizzle had started to fall.

We drove out along the broad highway to the elevated spot known as the Sparrow Hills, in order to take a look at Moscow from above, but owing to the grey shroud of rain we saw very little, only the broad semicircle of the valley with low clouds hanging above it like steam, for all the world like a tureen full of steaming broth.

As we were driving back, the sky brightened a little for the first time that day, and so we let the carriage go and set off on foot from the Kaluga Gate across the park. Their Highnesses walked ahead with Xenia Georgievna leading Mikhail Georgievich by the hand, so that he would not run off the path into the wet bushes, while Mademoiselle and I hung back slightly.

It was three months since His Highness had stopped having little accidents, and he had just reached four, at which age the Georgieviches are transferred from the care of an English nanny to the tutelage of a French governess, are no longer dressed in girls' frocks, and moved on from pantaloons to short trousers. His Highness found the change of attire to his liking, and he and the Frenchwoman got on quite excellently. I must confess that at first I had found Mademoiselle Declique's manners too free – for instance, encouragement in the form of kisses and punishment in the form of slaps, as well as noisy romping in the nursery – but as time passed I came to realise that there was a deliberate pedagogical method involved. In any case, after a month His Highness was already babbling away in French and loved singing little songs in that language, and in general he had become much more cheerful and free in his behaviour.

Recently I had noticed that I was glancing into the nursery much more frequently than before, and probably more frequently than was necessary. This discovery gave me cause for serious thought, and since it has always been my rule to be honest with myself in all things, I was rather quick to work out the reason: apparently I enjoyed Mademoiselle Declique's company.

I am accustomed to regard anything that is enjoyable with caution, because enjoyment goes hand in hand with relaxation, and from relaxation it is only one step to negligence and serious, even irreparable lapses in one's work. And so for some time I stopped visiting the nursery altogether (apart, naturally, from those instances when my duties required it) and became very cool with Mademoiselle Declique. But this did not last for long. She herself approached me and requested me with irreproachable politeness to assist her in improving her mastery of the Russian language – nothing special, simply to talk about various subjects with her in Russian from time to time and correct her crudest errors. Let me repeat that the request was framed so politely that a refusal would have appeared unjustifiably rude.

That was the beginning of our custom of daily conversations – on perfectly neutral and, naturally, respectable subjects.

Mademoiselle learned Russian quite amazingly quickly and already knew a very large number of words. Of course, her speech was grammatically incorrect, but this had its own charm which I was not always able to resist.

On this occasion also, as we strolled along the allée in the Neskuchny Park, we were speaking Russian. This time, however, the conversation was rather brief and uncomfortable. The problem was that Mademoiselle had been late in coming out for the drive and we had had to wait for her in the carriage for an entire thirty seconds (I was keeping track of the time with my Swiss chronometer). In the presence of Their Highnesses I restrained myself, but now that we were speaking *tête-à-tête*, I felt it necessary to issue a slight reprimand. I did not like reproving Mademoiselle, but my duty required me to do it. Nobody dares to keep members of the royal family waiting, not even for half a minute.

'It is not at all difficult always to be on time,' I said, pronouncing every word slowly so that she would understand. 'One merely has to live fifteen minutes ahead of things. Let us suppose you have an appointment with someone at three o'clock, then you must arrive at a quarter to. Or, say, in order to arrive at some place on time, you need to leave the house at two, then you must leave at a quarter to two. For a start I would advise you to simply to set your watch forward by fifteen minutes, until you become accustomed to it, and then punctuality will become a habit.'

What I had said was both practical and rational, but Mademoiselle Declique's reply was impertinent.

'Mr Ziukin, can I put my watch fohward by half a minute? (She could not manage the Russian 'r' – it came out rather like the Little Russian 'kh'.) I have neveh been lateh than half a minute in any case.'

I frowned at that and decided it would be best to pause, so we walked on in silence, and Mademoiselle even turned her head away.

Her Highness was telling her brother a fairy tale; I think it was

Chapeau Rouge[1]. In any case I heard the words: *'Et elle est allée à travers le forêt pour voir sa grandmaman.'*[2] Mikhail Georgievich, very proud of his new sailor suit, was trying to behave like a grown-up and hardly being naughty at all, except that every now and then he began skipping on one foot and once he threw his blue cap with the red pompom down on the ground.

Despite the overcast day we occasionally encountered people walking on the paths in the park. This, as my Moscow assistant had explained to me, was because the Neskuchny Park was not usually open to the public. Its gates had only been opened in connection with the festivities, and then just for a few days – until the ninth of May, when the emperor and empress would move here from the Petrovsky Palace. It was hardly surprising that some Muscovites had decided to take advantage of the rare opportunity to ramble through this forbidden territory, undeterred by the poor weather.

Approximately halfway back to the Hermitage we encountered an elegant middle-aged gentleman. He politely raised his top hat, exposing a head of smooth black hair with grey temples. He glanced at Xenia Georgievna inquisitively, but without offending against the proprieties, and walked on by. I would not have taken any notice of this gentleman if Her Highness had not suddenly looked round to watch him walk away and Mademoiselle Declique had not followed her example. At that point I took the liberty of looking round myself.

The elegant gentleman was walking on unhurriedly, swinging his cane, and I failed to notice anything whatsoever in his figure that ought to have made the grand princess and her governess glance round. But walking behind us, in the same direction as ourselves, there was a man of truly remarkable appearance: broad-shouldered and stocky, with a shaggy black beard. He ran the searing gaze of his ferocious coal-black eyes over me and

---

[1] *Little Red Riding Hood.*
[2] *And she went through the forest to see her grandmother.*

began whistling some *chansonette* or other that I did not know.

This individual appeared suspicious to me, and I promised myself that we would not come here again until the park was closed once more. Who could tell what kind of riff-raff – begging your pardon – might take a fancy to promenading here?

As if to confirm my misgivings, a bandy-legged, squat Chinese pedlar came waddling out from round the corner, carrying a tray of his dubious wares. The poor fellow had obviously thought that there would be many more people strolling in the park that day, but he had been unlucky with the weather.

When His Highness caught sight of a real live Chinaman, he pulled his hand free and went dashing towards the short, slant-eyed Oriental as fast as his legs would carry him.

'I want that!' Mikhail Georgievich shouted. 'I want that one!'

And he pointed at a poisonous-pink sugar lollipop in the form of a pagoda.

'*Ne montrez pas du doigt!*'[3] Mademoiselle cried.

Xenia Georgievna caught up with her brother, took hold of his hand again and asked: '*À quoi bon tu veux ce truc?*'[4]

'*Je veux, c'est tout!*'[5] His Highness snapped and jutted out his chin, demonstrating remarkable obstinacy for his age, and obstinacy is an excellent foundation for the development of character.

'Ah, Afanasii, buy him it,' Xenia Georgievna said, turning to me. 'He'll never stop pestering me now. He'll lick it once and throw it away.'

The grand princess had no money of her own and in general I believe that she did not even know what it looked like, or what it was worth. Why would she need to?

I looked at Mademoiselle, since it was her decision. She wrinkled up her nose and shrugged her shoulders.

---

3 *Don't point!*
4 *What do you want that rubbish for?*
5 *I just want it that's all.*

To give him his due, the Chinese did not make any attempt to impose his nightmarish merchandise on us; he merely peered at His Highness through the blank slits of his eyes. Some Chinese can be genuinely handsome – with delicate features, white skin and elegant movements – but this one was truly ugly. A flat face as round as a pancake and short hair that jutted straight up.

'Hey, pedlar, how much is that?' I asked, pointing at the pagoda and taking out my purse.

'One roubr,' the insolent Oriental replied, evidently having realised from my appearance that I would not try to haggle with him.

I gave the extortioner a 'canary', although the lollipop was worth no more than five kopecks at the most, and we walked on. The crude delicacy seemed to be to His Highness's liking – in any case, the lollipop was not discarded.

The railings of the Hermitage came into view at the far end of a side path, and we turned in that direction. There were no more than a hundred *sazhens* left to walk.

A crow on a branch cawed raucously and I looked up. But I didn't see the bird, only a patch of grey sky between the dark leaves.

I think that I would give anything at all to halt time at that precise moment, because it was destined to divide my existence into two halves: all that was rational, predictable and orderly was left behind in the old life, and the new consisted of nothing but madness, nightmares and chaos.

I heard the sound of footsteps approaching rapidly from behind and looked round in surprise. At that very instant a blow of prodigious force came crashing down on my head. I caught a glimpse of the face, distorted in incredible fury, of the bearded man I had seen not long before as I slumped to the ground and lost consciousness for a second. I say 'for a second' because when I raised my head, which felt as as if it were filled with lead, off the ground, the bearded man was only a few steps away. He threw Mikhail Georgievich aside, grabbed Her Highness by the arm and started dragging her back past me. Mademoiselle froze on the spot in bewilderment and I felt as if I had turned to stone. I raised one hand to my forehead, wiped away something wet and looked at it – it was blood. I didn't know what he had hit me with, brass knuckles or a lead cudgel, but the trees and bushes all around were swaying like ocean waves in a storm.

The bearded man gave a brigandish whistle and a black carriage harnessed to a pair of black horses emerged from round the corner that we had just turned. The driver, wearing a broad oilskin cloak, pulled back on the reins with a cry of 'Whoah!' and two other men, also dressed in black, jumped out of the carriage as it was still moving and came running towards us.

'This is a kidnapping, that's what it is,' a very calm, quiet voice stated somewhere inside me, and the trees suddenly stopped swaying. I got up on my hands and knees and shouted to Mademoiselle: '*Emportez le grand-duc!*'[6] and grabbed hold of the bearded man round the knees, just as he drew level with me.

He did not let go of Her Highness's hand, and all three of us tumbled to the ground together. I am naturally quite strong – everyone in our family is robust – and in my youth I served as a court outrunner, which is also excellent for strengthening the musculature, and so I had no difficulty in opening the hand with which the villain was clutching the hem of Her Highness's skirt, but that did not help very much. He struck me on the chin with the hand that had just been freed and before Her Highness could even get to her feet men in black were there already beside her. They took hold of the grand princess under the arms, lifted her up and set off towards the carriage at a run. At least Mademoiselle had managed to save Mikhail Georgievich – out of the corner of my eyes I had seen her pick the boy up in her arms and dive into the bushes.

My opponent proved to be adroit and strong. He struck me

---

[6] *Get the grand duke away!*

again, and when I tried to grab him by the throat, he put his hand in under his coat and brought out a Finnish knife with notches on the blade. I saw those notches as clearly as if he had held them up in front of my eyes.

The terrible man hissed something that was not Russian, but sounded like 'I'll kill you like a dog!' and his bloodshot eyes gaped wide as he swung the knife back.

I tried to remember the words of a prayer, but somehow I could not, although when, you might ask, should one pray, if not at a moment like that?

The knife was raised high, almost up into the sky, but it did not descend. In some magical fashion the wrist of the hand holding the knife was suddenly encircled by fingers in a grey glove.

The bearded man's face, already contorted, twisted even further out of shape. I heard the soft squelch of a blow, my would-be killer slumped gently to one side and there standing over me in his place was the elegant gentleman in the top hat, but instead of a cane he was holding a short sword, stained with red.

'Are you alive?' my rescuer asked in Russian, then immediately turned away and shouted something in a language unfamiliar to me.

I sat up and saw the Chinese pedlar dashing along the path, stamping his feet furiously, with his head down like a bull charging. He was no longer holding his tray; instead his hand was whirling a small metal sphere above his head on a piece of rope.

'Iiyai!' the Oriental grunted in an appalling voice and the sphere went hurtling forward, whistling by only a few *vershoks* above me.

I jerked round to see where its great speed was carrying it. It flew straight to its target, which proved to be the back of one of the kidnappers' heads. There was a repulsive crunch and the victim collapsed face down. The other man let go of the princess, swung round adroitly and snatched a revolver out of his pocket. Now I had a chance to take a better look at him, but I still did not see his face, because it was hidden behind a mask of black fabric.

The driver, who was sitting on the coach box, threw off his oilskin to reveal the same kind of black apparel as the two others were wearing, only without a mask. He jumped down onto the ground and ran towards us, also taking something out of his pocket on the way.

I turned to glance at my rescuer. (I am ashamed to admit that during those dramatic moments I lost my bearings completely and did nothing but turn my head this way and that, struggling to keep up with events.) The elegant gentleman took a short swing and flung his sword, but I did not see if he hit his target or not, because an even more improbable sight was presented to my astonished gaze: Mademoiselle Declique came dashing out of the bushes, clutching a hefty branch in one hand and holding up her skirt with the other to reveal a glimpse of well-turned ankle! As she ran towards us her hat flew off, her hair fluttered loose at her temples, but I had never seen her look more attractive.

'*J'arrive!*' she shouted. '*J'arrive!*'[7]

It was only then that I realised the shamefulness of my own conduct. I got to my feet and dashed to the assistance of the unfamiliar gentleman and the Chinese.

Alas, my assistance was no longer required.

The thrown sword had found its mark – the man in the mask was lying on his back, feebly stirring his legs, with a strip of steel protruding from his chest. It ended in a silver knob, and now I realised where the handsome gentleman had got his sword – it had been concealed in his cane.

And as for the coachman, the agile Chinese had dealt with him in excellent fashion. Before the bandit could even take his weapon out of his pocket, the Oriental leaped high into the air and struck his opponent a flying blow to the chin with his foot.

---

7 *I'm coming! I'm coming!*

The shattering impact jerked the coachman's head back with a crack so sharp that not even the very strongest of cervical vertebrae could possibly have withstood it. He threw up his arms and collapsed onto his back.

By the time Mademoiselle Declique joined us with her menacing branch, it was all over.

The first thing I did was to help Her Highness up – thank God, she was quite unhurt, simply feeling stunned.

Then I turned to the stranger.

'Who are you, sir?' I asked, although of course I ought first to have thanked him for saving us, whoever he might be.

Xenia Georgievna rectified my blunder.

'Thank you,' she said, looking intently at the man with the black hair and white temples. 'You saved us all. I am Grand Princess Xenia Georgievna. The boy who was with me is Mika, the Grand Duke Mikhail Georgievich. And these are my friends, Mademoiselle Declique and Mr Ziukin.'

The stranger bowed respectfully to Her Highness, doffed the top hat that had miraculously remained on his head throughout the commotion and introduced himself, stumbling over his words slightly, probably because he was quite understandably embarrassed to find himself facing a member of the royal family: 'Erast P-Petrovich Fandorin.'

He did not add anything else, from which it was possible to conclude that Mr Fandorin did not hold any position in the state service and was a private individual.

'And this is my valet, or perhaps b-butler, I'm not sure which is more correct. His name is Masa, he is Japanese,' said Fandorin, indicating the pugnacious pedlar, who in turn bowed low from the waist and remained bent over.

So it turned out that the elegant gentleman was not embarrassed at all but simply had a slight stammer, that the Chinese was not Chinese at all, and finally that the Oriental and I were in a certain sense professional colleagues.

'And who are these people, Erast Petrovich?' Her Highness

asked, pointing timidly to the hapless kidnappers lying completely motionless. 'Are they unconscious?'

Before replying, the dark-haired man went to each of the four men lying on the ground in turn, felt the arteries in their necks and shook his head four times. The last one he examined was the dreadful man with the beard. Fandorin turned him over onto his back and even to me, a man totally ignorant in such matters, it was perfectly clear that he was dead – the gleam of his motionless eyes was so completely lifeless. But Fandorin leaned down lower over the body, took hold of the beard between his finger and thumb and gave it a sudden jerk.

Her Highness cried out in surprise, and such crude familiarity with death seemed indecent even to me. However, the black beard parted easily from the face and was left in Fandorin's hand.

I saw that the dead man's crimson features were pitted with pockmarks and he had a forked white scar on his cheek.

'This is the famous Warsaw bandit Lech Penderetski, also known as Blizna, which means Marked One or Scar,' Fandorin stated calmly, as if he were introducing someone he knew well, and then added, almost to himself: 'So that's what's going on . . .'

'Are all these men really dead?' I asked, realising with a sudden shudder what a terrible situation the royal family could find itself in as a result of this incident. If some stroller were to peep round the corner now, the scandal that broke out would echo round the world. Just think of it . . . an attempt to kidnap a cousin of the Russian tsar! Four men killed! And some Warsaw bandit or other! The sacred solemnity of the coronation ceremony would be completely shattered!

'We have to get them into the carriage immediately!' I exclaimed with a fervour untypical of me in normal circumstances. 'Will your butler consent to assist me?'

While the Japanese and I piled the bodies into the carriage, I felt terribly anxious that someone might catch us engaged in this rather disreputable activity. Everything about the business was far from customary for me. Not only was there blood flowing down my face from my bruised forehead and broken lip, I had also stained my new promenading tunic with blood that was not my own.

And so I did not hear what Her Highness and Fandorin were talking about. But to judge from her flushed cheeks, she must have been thanking the mysterious gentleman again for saving her.

'Where is His Highness?' I asked Mademoiselle as soon as I recovered my breath.

'I left him in ze ...' She clicked her fingers, trying to remember the word, but could not. 'Ze quayside? Ze dock for ships?'

'The arbour,' I prompted her. 'Let's go together. His Highness must be feeling very frightened.'

Beyond the bushes there was a rather extensive lawn, with a lacy white wooden arbour standing at its centre.

When we did not find Mikhail Georgievich in it, we started calling for him, thinking that the grand duke must have decided to play hide and seek with us.

Our shouts brought Fandorin. He looked around on all sides and suddenly squatted down on his haunches, examining something in the grass.

It was the pink Chinese sugar lollipop, which had been crushed by some heavy object, probably a heel.

'Damn, damn, damn!' Fandorin exclaimed, striking himself on the thigh with his fist. 'I ought to have foreseen this!'

7 May

I shall not describe the events of the evening and the night that followed His Highness's disappearance, because in effect there were no events as such. The primary concern of those who were aware of what had happened was to keep the matter secret, and so from the outside everything appeared as if nothing had happened at all, except for the constant ringing of the telephones and the over-reckless pace at which horsemen raced round the triangle formed by the Hermitage, the Petrovsky Palace and the governor general's residence.

All of this carefully concealed but extremely frenetic (not to say chaotic) activity produced absolutely no result, since the most important thing remained unclear: who could have wanted to kidnap His Majesty's little cousin and why? And the mystery was not cleared up until the morning, when a letter without any stamp arrived at the Hermitage together with the ordinary municipal post – the postman himself was unable to say how it could have got into his bag in that condition.

As a result of this letter the sovereign himself, having received his grateful Asian subjects His Highness the Emir of Bukhara and His Grace the Khan of Khiva in the morning, postponed a parade at the Khodynsk Field at the last moment on the pretext of the cold and rainy weather and, accompanied only by the head of the court police, travelled in complete secret in an ordinary closed carriage with his personal valet, Seleznyov, on the coach box to join us at the Hermitage. That was when this palace in the park demonstrated the two great advantages for which it had received its name – its remoteness and privacy.

His Majesty's uncle the Grand Duke Kirill Alexandrovich and the Grand Duke Simeon Alexandrovich arrived in the same conspiratorial manner: the former came alone (his butler Luka Emelianovich was on the coach box) and the latter brought his adjutant, Prince Glinsky – the horses driven by the most highly respected of all living butlers, you might call him the elder of our trade, Foma Anikeevich.

Those in our house who knew about the emergency, apart from the family, were Mademoiselle Declique and I, the Englishmen, because in any case it would have been impossible to keep it secret from them, and Lieutenant Endlung, for the same reason and also because Pavel Georgievich had no secrets from his raffish friend. I did not explain anything to the servants living in the house and merely forbade them to leave the Hermitage for any reason whatever. As born court servants, they did not ask any questions. And the Moscow servants lodged above the stables were told that His Highness had gone to stay at Ilinskoe, the country palace of his uncle the governor general.

Naturally, Ekaterina Ioannovna in St Petersburg was not told anything. Why alarm Her Highness unnecessarily? And until the ominous letter arrived, we all still cherished the hope that some sort of misunderstanding had occurred and Mikhail Georgievich would soon return to the Hermitage unharmed and in good health.

Need I say that I barely slept a wink that night? I had terrible visions, each one worse than the one before. I imagined that His Highness had fallen into some invisible fissure overgrown with grass, and long after midnight I drove the servants out with blazing torches to search the park once again, telling them that Xenia Georgievna had lost a diamond earring. Then when I got back to my room, I suddenly imagined that Mikhail Georgievich had fallen victim to some monster of depravity who preyed on little boys, and my teeth started chattering in fright, so that I had to take valerian drops. But of course the assumption that seemed most likely was that the grand duke had been abducted by accomplices of the man with the false beard known as Blizna or Scar. While we were fighting some of the bandits for Xenia Georgievna, others had carried off the defenceless Mikhail Georgievich – and this was made all the more likely by the discovery of apparently fresh tracks from the wheels of another carriage not far from the fateful lawn.

But even though this thought was less horrific than the ones I have already mentioned, it was still agony to me. How was His Highness feeling now, surrounded by malicious strangers? Mika, the delicate, pampered little boy who had grown up in the firm belief that everyone around him loved him and they were all his friends. He did not even know what fear was, because nothing more frightening than a gentle slap on the hindquarters had ever happened to him. His Highness was so open, so trusting!

I was afraid even to approach Mademoiselle. All evening she sat as if she had been turned to stone and did not even attempt to offer any excuses. She merely wrung her hands and bit her lips, once so hard that they bled – I saw it and wanted to give her my handkerchief, because she had not even noticed the trickle of scarlet droplets, but I decided against it, in order not to place her in an awkward situation. That night she did not sleep either – I saw light coming from under her door and heard the sound of footsteps. As soon as the Moscow chief of police, Lasovsky, had finished questioning her, Mademoiselle Declique locked herself in her room. Twice, even three times during the night I walked up to her door and listened. The governess was still pacing to and fro, as regularly as clockwork. I wanted very much to knock at the door on some pretext and tell her that no one blamed her for what had happened, and I actually admired her courage. But knocking on a lady's door in the middle of the night is absolutely inconceivable. And in any case I would not have known how to talk to her.

★

42

The secret conference with the participation of His Majesty was held upstairs, in the small drawing room, as far away as possible from the Englishmen, who, with the tact typical of that nation, went out to walk in the garden as soon as His Majesty arrived, although the rain was simply lashing down and the weather not at all conducive to walking.

I served at the gathering. Naturally, it was quite impossible to allow any of the servants into this secret meeting, and in any case I would have regarded it as my duty and an obligation of honour to serve such brilliant company in person.

It is hard for the uninitiated to imagine the full complexity of this high art. It requires meticulous attention, unfailing deftness and – most important of all – total invisibility. It is as if one were transformed into a kind of shadow, an invisible man whom everyone very soon ceases to notice. Under no circumstances should one distract the members of an important conference with a sudden movement or sound, or even the unintentional gliding of a shadow across the table. At such moments I like to imagine that I am the disembodied master of the enchanted castle in the fairy tale *The Scarlet Flower*, regaling my dear guests: the drinks pour themselves into the glasses and cups; the matches flare up and are carried to the cigars without assistance from anyone; every now and then the ash that has accumulated in the ashtrays mysteriously disappears. When Simeon Alexandrovich dropped a pencil on the floor (His Highness is in the habit of constantly drawing little imps and cupids), I was on the alert. I did not crawl under the table, which would have attracted attention, but immediately handed the governor general another pencil, exactly the same, from behind his back.

I must say with some pride that not one of the participants in this highly delicate conference, which was, in a manner of speaking, crucial to the fate of the dynasty, ever once lowered his voice – in my opinion, that is the mark of supreme distinction for a servant. Of course, the conversation occasionally veered into French, but that did not happen because of me, it was simply that on the whole it was all the same to His Majesty and Their Highnesses whether they conversed in Russian or French. If they had wished to conceal the content of one part or another of the discussion from me, they would have started talking in English since, as I have already said, very few of the old generation of court servants know that language, while almost all of them speak French. Or, more precisely, they do not speak it, but they understand it, since it would be extremely strange if I, Afanasii Ziukin, were suddenly to address a member of the royal family or a noble at court in French. One must know one's place and not make oneself out to be something that one is not – that is the golden rule that I would recommend everyone to follow, regardless of his origins and position.

The sovereign, well-known for his patriotism, was the only one out of all those present who spoke nothing but Russian the whole time. It turned out that His Majesty remembered me from the time when I served as a table layer in the dining room of the late sovereign. Down at the entrance, before he went upstairs, the emperor was kind enough to speak to me: 'Hello, Afanasii Stepanovich. Was it you who had the canopy with my initial hung up? It's very beautiful, thank you.'

His Majesty's refined courtesy and astonishing memory for names and faces are well known. In fact, from early childhood all the grand dukes are specially trained to develop their memories – there is a special method for it – but His Majesty's abilities in this area are truly exceptional. Once he has seen someone, the sovereign remembers them forever, and this impresses many people tremendously. On the question of courtesy, the tsar and tsarina are the only members of the royal family who address their servants formally. Perhaps this is because we servants, while feeling an appropriate veneration for Their Majesties, are at the same time not very— However, hush. One does not talk of such things. Or even think of them.

The sovereign was sitting at the head of the table, gloomy and taciturn. Beside his tall, well-built uncles, His Majesty appeared quite small and insignificant, almost a stripling. And what can I say about our own Georgii Alexandrovich – a real mountain of a man: handsome, portly, with a dashingly curled moustache, and dressed in a blinding white admiral's uniform, compared with which the emperor's modest colonel's uniform looked rather shabby. Simeon Alexandrovich, the tallest and slimmest of the deceased sovereign's brothers, is like a medieval Spanish grandee, with his regular features that seem carved out of ice. And the eldest, Grand Duke Kirill Alexandrovich, the commander of the Imperial Guard, may not be as handsome as his brothers, but he is truly majestic and formidable, for he inherited the celebrated basilisk stare from his father the emperor. Officers who have committed some offence have been known to faint under that gaze.

In the presence of the doyens of the royal family, the youthful Pavel Georgievich was as quiet as a mouse and as meek as a lamb, and did not even dare to smoke. Also present was the head of the court police, Colonel Karnovich, a taciturn gentleman of huge resources and very meagre sentiment. He did not even sit at the table, but found himself a place in the corner.

Waiting outside on a chair in the corridor was our rescuer of the previous day, Mr Fandorin. I had been instructed to move him into the house, and for lack of any other accommodation I had put him in the nursery, judging that this gentleman would remain in the Hermitage only until Mikhail Georgievich returned to his own room. I had planned to lodge the Japanese in the stables, but he had wanted to stay with his master. He had spent the night on the floor with a plush teddy bear under his head and, to judge from his gleaming face, had slept excellently. Fandorin himself had not gone to bed at all, but spent the whole night until dawn prowling around the park with an electric torch. I did not know if he had found anything. He did not enter into any explanations with the chief of police, let alone with me, saying only that he would report everything he knew to His Majesty the emperor in person.

This same mysterious gentleman became the subject of discussion almost immediately the meeting began, although it did not begin with discussion as such, but with reading. Everyone sitting there took turns to read (or reread) the letter that had been received, the contents of which I did not know as yet. Then they all turned towards the sovereign. I held my breath in order to hear the precise words with which His Majesty would open this emergency meeting. The sovereign gave an embarrassed cough, glanced round from under his brows at the faces of all present and said quietly: 'This is appalling. Simply appalling. Uncle Kir, what shall we do now?'

The emperor had said his word, etiquette had been observed and somehow of its own accord the chairmanship of the meeting moved to Kirill Alexandrovich, who had been regarded as a covert joint ruler during the previous reign and had consolidated his position even further under the new sovereign.

His Highness spoke slowly, weighing his words: 'Above all, Nicky, self-control. How you conduct yourself will determine the fate of the dynasty. Over the next few days thousands of eyes will be trained on you, including some very, very shrewd ones. Not the slightest sign of agitation, not a hint of anxiety – do you understand me?'

The sovereign nodded uncertainly.

'We must all act as if nothing has happened. I understand, Georgie,' said Kirill Alexandrovich, turning to Georgii Alexandrovich, 'how hard this is for you. You are the father. But you and Pauly and Xenia must remain cheerful and calm. If rumours spread that some crooks or other have abducted a cousin of the Russian tsar with the whole world looking on, the prestige of the Romanovs, which has already been damaged by the fiendish murder of your father, will be completely undermined. There are eight foreign crown princes, fourteen heads of government and thirty special legations arriving in Moscow—'

Simeon Alexandrovich threw his pencil down on the table and interrupted his elder brother.

'This is all raving nonsense! Some doctor or other! What is this? Who is he? He's simply insane! Give him the Orlov! What insolence!'

I didn't understand anything that the governor general had said. A doctor? An Orlov? Which of the Orlovs – the arch-chamberlain or the deputy minister of the interior?

'Yes, yes, indeed,' His Majesty said with a nod. 'Is anything known about this Doctor Lind?'

Kirill Alexandrovich turned to the head of the court police, whose duty it was to know about everything that presented even the very slightest threat to the royal family, and therefore perhaps about everything in the world.

'What do you say, Karnovich?'

The colonel stood up, adjusted his spectacles with blue lenses and spoke in a voice that was almost a whisper but at the same time amazingly clear: 'There has not previously been any criminal with that name within the borders of the Russian empire.'

He sat down again.

There was a pause, and I sensed that the moment had come for me to abandon my role as a disembodied shadow.

I cautiously cleared my throat, and since the drawing room was absolutely silent, the sound was distinctly audible. Kirill Alexandrovich and Simeon Alexandrovich looked round in amazement, as if they had only just noticed my presence (in fact, that could indeed have been the case) and Georgii Alexandrovich, knowing perfectly well that I would sooner choke on my own cough than dare to attract attention to my own person unnecessarily, asked: 'Is there something you would like to tell us, Afanasii?'

At this point all of the other royal individuals directed their gazes at me, a state of affairs to which I was quite unused, so that I was unable to control the trembling of my voice.

'It is about Mr Fandorin, the gentleman who ... witnessed the outrage yesterday.' I mastered my agitation and continued in a steadier voice. 'This morning when, for obvious reasons, the

47

house was in something of a commotion, Mr Fandorin was sitting on the terrace and smoking a cigar in the calmest manner one could imagine—'

Simeon Alexandrovich interrupted me irritably: 'Do you really suppose it is so important for us and the sovereign emperor to know how Mr Fandorin spent the morning?'

I immediately fell silent and bowed to His Highness, not daring to continue.

'Be quiet, Sam,' Georgii Alexandrovich shouted abruptly at his younger brother.

Simeon Alexandrovich has an unfortunate peculiarity – no one likes him. Neither his relatives, nor his inner retinue, nor the Muscovites, nor even his own wife. It is hard to like such a man. They say that the late sovereign appointed him governor general of Moscow in order to see him less often. And also in order to rid the court of His Highness's entourage – all those pretty little adjutants and secretaries with dyed hair. Alas, Simeon Alexandrovich's habits are no secret to anyone – the whole of society gossips about them. On that very day, when he had just entered the hallway (having arrived last of all, even after the sovereign) His Highness had asked me in animated fashion: 'Who was that handsome chap I met just now on the lawn? The slim fellow with the yellow hair?' I politely explained to the grand duke that it must have been the Englishman, Mr Carr, but I felt a certain inward tremor: knowing the reason why the emergency conference had been convened, how was it possible to allow free rein to one's personal inclinations? It was not even so much a matter of inclinations – His Highness simply has a very bad character.

'Carry on, Afanasii,' Georgii Alexandrovich told me. 'We are all listening to you attentively.'

I could not help admiring my master's emotional restraint and fortitude. Any ordinary man whose child had been kidnapped would have been in a terrible state, screaming and tearing his hair out, but His Highness did not lose his self-control even for an instant, except that he kept smoking one *papyrosa* after another. At such moments one feels especially keenly what a great honour and inexpressible responsibility it is to serve individuals of the imperial blood. They are special people, unlike all the rest.

'Permit me to report,' I continued, 'that such imperturbability on the part of an individual aware of the disaster that has occurred struck me as strange. I approached Mr Fandorin and asked if he had discovered any more tracks in the park. He replied: "The second carriage, which was standing near the lawn and was used to abduct the boy, drove off in the direction of the Kaluga Highway. The attendant at the park gates saw a fast-moving carriage with the blinds tightly closed over the windows." "Then why haven't you told anyone?" I asked him. "You ought to inform the police immediately!" But he replied confidently: "But what for? There's nothing to be done now." And then he added this ...' At this point I deliberately made a brief pause and repeated Fandorin's words exactly as I remembered them: '"We have to wait for a letter from Lind." Yes, that was exactly what he said: "We have to wait for a letter from Lind." I must admit that I had no idea what letter he was talking about, and I didn't understand the last word at all. But now I remember quite clearly that he said "Lind". Then I was called to the telephone, and our conversation was interrupted. However, the inference is that Mr Fandorin knew in advance about the letter and about Lind. Permit me also to draw your Imperial Majesty's and your Imperial Highnesses' attention to the circumstance that Mr Fandorin's appearance at the scene of the kidnapping yesterday was clearly not fortuitous. He acted too resolutely for a chance passer-by, said some rather strange things and identified the leader of the bandits – he said his name was Penderetski.'

Colonel Karnovich spoke up from his corner.

'I have managed to discover something about Lech Penderetski, also known as Blizna. He is one of the leaders of the criminal world in the Kingdom of Poland. A bandit, extortionist and murderer, but cautious and crafty – no one had ever managed to catch him red-handed. According to rumour, Blizna has links with the criminal communities of many countries in Europe. The body has been sent to Warsaw for identification, but the description and other information do suggest that it really is Penderetski.'

'How did Fandorin come to know about this fellow?' Kirill Alexandrovich asked thoughtfully.

Simeon Alexandrovich laughed spitefully: 'Why, that's easy to find out. We have to arrest Fandorin and interrogate him thoroughly. He'll tell us everything. My Lasovsky knows how to loosen tongues. When he barks, even I get the shivers.'

And His Highness laughed, delighted with his joke, but no one else there shared his merriment.

'Uncle Kir, Uncle Sam,' His Majesty said in a quiet voice, 'you pronounce the name of this Fandorin as if you knew him. Who is he?'

The head of the court police answered for the grand dukes. He took a sheet of paper out of his pocket and reported as follows.

'Fandorin, Erast Petrovich. Forty years of age. Of the Ortho-dox confession. A hereditary noble. A knight of many orders, too many to mention. A retired state counsellor. For almost ten years he served as deputy for special assignments to the governor general of Moscow, Prince Dolgorukoi.'

'Ah yes, Fandorin again,' Kirill Alexandrovich said slowly, looking out through the window as if he were recalling some old story. 'I wonder where he has been all these years.'

From these words I concluded that His Highness really was acquainted with the retired state counsellor.

Then it emerged that Simeon Alexandrovich knew this gentle-man even better, and apparently not from his most flattering side.

'Fandorin has not shown his face in Moscow for about five years,' the governor general said, pulling a wry face. 'The scoundrel knows there's no place for him in my city. This man, Nicky, is an adventurer of the very worst kind. Sly and shifty, slippery and foul. The reports I have received say that after he left Moscow he prospered in all sorts of dirty business. He left his tracks behind him in Europe, in America and even in Asia. I must admit that I follow this gentleman's movements because I have a score to settle with him ... Well, anyway, reliable sources have informed me that Fandorin has fallen as low as it is possible to fall: he accepts commissions to carry out investigations for private individuals and is not squeamish about charging a fee – apparently a substantial one. The point is that his *clients* (Simeon Alexandrovich pronounced this word with emphatic disgust) include millionaires and even, unfortunately, some foreign monarchs. In five years of this infamous activity Fandorin has earned a certain reputation for himself. I have no doubt that he is privy to many dirty secrets, but we can manage our family business without his dubious services. My police are excellent at their job and my Lasovsky will run down this doctor in two shakes of a dog's tail.'

'I beg Your Highness's pardon,' Karnovich interjected with an imperturbable expression, 'but the protection of the imperial family falls within the purview of my department and I assure you that we will deal with this mission perfectly well without the participation of the Moscow police, not to mention any amateur detectives.' The colonel smiled gently and added in a quiet voice, as if he were talking to himself: 'We don't need any Sherlock Holmeses here.'

'Oh, Colonel, Fandorin is very far from being an amateur,' Kirill Alexandrovich objected. 'He is a man of exceptional abilities. If anyone can help us in this difficult and delicate matter, he can. And, in addition, he knows something about this villain Lind. It is also of some importance that as a private individual Fandorin is not restricted in the methods he can employ. No, Nicky, we won't be able to manage without this man. I am even inclined to think that he has been sent to us by God.'

'Rubbish! Absolute rubbish!' Simeon Alexandrovich cried, flinging his pencil into the corner. (I took another one out of my pocket.) 'I categorically protest!'

Kirill Alexandrovich, who was not accustomed to being addressed in this manner and also, as far as I was aware, regarded his younger brother with unmitigated contempt, lowered his leonine head and fixed the governor general with his famous withering stare. In response, Simeon Alexandrovich stubbornly jutted out his chin, which made his well-groomed beard look like the bowsprit of a ship, and assumed an absolutely uncompromising air.

There was an oppressive silence.

'But what are we going to do with this Fandorin?' the emperor asked plaintively. 'Call him in or not? Ask him to help or arrest him?'

Neither of Their Highnesses replied; they did not even change the direction of their gazes. This was an enmity of many years that had begun before the present sovereign was even born. Only, as the common folk put it, Simeon Alexandrovich was a bit 'weedy' in comparison with Kirill Alexandrovich. He had never been known to come off best against his elder brother.

By temperament Georgii Alexandrovich is much calmer and more easy-going than either of them, but if once he gets his temper up – then beware! And now he suddenly began flushing crimson, and seemed to swell up, making me afraid that the hooks on his collar would burst open, and it was clear that a storm was about to break.

His Majesty did not see this terrifying picture, since he was looking at Kirill Alexandrovich and Simeon Alexandrovich. If he had seen it, he would probably not have ventured to say anything, but as it was, he began in a conciliatory tone of voice: 'Uncle Sam, Uncle Kir, listen to what I think—'

There was a thunderous crash as Georgii Alexandrovich swung his fist down and slammed it into the table so hard that two wineglasses fell over, a coffee cup cracked and an ashtray was overturned, and Simeon Alexandrovich bounced on his chair in surprise.

'Shut up, Nicky!' the head of the Green House roared. 'And you two keep quiet as well! It's my son who has been kidnapped; I'm the one who should decide. And don't forget that it's only thanks to this, what's his name ... damn it, beginning with F, that my daughter was saved! Let him tell us everything that he knows!'

And so the matter was decided.

I slipped out of the drawing room silently in order to call Fandorin. Immediately outside the door there was a plush curtain, and then the corridor where the 'amateur detective', as Karnovich had called him, had been ordered to wait.

'Your lovely moustache – it's absolutely charming. And you don't shape it with tweezers? Or use fixative?'

On hearing these strange words, just to be on the safe side I peeped out from behind the curtain to see who could be speaking in such a manner.

Erast Fandorin was sitting where I had left him, with one leg crossed over the other, counting the jade beads on a rosary. The voice was not his, it belonged to the governor general's adjutant Prince Glinsky, a dainty young man with a pretty face like a girl's. The common folk have a saying about his kind: ''Tis a pity he's not a wench, at least he could wed.' The prince was standing in front of Fandorin, leaning down and carefully studying the retired official's slim, tidy moustache. Glinsky's own moustache was waxed – I could see that quite clearly now – and I think his lips were painted. But what was so surprising about that?

'No, sir, I do not use f-fixative,' Fandorin replied politely, looking up at the young man and not making the slightest attempt to move away.

'My God, what eyelashes you have!' the adjutant sighed. 'I think I would give absolutely anything for long black eyelashes like that, curved at the end. Is that your natural colour?'

'Absolutely natural,' Erast Petrovich assured him no less amiably.

At this point I interrupted this outlandish conversation and invited the state counsellor to follow me.

It is amazing, but on finding himself face to face with such a large number of members of the royal family, Erast Petrovich Fandorin betrayed not the slightest sign of discomfiture. The light but perfectly respectful bow that seemed to be addressed to all present but at the same time primarily to His Majesty would have done credit to a plenipotentiary ambassador extraordinary from some great power.

Kirill Alexandrovich, who had only just been extolling Fandorin's virtues, began abruptly, without any words of greeting, in what I thought was a rather hostile manner: 'Tell us what you know about Doctor Lind and about this whole business in general.'

Fandorin inclined his head as if to indicate that he understood the request, but what he said was not at all what they were expecting. The gaze of his cold blue eyes slid across the faces of the men sitting there and halted on the sheet of paper lying in the middle of the table.

'I see a l-letter has arrived. May I familiarise myself with its contents?'

'I warned you what an impudent beggar he is!' Simeon Alexandrovich exclaimed indignantly, but Fandorin did not even glance in his direction.

Kirill Alexandrovich took no notice of what he had said either.

'Yes, Georgie, read the letter out loud. Every word is important here.'

'Yes, yes,' His Majesty put in. 'I would like to hear it again too.'

With an air of disgust, Georgii Alexandrovich picked the sheet of paper up off the table and began reading out the message, which was written in French:

54

Messieurs Romanovs,

I offer you an advantageous arrangement: a little Romanov prince weighing ten kilograms for a little Count Orlov weighing 190 carats. The exchange will take place tomorrow, and do not take it into your heads to palm me off with a fake — I have my own jeweller. If you accept, give your reply at precisely noon from the semaphore apparatus at the Alexandriisky Palace. If you do not accept, the prince will be returned to you immediately. In pieces.

Yours sincerely,
Doctor Lind

PS I enclose the code for the light signal.

I had just begun to pour His Majesty's coffee, and I froze with the coffee pot in my hand, in my shock even spilling a few drops on to the floor, which had never happened to me before. The monstrousness of the letter had exceeded my very worst fears. His Highness in pieces? Oh my God, my God!

'What semaphore is this?' That was the only thing that interested Fandorin in this nightmarish missive.

It is improper to ask questions in the presence of His Majesty, but not only did the sovereign react indulgently to such a flagrant violation of etiquette, he actually replied himself, with his distinctive unfailing courtesy: 'An old light semaphore. Installed on the roof of the palace in my great-grandfather's time, and during my grandfather's reign it was fitted with electric lights for use in the dark and during overcast weather. Light signals sent from the semaphore can be seen from almost any point in the city.'

Instead of thanking His Majesty for his most gracious explanation, as a faithful subject ought to do, Fandorin merely nodded thoughtfully and asked: '"Orlov". Presumably we must take that to mean the diamond that adorns the imperial sceptre?'

'Yes,' His Majesty confirmed laconically. 'The diamond that Count Orlov bought in Amsterdam in 1773 on the instructions of Catherine the Great.'

'Impossible, absolutely unthinkable,' Simeon Alexandrovich snapped. 'The solemn presentation of the state regalia takes place in five days' time, and the coronation is two days after that. Without the sceptre the ceremony cannot go on. Let him have any amount of money but not the Orlov, under no circumstances.'

As one man they all turned towards Georgii Alexandrovich, whose opinion as the father was especially important in this matter.

And the grand duke proved worthy of his position and his rank. Tears sprang to his eyes, his hand tugged spontaneously at his tight collar, but His Highness's voice was firm: 'Impossible. The life of one of the grand dukes, even ... of my own son (at this point Georgii Alexandrovich did tremble after all) cannot be set above the interests of the monarchy and the state.'

That is what I call royal nobility – the summit that only those who have been marked and chosen by God himself can scale. The socialists and liberals write in their paltry newspapers and leaflets that the imperial house is wallowing in luxury. This is not luxury, this is the radiant halo of Russian statehood, and every member of the imperial family is prepared to sacrifice his own life and the lives of his loved ones in the name of Russia.

The room began swaying before my eyes and shimmering with iridescent colours. I blinked, shaking the tears off my eyelashes.

'And what if we replace the diamond with paste?' Karnovich's voice piped up from the corner. 'We can make such a good copy that no one will be able to tell the difference.'

'In such a short period of time it is not possible to produce a c-copy of such high quality,' Fandorin replied. 'And in any case Lind tells us that he has his own jeweller.'

Kirill Alexandrovich shrugged and said: 'There's one thing I don't understand. Why does he have to have the Orlov? The stone is priceless, and that means it has no market price. It's known all over the world; you can't sell it.'

'But why not, Your Highness?' Colonel Karnovich objected.

'You could cut it into three or four large diamonds and a few dozen medium and small ones.'

'And how much could you sell all that for?'

Karnovich shook his head, unable to answer the question.

'I know a little about such things,' said Fandorin. 'Three large diamonds of fifty carats or so can be worth approximately half a million roubles in gold each. And the small ones – well, let's say another half-million.'

'Two million?' said the emperor, and his face brightened. 'But we will not grudge a sum like that for our dear Mika!'

Fandorin sighed: 'Your Majesty, this is not at all a matter of two million. I know Lind's style. This is blackmail, and on a far grander scale than is obvious at first glance. We are not simply talking about the life of one of Your Majesty's eleven cousins. Lind's target is the coronation. He knows perfectly well that without the Orlov, the ceremony cannot go ahead. And the boy's life is only a means of applying p-pressure. The real threat is not that Lind will kill the young grand duke, but that he will disrupt the coronation and dishonour the name of Russia and the Romanov dynasty throughout the world by leaving parts of the boy's body in the most crowded areas.'

Everyone present, including myself, gave a groan of horror, but Fandorin continued remorselessly: 'You were saying, Your Majesty, that no buyer could be found for the Orlov anywhere in the world. But there already is a buyer, and one who cannot refuse to buy. That buyer is the house of Romanov. Essentially, what you have to buy from Lind is not the grand duke, but the Orlov diamond, for what is at stake here is not just the stone, but the c-coronation and the very prestige of the monarchy. I am afraid that it will cost more than two million. Very, very much more. And that is not the worst thing.' Fandorin lowered his head sombrely and I saw his hands clench into fists. 'You will pay for the safe keeping of the stone and the return of the grand duke, but Lind will not give the boy back alive. That is against the doctor's principles . . .'

An ominous silence fell, but only for a few moments, because Pavel Georgievich, who had so far been sitting quietly at the far end of the table, suddenly covered his face with his hands and burst into sobs.

'Pauly, get a grip,' Kirill Alexandrovich told him sternly. 'And you, Fandorin, stop trying to frighten us. You'd better tell us about Lind.'

'He is the most dangerous criminal in the world,' Fandorin began. 'I don't know why he is called Doctor, perhaps because he possesses knowledge in many surprising areas. For instance, he speaks numerous languages. Possibly even including Russian – I would not be surprised. Very little is known for certain about Lind. He is obviously relatively young, because ten years ago no one had heard of him. No one knows where he is from. Most likely he is American, because Lind committed the first crimes that brought him fame as a daring and ruthless villain in the United States of North America. He began by robbing banks and mail cars and moved on to become a true master of the arts of blackmail, extortion and kidnapping.'

Fandorin spoke with his eyes fixed on the table, as if he could see in its polished surface the reflection of pictures from the past that were visible only to him.

'And so, what do I actually know about this man? He is a confirmed misogynist. There are never any women n-near him – no lovers, no girlfriends. Lind's gang is an exclusively male preserve. A male brotherhood, if you like. The doctor seems to have none of the usual human weaknesses, and as a result no one has yet managed to follow his trail. Lind's assistants are slavishly devoted to him, something that is very rarely found in criminal associations. I have captured the doctor's men alive on two occasions, and both times I got nothing out of them. One was given hard labour for life, the other killed himself, but they did not betray their leader ... Lind's connections in international criminal circles are truly boundless and his authority is immense.

When he requires a specialist in any field at all – safe crackers, hired killers, engravers, hypnotists, burglars – the greatest experts of the criminal sciences regard it as an honour to offer him their services. I assume that the doctor is f-fabulously rich. In the time since I have taken an interest in him – which is a little over a year and a half – only in the cases that I know about he has appropriated at least ten million.'

'Francs?' Georgii Alexandrovich asked, intrigued.

'I meant dollars. That is approximately twenty million roubles.'

'Twenty million!' His Highness actually gasped at the figure. 'And the treasury gives me a pitiful two hundred thousand a year! Only a hundredth part of that! And the blackguard has the nerve to demand money from me!'

'Not from you, Uncle Georgie,' the sovereign commented dryly. 'From me. The Orlov is crown property.'

'Nicky, Georgie!' Kirill Alexandrovich shouted at both of them. 'Carry on, Fandorin.'

'I have had two meetings with Doctor Lind . . .' Fandorin said and then hesitated.

The room went very quiet. The only sound was the chair creaking under Colonel Karnovich as he leaned forward bodily in his eagerness.

'Although I do not know if I can really say that I met him, because we did not see each other's faces. I was wearing disguise and make-up, Lind was in a mask . . . We became acquainted with each other eighteen months ago, in New York. The Russian newspapers may perhaps have reported the kidnapping of the millionaire Berwood's twelve-year-old son? In America the story was front-page news for a month . . . Mr Berwood asked me to assume the responsibilities of intermediary for the delivery of the ransom. I demanded that the kidnappers first show me their prisoner. Lind himself took me to the s-secret room. The doctor was wearing a black mask that covered almost all of his face, a long cloak and a hat. And so the only observations I was able to make were that he was of average height and had a moustache –

but that could have been false. He did not utter a single word in my presence, and so I have never heard his voice.' Fandorin compressed his lips, as if he were struggling to contain his agitation. 'The boy was sitting there in the room, alive, with his mouth sealed. Lind allowed me to approach him, then led me out into the corridor, closed the door with three locks and handed me the keys. In accordance with our agreement, I handed him the ransom – a ring that belonged to Cleopatra, worth one and a half million dollars – and readied myself for a fight, since there were seven of them, and I was alone. But Lind studied the ring carefully through a magnifying glass, nodded and left, taking his men with him. I fiddled with the locks for a long time, since they proved a lot harder to open than to close, and when I finally managed to get into the room, Berwood junior was dead.'

Erast Petrovich pressed his lips together again, so hard that they turned white. Everybody waited patiently for him to recover his self-control – the members of the royal family are indulgent with those poor mortals who do not possess their supernatural self-control.

'I did not immediately understand why the boy was sitting so still and I leaned my head down low to look. It was only when I got very close that I saw there was a slim stiletto stuck straight into his heart! I couldn't believe my eyes. The day before, in anticipation of a trick, I had searched the room as thoroughly as possible, looking for a disguised hatch or a secret door, and I had not found anything suspicious. But later I recalled that as Lind let me pass him on the way out, he had lingered beside the chair – for a second, no more than that. But that second had been enough for him. What a precise blow, what cold-blooded calculation!'

It seemed to me that in addition to a bitterness and fury that time had not dulled, Fandorin's tone of voice expressed an involuntary admiration for the deftness of this satanic doctor.

'Ever since then I have set aside all other business until I settle scores with the doctor. I admit that a significant part in this decision was played by wounded vanity and the stain that the whole business left on my reputation. But there is more to it than mere vanity . . .' Fandorin wrinkled his high forehead. 'This man has to be stopped, because he is a true genius of evil, endowed with an incredibly fertile imagination and boundless ambition. Sometimes it seems to me that the goal he has set himself is to become famous as the greatest criminal in the whole of human history, and Lind certainly has more than enough rivals in that area. I had realised that sooner or later he would arrange some kind of catastrophe on a national or even international scale. And that is what has now happened . . .'

He paused again.

'Sit down, Erast Petrovich,' Kirill Alexandrovich said to him, and I realised that Fandorin's speech had obviously made a good impression on His Highness – the retired state counsellor was no longer being questioned, they were talking to him. 'Tell us how you hunted Doctor Lind.'

'First of all I turned the whole of New York upside down, but only succeeded in forcing the doctor to move his headquarters from the New World to the Old. I will not weary Your Majesty and Your Highnesses with a description of my searches, but six months later I managed to locate Lind's lair in London. And I saw the doctor for the second time – or rather I saw his shadow as he fled from his pursuers along one of the tunnels of the London Underground, shooting back with incredible accuracy. With two shots the doctor killed two constables from Scotland Yard outright, and he almost dispatched me to the next world.' Fandorin raised a lock of black hair off his forehead and we saw a scar running in a narrow white line across his temple. 'It's nothing, merely a glancing blow, but I lost consciousness for a moment, and in that time Lind was able to escape pursuit . . . I followed close on his heels from one country to another, and every time I was just a little too late. And then in Rome, about six months ago, the doctor simply vanished into thin air. It was only two weeks ago that I learned from a reliable source that the famous Warsaw bandit known as Blizna had boasted in intimate company that the doctor himself had invited him to Moscow for some very big job. As a Russian subject, Penderetski was well acquainted with the criminal world of Moscow – the gangs in both Khitrovka and the Sukharevka. That must be what Lind, who had n-never operated in Russia before, needed him for. I had been racking my brains to understand what could have attracted the doctor's interest in patriarchal Moscow. Now it is clear . . .'

'Impossible, absolutely impossible!' Simeon Alexandrovich exclaimed angrily, addressing His Majesty, not Fandorin. 'My boys in Khitrovka and the Sukharevka would never take part in a fiendish plot directed against the royal family! They will steal and cut throats as much as you like. But loyalty to the throne is in these Apaches' blood! On several occasions my Lasovsky has successfully used criminals to catch terrorists. Let me give you an example: for the duration of the coronation celebrations he has concluded a kind of gentlemen's agreement with the leader of all the Khitrovka thieves, a certain King, that the police will not detain pickpockets, but in exchange they must immediately report any weapons and other suspicious items that they discover in the pockets of the public. The King was quite happy to agree to this condition – he declared that in a certain sense he himself is an absolute sovereign, and monarchs must support each other. I can't vouch for the exact words that he used, but that was his meaning.'

This announcement lightened the gloomy mood of the company somewhat and Simeon Alexandrovich, encouraged by the smiles, added the following with a wily air: 'His Khitrovkan Majesty validated his promise with the formula: "I'm a mongrel if I don't!" Lasovsky tells me that this is the most cogent bandit oath of all.'

'How's that?' asked the sovereign, intrigued. 'A mongrel, as in a dog with no pedigree, eh? I'll tell Alice; she'll like that.'

'Nicky, Sam,' Kirill Alexandrovich said sternly. 'Let's listen to the rest of what Mr Fandorin has to say.'

'The King is not the only leader in Khitrovka and in any case he is certainly not an autocratic s-sovereign.' Although Erast Petrovich was replying to the governor general's statement, he did not look at him, but at the emperor. 'They are even saying that the King's days are numbered, that any day now he will be written off, that is killed by the so-called breakaways – pushy young bandits who are beginning to set the style in Khitrovka and Sukharevka. There is Rennet's gang, which operates in a new trade, dealing in opium, there is a certain Gristle – his speciality is "wet jobs", or killings, and extortion. A certain Stump has also appeared, with a gang in which the secrecy and discipline are tighter than in the Neapolitan Camorra.'

'Stump?' the emperor repeated in amazement. 'What a strange name.'

'Yes. A colourful character. His right hand was amputated and the stump ends in a plate onto which, according to requirements, he screws either a spoon or a hook or a knife or a chain with an iron apple on the end. They say it's a terrible weapon and its blow is deadly. The breakaways, Your Majesty, have no fear of spilling blood, do not acknowledge the thieves' laws, and the King is no authority for them. I suspect that Penderetski had connections with one of them. I followed the Marked One and his man from Warsaw, but very cautiously, in order not to frighten them off. He visited the Zerentui inn in Khitrovka twice, a place that is well known for not paying any tribute to the King. I was hoping that Blizna would lead me to the doctor, but nothing came of that. The Poles were in Moscow for ten days, and Penderetski went to the poste restante at the Central Post Office every day and spent a lot of time loitering near the Alexandriisky Palace and the Neskuchny Park. At least four times he climbed over the wall and strolled about in the park round the Hermitage. I realise now that he was looking for a convenient spot for an ambush. From noon yesterday he and his boys were hanging about in front of the exit from the park onto the Kaluga Highway, and there was a carriage waiting nearby. Some time after six a carriage with the grand duke's crest drove out of the gates and the Warsaw gang set out to follow it. I realised that the business was coming to a head. My assistant and I followed on behind in two cabs. Then two ladies, a boy and a man in a green tunic (Fandorin glanced towards me) got out of the grand duke's carriage. Penderetski, now wearing a false beard so that I did not recognise him immediately, walked after them. The carriage carrying the other bandits drove slowly behind him. Then my assistant and I entered the park from the other side, and I walked towards the strollers, watching out all the time in case Lind appeared . . .'

Erast Petrovich sighed dejectedly.

'How could I have miscalculated so badly? It never entered my head that there were two carriages, and not just one. But of course Lind had prepared two carriages, because he intended to abduct the girl and the boy, and then take them to separate hiding places. That was why Blizna only seized the grand princess. The second carriage was intended for the grand duke. That is probably where Lind was all the time, which really makes my blood boil. The governess unwittingly made their task easier when she carried the child to the very spot where the second group of kidnappers was lying in wait. Their plan only half-succeeded, but that does not change very much. Lind has still taken Russia by the throat . . .'

At these words His Majesty began gazing around with an expression of extreme unease, for some reason peering into the corners of the drawing room. I took a slight step forward, trying to guess what the emperor wanted, but my imagination was inadequate to the task.

'Tell me, Uncle Georgie, do you have an icon anywhere here?' the monarch asked.

Georgii Alexandrovich gave his nephew a glance of amazement and shrugged.

'Ah, Nicky, for God's sake!' Kirill Alexandrovich exclaimed with a frown. 'Let's manage without the anointed of God

64

business. You haven't been anointed yet in any case, and if the coronation is disrupted, you never will be.'

His Majesty replied with an air of profound sincerity: 'I do not see what can help here apart from prayer. All of us are in the hands of the Almighty. He has decided to arrange this trial for me, a weak and unworthy monarch, and so there must be some great meaning to it. We must trust in His will, and He will grant us deliverance.'

I recalled that I had seen a smoky little old icon, dark from age, in His Highness's study. Walking without making a sound, I went out for a minute and brought the sovereign the icon – after first having wiped it with a napkin.

While the emperor recited the words of a prayer with genuine fervour and even with tears in his eyes, the grand dukes waited patiently, except for Simeon Alexandrovich, who yawned as he polished his already impeccable nails with a piece of velvet braid.

'Can we continue, Nicky?' Kirill Alexandrovich enquired when the sovereign crossed himself for the last time and handed the icon back to me. 'Very well, let us sum up this lamentable situation. Mika has been abducted by a cruel and cunning criminal who threatens not only to kill the boy, but also to scupper the entire coronation. What else can we do apart from trust in the help of the Almighty?'

Karnovich rose to his feet and whispered from his corner: 'Find His Highness and free him from captivity.'

'Excellent,' said Kirill Alexandrovich, turning towards the chief of the court police. 'Then look for him, Colonel. Lind has given you until midday. You have an hour and a half at your disposal.'

Karnovich sat back down on his chair.

At this point Pavel Georgievich spoke for the first time. With his face contorted and still wet from tears, he said in a trembling voice: 'Perhaps we ought to give him it? After all, Mika is alive, and when all's said and done, the Orlov is only a stone . . .'

The eternal enemies Kirill Alexandrovich and Simeon Alexandrovich cried in a single voice: 'No! Never!'

The sovereign looked at his cousin with compassion and said gently: 'Pauly, Mr Fandorin has explained quite convincingly that handing over the diamond still will not save our Mika . . .'

Pavel Georgievich sobbed and wiped his cheek with his sleeve in an awkward gesture.

'Leave us, Pauly,' his father said sternly. 'Wait for me in your room. You make me feel ashamed.'

Pavel Georgievich jumped abruptly to his feet and ran out of the door. Even I had difficulty in maintaining an imperturbable expression, although of course no one even thought of looking at me.

Poor Pavel Georgievich, he found the burden of royal responsibility hard to bear. In the education of the grand dukes and princesses the greatest emphasis is placed on self-control, the ability to keep oneself in hand under any circumstances. Since early childhood Their Highnesses are taught to sit through long, exhausting gala dinners, and they are deliberately seated beside the least intelligent and most insufferable guests. They have to listen attentively to what the grown-ups say without showing that their company is boring or unpleasant and laugh at their jokes – the more stupid the witticism, the more sincere the laughter must be. And what about the Easter triple kiss for the officers and lower ranks of their affiliated regiments! Sometimes they have to perform the ritual kiss more than a thousand times in the course of two hours! And God forbid that they should show any signs of tiredness or revulsion. But Pavel Georgievich was always such a lively and spontaneous boy. He was not good at the exercises for developing self-control and even now, although His Highness has come of age, there is a lot that he still needs to learn.

After the door slammed shut behind the grand duke, there was a long, gloomy silence. Everyone started when the clock struck a quarter to eleven.

'However, if we do not let this Lind have the Orlov,' His Majesty said, 'then he will kill Mika, and tomorrow he will leave the body on Red Square or at the Cathedral of Christ the Saviour. And that will put me, the tsar, to shame in front of the entire civilised world!'

'And the entire house of Romanov with you,' Simeon Alexandrovich remarked.

Kirill Alexandrovich added gloomily: 'And the whole of Russia.'

'As God is my witness,' the sovereign sighed woefully, 'I never wanted the crown, but clearly it is my cross. It was no accident that I appeared in this world on the day of St Job the Long-Suffering. O Lord, teach me, enlighten me. What am I to do?'

God's answer was given by Fandorin, who enunciated a single brief phrase very clearly: 'Rent the stone.'

'What?' asked His Majesty, raising his eyebrows in amazement.

I also thought that I had misheard.

'We have to rent the stone from Lind until the end of the coronation.'

Simeon Alexandrovich shook his head.

'He's raving!'

However, the eldest of the grand dukes narrowed his eyes in thoughtful concentration, trying to penetrate the meaning of this bizarre suggestion. Having failed, he asked: 'How do you mean, "rent" it?'

Fandorin explained dispassionately.

'We have to tell Lind that his terms have been accepted, but for obvious reasons they cannot be met before the coronation. And therefore, for each day of delay he will receive a certain sum of money, a most substantial one – as if we are renting the Orlov from him. There is a week still to go until the coronation, is there not?'

'But what will that give us?' asked Georgii Alexandrovich, clutching his magnificent moustache.

'What do you mean, Georgie – time!' explained Kirill Alexandrovich. 'A whole week of time!'

'And a better chance of saving the child,' Fandorin added. 'Our terms will be as follows: the payments are made daily, and at each handover we must have unequivocal proof that the boy is alive. That is seven extra d-days of life for His Highness. And seven chances to pick up a thread that will lead us to the doctor. Lind may be extremely cunning, but he can make a mistake. I shall be on the alert.'

Georgii Alexandrovich jumped to his feet and drew himself up to his full impressive height. 'Yes, now I see that it is an excellent idea!'

The idea really did seem most felicitous – not even Simeon Alexandrovich could find any objections to make against it.

'And I will assign my most capable agent as an intermediary,' Karnovich suggested.

'I have genuine lions in the Department of Security,' the governor general of Moscow immediately retorted. 'And they know the city very well, unlike your Tsarskoe Selo carpet scrapers.'

'I b-believe it would be best if I were to take on the role of the intermediary,' Erast Petrovich said quietly. 'Naturally, in some kind of disguise. I know Moscow very well, and I know Lind's habits too.'

Kirill Alexandrovich put an end to the argument by declaring firmly: 'We will decide this later. The important thing is that now at least we have some kind of plan of action. Nicky, does it have your approval too?'

The question was clearly asked for form's sake, for His Majesty had never been known to object to anything that had been approved by his eldest uncle.

'Yes, yes, Uncle Kir, absolutely.'

'Excellent. Sit down, Colonel, take the code and write this message . . .' said His Highness, clasping his hands behind his back and striding across the room. '"Agreed. We need a respite of seven days. For each day we are willing to pay a hundred . . . no, two hundred thousand roubles. Payment by daily instalments, in any place at any time, but the prisoner must be produced." Well, how's that?' he asked, not addressing the question to his royal relatives, but to Fandorin.

'Not bad,' Fandorin replied most impudently to the commander of the Imperial Guard. 'But I would add: "Otherwise there will be no deal." Lind must understand we acknowledge that he has a strong hand and are prepared to pay a high price, but are not prepared to jump to his every beck and call.'

Our exalted visitors did not go home even after taking this difficult decision, for Fandorin expressed the opinion that a reply from Lind would follow almost immediately, either by semaphore light signal, telegraph – there was an apparatus in the Alexandriisky Palace – telephone call or some other, entirely unusual means. He said that on one occasion in similar circumstances a message from the doctor had come flying in through the window, attached to an arrow fired from a great distance.

Just imagine it – the autocrat of all Russia, the admiral-general of the fleet, the commander of the royal guards and the governor general of Moscow waiting patiently for some adventurer to deign to reply to them! I'm sure that nothing of the sort had happened in Russian history since the negotiations with the Corsican at Tilsit – but at least Bonaparte was an emperor.

In order not to waste time, the grand dukes began instructing their nephew the emperor in how to receive the foreign ambassadors and monarchs who had arrived for the celebrations. These meetings constituted the main political significance of the coronation, since it is quite common for extremely delicate questions of interstate relations to be decided, highly responsible diplomatic initiatives to be launched and new alliances to be concluded under the guise of ceremonial audiences.

His Majesty definitely still lacked experience in such subtleties and was in need of guidance and instruction. Not to mention the fact that the late sovereign, not having a very high opinion of the tsarevich's intellectual abilities, had not felt it necessary to initiate him into the secrets of higher diplomacy. For example, not until he had already ascended the throne, and even then not immediately, did the new emperor learn that in some mysterious fashion the direction of Russian foreign policy had been completely reversed: although to all appearances we remained a friend of His Majesty the Kaiser, we had concluded a secret defence pact with France, Germany's most bitter enemy. And this was by no means the only surprise awaiting the young successor to the throne.

The briefing was extremely sensitive in nature and, having ascertained that everything necessary was on the table, I thought it best to withdraw. The sensitivity arose not so much from the secrecy of the information as from the intimate family tone that the conversation assumed. His Imperial Majesty was actually not all that quick at absorbing what he was told, and his most august uncles began losing patience with their nephew, sometimes employing expressions that might perhaps be permissible between close relatives but are unthinkable in the presence of servants.

Well, I had my own guests, who might be less eminent but were far more demanding. Having installed Mr Fandorin, Colonel Karnovich and Prince Glinsky in the large drawing room, where my assistant Somov served them coffee and cigars, I went to the servants' parlour, a small, cosy little room located beside the kitchen on the ground floor. The governor general's butler Foma Anikeevich, the senior grand duke's butler Luka Emelyanovich, His Majesty's valet Dormidont Seleznyov and Fandorin's Japanese servant Masa were taking tea there. I had asked Mademoiselle Declique to look in on my guests from time to time to make sure that they did not feel abandoned – and also to give the poor woman, who was crushed by the misfortune that had overtaken her, something to keep her occupied. I know only too well from my own experience that at moments of such moral suffering there is no better medicine than performing mundane duties. It helps one to keep control.

On entering the servants' parlour, in addition to the pale but evidently quite calm governess, I also found Mr Freyby there, sitting a little apart from the general group with his interminable book in his hands. But there was not really anything to be surprised at in that. It was raining outside, the English gentlemen had gone for their enforced promenade, and Mr Freyby had no doubt grown bored of sitting in his room. Every butler knows that the servants' parlour is something like a drawing room or, to put it in the British manner, a club for the senior servants.

For a brief moment I was perturbed by the Englishman's presence, since I was intending to hold my own secret council meeting with my guests, but then I remembered that Mr Freyby did not understand a single word of Russian. Very well, let him sit there and read.

We were served by the new footman Lipps, whose experience and level of training I had not yet had time to ascertain. He himself understood perfectly well the importance of the examination to which he was being subjected, and he did everything immaculately. I observed him with as critical an eye as possible but failed to spot any blunders. I told Lipps to wait outside the door, for the conversation was not intended for his ears, and when something had to be brought in or taken away, I rang the bell. The man from the Baltic did what was required quickly but without hurrying – that is exactly as it should be done, and disappeared behind the door again.

You could probably not find judges of the servant's art sterner and better informed than my guests anywhere in the world. And that applied in particular to the venerable Foma Anikeevich.

I ought to explain that we servants have our own hierarchy, which does not depend at all on the status of our masters, but exclusively on the experience and merits of each one of us. And in terms of this hierarchy beyond all doubt the most senior among us was Foma Anikeevich, butler to Simeon Alexandrovich, the youngest of His Majesty's uncles. Luka Emelyanovich and I were approximately on the same level, while Dormidont, for all the brilliance of the position that he held, was regarded in our circle as still an apprentice. He knew his place and sat there modestly without leaning back in his chair, trying to listen to everything and not speak too much. The general opinion concerning him was that he was competent, observant, capable of learning and would go a long way. He came from a good court servant family, which was obvious from his given name and patronymic – Dormidont Kuzmich. At christening we hereditary servants are all given the simplest of the old names, so that the order of the world will be preserved and every human will have a name to suit his calling. What kind of servant or waiter could be called Vsevolod Apollonovich or Evgenii Viktorovich? That would only cause hilarity and confusion.

In the year and a half of the new reign Dormidont had grown tremendously in the opinion of court connoisseurs. For instance, there was the important incident in Livadia, immediately after the death of the previous sovereign, when the new emperor, being in a rather distraught state, almost received the visitors who had come to pay their condolences in his shoulder straps and without his black armband. Seleznyov caught His Majesty by the elbow when the doors were already open, and in five seconds changed the straps for epaulettes and even managed to attach mourning crêpe to His Majesty's shoulder knot. What an embarrassing faux pas that would have been!

But of course he still has a long way to go to reach the level of high-flying eagles like Foma Anikeevich or the late Prokop Sviridovich. Foma Anikeevich endures the heavy cross of being attached to an individual like Simeon Alexandrovich. In a word – his lot is not to be envied. The number of times that Foma Anikeevich has saved His Highness from shame and scandal! If the governor general's rule still possesses any authority in Moscow, it is only thanks to the Grand Duchess Elizaveta Feodorovna and his butler.

And our circle tells legendary stories about Prokop Sviridovich, who served as a valet to Tsar Alexander the Liberator.

Once, during the Balkan campaign, in the middle of the third battle of Plevna, a stray Turkish grenade fell right in front of the sovereign, who happened at that moment to be taking his afternoon snack. Prokop Sviridovich was standing close by, just as he ought to have been, holding a tray on which there was a cup of broth, a bread roll and a napkin.

Suddenly this ball of fire appeared out of nowhere! It fell into a small hollow overgrown with grass, hissing, hopping up and down and spitting smoke, all set to go off bang at any moment. The entire entourage froze and the butler was the only one not to lose his head: without dropping his tray, he took two short steps towards the hollow and poured the broth onto the grenade! The fuse went out. The most remarkable thing is that His Majesty, engrossed in his snack, did not even notice this incident and was only surprised at how little broth there was in the cup that was served to him. Kommissarov was awarded a noble title for deflecting the would-be regicide Karakozov's pistol, but Prokop Sviridovich ended up, as simple folk say, with twice nothing because none of the witnesses – the duty generals and aides-de-camp – bothered to explain anything to the tsar. They were ashamed that a butler had proved pluckier and more reso- lute than them, and Prokop Sviridovich was not one to boast of his achievements.

However, this outstanding servant demonstrated even greater bravery on the front of intimate relations. You might say that he saved the peace and tranquillity of the imperial family. On one of the empress's saint's days His Majesty committed a serious blunder: as he took her present out of his pocket – it was a ring with a large sapphire in the form of a heart and the empress's initials – he dropped another ring that was absolutely identical except that it bore the initials of the Princess Tverskaya.

'What's that, Sandy?' the empress asked, peering short-sight- edly at the small round shape that had gone tumbling across the carpet and taking her lorgnette out of her handbag.

The sovereign was dumbstruck and had no idea what to say. But Prokop Sviridovich quickly bent down, picked up the ring and swallowed it on the spot, after which he politely explained:

'I beg your pardon, Your Imperial Highness, I dropped one of my catarrh lozenges. I have been having terrible trouble with my stomach.'

That's the sort of man he was. The surgeon Pirogov himself cut the ring out of his stomach later.

It was precisely Prokop Sviridovich's example that inspired me last year when, as I dare to think, I rescued Georgii Alexandrovich from an almost identical delicate situation involving a letter from the ballerina Snezhnevskaya. Thank God, paper is not sapphire, and so no surgical intervention was required.

When I joined the honourable company, they were discussing the imminent festivities. Dormidont, who was clearly excited, and no wonder – he did not often have an opportunity to speak in such company – was telling the others something interesting about the sovereign. Foma Anikeevich and Luka Emelyanovich were listening benignly. The Japanese was drinking his tea from the saucer, puffing out his cheeks and goggling wildly. Mademoiselle was nodding politely, but I could see from her eyes that her thoughts were far away – I believe I have already mentioned that, for all her self-restraint, she did not have much control over the expression of her eyes. Mr Freyby was puffing away comfortably on his pipe and leafing through the pages of his book.

'... toughen their characters,' Dormidont was saying just as I walked into the servants' parlour. When he saw me he sat up respectfully and continued: 'They themselves are very superstitious, but they want to get the better of destiny, at any price. They deliberately arranged the arrival in Moscow for an unlucky day, the festival of St Job the Long-Suffering, and the move from the city to the Kremlin for the thirteenth, although it could easily have been earlier. I think it's all wrong – what point is there in tempting fate? You've seen for yourselves how Saint Job's day turned out yesterday.' And he gave me an eloquent glance, evidently feeling it was inappropriate to comment in greater detail on the disaster that had overtaken the Green Court.

'What do you say to that, Luka Emelyanovich?' Foma Anikeevich asked.

Kirill Alexandrovich's butler, a stolid and dignified man, thought for a moment and said: 'Well now, strengthening the will is no bad thing for a monarch. His Majesty could do to have a firmer character.'

'Is that what you think?' Foma Anikeevich asked with a shake of his head. 'I think it's not good. Ruling is like living: it should be done naturally and joyfully. Fate is kind to people like that. But if someone calls down misfortune on his own head, Fate heaps the dark clouds up over him. Our state isn't exactly a cheery place in any case, and if the sovereign himself starts prophesying gloom and doom ... And then again, Her Majesty has a heavy and joyless character. When the tsar grows a bit older and stronger, he'll choose ministers who are just as gloomy and unlucky. Every one knows the tsar's kennel man is just like the tsar.'

I was astounded, not by the fact that Foma Anikeevich spoke so freely about His Majesty (that is perfectly normal in our circle, and it is a good thing for the work) but that he was not in the least bit wary of an outsider – the Japanese. Obviously in my absence Fandorin's servant must have done something to win Foma Anikeevich's special trust. He is a perspicacious man who sees right through people and understands perfectly what can be said in front of them and what cannot.

The Oriental's smooth, impassive features gave no clue as to whether he understood what the conversation was about or was simply filling himself up with tea.

'And what is your opinion about this, Afanasii Stepanovich?' Foma Anikeevich asked me, and I realised from his quizzical glance that the question actually meant something quite different: did I think we could discuss the most important subject, or should we limit ourselves to conversation on abstract themes?

'Time will tell,' I replied, sitting down and ringing the bell for

Lipps to pour me some tea. 'There have been cases in history when extremely weak-willed successors to the throne have proved to be most worthy rulers in time. Take Alexander the Blessed, for instance, or even Franz-Josef.'

We spoke about one thing and thought about another: did I have any right to mention the decision that had been taken upstairs?

The Japanese would learn about it from his master in any case. Mademoiselle could not be kept in ignorance either – that would be too cruel. Foma Anikeevich and Luka Emelyanovich could give useful advice. The only awkwardness was occasioned by the presence of Mr Freyby.

Catching my glance, the Briton raised his eyes from his book and mumbled something incomprehensible, with his pipe swaying up and down.

'I know everything,' Mademoiselle translated into Russian, pronouncing the word 'efrything'. 'My lord has told me.'

The butler stuck his nose back in his book to let us know that we need not take any notice of him.

Well then, so in England gentlemen had no secrets from their butlers. So much the better.

I briefly told my comrades about the letter, the sinister doctor and the decision that had been taken at the secret council. They heard me out in silence. It was only when I told them that Doctor Lind never returned his captives alive that Mademoiselle broke down and gasped, clenching her firm little fists above the table. To assist her in mastering her understandable agitation, I digressed briefly to talk about the remarkable self-control shown by Georgii Alexandrovich. But, as was often the case, Mademoiselle's comment took me by surprise.

'Georgii Alexandrovich has six sons from Heh Highness and two from a young ballehina. If Doctor Lind had abducted His Highness's only daughteh – O, he would have behaved quite diffehently.'

I must confess that I was flabbergasted – both by the

76

judgement itself (which might not have been entirely unjustified, since Xenia Georgievna really was Georgii Alexandrovich's favourite) and by the tactless reference to Miss Snezhnevskaya.

Foma Anikeevich changed the subject and smoothed over the awkward moment.

'Is there not anything that we servants can do, for our part?'

There you have a genuine butler – with only a few scant words he swept away the dross and defined the most important point. Compared to him we are all of us mere dwarves.

'Pardon me for saying this, Afanasii,' Foma Anikeevich continued with his unfailing politeness, 'but we are not talking here just about the life of Mikhail Georgievich, but about even more significant matters – the fate of the monarchy and of Russian statehood itself. If you take all our internal upheavals, disorder and vacillation, as well as the sovereign's obvious weakness and lack of experience, then add a blow like this, with the whole of society, the whole world looking on ... The consequences are quite unimaginable. We, the servants of the Romanovs, must not allow it to happen.'

The Japanese banged his saucer down on the table and bowed his forehead down to the tablecloth so abruptly that I was afraid he was having an apoplectic fit. But no, it turned out to be a bow. With his forehead still touching the tablecloth, the Oriental addressed Foma Anikeevich, speaking with passion.

'These words of genuine samurai, Foma-sensei, you nobur man.'

I had read that a samurai is a kind of Japanese knight, but I did not know the meaning of *sensei*. I can only assume it is some kind of respectful oriental form of address, similar in kind to *cher maître*.

Foma Anikeevich replied with a polite bow and the Japanese straightened up.

'We have to hewp my masta,' he declared in his outlandish but perfectly comprehensible Russian. 'Onry my masta can save ritter *odzi* and honow of the empia.'

'I have heard a lot about Erast Petrovich, Mr Masa,' said Foma Anikeevich. 'I believe that during the governorship of Prince Dolgorukoi here in Moscow he performed no small number of remarkable deeds.'

I had not known that Foma Anikeevich was informed about Fandorin, but was not in the least surprised.

The Japanese replied staidly: 'Yes, ver', ver' many. But that no' importan'. Importan' that my master will not wive if Dokutor Rind wive.'

It was not said in the most elegant fashion, but I understood the meaning.

Mademoiselle spoke in a different accent, far more pleasing to the ear: 'But what can he do, your master?'

'Evewyfin',' Masa said laconically. 'Master can do anyfin'. Dokutor Rind will not wive.'

'Lady, gentlemen, I propose the following ...'

It immediately went quiet, and even Mr Freyby looked up from his book, peering curiously at Foma Anikeevich over the top of his spectacles.

'Our gentlemen, unfortunately, are not on good terms with each other. That could be bad for the cause. Let us therefore agree that at least we servants will act together. We shall keep each other informed and protect His Majesty and Their Highnesses against making mistakes. Insofar as it lies in our power.'

That was how he spoke – simply and wisely.

At this point my assistant Somov stuck his head into the servants' parlour and pressed his hand to his heart as he apologised: 'Afanasii Stepanovich, gentlemen, I beg your pardon, but Her Highness is asking for Mademoiselle Declique.'

Then he bowed and withdrew.

'Ah, yes, Monsieur Ziukin,' the governess said to me. 'Poor Xenia does not know. What can I tell her?'

'Do not tell *Her Imperial Highness* about Lind's threats,' I said sternly, somewhat annoyed by such familiarity in speaking of Xenia Georgievna. 'Simply tell *Her Imperial Highness* that the kidnappers are demanding a ransom and the money will be paid.'

I believe that she left the room feeling duly chastened.

A few minutes later I had reason to regret Mademoiselle's absence, because Mr Freyby suddenly parted his lips to utter a brief phrase.

'What was that you were so good as to say?' Foma Anikeevich asked.

'He say "A spy",' Masa translated – apparently he understood English.

'A "spy" in what sense?' I asked, puzzled.

The Briton looked hopefully at Foma Anikeevich, who suddenly frowned pensively.

'Mr Freyby is quite right. There must have been a spy at work. The kidnappers were too well informed about your movements yesterday. I do not wish to upset you, Afanasii Stepanovich, but it is very probable that Doctor Lind's spy is one of your staff. Can you vouch for your servants?'

I felt the colour drain from my face.

'Not completely. I can vouch for those from St Petersburg. All of them apart from Lipps – the one who is serving us – are old and well-tried colleagues. But I have a temporary staff of nine here and I don't know the local staff at all; Somov is in charge of them.'

'Then extreme caution is required,' Luka Emelyanovich declared solemnly.

Foma Anikeevich spoke to the Englishman: 'Thank you, Mr Freyby, for a most pertinent comment.'

The English butler shrugged in incomprehension, and I remembered that I had the lexicon he had given me in my pocket.

I looked up the words and said: 'Tenk yoo, Meester Freebee.'

He nodded and stuck his nose back into his Trollope (I had looked in the library and now knew that this was the name of an English novelist).

For a while we carried on discussing the means by which we could maintain confidential contact with each other, and then the meeting was interrupted by Somov sticking his head in at the door again. From the expression on his face I realised that something out of the ordinary had happened.

I excused myself and went out into the corridor.

'Look here,' Somov said, whispering for some reason, and held out a white envelope. 'This has been found. The doorman picked it up. No one knows where it came from.'

I took the envelope and read the message in capital letters that was written on it in pencil: AVEC LES COMPLIMENTS DE DR LIND.

It cost me an incredible effort of will to maintain my composure.

'Where was it found?'

'On the porch, right outside the doors. The doorman went out to see if the rain had stopped, and it was lying there.'

That means it could have been left from the outside, I thought. They climbed over the fence and left it, very simple. That made me feel better, but only a little.

Of course, I did not open the envelope, although it was not sealed – I took it up to the first floor. If Somov had not been watching me, I would have run.

Before entering the small drawing room, I stopped and listened at the door. I always do this, but not in order to eavesdrop, only to avoid interrupting any important conversations or intimate moments by knocking.

I heard Kirill Alexandrovich's thick, angry voice speaking in the room: 'Nicky, how can you be such a blockhead! You mustn't say anything about concessions during the audience with Li Hunchan! Under no circumstances! You'll ruin everything!'

I could not help shaking my head and thinking that things could not go on like this for much longer. The sovereign was by no means as weak-willed as Their Highnesses imagined. And he had a vindictive streak.

I knocked loudly, handed over the message and immediately went back out into the corridor.

I had to wait no more than five minutes. Georgii Alexandrovich looked out and beckoned to me with his finger. His expression seemed rather strange to me.

The sovereign and the other grand dukes also looked at me in the same way – as if they were seeing me for the first time or, perhaps, as if they had only just noticed that there was a man by the name of Afanasii Stepanovich Ziukin living in the world. I did not like it at all.

'You know French, don't you?' Kirill Alexandrovich asked. 'Here, read this.'

I took the unfolded sheet of paper with a certain degree of trepidation and read:

Your terms are accepted, but the payment for each day of deferment is one million. Tomorrow at three in the afternoon your intermediary must drive along the Garden Ring Road alone, in an open carriage, from Kaluga Square in the direction of Zhitnaya Street. The money must be in a suitcase, in twenty-five-rouble treasury notes. I shall regard the slightest sign of foul play from your side as releasing me from all commitments and shall return the prince to you as promised — in pieces.

One final thing. The intermediary must be the servant who was in the park: with a wart on his cheek and the doggy sideburns.

Yours sincerely,
Doctor Lind

The first response I felt was resentment. *Favoris de chien?*[1] How dare he call my well-groomed whiskers that?

It was only afterwards that the full, frightening meaning of the message struck me.

---

[1] *Doggy sideburns.*

8 May

Following long telephone conversations between the Petrovsky Palace, the governor general's residence and the Hermitage, control of the operation was entrusted to Colonel Karnovich. The high police master of Moscow was instructed to provide every possible assistance, while Fandorin was assigned the rather indefinite role of adviser, and even then only at the stubborn insistence of Georgii Alexandrovich who, following the rescue of his daughter, believed fervently in the exceptional qualities of the retired deputy for special assignments.

Like everyone else, I knew very little about Karnovich, because this mysterious man had only made his appearance at the foot of the throne very recently. He was not obviously fitted for this responsible, indeed one might say crucially important, post either by age, or rank or social connection, especially since before this exalted appointment Karnovich had performed the modest duties of head of one of the provincial offices of gendarmes. However, following the sensational exposure of an anarchist terrorist organisation, people had begun speaking of the colonel as the rising star in the field of political detective work, and soon this quiet, unprepossessing gentleman, who always kept his eyes hidden behind blue-tinted spectacles, was the head of His Majesty's bodyguard – a truly prodigious advancement which did not endear Karnovich to the members of the court. But then, when had the head of the court police, who, by the very nature of his job, is exceptionally well informed about the weaknesses and secrets of individuals who stand close to the throne, ever enjoyed the sympathy of the court? Such is the nature of the job.

In contrast, High Police Master Lasovsky was very well known, a figure of almost legendary status in both capital cities. The St Petersburg newspapers loved to describe the eccentric and despotic behaviour of this modern-day Ivan the Terrible (the Moscow papers did not dare): his love of driving round the streets in the famous police master's carriage with the finest horses in the entire city, his particular enthusiasm for the fire brigade, his exceptional strictness with yard keepers and his famous orders, printed every day in the *Moscow Municipal Police Gazette*. That very morning, on the front page of this remarkable newspaper, I myself had read the following order:

While driving out on 7 May I observed the following: on Voskresenskaya Square opposite the Bolshaya Moskva hotel I detected the foul odour of rotting herrings that had not been cleared away by the yard keepers; at 5.45 a.m. two nightwatchmen standing by the Triumphal Gates were making idle conversation; at 1.20 in the afternoon the constable was not at his post on the corner of Bolshay Tverskaya-Yamskaya Street and the Triumphal Gates Square: at 10 p.m. on the corner of Tverskaya Street and Voskresenskaya Square, the constable stepped up on to the pavement and began arguing with a cab driver.

I hereby order all the guilty constables, watchmen and yard keepers to be arrested and fined.

Acting High Police Master of
Moscow, Colonel Lasovsky

Of course, the head of police in a city of a million people ought not to concern himself with such petty matters, but in my view we could well introduce some of Moscow's innovations in St Petersburg. For instance, we could station constables at crossroads in order to direct the movement of carriages – on Nevsky Prospect and the embankments the crush is so thick that you cannot pass either on foot or in a vehicle. And it would also be a good idea to follow the example of Moscow and forbid cab drivers to swear and drive unwashed carriages on pain of a fine.

But Colonel Lasovsky's temperament was genuinely gruff and whimsical, as I had the opportunity to observe during the briefing meeting before the beginning of the operation.

Although my main supervisor was Karnovich, the high police master constantly interrupted with his own remarks, and his entire manner suggested that he, Lasovsky, and not the upstart from out of town was the true master in the old city. Arguments flared up repeatedly between the two colonels as to whether one ought to arrest the doctor's messenger when he came for the money: the Moscow colonel was emphatically in favour of an immediate arrest and swore he would shake the son of a bitch's very soul out of him, together with the rest of his innards, while the colonel from Tsarskoe Selo spoke no less emphatically in support of caution and emphasised the threat to Mikhail Georgievich's life. Fandorin was present in the drawing room, but he did not get involved in the argument.

Karnovich took a number of measures that appeared very sensible to me. Three disguised carriages with police agents in civilian dress were to drive ahead of my carriage. The agents would all be from the court police – fine strapping young men. Their task would not be to seize Lind's messenger, but to 'sit on his tail' (as the colonel put it) and 'tail' him to the kidnappers' lair. In addition, since the previous evening a special group of treasury officials had been engaged in copying out the numbers of all the banknotes to be handed over to Lind, each of these would then leave its own trail to be followed.

My task appeared simple: to drive without hurrying along the Garden Ring Road and wait for the villains to show themselves, then demand that their man take me to His Highness, and until I saw Mikhail Georgievich alive and well, not to let them have the suitcase under any circumstances. If the bandit or bandits used force, the disguised agents would intervene.

'You should grab the fellow by the scruff of the neck straight away,' the stubborn police master repeated for probably the tenth time already. 'And hand him over to me. After I've had a talk with him, there'll be no need to sit on his tail. He'll tell you everything you want to know and show you everything you want to see. But you, Mr Colonel, are trying to be too clever by half and making a mess of things.'

Karnovich nervously adjusted his spectacles, but he vented his irritation on Fandorin instead of his Moscow colleague.

'Listen here, sir, what use to me is an adviser who never opens his mouth? Do you have any thoughts?'

Fandorin sceptically raised one eyebrow, as elegant as if it were painted on.

'Lind is very cunning and inventive. He can guess all the actions that you might take in advance. And copying out the numbers of the banknotes is simply a joke. Are you really going to hang up lists of forty thousand seven-digit numbers in all the shops and bureaux de change?' He turned to address me. 'The most important thing depends on you, Ziukin. Acute observation, attention to the most minute details – that is what is required. Remember that today is only the first meeting; there are at least six more to come. All you need to do now is get a good look at things. And as for a tail,' he said, speaking to Karnovich now, 'it can be tried, but don't push too hard, otherwise we'll be handed a corpse.'

'A most valuable recommendation, *merci*,' the head of the court police replied with a sardonic bow. 'Are you intending to pay the respected doctor a million roubles six more times? Are you not perhaps receiving a commission from Dr Lind for giving such advice?'

Fandorin got up and walked out without saying anything in reply.

'That's the one we ought to put a tail on,' Lasovsky hissed in the direction of the door after it closed. 'A highly suspicious individual.'

'If the need arises, we will,' Karnovich promised. 'He really is a most disagreeable fellow.'

I shared this judgement with all my heart, for my view of Mr Fandorin, who had initially produced a positive impression on me, had changed completely. And with good reason.

The first half of the day had dragged by at a distressingly slow pace. While the higher spheres were arguing over which department would head the operation, everyone had left me alone, and I was tormented by both alarm and inactivity. Owing to my forthcoming responsible assignment I was released from my usual responsibilities, which were transferred to Somov. Georgii Alexandrovich said that only one thing was required from those of us who were privy to the secret: not to let anything show and to maintain an air of serene imperturbability. Endlung was given the task of cheering up the dejected Pavel Georgievich. In order to perform this important mission, the lieutenant was given a certain sum of money. He adopted an exceptionally brisk and lively air, put his ward in a carriage first thing in the morning and drove him off to the gypsy restaurant at Tsaritsyno – for a 'razzle' as Endlung put it.

His Highness entrusted Xenia Georgievna to me, and my task did not appear to be simple. The grand princess came down to breakfast with red eyes, looking pale and sad, and that evening she would have several visits to make and then drive to the Petrovsky Palace for supper and a serenade in a narrow circle.

Georgii Alexandrovich consulted me on what should be done, and we came to the conclusion that the most effective way of dispelling melancholy was physical exercise. Let her play tennis, His Highness decreed, since the day had turned out dry, if overcast. After that he dressed in civilian clothes and left on some business that I did not know about, having instructed me to arrange the game.

'But Afanasii, with whom can I play?' Xenia Georgievna asked.

Indeed, as it turned out, there were no partners for Her Highness. On instructions from Simeon Alexandrovich, Prince Glinsky had called for the Englishmen and driven them to Sokolniki Park to go riding, and from there to lunch at the governor general's residence. Remembering the interest that His Highness had taken in the elegant Mr Carr the previous day, I felt alarmed, but not greatly so, since I had more serious concerns on my mind.

After thinking for a little while, Xenia Georgievna said: 'Go to Erast Petrovich and ask him. There isn't anyone else, after all.'

So I went to Fandorin's room. Before knocking, I listened at the door and heard very strange sounds: dull blows, loud snorts and the jangling of glass. Alarmed, I knocked gently and opened the door slightly.

The sight that met my eyes was amazing. Mr Fandorin and Mr Masa, both wearing nothing but white underpants, were performing some strange kind of ritual, taking turns to run, jump to a quite incredible height and strike the wall with one foot, which was the cause of the jangling sound that had frightened me. Erast Petrovich performed this outlandish exercise in total silence, but his servant panted and snorted, and after each attack on the wall, he did not simply bounce back, but tumbled across the floor like a ball.

'What can ... I do for you?' Fandorin enquired jerkily, interrupting his question halfway through for another blow.

A good butler is never surprised by anything. And if he is, then he does not show it. So I simply bowed as if everything was perfectly normal and conveyed Xenia Georgievna's request.

'Thank Her Highness for the honour,' he replied, wiping away his sweat, 'but I do not know how to play tennis.'

I went back to the grand princess, but she had already changed into a loose-fitting tennis dress and white shoes.

She was very upset by Fandorin's refusal: 'What am I supposed to do, serve the ball to myself? Ask him anyway. Say I'll teach him.'

There were tears in her eyes.

I hurried back to Fandorin and this time I asked him properly, and also mentioned Georgii Alexandrovich's instructions to me.

Erast Petrovich sighed and gave way. In an instant I brought him Pavel Georgievich's tennis clothes, which were almost a perfect fit, except for being a little tight in the shoulders.

The lesson began. I watched from the side of the net, since I had nothing to busy myself with. Soon I was joined by Masa, and a little later Mr Freyby also came out, attracted by the sound of a bouncing ball, so enchanting to the English ear.

Fandorin proved to be a rather good pupil and after a quarter of an hour the ball was already flying backwards and forwards over the net as many as ten times in a row. Xenia Georgievna became more cheerful, roses appeared in her cheeks and a few strands of light hair crept out from under her hat – she was a joy to look at. Her partner was also a fine sight. He held the racket wrongly and struck the ball powerfully, as if he were slashing with a sabre, but his movements around the court were agile, and it must be admitted that he looked very handsome.

'They make a lovely couple, don't they?' said Mr Freyby.

'Beootifur per,' Masa translated succcinctly.

I was astounded by this remark and attributed it to a distortion of meaning in the translation. Of course, Mr Fandorin could not possible make a 'pair' with Her Highness, not in any sense of the word. However, after those words of Mr Freyby's I looked more closely at Xenia Georgievna and for the first time, as the common folk say, felt a cat scratching at my soul. I had never seen Her Highness look so radiant, not even before her first 'grown-up' ball.

'That's all now, Erast Petrovich, no more time-wasting!' she shouted. 'You already know enough for us to play one game keeping score. The rules are very simple. I'll serve, because you don't know how to anyway. First I'll hit the ball into this square, then into that one, and so on by turns until the game is won. And you hit it back, only into the court. Is that clear? The loser will crawl under the net. And I'll ask the Englishman to be umpire.'

She spoke to Mr Freyby in English and he bowed with a serious air and walked up to the net. However before signalling for the game to start, he turned to us and said something.

'He want bet,' Masa explained, and sparks of mischief glinted in his little eyes. 'Two to one on rady.'

'On the what?' I asked, mystified.

'On young rady,' the Japanese replied impatiently and then he also started babbling away in English, pointing to his master and to Her Highness by turns.

'All right,' the Briton agreed. 'Five to one.'

Masa translated.

With a despairing sigh, he took a brightly coloured wallet out from somewhere under his clothes, showed Mr Freyby a five-rouble note and put it down on the bench.

The Englishman immediately took out a squeaky wallet of fine leather and extracted a twenty-five-rouble note from it.

'What about you, Mr Ziukin?' he asked, and I understood that without any translation.

To my mind the idea of betting was not entirely decent, but as Georgii Alexandrovich was leaving, he had ordered me: 'Fun and relaxation, Afanasii. I am relying on you.' So I decided to behave in a relaxed fashion.

And anyway, the bet looked like a certainty. Xenia Georgievna had been exceptionally flexible and agile ever since she was a child, and there was no one among the ladies who could match her at tennis. And not just among the ladies, either – I had often seen her outplay Pavel Georgievich, and Endlung, while Fandorin had never even held a racket before today. Masa could only have bet on his master out of a sense of loyalty. I have heard that among Japanese servants loyalty extends to a fanaticism that knows no bounds. They write (I do not know if it is true) that a

89

Japanese servant will rather rip open his own stomach than fail his master. Such self-sacrifice, in the spirit of the butler Vatelle, who fell on his own sword when the fish dish was not served in time, cannot occasion anything but respect. However, the spilling of one's own intestines on a polished parquet floor is an act that is quite inconceivable in a respectable house.

I began feeling curious as to how far the Japanese valet's self-sacrifice extended. I happened to have exactly fifty roubles in my purse, set aside to be deposited in my savings account at the bank. I took out the notes and put them in the same place on the bench.

To give the Japanese his due, he didn't turn a hair. He took another ten-rouble note out of his wallet, and then Mr Freyby shouted: 'Go!'

I knew the rules of the game very well, so I did not need to pay attention to what the Englishman shouted.

Xenia Georgievna arched over gracefully and served the ball so powerfully that Fandorin barely managed to get his racket in the way. The ball flew off at an angle, caught the top of the net, hesitated for a while over which way to fall, then tumbled over on Her Highness's side.

Love–fifteen to Erast Petrovich. He was lucky.

Her Highness moved to the other side of the court and hit a very tricky serve with a powerful swerve, then ran rapidly up to the net, knowing in advance where her opponent would return the ball – if he returned it at all.

Fandorin did return it, but so powerfully that the ball would certainly have flown out of the court if only it hadn't struck Her Highness on the forehead.

Xenia Georgievna looked rather shaken, and Fandorin seemed frightened. He dashed to the net and applied a handkerchief to Her Highness's forehead.

'It's all right, it's nothing,' she murmured, holding Fandorin's wrist. 'It doesn't hurt at all. You are a lucky beggar, though. Love–thirty. But now I'll show you.'

The third serve was one of those that are quite impossible to get. I didn't even see the ball properly – only a streak of lightning that flashed above the court. By some miracle Fandorin managed to catch the ball with his racket, but extremely awkwardly: the small white sphere flew up onto the air and began falling back down straight onto the net.

Xenia Georgievna ran forward with a triumphant exclamation, prepared to hammer the ball into the court. She swung and smashed the ball hard, and once again it caught the top of the net, only this time it did not tumble over on to the opponent's side, but fell back to Her Highness's feet

The grand princess's face expressed confusion at the strange way the game was turning out. No doubt it was this confusion that caused Her Highness to miss twice on her last serve, a thing that had never happened before, and the game was lost 'to love', as the sportsmen say.

I felt my first twinge of dislike for Fandorin as his valet coolly stuffed his substantial winnings into his bright-coloured purse. It would take me quite a while to get used to the idea of losing fifty roubles in such an absurd fashion.

And I did not like the scene that was now played out on court at all.

As it had been agreed that the losing party would do, Her Highness went down on all fours and crawled under the net. Fandorin bent down hastily to help Xenia Georgievna get up. She looked up at him and she froze in that absurd pose. Embarrassed, Erast Petrovich took her by the hand and pulled, but too strongly – the grand princess fell against him with her chest and her hat went flying to the ground, taking her hairpins with it, so that her thick locks scattered loose across her shoulders.

'I beg your pardon,' Fandorin mumbled. 'Thank you for the lesson. I must be going.'

He bowed awkwardly and strode off towards the house, with the Japanese waddling after him.

'Lucky devil,' said Mr Freyby.

Then he translated it:

'*S-cha-stlivy . . . chort.*'

And he began counting the money remaining in his wallet with an obvious air of regret.

But I was no longer thinking about the money I had lost. My heart was wrung by a feeling of alarm and a sense of foreboding.

Ah, how Xenia Georgievna gazed after Fandorin as he moved away from her! The cunning beast walked as if nothing at all had happened and only looked round at the very last moment – just before he turned the corner. He glanced briefly at Her Highness and immediately turned away. A low trick, very low, perfectly calculated for its effect on a young, inexperienced girl!

The grand princess flushed bright red at that lightning-fast glance, and I realised that something monstrous, something quite scandalous had occurred – one of those events that shake the very foundations of the monarchy. An individual of the imperial blood had fallen in love with a person who was inappropriate. There could be no mistake about it, although I can certainly not be considered an expert on the subject of women and their feelings.

Afanasii is an old bachelor and will evidently remain one. Our honourable dynasty is destined to end with me because, although I have a brother, he has forfeited the right to continue the Ziukin line of court servants.

My father, Stepan Filimonovich, and before him his father, Filimon Emelyanovich, were married at the age of seventeen to girls from similar court servant families and at the age of eighteen they had already produced their eldest sons. God grant to every-one the respect and love in which they lived with their spouses. But with me our family's good fortune faltered and stumbled. The Ziukins will die out because I was given a feeble soul incap-able of love.

I have not known love for the female sex. Adoration, though, is a different matter: I experienced that feeling when I was still a youth, and it was so powerful that afterwards I seemed to have no strength left for ordinary love.

From the age of fourteen I was a servant at a certain grand-ducal house too well known for me to name it. One of the grand princesses, whose name I will also not mention, was the same age as myself, and I often accompanied her when she went riding. In all my life since then I have never met a girl or a lady who could even remotely compare with Her Highness – not in beauty, although the grand princess was quite indescribably lovely, but in that special glow that radiated from her face and her entire person. I cannot explain it any better than that, but I saw that radiance quite clearly, as others see the moon's rays or the light from a lamp.

I do not recall ever making conversation with Her Highness or asking her a question. I simply dashed to carry out any order that she deigned to give me without saying a word. In those years my life consisted of days that happened and days that somehow didn't. When I saw her, it was a good day; when I did not see her, it was as if there was no day, nothing but blackness.

She must have thought that I was dumb, and she either pitied or simply grew used to me, but sometimes she would look at me with such an affectionate smile that I simply froze. It happened once during a horse race through the forest. Her Highness looked round at me and then smiled in that way, and in my happiness I let go of my reins. When I came round I was lying on the ground with everything swimming around me and Her Highness's radiant face bending down over me, with tears in her eyes. I believe that was the happiest moment in my entire life.

I was a boy servant at that court for two years, seven months and four days, and then the grand princess was married to a German prince, and she went away. It did not happen all at once – in imperial households marriages are arranged slowly – and all that time I had only one dream – to be among the staff of servants that would go to Germany with Her Highness. There was a vacancy for a junior footman.

But it did not happen. My father, the wise man, would not allow it.

I never saw Her Highness again. But at Christmas that year I received a letter she had written to me in her own hand. I still keep it to this day, with my parents' wedding rings and my bank book, but I never open it to look at it – I know it off by heart in any case. It is not even a letter really, more of a note. Her Highness sent one like it to all her former servants who had stayed at home.

Dear Afanasii

All is well with me, and soon I shall have a little baby – a son or a daughter. I often remember our rides together. Do you remember the time you fell and I thought you had been killed? Not long ago I dreamed of you, and you were not a servant but a prince, and you told me something very happy and very nice, only I don't remember what it was.

Be happy, Afanasii, and remember me sometimes.

That was the letter that I received from her. But there were no more letters because Her Highness passed away during her first labour and for almost thirty years now she has been with the angels, which is certainly a more suitable place for her than our sinful earth.

And so my father was proved right all round, although for a long time, right up until his death, I was unable to forgive him for not letting me go to Germany. Soon after Her Highness's departure I turned seventeen, and my parents wished to marry me to the daughter of the senior doorman at the Anichkov Palace. She was a fine girl, but I would have nothing of it. Despite my equable and accommodating character, I would sometimes be overcome by stubbornness like that. My father struggled and struggled with me, and then finally gave up. He thought that in time I would come to my senses. And so I did, but I never did feel the desire for family life.

And that is the best way for a genuine butler – there is nothing to distract you from serving. Foma Anikeevich is not married either. And as for the legendary Prokop Sviridovich, although he had a wife and children, he kept them in the country and only visited them twice a year – at Christmas and at Easter.

A genuine butler knows that his service is not a duty but a way of life. It is not a matter of being a butler from morning until evening and then going home and simply being Afanasii Ziukin. A butler is like a nobleman, they both serve at court, only we are a lot stricter with ourselves than the nobility. That is what makes us worth so much.

Many people would like to lure away a genuine butler from the court of the tsar or a grand duke and they have been known to offer huge amounts of money. Any rich man is flattered to have his own home ordered in the same manner as the imperial palaces. My own brother Frol could not resist the temptation: he felt flattered by a handsome offer . . . Now he serves as a butler – no, they call it a major domo – for a Moscow millionaire, the banker Litvinov, a Jew. Frol was given five thousand for making the move and three thousand a year, all found, with an apartment and gratuities. There was a butler once, but no more.

I severed all relations with my brother. And he does not bother me either – he understands the sin he has committed. And never mind millionaires, I would not even go to Prince Borontsov, although he offered me everything you could possibly imagine. One can only serve someone with whom one will not compare oneself. Distance is required. Because on one side there is the human, and on the other side the divine. Distance will always help to maintain respect. Even when one discovers Georgii Alexandrovich in the black chef Manefa's little room or when Pavel Georgievich, unconscious and covered in vomit, is delivered home by cab in the middle of the night. But who is Prince Borontsov – merely a noble, and what is so special about that?

Even we Ziukins were nobles once, although not for long.

This is an unusual story concerning one of our ancestors, my great-grandfather Emelyan Ziukin. I think it is probably worth telling – it is highly edifying, since it demonstrates once again that the foundation of the world is the established order, and God forbid that one should disrupt this order – no good will ever come of it in any case.

The Ziukins have their origins among the serfs of the Zvenigorod district of the province of Moscow. My ancestor, Emelyan Silanti-evich – at that time simply Emelka – was taken as a child to serve the master and his family, and his quick wit and efficiency made him well-liked, so that after a while they began treating him specially: they dressed him in clean clothes, kept him away from dirty work and taught him to read and write. He was attached to the young master as a kind of play friend. He read a lot of books, picked up some manners and even learned a certain amount of French, but the worst thing was that he started to feel ashamed of being a serf. And I believe that is why he started looking at the young lady of the house, the landowner's daughter, not as one looks at a grand princess, with reverential devotion, but with the most audacious of intentions: he was determined to marry the object of his interest. You might think, who has ever heard of a peasant boy marrying a noblewoman? Anyone else would have dreamed for a while and then given up, but Emelyan was a stubborn character – he thought a lot and planned a long way ahead and, as they would say nowadays, he believed in his star.

He did not tell a single living soul about his dream (although one could call it a plan, not a dream), especially not the young lady, but when recruits were being enlisted – they were fighting the French at the time – he suddenly asked to go for a soldier instead of the miller's son, whose name had been drawn in the lottery. Emelyan was not yet old enough, but he was a fine strapping lad, and he added a year or two to his age. He was willingly let go, because by that time he had become insolent and disobedient – the master and his family no longer knew what to do with him.

So my great-grandfather put on a soldier's uniform and took a payment in compensation from the miller, the richest man in the village, of seven hundred roubles in paper money, which he didn't give to his father but put in the bank in his own name. That was in order to carry out his plan.

Emelyan was sent straight to the war, to fight in the Austrian campaign, and he fought for seven or eight years without a break – against the French and the Persians and the Swedes and the Turks and then the French again. He found his way into the very hottest spots and always volunteered for every desperate adventure. He was wounded many times and awarded medals, won a corporal's stripes, and still that was not enough for him. And in the campaign of 1812, at the battle of Smolensk, when all the commanders in his company were killed, Emelyan won his cherished reward: General Bagration himself kissed him and promoted him to officer's rank, something that almost never happened in those times.

After that Emelyan Ziukin fought for another two years and went as far as Paris with the army, but as soon as the armistice came, he asked for extended leave, although he was regarded most highly by his superiors and could have hoped for further advancement in the army. But my great-grandfather wanted something else – his impossibly bold plan was finally coming close to fulfilment.

Emelyan returned to his native parts not simply as a nobleman and a lieutenant in the grenadiers, he also had his own small capital, because in all those years he had not spent his pay, and when he was discharged he received bonuses and medical payments, and his initial seven hundred roubles had also almost doubled owing to accrued interest.

And in his home village everything could not have gone better. The estate had been burned by the French, so that the master and his family were absolutely ruined and now lived in the priest's house. The young master, Emelyan's former playmate, had been killed at Borodino, and the maiden who had inspired my great-grandfather to play his desperate game with fate had been left without a bridegroom, for he had laid down his life at Leipzig. All in all, Emelyan appeared to the object of his dreams almost in the guise of an angel sent to rescue her.

He presented himself at the priest's log-built village but in his dress uniform, wearing his medals. The young lady came out in an old patched dress, and the trials she had suffered had spoiled her looks, so that he did not recognise her immediately. But that did not matter to him, because it was not the young lady he loved but his own impossible dream.

Only nothing came of it. The young lady greeted him affectionately enough at first – she was delighted to see an old acquaintance – but she replied to the offer of his hand and his heart with an insulting amazement, and said she would rather live under sufferance with her relatives than ever become 'Mrs Ziukin'.

These words clouded Emelyan's reason. He had never drunk intoxicating liquor before in his life, but now he launched into a wild binge, and it ended very badly. In his drunken state he tore off his epaulettes and medals in public and trampled them into the ground, all the while bawling out an incoherent stream of words. He was tried for bringing disgrace on the uniform, stripped of his officer's rank and expelled from the nobility. He would have been completely destroyed by drink but, by a fortunate chance, he was spotted by his former regimental commander, Prince Drubetskoi, who took pity on the down-and-out and for the sake of his former meritorious services found him a place as a manservant at Tsarskoe Selo.

And so the fate of our family line was decided.

When an individual of low origins cherishes inadmissible dreams regarding a person of higher standing, this is deplorable and even perhaps outrageous, but not really so very dangerous for, as they say, a wicked cow has short horns. But an infatuation that runs in the opposite direction, not up from below but down from above, is fraught with far-reaching consequences. The case of Grand Duke Dmitrii Nikolaevich is still fresh in everyone's memory. He defied the tsar's will and married a divorced lady, for which he was banished from the empire. And we court servants also know that when the present tsar was still the tsarevich, he begged his august father with tears in his eyes to release him from succeeding to the throne and allow a marriage beneath his station to the ballerina Snezhnevskaya. That had everybody trembling, but any damage was prevented by the grace of the Lord and the abrupt temperament of the late tsar.

Therefore, the sense of alarm that came over me following that infamous game of tennis is entirely understandable, especially since Xenia Georgievna already had a fiancé in the shape of a Scandinavian prince with good prospects of becoming king (everybody knew that his elder brother, the heir to the throne, had consumption).

I needed urgently to consult someone who understood the workings of a young girl's emotions, for I myself, as must be clear from what has already been said, can not consider myself an authority in such matters. After long hesitation, I decided to take Mademoiselle Declique into my confidence and I informed her of my apprehensions in the most general and delicate of terms. Mademoiselle nonetheless understood me perfectly well and – to my dismay – was not at all surprised, indeed she took what I said in a spirit of quite incredible frivolity.

'Yes, yes,' she said, nodding absent-mindedly. 'I noticed that too. He is a handsome man, and she is at that age. It is all right. Let Xenia know a little love before they put her in a glass case.'

'How can you say such a thing!' I exclaimed in horror. 'Her Highness is already engaged!'

'Ah, Monsieur Ziukin, I saw her fiancé Prince Olaf, in Vienna,' Mademoiselle said, wrinkling up her nose. 'What was that folk saying you taught me . . . one of God's own fools, yes?'

'But if the elder brother should die – and everyone knows that he is consumptive – Prince Olaf will be first in line to inherit the throne. Which means that Xenia Georgievna could be a queen!'

Of course, the governess's remark that I found so jarring should be attributed to her state of dejection. I had noticed that Mademoiselle was absent that morning and believed I had guessed why. No doubt, with her active and energetic temperament, she had been unable simply to do nothing and had attempted to undertake some searches of her own. But what could she do in a foreign country and an unfamiliar city when even the police felt helpless?

Mademoiselle had returned looking so tired and miserable that it pained me to look at her. And it was partly because of this that I began the conversation about the subject of my concern – in a desire to distract her from her thoughts about the little grand duke. In order to calm her a little, I told her the direction that things had taken and mentioned the responsible mission that had fallen to my lot – naturally without any undue inflation of my own role in matters.

I had expected Mademoiselle to be delighted by the news that now there was a glimmer of hope, but after hearing me out she looked at me with a strange, frightened expression and suddenly said: 'But that is very dangerous.' And turning her eyes away, she added: 'I know you are brave . . . but don't be too brave, all right?'

I was quite nonplussed by that, and there was a rather uncomfortable pause.

'Ah, what bad luck,' I eventually said to recover the situation. 'It has started raining again. And the combined choir serenade for Their Imperial Majesties is set for this evening. The rain could spoil everything.'

'You'd better think of yourself. You have to ride in an open carriage,' Mademoiselle said in a quiet voice, pronouncing the final phrase almost perfectly. 'It's very easy to catch cold.'

When I drove out through the gate in the gig with the top back, the rain was already lashing down in earnest and I was soaked through before I even reached Kaluga Square. That was bad enough, but in the stream of carriages rolling along Korovii Val Street, I was the only person behaving in this intrepid manner, which must have appeared strange to any onlookers. Why would a respectable-looking man with a large moustache and whiskers not wish to put up the leather hood on his carriage? The water was streaming off the sides of my bowler hat, and my face was inundated too, while my fine tweed suit clung to me like a wet sack. But how else would Doctor Lind's people have been able to recognise me?

Standing at my feet was a heavy suitcase stuffed full of twenty-five-rouble notes. Colonel Karnovich's agents were driving in front of me and behind me, maintaining a cautious distance. I was in a strangely calm state of mind and did not feel any fear or excitement – my nerves had probably been numbed by the long wait and the damp.

I did not dare to look round, for my instructions had strictly forbidden it, but I did glance to the sides every now and then, examining the occasional pedestrian passers-by. Half an hour before I left, Foma Anikeevich had telephoned me and said: 'Mr Lasovsky has decided to take measures of his own. I heard him reporting to His Highness. He has positioned his sleuths from Kaluga Square all the way down to the Moscow River, spaced fifty paces apart, and told them to stay alert and arrest anyone who comes close to your carriage. I am afraid this might put Mikhail Georgievich in danger.'

I had no difficulty in spotting the sleuths – who, apart from them, would be out strolling with such an air of boredom in a downpour like this? Except for these gentlemen with identical black umbrellas there was almost no one on the pavements. There were just carriages driving in both directions, crowded close together, almost wheel-to-wheel. After Zatsepsky Val Street

(I read the name on the street sign) a priest came up beside me in an old rattletrap of a carriage with its tarpaulin cover up. He was in a ferocious mood, in a hurry to get somewhere, and he kept shouting at the driver in front: 'Come on, get a move on, servant of God!' But how can anyone get a move on when he's stuck behind a solid line of carriages, wagons, charabancs and omnibuses?

We crossed a little river or canal, then a river that was a bit wider. The chain of sleuths had ended long ago, and still no one had hailed me. I was already quite convinced that Lind had spotted the police agents and decided to call the meeting off. The flow of traffic halted at a wide crossroads, with a constable in a long oilskin raincoat whistling frantically as he gave right of way to traffic from the street crossing ours. The newspaper boys took advantage of the hold-up and darted in between the carriages, screeching: *'One-Kopeck News!'*, *'Moscow Gazette!'*, *'Russian Word!'*

One of them, with a flaxen forelock stuck to his forehead and a plush shirt turned dark by the rain hanging outside his trousers, suddenly grabbed hold of my carriage shaft with one hand and adroitly plumped himself down beside me on the seat. He was so small and so nimble that probably no one in the carriages behind had noticed him through the curtain of rain.

'Turn right, Mister,' the little lad said, nudging me in the side with his elbow. 'And orders are not to turn your head.'

I wanted very much to look back to see if the police agents had missed this unexpected messenger, but I did not dare. They would see me take the turn anyway.

I pulled the reins to the right, cracked the whip, and the horse turned into a slanting side street that looked most respectable, with fine stone houses.

'Move on, Mister, move on!' the boy cried, looking back. 'Come on now!'

He grabbed the whip from me, gave a wild whistle, lashed the chestnut horse, and it started clopping its hooves over the cobblestones for all it was worth.

'Turn in there!' said my guide, jabbing one finger to the left.

We went flying into a street that was a bit smaller and less grand, hurtled past one block of buildings and took another turn. Then another, and another.

'Go that way, into the gateway,' the newspaper boy ordered.

I pulled back slightly on the reins, and we drove into a dark narrow archway.

Less than half a minute later two carriages carrying police agents went rumbling and clattering past, and then all was quiet except for the splashing of the rain as it lashed even harder against the surface of the road.

'And what now?' I asked, taking a cautious look at the messenger.

'Wait,' he said grandly, blowing on his chilly hands.

It was clear that I could not expect any help from the court police and I would have to fend for myself. But I was not afraid, for I could deal with an opponent like this on my own. A small boy was no problem. Grab him by his skinny shoulders, give him a good shaking and he would tell me who had sent him. Then I could follow the trail.

Then I took a better look at the little fellow, noting the swollen mouth not at all like a child's and the screwed-up eyes. A wild wolf cub, a real wolf cub. One could never shake the truth out of a boy like that.

Suddenly I heard the sound of another carriage approaching in the distance. I craned my neck to look, and the boy immediately took his chance. I heard a rustling sound and when I looked back I saw there was no longer anyone beside me – there was nothing but a blurred smear on the wet seat.

The rumbling was very close now. I jumped down off the coach box, ran out of the archway to the pavement and saw a foursome of sturdy blacks pulling a carriage with all the curtains tightly closed at a spanking pace. The driver had a hood lowered over his face and he was cracking a long whip loudly over the gleaming backs of the horses. When the carriage drew abreast of the archway, the curtains suddenly parted and there in front of me I saw His Highness's pale little face framed in golden curls and that familiar sailor's hat with the red pompom.

Mikhail Georgievich also saw me and started shouting loudly: 'Afon! Afon!'

That was what he had always called me.

I tried to shout too and I opened my mouth, but only sobbed.

Lord, what was I to do?

The tricky procedure of backing the gig out of the gateway would take me too long. Not even realising what I was doing in my agitation, I dashed after the carriage as fast as I could run. I did not even notice when the wet bowler hat went flying off my head.

'Stop!' I shouted. 'Stop!'

I could see the driver's round hat above the roof of the carriage, and his flailing whip.

I had never run like that before in all my life, not even during my time as a court outrunner.

Of course, there was no way I could have caught a team of four horses if the street had not suddenly taken a tight bend. The carriage slowed down, heeling over slightly to one side. I took several huge bounds to reduce the distance, jumped and clung onto the luggage rack with both hands. I pulled myself up and was just on the point of climbing onto the monkey board, but the driver, without even looking round, lashed his whip back over the roof, stinging my temple, and I fell off. I landed face down in a puddle and then rolled across it, sending up a fountain of spray. When I lifted myself up on my hands the carriage was already turning a corner.

I limped back to the gig, wiping my dirty face with my sleeve, but when I got there the suitcase of money was gone.

9 May

The ceremonial procession had already passed the Triumphal Gates when I jumped out of my hired carriage, panting hard and streaming with sweat, and started working away brusquely with my elbows to force my way through the dense crowd lining both sides of Bolshaya Tverskaya-Yamskaya Street.

There were cordons of troops along the edge of the roadway and I squeezed my way through as close as possible to an officer, attempting as I went to extract from my pocket the decorative cardboard ticket that gave me the right to take part in the procession. But that proved to be far from simple, for in the crush it was not possible for me to straighten out my elbows. I realised that I would have to wait until the sovereign passed by and then slip through into the tail of the column.

There was a festive, radiant sun in the sky – for the first time after so many overcast days. The air was filled with the pealing of bells and shouts of 'Hoorah!'

The emperor was making his ceremonial entry into the old capital, following the route from the suburban Petrovsky Palace to the Kremlin.

There were twelve horse gendarmes riding huge stallions at the front of the procession, and a mocking voice behind my back said rather loudly: '*C'est symbolique, n'est-ce pas?*[1] It's easy enough to see who's in charge in Russia.'

---

[1] *Symbolic, isn't it?*

I looked round and saw two students gazing in disgust at the parade through the spectacles on their smug faces.

Behind the gendarmes came the Cossacks of the the imperial escort, swaying in their saddles, with the silver embroidery of their crimson Circassian coats glittering in the sun.

'And they've got their whips too,' the same voice remarked.

Then the Don Cossacks rode past in a rather untidy square, followed by a deputation from the Asiatic subjects of the empire, dressed in their colourful costumes, riding without any formation whatever, with carpets for saddles on their slim-legged, prancing steeds. I recognised the Emir of Bukhara and the Khan of Khiva, both wearing medals and gold general's epaulettes, which looked strange on their Central Asian robes.

I still had a long time to wait. A long procession of representatives of the nobility passed by in their full-dress uniforms, and behind them came Head of the Bedchamber Bulkin, who was leading the court servants: footmen, blackamoors in turbans, Cossacks of the bedchamber. Then at last the people on the balconies decorated with flags and garlands began cheering, waving their hands and scarves, and the spectators pressed forward, stretching the cables taut, and I guessed that the central core of the column was approaching.

His Majesty was riding alone, looking most impressive in his Semyonovsky regimental uniform. His graceful snow-white mare Norma twitched her slim ears sensitively and squinted to one side and the other with her moist black eyes, but her ceremonial stride never faltered. The tsar's face was motionless, frozen in a fixed smile. His white-gloved right hand was suspended beside his temple in a martial salute while his left hand toyed gently with the gilded bridle.

I waited for the grand dukes to pass by, and also the open landaus with Their Majesties the dowager and reigning empresses, and then showed my pass to the cordon and ran hastily across the open space.

Finding myself in the column of senators walking on foot, I made my way into the very centre, as far away as possible from the public gaze, and then started zigzagging my way forward, muttering my apologies as I slipped through. The important gentlemen, many of whom I knew by sight, glanced in bewilderment at this ignorant fellow in the green livery of the house of the Georgieviches, but I had no time to be concerned about the proprieties. The letter from Doctor Lind was burning my chest.

I caught a glimpse of Colonel Karnovich sitting on the monkey board of the empress-mother's carriage. He was dressed as a footman of the chamber, with a tunic and a powdered wig, but was still wearing his eternal blue-tinted spectacles. At that moment however the head of the tsar's bodyguard could not be of any help to me. I needed urgently to talk with Georgii Alexandrovich, although even he would not be able to resolve the problem that had arisen. The tsar himself was required for that. And, even worse, the tsarina.

Following the previous day's embarrassing failure, Colonel Karnovich had received a vociferous dressing-down from Georgii Alexandrovich for preparing his agents poorly. I got my share too, from both of them, for not getting a good look at anything and not even detaining the newspaper boy. Fandorin was not present at this distressing scene. As Somov later informed me, the state counsellor and his Japanese had gone off somewhere even before I left for the meeting with Doctor Lind's people, and they had not been seen since.

Their absence worried me greatly. Several times in the course of the evening and once long after midnight I went outside and looked at their windows. There was no light.

In the morning I was woken by a sharp, nervous knocking. I thought it must be Somov and opened the door in my nightcap and dressing gown. Imagine my embarrassment when I saw Her Highness standing there!

Xenia Georgievna looked pale, and the shadows under her eyes suggested that she had not gone to bed at all.

'He's not here,' she gabbled. 'Afanasii, he wasn't here last night!'

'Who, Your Highness?' I asked in fright, pulling off my nightcap and bending my legs slightly, so that the hem of the dressing gown touched the floor and concealed my bare ankles.

'What do you mean? Erast Petrovich! Do you perhaps know where he is?'

'I have no idea,' I replied, and my heart sank because I did not like the expression on Her Highness's face at all.

Fandorin and his servant made their appearance after breakfast, when the grand dukes had already left for the Petrovsky Palace for the preparations for the ceremonial entry into the city. The house was full of police agents because a further message from the kidnappers was expected. I myself stayed as close as possible to the telephone and kept sending Somov out to the entrance to see if another note had been left. In fact, that was quite unnecessary, since Colonel Lasovsky had sleuths on duty in the bushes all the way along the avenue leading to the house. This time no one would be able to climb over the fence and approach the Hermitage unnoticed.

'Did you see the child?' Fandorin asked instead of greeting me. 'Is he alive?'

I told him the bare bones of what had happened the previous day, anticipating another helping of reproaches for letting the newspaper boy get away.

In order to forestall any reprimands, I said: 'I know I am at fault. I ought to have grabbed that little scoundrel by the scruff of his neck and not gone chasing after the carriage.'

'The most important thing is that you got a good look at the boy and that he is unharmed,' said Fandorin.

I could have stomached his reproaches, because they were well deserved, but I found such condescension objectionable.

'But now the only clue has been lost!' I exclaimed angrily,

letting him see that I had no need of his false magnanimity.

'What clue?' he asked with a mild gesture of the hand. 'A perfectly ordinary mop-headed little scamp, eleven and a half years old. Your Senka Kovalchuk doesn't know a thing, and there's no way he could have. Just who do you think Doctor Lind is?'

My jaw must have dropped, because before I began to speak I felt my lips slap together in a most foolish fashion.

'Se-Senka? K-Kovalchuk?' I repeated, suddenly developing a stammer. 'You mean you have found him? But how?'

'Nothing to it. I got a good look at him when he dived into your g-gig.'

'A good look?' I echoed and felt furious with myself for talking like a parrot. 'How could you get a look at anything, when you weren't even there?'

'How do you mean, I wasn't there?' Fandorin protested with a dignified air. He knitted his brows together and suddenly boomed in a deep voice that seemed incredibly familiar: "Come on, servant of God, get a move on!" Didn't you recognise me? I was there beside you all the time, Ziukin.'

The priest, the priest in the rattletrap with the tarpaulin cover!

I took myself in hand and gave vent to my righteous indignation.

'So you were there beside us, but you didn't follow us!'

'What on earth for?' The gaze of his blue eyes was so cool that I suspected he was mocking me. 'I had s-seen quite enough. The boy had the *Moscow Pilgrim* newspaper in his bag. That is one. The printer's ink had eaten deep into his fingers, so he really was a newspaper boy who handled hundreds of copies every day. That is two ...'

'But there are plenty of boys who sell the *Pilgrim*,' I exclaimed in frustration. 'I've heard that almost a hundred thousand copies of that yellow rag are sold in Moscow every day!'

'The boy also had six fingers on his left hand – did you not notice that? And that is three,' Fandorin concluded serenely.

'Yesterday evening Masa and I went round all the ten depots where *Moscow Pilgrim* news boys collect their wares and we had no difficulty in establishing the identity of the individual who interests us. We had to search for a while before we found him, it is true, and when we found him we had to run a bit too, but it is quite hard to run away from Masa and me, especially for such a young individual.'

So simple. Lord, it was so simple – that was the the first thought that came into my head. In fact, all I needed to have done was look more closely at the kidnappers' messenger.

'What did he tell you?' I asked impatiently.

'Nothing of any interest,' Fandorin replied, suppressing a yawn. 'A perfectly ordinary little Senka. He sells newspapers to earn his own daily bread and his alcoholic mother's vodka. Has no contacts with the criminal world. Yesterday he was hired by a certain "mister" who promised him three roubles and explained what he had to do. And he threatened to rip the boy's belly open if he got anything confused. Senka says he was a serious mister, the kind who really would rip you open.'

'And what else did he say about this "mister"?' 'I asked with a sinking heart. 'What he looked like? How he was dressed?'

'Ordnery,' Fandorin said with a gloomy sigh. 'You see, Ziukin, our young friend has a very limited vocabulary. His answers to every question are "Ordnery" and "Who knows?" The only distinctive f-feature of his employer that we have established is that he has a "bold face". But I am afraid that will not be of much help to us . . . All right, I'll go and get a bit of rest. Wake me when the message from Lind arrives.'

And the unpleasant man went to his room.

I, however, still could not bring myself to move far away from the telephone apparatus standing in the hallway. I paced up and down, trying to maintain a dour, pensive air, but the servants were already casting glances of frank bewilderment in my direction. Then I stood at the window and pretended to be observing Lord Banville and Mr Carr, both dressed in white trousers and check caps, as they played croquet.

Properly speaking, they were not actually playing, merely strolling around the croquet pitch with sour expressions on their faces, while His Lordship spoke incessantly about something or other, seeming to become more and more angry. Finally he stopped, turned towards his companion and flew into a genuine fury – he waved his hands and started shouting so loudly that even I could hear him through the glass. I had never seen English lords behave in such a manner before. Mr Carr listened with a bored expression on his face, sniffing at his dyed carnation. Freyby was standing a short distance away, smoking his pipe without looking at his gentlemen at all. The butler had two wooden mallets with long handles tucked under his arm.

Suddenly Lord Banville shouted something especially loudly and gave Mr Carr a resounding slap which knocked the gentleman's cap off his head. I froze in horror, afraid that the Britons would start up their barbarous 'boxing' right there on the lawn, but Mr Carr only threw his flower down at Banville's feet and walked away.

His Lordship stood there for no more than a few moments, and then dashed after the friend of his heart. He overtook him and grabbed him by the arm, but Mr Carr tore himself free. Then Lord Banville went down on his knees and waddled after the man he had struck in that unflattering position. Freyby followed them with the mallets, yawning.

I didn't understand what had happened and, to be quite honest, I was not interested in their English passions. And in any case I had just had a good idea that would free me from my enslavement to the telephone. I sent for the senior police agent and asked him to take my place in the hallway and send to the conservatory for me immediately there was a call from the kidnappers.

I believe that when I described the Hermitage I forgot to mention the most delightful space in this old palace – a glass-roofed winter garden with tall windows overlooking the Moscow river.

I chose this secluded spot, so conducive to intimate conversation, in order to deal with a matter that had been tormenting me for three days. I had to overcome my accursed shyness and finally tell poor Mademoiselle Declique that it was high time for her to stop suffering, that she had not done anything for which she deserved to be punished. How on earth could she have known that there was another carriage hidden behind the bushes? Not even the cunning Fandorin, who knew about Doctor Lind, had guessed that.

I ordered Lipps to lay a table in the conservatory and sent to Mademoiselle to ask whether she would care to take tea with me. (In St Petersburg the two of us often often used to sit for a while over a cup or two of good Buryatian oolong.) I had selected a lovely little corner, completely cut off from the rest of the conservatory by luxuriant bushes of magnolia. I waited for the governess, feeling very nervous as I tried to choose the right words – quite unambiguous and yet at the same time not too intrusive.

However, when Mademoiselle arrived, looking sad in a severe, dark grey dress with a shawl across her shoulders, I could not bring myself to address the ticklish subject immediately.

'It's funny,' I said, 'there's a garden in here and a garden out there.'

I meant that we were sitting in the winter garden, and there was a garden outside the window too, only a natural one.

'Yes,' she replied, lowering her head and stirring her tea with a spoon.

'You shouldn't . . .' I blurted out, but then she lifted her head and glanced at me with her luminous eyes, and I finished in a way I had not intended ' . . . dress so warmly. Today is a genuine summer day, even rather hot.'

The light in her eyes went out.

'I don't feel hot,' Mademoiselle said quietly and then neither of us spoke any more.

It was this silence that allowed it all to happen.

There was the sound of footsteps in the conservatory and we heard Xenia Georgievna's voice: 'Yes, yes, Erast Petrovich, this is just the right spot. No one will disturb us here.'

I was about to push my chair back and get up, but Mademoiselle Declique suddenly squeezed my wrist in her fingers, and I froze in surprise, because in all the time we had known each other this was the first time she had touched me in that way. By the time I recovered my wits it was already too late to speak up – things had gone too far between Her Highness and Fandorin.

'What do you want to tell me?' he asked quietly and – so I thought – cautiously.

'Just one thing . . .' Xenia Georgievna replied in a whisper, but she did not add anything else – the only sound was a rustle of material and a very faint squeak.

Concerned, I parted the thick bushes and was absolutely astounded: Her Highness was standing on tiptoe (it was her shoes that had squeaked, I realised) with both of her arms round Fandorin's neck, pressing her lips against his. The detective adviser's hand was held out helplessly to one side; the fingers clenched and unclenched and then suddenly, as if they had finally come to some decision, flew up and began stroking the delicate nape of Xenia Georgievna's neck with its fluffy strands of light hair.

I heard the sound of rapid breathing right beside my ear – it was Mademoiselle, who had also parted the bushes and was watching the kissing couple. I was astounded by the strange expression on her face, her eyebrows seemingly raised in a kind of merry amazement, a half-smile trembling on her lips. The doubly scandalous nature of the situation – the kiss itself and my inadvertent spying – brought me out in a cold sweat. But my accomplice apparently felt no awkwardness at all.

The kissing went on for a very, very long time. I had never imagined that it was possible to kiss for so long without any pause for breath. But I did not actually look at my watch, and perhaps the wait seemed so interminable to me because of the sheer nightmarishness of the situation.

Eventually they released their hold on each other, and I finally saw the radiant glow in Her Highness's eyes and the perplexed expression, so unlike his usual one, on the face of her seducer. Then Xenia Georgievna took Fandorin by the hand in a most determined fashion and led him away.

'What do you think; where is she taking him?' I asked in a whisper, avoiding looking at Mademoiselle.

There was strange sound rather like giggling. I glanced at the governess in surprise, but she looked perfectly serious.

'Thank you for the tea, Afanasii Stepanovich,' Mademoiselle said with a demure little bow and left me there alone.

I tried to gather my thoughts. What should I do? The honour of the imperial house was under threat – God only knew what this infatuation might lead to if someone did not intervene in time. Perhaps I should inform Georgii Alexandrovich? But to burden him with this additional problem seemed quite impossible. I had to think of something myself.

However, I was prevented from concentrating effectively on this most important matter by entirely extraneous questions.

Why had Mademoiselle taken hold of my wrist? I could still feel the dry heat of her hand.

And what was the meaning of that giggling – if, of course, I had not imagined it?

The window panes sudden quivered from a plangent blow and I heard a mighty rumbling – it was the cannon firing from the Kremlin towers to announce the commencement of the procession. And that meant it was noon already. And almost that very same moment I was called to the hallway. The postman had delivered the daily correspondence, and among the usual envelopes containing all sorts of invitations, notifications and charity appeals, one envelope without a stamp had been discovered.

We assembled round this rectangle of white paper lying in the centre of the small table under the mirror: myself, two police agents and Fandorin – looking unusually ruddy and with his collar distinctly lopsided.

While he questioned the postman about which route he had followed and whether he might have left his bag anywhere, I opened the envelope with trembling fingers and took out, together with a sheet of paper folded into four, a lock of soft, golden hair.

'Oh Lord,' I exclaimed involuntarily, because there could be no doubt at all that the hair belonged to Mikhail Georgievich.

Fandorin left the frightened postman and joined me. We read the message together.

Gentlemen, you have violated the terms of our arrangement. Your intermediary attempted to reclaim the goods by force without having made the payment agreed. As a first warning I am sending you a strand of the prince's hair. Following the next breach of faith on your side, you will receive one of his fingers.

The gentleman with the doggy sideburns can no longer be trusted. I refuse to deal with him. Today the prince's governess, whom I saw in the park, must come to the meeting. So that the lady will not be encumbered with the burden of a heavy suitcase, this time please be so good as to make the next payment to me in the form of the sapphire bow collar made by the court jeweller of the Tsarina Elisaveta – in the opinion of my specialist this bauble is worth precisely a million roubles, or perhaps slightly more, but you will not cavil at petty trifles, surely?

Beginning from six o'clock this evening the governess, completely alone, must stroll along the Arbat and the streets around it, following any route that she wishes, but choosing the places that are less crowded. She will be approached.

Yours sincerely,
Doctor Lind

'I am afraid that this is impossible,' was the first thing I said.

'B-but why?' Fandorin asked.

'The inventory of the crown jewels lists the neckband in the *coffret*[2] of the ruling empress.'

'And what of that?'

I simply sighed. How was he to know that for Her Majesty, so jealously protective of her somewhat ethereal status, the crown jewels held a special, rather morbid importance?

According to established ceremonial, the dowager empress was obliged to pass on the *coffret* to her successor immediately upon the new tsarina's accession to the throne. However, Maria Feodorovna, being a connoisseur of the beautiful as well as a capricious and wilful individual – and also let us be quite frank, not overfond of her daughter-in-law – had not wished to be parted from the jewels and had forbidden her crowned son to pester her with conversations on the subject.

A painful situation had resulted in which His Majesty, being on the one hand a dutiful son and, on the other, a loving husband, found himself, as they say, caught between the devil and the deep blue sea, and did not know what to do. The confrontation had continued for many months and had only been ended very recently by an unexpectedly decisive move on the part of the young empress. When, following numerous hints and even direct demands, Maria Feodorovna sent her only a small part of the jewels, mostly emeralds, which she did not like, Alexandra Feodorovna announced to her husband that she regarded the wearing of jewellery as in bad taste and henceforth she would not wear any diamonds, sapphires, pearls, gold and other vain ornaments at any ceremonial occasions. And she referred to the Scriptures, where it is said: 'A good name is better than great riches, and a good reputation is better than silver and gold.' After this threat the empress-mother was obliged to part with her jewels after all and, as far as I was aware, Alexandra Feodorovna

---

[2] *Casket.*

had brought the entire contents of the *coffret* to Moscow so that she could appear in all her splendour at the numerous balls, receptions and ceremonies.

I had to reach Georgii Alexandrovich urgently.

I had to delay a little while before running from Maria Feodorovna's landau to the mounted group of grand dukes, for the procession had just entered the Triumphal Square and my manoeuvre would have been blatantly obvious. My watch already showed half past one. Time was running out.

A convenient opportunity presented itself when rockets went soaring up into the sky from the roof of a large building on the corner of Tverskaya Street, leaving trails of coloured smoke behind them. As if by command, the assembled members of the public jerked up their heads and started buzzing in rapturous delight, and I quickly cut across the open space and hid among the horses. In accordance with ceremonial, each of the horses on which Their Highnesses were sitting was being led by the bridle by one of the companions of the court. I saw Pavel Georgievich, wearing a weary, anxious expression on his bluish-green face; Endlung, sprightly and rosy-cheeked, was striding out beside him.

'Afanasii,' His Highness called to me in a pitiful voice. 'I can't go on. Get me some pickle water. I swear to God, I'm going to be sick ...'

'Hold on, Your Highness,' I said. 'The Kremlin is coming up soon.'

And I carried on squeezing my way through. A dignified gentleman squinted sideways at me in bewilderment. To judge from the red welts on his cuffs and the buttons with hunting horns on them, he must have been a master of hounds, but so many of those had appeared during the new reign that it was impossible to remember them all.

His Majesty's three uncles made up the front row of the procession of grand dukes. I worked my way through to Georgii

Alexandrovich's sorrel Turkmen, took hold of its bridle (so that there were now two of us leading it – myself and the stall-master Count Anton Apollonovich Opraksin) and passed the note from Lind to His Highness without speaking.

When he saw the lock of hair, Georgii Alexandrovich's face changed. He quickly ran his eye over the lines of writing, touched his spurs to the lean, muscular sides of his mount and began slowly overhauling the solitary figure of the sovereign. The count let go of the bridle in horror. And so did I.

There could be no doubt at all that a genuine storm would blow up in international politics. It was a certainty that today the coded telegrams would go flying to foreign courts and delegations: Admiral-General Georgii Alexandrovich demonstrates his special relationship with the tsar, and from now on can probably be regarded as the most influential individual in the Russian empire. So be it. There were more important things to deal with.

With his hands held proudly on his hips exactly like his nephew, His Highness approached the sovereign unhurriedly and rode on beside him, just half a length behind; the admiral-general's portly figure made a far more majestic sight than the autocrat's thin silhouette. From the twitching of His Highness's magnificent moustache, I guessed that Georgii Alexandrovich was telling the emperor about the letter, without even turning his head. The tsar's head quite clearly jerked to one side. Then his moustache, less magnificent than Georgii Alexandrovich's, twitched in exactly the same way, and the grand duke began gradually falling back, until he was level with his brothers again.

Since I was so close, I could hear Kirill Alexandrovich hiss furiously: '*Tu es fou, Georgie, ou quoi?*'[3]

I do not know if the people of Moscow noticed that when the procession entered Tverskaya Street the column began moving

---

[3] *Are you mad, Georgie, or what?*

significantly more quickly, but in any case twenty minutes later the sovereign rode in through the Spassky Gate of the Kremlin and a quarter of an hour after that closed carriages drove away one after another from the porch of the Large Kremlin Palace. The individuals who were privy to the secret were hurrying to the Hermitage for an emergency meeting.

This time the visitors included our sovereign lady, whose decision would determine the outcome of the whole affair.

Since I had to arrange in haste for light hors d'œuvres, coffee, seltzer water and orangeade for Her Majesty (nothing so inflames the thirst and the appetite as a prolonged ceremonial procession), I missed the beginning of the discussion and had to reconstruct its course in retrospect, from what I heard the participants say.

For example, the delicate explanation to the tsarina concerning the sapphire neckband took place in my absence. When I came in, I found Her Majesty in an angry mood but already reconciled to the inevitable.

'However, His Anointed Majesty has promised to me that this thing will quite definitely be returned to me entire and undamaged,' our sovereign lady was saying to High Police Master Lasovsky just as I entered with the tray.

From these words, and also from the fact that Colonel Karnovich was sitting there with a rather sulky air, I concluded that following the previous day's failure control of the operation had been transferred to the Moscow police. Fandorin was also here – I assumed in his capacity as an adviser.

Her Majesty had not had time to change, and she was still wearing her ceremonial dress of white brocade studded all over over with precious stones, and a heavy diamond necklace. The grand dukes had had no time to remove the stars of their various decorations, the watered silk ribbons of their medals and their chains of St Andrew, and all this iridescent shimmering made the room seem like a closet where the New Year's tree decorations are kept.

'Your Majesty,' Lasovsky declared, 'I warrant on my own head that the sapphires will remain perfectly safe, we will rescue Mikhail Georgievich, and we will nab the entire gang.' He rubbed his hands together eagerly and Alexandra Feodorovna wrinkled up her nose at this rather vulgar gesture. 'Everything will go absolutely perfectly, because this time that villain Lind has laid the trap for himself. Allow me to explain – I have drawn up a plan.'

He moved aside all the glasses and cups that I had arranged so carefully, grabbed a starched napkin and set it down at the centre of the table.

'This is Arbat Street and the area around it, the Second Pre-chistensky District. The governess will get out of her carriage here, at Maly Afanasievsky Lane, hesitate for a while as if uncertain which way to go, then turn in here, on to Bolshoi Afanasievsky Lane, from there on to Sivtsev Vrazhek Lane, and then . . .'

He carried on listing the turns for a quite a long time, checking them against a sheet of paper. Everyone listened attentively, although Her Majesty, if the disdainful set of her mouth was anything to go by, was thinking more about the odour of sweat that was clearly emanating from the overheated chief of police.

'I have already calculated that she will pass twelve blocks in all, on which there are two hundred and thirty houses.' Lasovky looked round triumphantly at the sovereign and rapped out: '*And in every one of those houses there will be one of my men. In every one!* My assistants are arranging it at this very moment. And so, although the governess's route will appear random, she will actually be in our field of vision all the time, but the villains will never realise it, since the detectives, agents and constables in plain clothes will be located inside the residents' houses and apartments. If she walks the entire route and no one approaches her, she will go round a second time, and then a third – as many times as necessary.'

'Rather smart, isn't it?' Simeon Alexandrovich asked smugly, very proud of his chief of police.

'P-permit me to ask, Colonel,' Fandorin suddenly put in. 'Are you certain that Mademoiselle Declique, who has never been to Moscow before, will not be confused by your complicated route?'

Lasovsky frowned, knitting his brows.

'I shall personally lock myself away in a room with her and make her learn off all the corners and turns by heart. We shall have an entire hour to do it.'

Fandorin seemed to be satisfied with this answer and he did not ask any more questions.

'We have to send for the neckband,' the sovereign said with a sigh. 'And may God be with us.'

At half past four, as Mademoiselle, pale-faced and with clear bite marks on her lips, was on her way to the carriage, where two gendarmes officers in civilian clothes were waiting for her, Fandorin approached her in the corridor. I happened to be nearby and I heard every word.

'There is only one thing required of you, My Lady,' he said in a very serious voice. 'Do not put the life of the boy at risk. Be observant, that is your only weapon. I do not know what scheme Lind has in m-mind this time, but be guided by your own understanding, listen to no one and trust no one. The police are less interested in the life of your pupil than in avoiding publicity. And one more thing ...' He looked her straight in the eye and said what I had tried to say so recently, but had not known how. 'Do not blame yourself for what happened. If you had not left the boy alone, your presence would still not have made any difference. There would only have been another unnecessary casualty, because Doctor Lind does not leave witnesses.'

Mademoiselle fluttered her eyelashes rapidly, and I thought I saw a teardrop fall from them.

'*Merci, monsieur, merci. J'avais besoin de l'entendre.*'[4]

She put her hand on Fandorin's wrist – exactly as she had done so recently with mine – and squeezed it. He squeezed her elbow in a highly familiar manner, nodded and walked rapidly away in the direction of his room, as if he were in a great hurry to get somewhere.

I shall jump ahead of my story at this point – why will become clear later – and tell you what came of the Moscow police's operation.

Colonel Lasovsky's plan was not bad at all, and no doubt it would have been crowned with success if Lind had complied with the conditions that he himself had set for the meeting. But that, unfortunately, is precisely what the guileful doctor did not do.

And so the governess was driven to Arbat Street. She had a velvet reticule holding the priceless treasure in her hands, and there were two gendarmes with her: one sitting opposite her, the other on the coach box.

Immediately after Krymsky Most Street, when the carriage turned into another street which, if I am not mistaken, is called Ostozhenka Street, Mademoiselle suddenly stood up, turned round to look after a carriage that had driven past in the opposite direction and shouted in a piercing voice: 'Mika! Mika!'

The officers also looked round, just in time to glimpse a little blue sailor's cap between the swaying curtains of a rear window.

They had no time to turn their carriage – just as I did not the day before, but fortunately there was a cab driving towards them.

The gendarmes told Mademoiselle to stay in the carriage, threw the cabby off his own rig and set off in pursuit of the carriage that had driven away with Mikhail Georgievich.

They were unable to catch it, however, because the cab horse was no match for a fine four-in-hand. Meanwhile, as Made-

---

4 *Thank you, sir, thank you. I needed to hear that.*

moiselle Declique squirmed in confusion on her seat, a gentleman wearing a beard and moustache approached her, politely
doffed his Office of Mines peaked cap and addressed her in broken
French: 'The terms have been met – you have seen the prince.
And now, if you don't mind, the payment.'

What could Mademoiselle do? Especially since there were two
other men, whom she described as looking far less gallant than
the polite gentleman, strolling about not very far away.

She gave them the reticule and tried to follow Fandorin's
instructions by memorising the three men's appearances.

Well, she memorised them and later described them in the
greatest possible detail, but what good would that do? There was
no reason to think that Doctor Lind was short of men.

I did not learn about the failure of the operation conceived
by the high police master until later, because I was not at the
Hermitage that evening. When Mademoiselle returned, never
having reached the cunning trap set around Arbat Street, I had
already left the Neskuchny Park.

After I had seen the governess off on her way to the risky
undertaking in which she was obliged to participate because I
had behaved stupidly and bungled my own assignment, I found
the inactivity simply too painful. I paced backwards and forwards
in my room, thinking what a monster Fandorin was. That gutta-
percha gentleman ought not to be allowed anywhere near young
girls and respectable women. How shamelessly he had turned
Her Highness's head! How craftily he had won the good favour
of Mademoiselle Declique! And after all, what for? What could
this slick seducer and experienced man of the world want with a
modest governess who was no great beauty and no *grande dame*?
Why would he talk to her in that velvety voice and squeeze her
elbow so tenderly? Oh this specimen never did anything without
a reason.

At this point my thoughts suddenly turned in a completely
unexpected direction. I remembered that Simeon Alexandrovich,

who had known Fandorin in his previous life, had called him 'an adventurer of the very worst sort' from whom you could expect absolutely anything at all. I had formed the very same impression.

The suspicions came crowding into my mind one after another, and I attempted to make sense of them by setting them out in order, in Fandorin's own manner.

First. After a little reflection, the story about the finding of the newspaper boy appeared suspicious. If one supposed that Fandorin really had displayed quite uncommon resourcefulness and sought out the little rogue, then why would he have let him go? What if the boy had kept something back or quite simply lied, and then gone running to report to Lind?

Second. Why had Fandorin tried to dissuade Mademoiselle from following the instructions of the police and recommended her to act as she thought best? A fine adviser Lasovsky had, no two ways about it!

Third. If he found the high police master's plan so disagreeable, then why had he not said so at the meeting?

Fourth. Where was he off to in such a hurry after he said goodbye to Mademoiselle Declique? What kind of urgent business could he suddenly have when the operation was being conducted without his involvement? Yet another trick like yesterday's?

And fifth, and most importantly. Had he told me the truth about his relations with Lind? I could not be certain about that either.

It was this last thought, coupled with my feeling of guilt for the risk to which Mademoiselle had been exposed thanks to my good offices, that drove me to commit an act the like of which I had never committed before in my life. I could never even have imagined that I was capable of anything of the sort.

I walked up to the door of Fandorin's room, looked around and put my eye to the keyhole. Peeping through it proved to be extremely uncomfortable – my back soon turned numb and my

124

bent knees began to ache. But what was going on in the room rendered such minor discomforts entirely irrelevant. They were both there – the master and the servant. Fandorin was sitting in front of the mirror, naked to the waist and performing some incomprehensible manipulations with his face. It looked to me as if he was putting on make-up, just as Mr Carr did every morning, with his door open and without the slightest sign of embarrassment in front of the servants. Masa did not fall within my limited range of vision, but I could hear him snuffling some-where in the immediate vicinity of the door.

Fandorin reached out his hand, pulled a crimson silk Russian shirt over his head and then stood up so that I could not see him any longer, but I did hear squeaking and tramping sounds, as if someone were pulling on a pair of blacked boots.

What was this masquerade in aid of? What shady business was afoot here?

I was so completely absorbed that I let my guard down and almost banged my head against the door when I heard a gentle cough behind my back.

Somov! Ah, this was not good.

My assistant was gazing at me in utter amazement. Things were doubly bad because that morning I had put a flea in his ear for his lack of discretion – as I walked along the corridor before breakfast I had caught him coming out of Mademoiselle Declique's room, where he had absolutely no business to be. In reply to my stern question, Somov had blushed and admitted that in the mornings he studied French on his own, and he had asked the governess to explain a particularly difficult point of grammar. I told him that although I encouraged the study of foreign languages by the staff, Mademoiselle Declique had after all been hired to teach His Highness and not the servants. It seemed to me that Somov resented my remarks, but of course he did not dare to answer me back. And now this embarrassing blunder!

'The door handles and keyholes have not been polished as

well as they might,' I said, concealing my embarrassment. 'Here, take a look for yourself.'

I squatted down, breathed on the brass handle and, thank God, fingerprints appeared on its misty surface.

'But a guest only has to take hold of the handle once, and a mark will be left. Afanasii Stepanovich, no one will ever spot trifles like that!'

'In our work, Kornei Selifanovich, there are no trifles. And that is something you ought to get clear before you try to master French,' I said with a severity that was perhaps inordinate but justified by the circumstances. 'Be so good as to go round all the doors and check. Begin with the upper floors.'

When he had left, I put my eye to the keyhole again, but the room was quiet and deserted, and the only movement was the curtain swaying at the open window.

I took a master key that fitted all the doors in the house out of my pocket, went inside and ran across to the window.

I was just in time to see two figures dive into the bushes: one was tall, wearing a black pea jacket and a peaked cap, the other was a squat figure in a blue robe, with a long plait and a bowler hat. That was exactly how Masa had looked when he was playing the part of the Chinese pedlar on the day we first met. 'Strollers' like that had spread all over St Petersburg in the last few years, and apparently all over Moscow too.

I did not have any time to think.

I clambered determinedly over the window sill, jumped down onto the ground, hunched over and ran after them.

It was easy enough to determine the direction in which the disguised men were running from the shaking of the bushes. I tried hard not to fall behind, but I avoided getting too close to them, in order not to give myself away.

With an agility that I found impressive, Fandorin and Masa scaled the railings and jumped down on the other side. My attempt to overcome this barrier, a *sazhen* and a half in height, went less smoothly. I fell off twice, and when I finally did find

126

myself on the top I did not dare jump for fear of breaking my leg or spraining my ankle, and I carefully slid down the thick railings, catching the coat-tail of my livery and lacerating the entire flap, and also getting dirt on my culottes and white stockings. (It later became clear that if we had gone along the main avenue instead of through the garden, we would have run into Mademoiselle Declique on her way back from her unexpectedly brief expedition.)

Fortunately Fandorin and Masa had not got very far. They were standing arguing with a cabby who apparently was very reluctant to let such a suspicious-looking pair into his vehicle. Eventually they got in and drove off.

I glanced to the left and then to the right. There were no more cabs to be seen. The Kaluga Highway is just that, not really a street, more like a country high road, and cabbies are a rare commodity there. But once again my experience as a footman came in useful. I set off trotting smoothly at an easy pace, keeping close to the railings of the park, since the cab was not moving very fast. I did not come across a cab until I reached the Golitsyn Hospital, when I was beginning to get out of breath. Puffing and panting, I slumped on to the seat and told him to follow the other cab, offering to pay him twice the usual rate.

The driver looked respectfully at my green livery with braid trimmings and the gold epaulette with aiguillettes (in order to get into the ceremonial parade, I had decked myself out in my dress uniform, and afterwards there had been no time to change back – thank goodness that at least the three-cornered hat with the plumage had been left at home) and called me 'Your Excellency'.

At Kaluga Square we took a turn to the left, came out on the embankment just before the bridge and then we did not make any more turns for a long time. Thank God, the passengers in the carriage in front did not turn round even once – my green and gold outfit must have been clearly visible from a long distance away.

The river divided into two. Our route lay along the the narrower of the two channels. On the left I could see the Kremlin towers and eagles between the buildings, and still we kept on driving, further and further, so that I no longer knew what part of Moscow we had reached.

At long last we made another turn and rumbled across a short cobblestoned bridge, then across a long wooden one, then across a third, which bore a plaque: 'Small Yauza Bridge'.

The houses became poorer and the streets dirtier. And the longer we drove along that atrocious, rutted embankment, the more wretched the buildings became, so that I could not think of any other word to describe them except slums.

The driver suddenly halted his horse.

'You do what you like, guv'nor, but I'm not going into Khitrovka. They'll rob me. Take me horse and give me a good battering into the bargain, if not worse. Everyone knows what the place is like, and evening's coming on.'

And indeed dusk was already falling – how had I failed to notice that?

Realising that it was pointless to argue, I got out of the cab immediately and handed the driver three roubles.

'Oh no!' he said, grabbing me by the sleeve. 'You just look how far we've rode, and you promised me double, Your Excellency!'

Fandorin's carriage disappeared round the corner. In order not to fall behind, I tossed the insolent fellow another two roubles and ran in pursuit.

The people I encountered on the street were unsavoury in the extreme. To put it more simply, they were riff-raff, the same sort as we have on the Ligovka in St Petersburg only probably even worse. What I found particularly unpleasant was that every last one of them was staring at me.

Someone shouted after me familiarly: 'Hey, you dandy drake, what have you lost around here?'

I pretended not to hear.

The cab was not there round the corner – there was nothing

but an empty, crooked little street, crooked street lamps with broken glass covers and half-ruined little houses.

I dashed to the next turn and then jerked back sharply, because right there, only about fifteen paces away, the men I was looking for were getting out of their carriage.

I cautiously peeped round the corner and saw a crowd of repulsive ragamuffins gather round the new arrivals from all sides, gaping curiously at the cabby, from which it was possible to conclude that the appearance of a cab in Khitrovka was a rather extraordinary event.

'Well, what about a rouble and a half, then?' the driver whined plaintively, addressing the disguised state counsellor.

Fandorin swayed back on his heels, keeping his hands in his pockets, baring his teeth in a fierce grin with a glint of gold caps, which had appeared in his mouth out of nowhere, and spat neatly on the driver's boot. Then he asked mockingly: 'What about a kick and a poke?'

The idle onlookers chortled.

Oh, what a fine state counsellor this was!

The cabby pulled his head down into his shoulders, lashed his horse and drove off, accompanied by whistling, hallooing and shouts of an obscene nature.

Without even glancing at each other, Fandorin and the Japanese walked off in different directions. Masa ducked into a gateway and seemed to dissolve into the gathering gloom, while Erast Petrovich set off along the very middle of the street. After hesitating for a while, I followed the latter.

It was incredible how much his walk had changed. He waddled along as if he were on invisible springs, with his hands in his pockets and his shoulders hunched over. He spat zestfully twice to once side and kicked an empty tin can with his boot. A crudely painted wench in a bright-coloured dress came walking towards him, wiggling her hips. Fandorin deftly extracted one hand from his pocket and pinched her on the side. Strangely enough, this style of courtship seemed very much to the lady's liking – she squealed, broke into peals of laughter and shouted such a pithy phrase after her admirer that I almost stumbled over my own feet. If only Xenia Georgievna could have seen how little this gentleman cared for her tender feelings!

He turned into a dark narrow alleyway – no more than a chink between two buildings. I went in after him, but before I had even taken ten steps I was grabbed by the shoulders from both sides. A whiff of something rotten and sour blew into my face and a young, nasal voice drawled: 'Ea-sy now, Mister, ea-sy.'

There were two figures that I could only vaguely make out in the twilight, one standing on my left and one on my right. Right in front of my eyes an icy spark glinted on a strip of steel, and I felt the strange sensation of my knees turning soft, as if they might suddenly bend in the wrong direction, in defiance of all the laws of anatomy.

'Lookee 'ere,' hissed a different voice, a bit older and hoarser. 'A wallet.'

The pocket in which my *porte-monnaie* was lying suddenly felt suspiciously light, but I realised it would be best not to protest. In any case, the noise might bring Fandorin, and my surveillance of him would be exposed.

'Take it quickly and leave me in peace,' I declared quite firmly, but then gagged on my words because a fist came hurtling out of the gloom and struck me on the base of the nose, so that I was immediately blinded, and something hot ran down my chin.

'Well, isn't he the feisty one?' I heard someone say as if he was speaking through a pane of glass. 'And the skins, look at the skins, with gold trimmints.'

Someone's hands grabbed hold roughly of my shirt and pulled it out from under my belt.

'You did wrong to bloody his snout, Seka. That shirt of his is pure cambric, and now look, the whole front's spattered something rotten. And his pants are good too.'

It was only then I realised that these criminals intended to strip me naked.

'Them's women's pants, but the cloth's right enough,' the other voice said and someone tugged at the edge of my culottes. 'They'll do Manka for pantaloons. Get 'em off, Mister, get 'em off.'

My eyes had grown accustomed to the dull light, and now I could make out my robbers better.

It would have been better if I hadn't – the sight was nightmarish. Half the face of one of them was swollen up and covered by a bruise of monstrous proportions, the other was wheezing through a damp, sticky collapsed nose.

'Take the livery, but I won't give you the breeches and the shoes,' I said, for the very idea that I, the butler of the Green Court, might go wandering around Moscow in the nude, was inconceivable.

'If you don't get 'em off, we'll pull 'em off yer corpse,' the hoarse one threatened and pulled a razor out from behind his back – a perfectly ordinary razor, the same kind that I shave with, except that this one was covered in rust and badly notched.

I began unbuttoning my shirt with trembling fingers, cursing my own folly. How could I have got into such a loathsome mess? I had let Fandorin get away, but that was the least of my worries now – I would be lucky to get out of there alive.

Another shadow appeared behind the backs of the Khitrovka savages and I heard a lazy, sing-song voice say: 'And what's this little comedy we 'ave 'ere, then? Right, shrimp, scarper, and quick.'

Erast Petrovich! But where had he come from? He had walked away!

'You what? You what?' the young robber shrieked, but his voice sounded nervous to me. 'This here's our sheep, mine and Tura's. You live your life, toff, and let honest dogs live too. There's no law says you can take a sheep off us dogs.'

'I'll give you a law,' Fandorin hissed, and put his hand inside his jacket.

The robbers instantly pushed me away and took to their heels. But they took with them the livery and my wallet – with forty-five roubles and small change inside it.

I did not know if I could consider myself saved or, on the contrary, I had simply fallen out of the frying pan into the fire, as they say. That wolfish grin distorting Fandorin's smooth features could hardly bode me any good, and I watched in horror as his hand drew something out of his inside pocket.

'Here, take that.'

It was not a knife or a pistol, merely a handkerchief.

'What am I going to do with you, Ziukin?' Erast Petrovich asked in his normal voice and the appalling grimace was replaced by a crooked smile which, to my mind, was equally repulsive. 'Of course, I spotted you back at Neskuchny Park, but I didn't expect you to stay in Khitrovka – I thought you would take fright and retreat. However, I see you are not a man who frightens easily.'

I did not know what to say to that, so I said nothing.

'I ought to leave you here wandering around naked. It would be a lesson to you. Explain to me, Ziukin, what on earth made you come traipsing after us?'

The fact that he was no longer speaking like a bandit but in his usual gentleman's voice made me feel a bit calmer.

'What you told me about the boy was not convincing,' I replied. I took out my own handkerchief, threw my head back and squeezed my bloodied nose. 'I decided to check on you.'

Fandorin grinned.

'Bravo, Ziukin, b-bravo. I had not expected such perspicacity from you. You are quite right. Senka Kovalchuk told me everything he knew, and he's an observant boy – it's part of his p-profession. And he's bright – he realised that I wouldn't let him go otherwise.'

'And he told you how to find the "bold face" who hired him?'

'Not exactly, for that of course is something that our young acquaintance does not know, but he gave an exhaustive description of his employer. Judge for yourself: a bold face, slit eyes, clean-shaven, thick lips, a "general's" cap with a lacquer peak, a red silk shirt, boots with a loud squeak and lacquer galoshes ...'

I looked at Fandorin's own attire and exclaimed: 'That's amazing, you're dressed in exactly the same way. There are plenty of young fellows like that around in Moscow.'

'By no means,' he said, shaking his head. 'You certainly won't see them around Moscow very often, but in Khitrovka you can meet them, although not in such v-very large numbers. It's not just a matter of clothes, this is the supreme Khitrovka chic – the red silk and the lacquer galoshes. Only the toffs, that is bandits at the very top of the hierarchy, can presume to wear this outfit. To make it easier for you to understand, Ziukin, to them it is something like a gentleman-in-waiting's uniform. Did you see the way those d-dogs scarpered at the sight of me?'

'Scarpered', 'dogs' – what sort of way is that to talk? I could see that there was very little of the state counsellor left in Fandorin. This man rather reminded me of cheap gilded tableware from which the upper layer has peeled away, exposing the vulgar tin.

'What "dogs" do you mean?' I asked, to make it clear that I would not agree to converse in criminal argot.

'"Dogs", Ziukin, are petty thieves and ruffians. For them, toffs like me are b-big bosses. But you interrupted me before I could tell you the bold face's most important characteristic.' He paused and then, with a pompous air, as if he were saying something very important, he said: 'All the time he was talking to Senka – and he spoke to him for at least half an hour – this individual never took his right hand out of his pocket and kept jingling his small change.'

'You believe that this habit is enough for you to find him?'

'No,' Fandorin sighed. 'I believe something quite different. But anyway it will soon become clear whether my assumption is correct or not. Masa has to establish that. And if I am right, we intend to look for Mr Bold Face while Doctor Lind is playing cat and mouse with the police.'

'And where is Mr Masa?'

Erast Petrovich waved his hand vaguely.

'Not far from here, in a basement, a secret Chinese opium den. It moved from Sukharevka to Khitrovka after a police raid the year before last. Those people know all sorts of things.'

'You mean that Mr Masa can speak Chinese?'

'A little. There are many Chinese in his home town of Yokahama.'

Just then we heard an intricate bandit-style whistle from around the corner and I cringed.

'There he is now,' Fandorin said with a satisfied nod. He folded his fingers together in some special manner and whistled in exactly the same way, only even more piercingly – it actually left me deaf in one ear.

We walked on along the narrow side street and very soon met the Japanese. He was not at all surprised to see me and merely bowed ceremonially. I nodded, feeling extremely stupid without my livery and with blood spattered on my shirt.

They babbled away to each other in some incomprehensible language – I don't know whether it was Japanese or Chinese – and all I could make out was the constant repetition of the word stump, which failed to make anything clearer to me.

'I was right,' Fandorin eventually condescended to explain. 'It really is Stump – he has lost one hand and is in the habit of holding the stump in his pocket. He is a very serious bandit, the head of one of the new and most dangerous gangs in Khitrovka. The Chinese say their hideout is on Podkopaevka Street, in an old wine warehouse. It won't be easy to get in there – they post sentries as if it was an army barracks, and they have even introduced a "scrip", that is a password...

That's all very well, but what am I going to do with you, Ziukin? You've made yourself a real problem now. I can't let you go wandering round Khitrovka on your own. You never know, you could get your throat cut.'

I was greatly piqued by these words and was on the point of saying that I would manage very well without anyone else looking after me – although, I must admit, I did not find the thought of a solitary stroll through the Khitrovka evening very attractive – when he asked: 'Tell me, Ziukin, are you a physically robust man?'

I straightened my shoulders and replied with dignity: 'I have served at court as a footman and postilion and on excursions. I do French gymnastics every morning.'

'All right then, we'll s-see,' said Fandorin, with an insulting note of doubt in his voice. 'You'll come with us. Only on one condition: don't take any action on your own; you must obey Masa and myself unquestioningly. Do you give me your word?'

What else could I do? Go back with nothing, as they say, for all my pains? And would I be able to get out of this cursed place on my own? And then it would be very much to the point to find this Stump. What if Fandorin was right, and the police operation on Arbat Street failed to produce any results?

I nodded.

'Only your appearance isn't really suitable for Khitrovka, Ziukin. You could compromise Masa and myself. Who can we turn you into? Well, at least a servant from a good house who has taken to drink.'

And, so saying, Fandorin leaned down, scooped up a handful of dust and poured it on the crown of my head, then wiped his dirty hand on my shirt, which was already stained with red blotches.

'Ye-es,' he drawled in satisfaction. 'That's a bit better.'

He squatted down and tore the gold buckles off my shoes, then suddenly took hold of my culottes and jerked hard, so that the seam at the back split and parted.

'What are you doing?' I cried in panic, jumping back.

'Well, how's that, Masa?' the crazed state counsellor asked the Japanese, who inclined his head, looked me over and remarked: 'Stockings white.'

'Quite right. You will have to t-take them off. And you are far too clean-shaven, that is not *comme il faut* around here. Come on ...'

He stepped towards me and, before I could even protest, he had smeared dust from the crown of my head right across my face.

I gave up. I took off my white silk stockings and put them in my pocket.

'All right, that will do in the dark,' Fandorin said condescendingly, but his valet actually favoured me with praise: 'Ver' good. Ver' beeutfuw.'

'Now where? To this Stump?' I asked, burning with desire to get down to business.

'Not so f-fast, Ziukin. We have to wait for night. Meanwhile, let me tell you what is known about Stump. He has the reputation of a mysterious individual with a big future among the criminals of Moscow. Rather like Bonaparte during the Directoire period. Even the King himself is rather afraid of him, although no state of war has been declared between the two of them. The one-armed bandit's gang is small but select – everyone pulls their weight. Nothing but toffs, all well tried and tested. My man in the criminal investigation department, a highly authoritative professional, believes that the future of the Russian criminal world belongs to leaders like Stump. There are no drinking binges or fights in his gang. They won't touch any small-time business. They plan their raids and robberies thoroughly and execute them cleanly. The police do not have a single informer among Stump's men. And this gang's hideaway, as I have already had the honour of informing you, is guarded with great care, military fashion.'

This all sounded most discouraging.

'But how are we going to reach him, if he is so cautious?'

'Over the rooftops,' said Fandorin, gesturing for me to follow him.

We made our way through dark, dismal, foul-smelling court-yards for a while, until eventually Fandorin stopped beside a blank windowless wall that was indistinguishable from the others beside it. He took hold of a drainpipe, shook it hard and listened to the rattling of the tin plate.

'It will hold,' he muttered as if he were talking to himself, and then suddenly, without the slightest apparent effort, he started climbing up the flimsy structure.

Masa thrust his bowler further down onto his head and climbed after him, looking like a fairground bear who has been taught to scramble up a pole to get a sugarloaf.

As the common people say, in for a kopeck, in for a rouble. I spat on my hands the way our kitchen servant Siavkin does when he is chopping firewood, crossed myself and took hold of an iron bracket. Right, one foot on the step in the wall, now the other – hup! Reach up to that hoop, now get my other arm over that ledge . . .

In order not to feel afraid, I started adding up my financial losses over the last few days. The day before before I had lost fifty roubles on the bet with Masa, today I had spent two and a half roubles on a cab in the morning and five in the evening, making seven and a half in all, and then the Khitrovka 'dogs' had gone off with my *porte-monnaie* and forty-five roubles. Then add to that my ruined clothes – they might only be my official uniform, but even so it was upsetting.

At this point I accidentally looked down and immediately forgot all about my losses because the ground was a lot further away than I had thought. The wall had not seemed all that high from below, only three storeys, but looking down made my heart skip a beat.

Fandorin and Masa had clambered onto the roof a long time

ago, but I was still creeping up the drainpipe, trying not to look down any more.

When I reached the overhang of the roof, I suddenly realised that there was absolutely no way I could climb over it – all my strength had gone into the climb. I hung there, with my arms round the drainpipe, for about five minutes, until a round head in a bowler hat appeared against the background of the purple sky. Masa took hold of my collar and dragged me up onto the roof in a jiffy.

'Thank you,' I said, gulping in the air.

'No need gwatitude,' he said, and bowed although he was on all fours.

We crawled over to the other side of the roof, where Fandorin was spreadeagled on his belly. I settled down beside him, impatient to find out what he was watching for.

The first thing I saw was the crimson stripe of the fading sunset, pierced by the numerous black needles of bell towers. Fandorin, however, was not admiring the sky, but examining a lopsided old building with boarded-up windows located on the opposite side of the street. I could see that once, a long, long time ago, it had been a fine strong building, but it had been neglected, fallen into disrepair and begun to sag – it would be easier to demolish than renovate.

'Back at the beginning of the century this used to be a warehouse that belonged to the Mobius brothers, the wine merchants,' Erast Petrovich began explaining in a whisper, and I noticed that when he whispered the stammer disappeared completely from his speech. 'The basement consists of wine cellars that go very deep. They say that they used to hold up to a thousand barrels of wine. In 1812 the French poured away what they didn't drink and supposedly a stream of wine ran down the Yauza. The building is burnt out from the inside and the roof has collapsed, but the cellars have survived. That is where Stump has his residence. Do you see that fine young fellow?'

On looking more closely, I observed a ramp sloping down

from the road to a pair of gates set well below the level of the street. There was a young fellow wearing a peaked cap just like Fandorin's, standing with his back to the gates and eating sunflower seeds, spitting out the husks.

'A sentry?' I guessed.

'Yes. We'll wait for a while.'

I do not know how long the wait lasted, because my chronometer was still in my livery (something else to add to the list of losses: a silver Breguet awarded for honourable service – I regretted that most of all) but it was not just one hour or two, but more – I was already dozing off.

Suddenly I sensed that Fandorin's entire body had gone tense, and my sleepiness disappeared as if by magic.

I could hear muffled voices from below.

'Awl,' said one.

'Husk,' replied the other. 'Come on through. Got a message?'

I did not hear the answer to this incomprehensible question. A door in the gates opened and then closed, and everything went quiet again. The sentry lit up a hand-rolled cigarette and the lacquer peak of his cap glinted dully in the moonlight.

'Right, I'm off,' Fandorin whispered. 'Wait here. If I wave, come down.'

Ten minutes later a slim figure approached the building, walking in a loose, slovenly manner. With a glance back over its shoulder, it loped springily down to the sentry.

'Wotcher, Moscow. Guarding the wall?'

It was Fandorin of course, but for some reason his speech had acquired a distinct Polish accent.

'Shove off back to where you came from,' the sentry replied hostilely. 'Or shall I tickle your belly with a pen?'

'Why use a pen?' Fandorin laughed. 'That's what an awl's for. An awl, get it?'

'Why didn't you say so before?' the sentry growled, taking his hand out of his pocket. 'Husk. So who would you be then, a Polack? One of that Warsaw mob, are you?'

'That's right. I need to see Stump.'

'He's not here. And he said as he wouldn't be back today. Expect him tomorrow, he said, by nightfall.' The bandit lowered his voice, but in the silence I could still hear what he said, and asked curiously, 'They say as the narks done for your top man?'

'That's right,' Fandorin sighed. 'Blizna, and three other guys. So where's Stump, then? I've got some business to talk over with him.'

'He don't report to me. You know the way the music plays nowadays, Polack. He's on the prowl somewhere – ain't shown his face since early morning. But he'll be here tomorrow, for sure. And he's put out the word for all the lads to come to a meet ... Many of your Warsaw mob left?'

'Just three,' Fandorin said with a wave of his hand. 'Vatsek One-Eye's in charge now. How many of yours?'

'Counting Stump, seven. What's this bazaar tomorrow, d'you know?'

'Na-ah, they don't tell us anything, treat us like mongrels ... What's your handle, Moscow?'

'Code. And who are you?'

'Striy. Shake?'

They shook hands and Fandorin glanced around and said: 'Vatsek was spieling about some *doktur* or other. Did you hear anything?'

'No, there wasn't no yak about no doktur. Stump was talking about some big man. I asked him what sort of man it was. But you can't get nothing out of him. No, he didn't spiel about no doktur. What doktur's that?'

'Devil knows. Vatsek's got a tight mouth too. So Stump's not here?'

'I told you, tomorrow, by nightfall. Come on in and have a banter with us. Only you know, Striy, our den's not like the others – you won't get no wine.'

'How about a bit of hearts are trumps?'

'Not done around here. For cards Stump'll smash your neb in

with his apple without thinking twice. Heard about the apple, have you?'

'Who hasn't heard about it. No, I won't come in. It's more fun round at our place. I'll call round tomorrow. By nightfall, you say?'

And just then there was the sound of a clock striking the hour from the German church, a vague dark outline in the distance. I counted twelve strokes.

10 May

'Roll up when them bells is clattering,' said Code, jerking his head in the direction of the church. 'Stump ordered the meet for midnight sharp. Righty-ho, Polack, be seeing you.'

Fandorin waddled away, and the Japanese jabbed me in the back and gestured to indicate that it was time to get down off the roof.

I will not tell you how I climbed down the drainpipe in the total darkness. It is best not to remember such things. I skinned my hands, ripped my long-suffering culottes wide open and finally jumped down straight into a puddle, but the important thing is that I did not break my arms or legs, for which, O Lord, I thank Thee.

We were unable to hire a cab for a long time, even after we left Khitrovka. Once they got a good look at the three of us, the night-time cabbies simply lashed on their horses without saying a word and disappeared into the night. Moreover, I got the impression that the drivers' doubts were aroused, not so much by Fandorin and Masa, as by my own tattered and spattered personage.

Finally we got a cab – when we had already reached the Kitaigorod Wall. All the way back I was worried that Erast Petrovich would refuse to pay again, and I didn't have a kopeck on me. But no, this time he did pay, and in fact more generously than he need have done, as if he were paying for both journeys at once.

In my condition it seemed inappropriate to go in through the gates and I suggested, with some embarrassment, that we should climb over the fence again, although, God knows, in the day just past I had done more than enough climbing over fences and roofs. However, Fandorin glanced at the brightly lit windows of the Hermitage glimmering through the trees and shook his head.

'No, Ziukin, we'd better go in through the gates. Otherwise we'll probably get shot as well.'

It was only then I realised that light in the windows at such a late hour was a strange and alarming sign. There were two men in civilian clothes standing beside the usual gatekeeper. And, on looking more closely, I noticed that there were indistinct figures in the garden on the other side of the railings. Gentlemen from the court police, there was nobody else they could possibly be. And that could only mean one thing: for some reason the sovereign had come to visit the Hermitage in the middle of the night.

After long explanations at the entrance which concluded with Somov being sent for and the humiliating confirmation of my identity (the expression on my Moscow assistant's face was a sight to behold when I appeared before him in such a state) we were admitted, and as we walked along the drive to the house I saw several carriages. Something out of the ordinary was clearly going on.

In the hallway there was another ordeal in store for me: I came face to face with the governess.

'*Mon Dieu!*' she exclaimed, fluttering her eyelashes, and in her agitation forgetting our agreement to speak to each other only in Russian. '*Monsieur Ziukin, qu'est-ce qui s'est passé? Et qui sont ces hommes? C'est le domestique japonais?*'[1]

---

[1] *My God! Mr Ziukin, what has happened? And who are these men? Is this the Japanese servant?*

'It is I, Mademoiselle,' Fandorin said with a bow. 'Afanasii Stepanovich and I have been taking a brief tour of the sights of Moscow. But that is of no importance. Please tell me how your meeting went. Did you see the boy?'

That was when I learned the circumstances under which Her Majesty had lost her sapphire collar.

'It's very bad that the gendarmes went off in pursuit,' Erast Petrovich said anxiously. 'They should not have done that under any circumstances. Describe the c-carriage for me.'

Mademoiselle wrinkled up her forehead and said: 'Black, dusty, a window with a *rideau* ... The wheel had eight *rais* ... Spikes?'

'Spokes,' I prompted.

'Yes, yes, eight spokes. On the door – a brass handle.'

'That's right!' I exclaimed. 'The handle on the door of the carriage that I saw was in the form of a brass ring!'

Fandorin nodded. 'Well then, they have used the same carriage twice. Lind is too sure of himself and has too low an opinion of the Russian police. And that's not a bad thing. Describe the man who took the reticule from you.'

'Tall, brown eyes. His nose a little crooked. His moustache and beard ginger, but I think they were not real, glued on. *Outre cela.*[2] ...' Mademoiselle thought. '*Ah, oui!* A mole on the left cheek, just here.' And she touched my cheek with her finger, making me start.

'Thank you, that is something at least,' Fandorin told her. 'But what is going on here? I saw the carriages of the tsar and the grand dukes in front of the house.'

'I don't know,' Mademoiselle said plaintively, switching completely into French. 'They don't tell me anything. And they all look at me as I were to blame for everything.' She took her elbows in her hands, gulped and said in a more restrained voice, 'I think something terrible has happened. An hour ago a package

---

[2] *Apart from that.*

144

was delivered to the house, a small one, and everyone started running around, and the phones started ringing. Half an hour ago His Majesty arrived, and Grand Dukes Kirill and Simeon have just arrived too ...'

At that moment Colonel Karnovich glanced out into the hallway with his brows knitted and his lips tightly compressed.

'Fandorin, is that you?' he asked. 'I was informed you had arrived. What sort of idiotic masquerade is that? Still playing the gentleman detective? They're waiting for you. Please be so good as to make yourself decent and and get up to the large drawing room immediately. And you too, madam.'

Erast Petrovich and Mademoiselle walked away, but Karnovich looked me over from head to foot and shook his head fastidiously.

'What do you look like, Ziukin? Where have you been? What was Fandorin up to? It's most opportune that he should have taken you into his confidence. Come on, tell me; you and I are from the same department.'

'It was all pointless, Your Honour,' I said, without knowing why. 'We just wasted our time. Who is serving His Majesty and Their Highnesses?'

'The sovereign's valet and Simeon Alexandrovich's butler.'

Oh, how shameful!

Never before had I washed and changed with such speed. Just ten minutes later, after putting myself in order, I quietly entered the drawing room and thanked Foma Anikeevich and Dormidont with a bow.

There were no drinks or hors d'œuvres on the table – only ashtrays and a rather small brown paper package that had already been opened. Just to be on the safe side I took a tray from the side table and started setting out glasses on it, and in the meantime I stole a quick glance at the faces of those present, trying to guess what had happened.

The sovereign was nervously smoking a *papyrosa*. Kirill Alexandrovich was wearily rubbing his eyelids. The governor general was drumming his fingers on the table. Georgii Alexandrovich was gazing fixedly at the package. Pavel Georgievich looked unwell – his lips were trembling and there were tears in his eyes. But I found Mademoiselle Declique's appearance most frightening of all. She was sitting with her face in her hands, her shoulders were trembling, and there were convulsive sobs escaping through her fingers. I had never seen her cry before, in fact I had never even imagined that it was possible.

The high police master was sitting apart from the other men, beside the impassive Karnovich, and constantly mopping his forehead and bald temples with a handkerchief. He suddenly hiccuped, flushed bright crimson and muttered: 'I beg your pardon.'

Then he immediately hiccuped again. In the total silence the indecorous sound was distinctly audible.

I suddenly felt very afraid. So afraid that I swayed on my feet. Oh Lord, surely not?

'May I take a look?' Fandorin asked, breaking the silence.

Erast Petrovich had evidently entered the drawing room a minute or two before me. He had changed into a severe English frock coat and even found time to put on a tie.

What was it that he wanted to look at? The latest letter from Lind?

'Yes,' Kirill Alexandrovich said morosely. He had evidently taken on the role of chairman out of force of habit. 'Feast your eyes on it.'

Fandorin took a small bundle, about the size of a fruit drop, out of the package. He unwrapped it, and I saw some small object, pink and white, inside it. Erast Petrovich quickly extracted a magnifying glass from his inside pocket and bent down over the table. The expression on his face was as sour as if he had bitten a lemon.

'Is this d-definitely His Highness's finger?'

The silver tray slipped out of my hands, the glasses were smashed to smithereens. Everybody started and looked round at me, but I didn't even apologise – I barely managed to grab hold of the corner of the table in order to stop myself falling.

'What kind of stupid question is that?' Simeon Alexandrovich growled angrily. 'Of course it's Mika's little finger! Who else's could it be?'

Foma Anikeevich walked silently across to me and supported me by the elbow. I nodded to him gratefully, trying to indicate that it would soon pass.

'Listen to what it says in the letter,' said Kirill Alexandrovich, and I noticed that there was a sheet of paper lying in front of him.

The grand duke put on his pince-nez and read out the message which, like the previous ones, was written in French.

Gentlemen, you still do not seem to have realised that I am not joking.

I hope that this little parcel will convince you of the seriousness of my intentions. The severed finger is the punishment for your people's repeated violation of our agreement. The next time there is any foul play, the boy's ear will be cut off.

Now concerning our business. For the next payment I am expecting you to deliver the diamond bouquet with a spinel from the collection of the empress. The governess must be at mass in the Cathedral of Christ the Saviour from three o'clock in the afternoon. Alone, naturally.

If she is shadowed, you have only yourselves to blame for the consequences.

Yours sincerely,
Doctor Lind

What astounded me most of all was how well-informed the villain was about Her Majesty's coffret. The small diamond bouquet with a spinel was one of the genuine masterpieces of the imperial collection. It had become the property of the crown as part of the dowry of the bride of Pavel Petrovich, the future Emperor Paul I. This great masterpiece of eighteenth-century jewellery work was valued not so much for the size and purity of the stones of which it was composed as for its sheer elegance. To my mind there was no more beautiful jewel in the entire Diamond Room collection.

'Oh Lord, poor Alice,' the emperor said miserably. 'She is suffering so badly over the loss of the neckband—'

One ought perhaps to have sympathised with His Majesty, especially bearing in mind the the temperament of the tsarina, but at that moment I was quite unable to feel pity for anyone apart from poor little Mikhail Georgievich.

'We have all had our say, Fandorin,' said Kirill Alexandrovich, rather brusquely interrupting the sovereign. 'What do you think? It's clear now that you were right. Lind is an absolute monster: he will not stop at anything. What are we to do?'

'Ah, poor little Mika,' said the tsar, hanging his head disconsolately.

'We all feel sorry for Mika, of course,' said Simeon Alexandrovich, striking his fist on the table, 'but you, Nicky, ought to be feeling sorry for yourself. If the world finds out that some crook has kidnapped your nephew during the coronation of the Russian tsar and is slicing him up like salami—'

'Sam, for heaven's sake!' Georgii Alexandrovich roared in a voice like thunder. 'You're talking about the fate of my son!'

'I'm talking about the fate of our dynasty!' the governor general answered in kind.

'Uncle Sam! Uncle Georgie!' His Majesty cried, raising his hands to heaven in a gesture of conciliation. 'Let us listen to what Mr Fandorin has to say.'

Erast Petrovich picked the package up off the table and turned it this way and that.

'How was it delivered?'

'Like the previous messages,' said Kirill Alexandrovich. 'By ordinary post.'

'And again there is no stamp,' Fandorin said pensively. 'Has the postman been questioned?'

Colonel Karnovich replied: 'Not only has he been questioned, but all three postmen who deliver the municipal mail to the Hermitage by turns have been under surveillance since yesterday afternoon. They have not been seen doing anything suspicious. Furthermore, the mailbags with the post sent from the Central Post Office to this postal district are constantly under observation by plain-clothes police. No outsiders came close to the bag during the journey from Myasnitskaya Street to Kaluzhskaya Street or later, after the postman set out on his round. We don't know where Lind's messages come from. It's a real mystery.'

'Well then, until we can solve it, this is what we must do,' Erast Petrovich said morosely. 'Give him the bouquet. That is one. No attempts to follow Lind's people. That is two. Our only hope lies in Mademoiselle Declique's powers of observation – fortunately, they are very keen. That is three. I have no other recommendations to make. The slightest indiscretion by the police now, and you will not receive the boy's ear but a corpse and an international scandal. Lind is furious, that much is obvious.'

As one man, everybody turned to look at the governess. She had stopped crying and was no longer hiding her face in her hands. Her features seemed frozen to me, as if they were carved out of white marble.

She said quietly, '*Je ferai tout mon possible.*'[3]

'Yes, yes,' the sovereign pleaded. 'Please, do try. And Alice and I will pray to the Almighty. And we will start a fast immediately. According to ancient ritual that is the right thing to do before a coronation ...'

'Excellent, everyone will make the best contributions they can.' Kirill Alexandrovich laughed dismally. 'Colonel Lasovsky must be removed from command of the search.' (At these words the high police master hiccuped even more loudly than previously, but he did not apologise any more.) 'The responsibility will be returned to you, Karnovich, but this time no rash moves.

---

3 *I will try my best.*

Let everything be as Fandorin said. You will move into the Hermitage temporarily and run the search from here. There are too many visitors at the Alexandriisky Palace. Ziukin, find the colonel some sort of room and run a phone line to it. That's all. Let's go home. We all have a hard day tomorrow and you, Nicky, have to receive the ambassadors. Your bearing must be absolutely irreproachable.'

After the exalted guests had left, I continued serving tea to Their Highnesses for a long time, and many tears were shed – mostly by Pavel Georgievich, but Georgii Alexandrovich also wiped his fleshy cheeks with his cuff more than once, and as for me, I went completely to pieces. On two occasions I was obliged to hurry out of the drawing room in order not to upset the grand dukes even more with the sight of my crooked, tear-stained face.

Some time after three in the morning I was plodding along the corridor in the direction of my room when I came across Mr Masa in a very strange pose outside Fandorin's door. He was sitting on the floor with his legs folded under him and his head nodding drowsily.

When I stopped in amazement, I heard muffled sobs coming from inside the room.

'Why are you here and not inside?' I asked. 'Who is in there with Mr Fandorin?'

A terrible suspicion made me forget all the other shocks of the day.

'Pardon me, but there is something I must tell Mr Fandorin,' I declared resolutely, taking hold of the door handle, but the Japanese rose nimbly to his feet and blocked my way.

'Not arrowed,' he said, fixing me with his little black eyes. 'Genterman cry. Suffering much for ritter boy. Cannot rook. Is shamefur.'

He was lying. I realised immediately that he was lying!

Without saying another word, I ran up to the first floor and knocked at Xenia Georgievna's door. There was no answer. I cautiously opened the lock with my master key. The room was empty. And the bed had not been disturbed.

Everything went hazy in front of my eyes. She was down there, alone with that heartbreaker!

Oh Lord, I prayed, guide me and show me what I must do. Why have you visited such trials on the house of Romanov?

I hurried to the doorkeepers' room, where I had installed Colonel Karnovich only an hour earlier after laying a telephone line from the hallway.

The head of the court police opened the door to me wearing nothing but his nightshirt and without his usual tinted spectacles. His eyes proved to be small and piercing, with red eyelids.

'What is it, Ziukin?' he asked, screwing up his eyes. 'Have you decided to tell me what your friend is up to after all?'

'Her Highness is spending the night in Mr Fandorin's room,' I announced in a whisper. 'I heard her crying. And I am afraid . . . that she went there of her own accord.'

Karnovich yawned in disappointment.

'That is all very racy of course, and as head of the court police it is my business to know with whom the young ladies of the imperial family spend the night. However, you could have told me about it in the morning. Believe it or not, Ziukin, I had gone to bed to get a bit of sleep.'

'But Her Highness has a fiancé, Prince Olaf! And, apart from that, she is a virgin! Colonel, it may still not be too late to prevent this!'

'Oh no,' he said, yawning again. 'Interfering in grand princesses' affairs of the heart is more than my life's worth. They don't forgive my kind for that sort of indiscretion. And as for being a virgin, I expect she was, but she's got over that now,' Karnovich said with a crooked smile. 'Everyone knows it's a short step from weeping to consolation, and that Fandorin of yours has a considerable reputation as a ladykiller. But don't you worry, the prince won't lose a thing. He's marrying the House of Romanov, not the girl. Virginity is a load of bunk. But what is not a load of bunk are these sly tricks of Fandorin's. I'm very concerned about our very own Pinkerton's maverick activities. If you want to help me and help the sovereign at the same time, tell me everything you know.'

And so I told him – about Khitrovka and about Stump, and about the bandits' gathering the next day.

'Bosh,' Karnovich commented succinctly when he had heard me out. 'A load of bosh. Which was just what I expected.'

Sleep was entirely out of the question. I walked up and down the corridor of the first floor, wringing my hands. I was afraid that I might wake Georgii Alexandrovich with my tramping, but at the same time in my heart that was what I wanted. Then His Highness would have asked what I was doing there and I could have told him everything.

But this was a petty and unworthy hope. After what the grand duke had been through that day, I could not add this to his burdens. And so I stopped walking about and sat down on the landing.

At dawn, when the newborn sun timidly extended its first rays across the gleaming parquet, I heard light steps on the stairs, and I saw Xenia Georgievna walking up, wrapped in a light lace shawl.

'Afanasii, what are you doing here?' she asked, not so much in surprise, more as if she didn't think our meeting like this at such an unusual hour was of any great importance.

Her Highness's face was strange. I had never seen it look like that before – as if it were completely new.

'How incredible all this is,' Xenia Georgievna said, sitting down on one of the steps. 'Life is so strange. The horrible and the beautiful side by side. I've never felt so unhappy or so happy before. I'm a monster, aren't I?'

Her Highness's eyes and lips were swollen. The eyes – that was from her tears. But the lips?

I simply bowed without saying anything, although I

understood the meaning of her words very well. If I had dared, I would have said: 'No, Your Highness, it's not you who is the monster, but Erast Petrovich Fandorin. You are only a young, inexperienced girl.'

'Good night, Your Highness,' I said eventually, although the night was already over, and went to my room.

I slumped down in an armchair without getting undressed and sat there blankly for a while, listening to the dawn chorus of birds whose names I did not know. Perhaps they were nightingales or some kind of thrushes? I had never known much about such things. I went on listening and fell asleep without realising it.

I dreamed that I was an electric light bulb and I had to illuminate a hall full of waltzing couples. From my position up on high I had an excellent view of the gleaming epaulettes, glittering diamond coronets and sparkling gold embroidery on the uniforms. There was music playing, and the echoes of many voices washing about under the high vaulted ceiling, merging into a single, indistinct rumbling. Suddenly I saw two dancing couples collide. Then another two. And another two. Some people fell over, and some of them were taken by the arms and helped up, but the orchestra kept playing faster and faster, and the dancers never stopped circling even for a second. Suddenly I realised what the problem was. I was not coping with my job – my light was too dim, that was what was causing the turmoil. Panic-stricken, I strained as hard as I could to burn brighter, but I failed. In fact the twilight in the hall was growing thicker and thicker with every second that passed. Two resplendent couples flew straight towards each other, spinning as they went, and they could not see that a collision was inevitable. I did not know who they were, but the respectful way in which the other couples moved aside to make way for them suggested that they were no ordinary guests but members of the royal family. I made an absolutely incredible effort that set my thin glass shell tinkling, strained with all my might and a miracle happened: I and the world around me were suddenly flooded with a blinding light that illuminated everything. The intense bliss I experienced in that magical moment set me trembling, I cried out in rapture – and woke up.

I opened my eyes and immediately squeezed them shut again to keep out the brilliant sunlight that must have reached my face at just that second.

The final peals of my chimerical rapture slowly gave way to fright: the bright disc was so high in the sky that the hour had to be late. In any case, breakfast time must certainly be over.

I jumped to my feet with a gasp, then remembered that I had been excused from all domestic duties – Somov was performing them for the time being. Then I listened and realised how quiet the house was.

Well, naturally. Everyone had gone to bed so late that probably no one had got up yet.

I took a wash and freshened up my clothes, then walked round all the places where work should be going on to make sure that the servants at least were not sleeping and the table had already been laid for breakfast.

I went out into the yard to see if the carriages were ready for driving out and then turned into the garden to pick some tulips for Xenia Georgievna and pansies for Mademoiselle Declique.

I ran into Mr Fandorin on the lawn. Or rather, I saw him first and instinctively ducked behind a tree.

Erast Petrovich took off his white shirt and performed some complicated gymnastic movements. Then suddenly he leapt up and hung from the lowest branch of a spreading maple tree. First he swung to and fro and then he started doing something completely fantastic, flying from branch to branch with deft, confident movements of his arms and hands. He made a complete circuit round the maple tree in this way, and then repeated the procedure.

I could not tear my eyes away from his lean, well-muscled body, and I felt a quite untypical feeling of burning hatred seething helplessly inside me. Oh, if only I were a magician, I would have turned that man into some kind of monkey, then he could gambol around in the trees as much as he liked.

Turning away with an effort, I saw the curtain was drawn back at one of the windows on the ground floor – I thought it was Mr Carr's room. Then I saw the Englishman himself. He was following Fandorin's gymnastic routine with a fixed stare: his lower lip was gripped between his teeth, his fingers were gently stroking the window pane and there was a dreamy expression on his face.

The day that had started so late dragged on at an agonising, leisurely pace. I tried to occupy myself with work around the house and preparations for the imminent receptions, routs and ceremonies, but very soon abandoned all important matters, because they needed to be tackled seriously, with total concentration, and my thoughts were infinitely far removed from discussing a menu, polishing silver tableware and airing ceremonial uniforms and dresses.

I did not even have a chance to exchange a few words with Mademoiselle, because Karnovich was with her all the time. He kept on trying to get her to understand something about the next meeting with the kidnappers until at two o'clock the governess was put into a carriage and driven away – I only saw her from behind as she walked down the steps of the porch with her head held high. She was carrying a handbag which, I presumed, contained the Lesser Diamond Bouquet, that beautiful creation of the court jeweller Pfister.

After Mademoiselle left, I sat on a bench in the company of Mr Freyby. Only a little earlier, I had come out consumed by anxiety to walk round the palace and had spotted the English butler on the lawn. On this occasion he was without his book, simply sitting there with his eyes closed, luxuriating in the sunshine. Mr Freyby looked so calm and peaceful that I stopped, overcome by a sudden envy. There is the only person in this entire insane house who radiates normality and common sense, I thought. And I suddenly felt an overwhelming desire simply to enjoy the fine day with the same appetite for it as he had, to sit for a while on a bench warmed by the sun, turn my face to catch the light breeze, and not think about anything at all.

In some mysterious way the Briton must have guessed my desire. He opened his eyes, raised his bowler hat politely and gestured to me, as if to say: 'Would you care to join me?' And why not? I thought to myself. At least it will calm my nerves.

I thanked him ('Tenk yoo') and sat down. It was really wonderful there on the bench. Mr Freyby nodded to me, I nodded to him, and this ritual made a perfect substitute for conversation, which in my exhausted state would probably have been beyond my powers.

After the carriage took Mademoiselle Declique away to the Cathedral of Christ the Saviour on Volkhonka Street, I became agitated again and began squirming about on the bench, but the butler took a flat leather-bound flask out of his voluminous pocket, unscrewed its silver top, poured some amber liquid into it and held it out to me. He himself made ready to drink directly from the mouth of the flask.

'Whisky,' he exclaimed, noticing my indecision.

I had heard a lot about this British beverage, but I had never had occasion to sample it. I should tell you that I never take strong spirits, and only use less-strong drink – a glass of Malvasen – twice a year, at Easter and on Georgii Alexandrovich's name day.

However, Freyby sipped his drink with such evident enjoyment that I decided to try it. I threw my head back and drank it down, in the way that Lieutenant Endlung deals with his rum.

My throat felt as if it had been stripped raw by a file, tears sprang to my eyes and I was completely unable to breathe. I looked round in horror at the perfidious Englishman, and he winked approvingly at me, as if he were delighted with his cruel trick. Why on earth do people drink horrid things like that?

But on the inside I began to feel a warm, sweet sensation, my anxiety disappeared and was replaced by a quiet sadness – not for myself but for people who turned their lives into an absurd confusion and then suffered torment as a result.

We enjoyed a glorious silence. Here is the person who can give me some advice about Xenia Georgievna, I suddenly thought. It is obvious that he is a level-headed individual who is never at a loss in any situation. No one would envy him the master that he has, and yet he maintains such an air of dignity. However, it was absolutely impossible for me to talk to the Englishman about such a ticklish subject. I heaved a sigh.

And then Freyby turned his head slightly towards me, opened one eye and said: 'Live your own life.' He took out the dictionary and translated: 'Zhit' . . . svoy . . . sobstvenniy . . . zhizn'.'

After that he leaned back contentedly, as if the subject were exhausted, and closed his eyes again.

These strange words were spoken in the tone of voice in which good advice is given. I started wondering what living one's own life might mean. 'Live your own life.' In what sense?

But then my gaze fell on the flower clock and I saw it was already three, and I shuddered.

May the Lord Almighty preserve Mademoiselle Declique.

An hour passed, then two, three. And still the governess did not return. Karnovich stayed by the telephone the whole time, but none of the calls was the one he wanted.

There were three telephone calls from the Alexandriisky Palace on behalf of the tsar and two from Kirill Alexandrovich. And then shortly after six Simeon Alexandrovich arrived with his adjutant. He declined to enter the house and ordered cold fruit punch in the arbour. Cornet Glinsky, who was accompanying the governor general, was about to join His Highness, but the grand duke told him rather sharply that he wished to be alone, and the young man was left waiting outside the railings with the air of a beaten dog.

'How are your Englishmen getting on?' Simeon Alexandrovich

asked when I served the fruit punch. 'They probably feel completely abandoned because of . . .' He gestured vaguely with one hand. 'Because of all this. How is Mr Carr?'

I did not reply immediately to this question. Only a little earlier I had heard the sounds of a rather noisy argument between Lord Banville and his friend as I was walking down the corridor.

'I expect, Your Highness, that His Lordship and Mr Carr are upset by what has happened.'

'Mmm, well, that is not hospitable.' The grand duke flicked a cherry-red drop off his pampered moustache and drummed his fingers on the table. 'I tell you what, brother, invite Mr Carr to join me here. There is something I wish to discuss with him.'

I bowed and set off to carry out his instructions. I was struck by the tragic expression on the face of Prince Glinsky – drooping eyebrows, pale lips, a despairing look in the eyes. Ah, sir, if I only had your problems, I thought.

Mr Carr was sitting in front of the mirror in his room. He had a lacy net over his remarkable yellow hair, and his scarlet dressing gown with dragons was wide open across his white hairless chest. When I conveyed His Highness's invitation in French, the Englishman turned pink and asked me to say that he would be there immediately. '*Tout de suite*'[4] extended in practice to a good quarter of an hour, but Simeon Alexandrovich, well known for his impatience and irritability, waited without a murmur.

When Mr Carr came out to go to the arbour, he looked a real picture. The rays of the sun glittered and sparkled on his impeccable coiffure, the collar of his blue shirt supported his rouged cheeks exquisitely, and the snow-white dinner jacket with a green forget-me-not in the buttonhole was simply dazzling.

I do not know what His Highness and the beautiful gentleman spoke about, but I was shocked when Mr Carr responded to some comment from Simeon Alexandrovich by laughing and striking him across the wrist with two fingers.

---

4 *Immediately.*

I heard convulsive sobbing and on turning round saw Prince Glinsky dashing away, kicking out his long legs in uhlan breeches just like a little girl.

My God, my God.

Mademoiselle returned at six minutes to eight. As soon as Karnovich, who had been waiting together with me on the porch, saw the long-awaited carriage at the end of the drive, he immediately sent me to get Fandorin, so that I only had a brief glimpse of the familiar white hat behind the broad figure of the driver.

I trudged along the corridor to Erast Petrovich's door and was about to knock on it, but the sounds coming from inside literally paralysed me.

It was the same kind of sobbing that I had heard the night before.

I could not believe my ears. Could Xenia Georgievna possibly have taken leave of her senses so far that she was visiting here during the day? I recalled that I had not seen Her Highness even once that morning – she had not come to either breakfast or lunch. What on earth was going on?

After glancing around, I pressed my ear to the keyhole with which I was already so familiar.

'Enough of that n-now, enough,' I heard Fandorin say with his distinctive stammer. 'Later you will be sorry for speaking to me so frankly.'

A thin, faltering voice replied: 'No, no, I can see from your face that you are a noble man. Why does he torment me so? I shall shoot this detestable British flirt and then shoot myself! In front of his very eyes!'

No, it was not Xenia Georgievna.

Reassured, I knocked loudly.

Fandorin opened the door to me. Simeon Alexandrovich's adjutant was standing at the window with his back to me.

'Please come to the drawing room,' I said in a calm voice,

looking into those hateful blue eyes. 'Mademoiselle Declique has returned.'

'I waited for at least forty minutes in that big half-empty church, and no one approached me. Then an altar boy came up and handed me a note with the words: "I was told to give you this."' Mademoiselle pronounced the last phrase in Russian.

'Who told him, did he say?' Karnovich interrupted.

'Where is the note?' said Simeon Alexandrovich, holding out his hand imperiously.

The governess looked in confusion from the colonel to the governor general, as if she did not know who to answer first.

'Don't interrupt!' Georgii Alexandrovich roared menacingly.

Pavel Georgievich and Fandorin were also present in the drawing room, but they did not utter a single word.

'Yes, I asked who the note was from. He said: "From a man" and walked away.'

I saw Karnovich write something down in a little notebook and I guessed that the choirboy would be found and questioned.

'They took the note away from me later, but I remember what it said word for word: "Go out into the square, walk along the boulevard and round the small church." The text was in French, and it was written in cursive handwriting, not printed. The writing was fine and it slanted to the left.'

Mademoiselle looked at Fandorin, and he gave her a nod of approval. My heart was wrung.

'I did what it said. I stood beside the church for about ten minutes. Then a tall broad-shouldered man with a black beard and a hat pulled down over his eyes nudged me with his shoulder as he was walking by, and when I glanced round, he gestured inconspicuously for me to follow him, and I did. We walked up to the top of the side street. There was a carriage waiting there, but not the same one as yesterday, although it was black too, with its blinds tightly closed. The man opened the door and helped me in, feeling my dress as he did so. He was obviously looking for weapons.' She shuddered in disgust. 'I said to him: "Where is the boy? I won't go anywhere until I have seen him." But he seemed not to have heard me. He shoved me in the back and locked the door from the outside, and then he climbed onto the coach box – I could tell that from the way the carriage leaned over – and we set off. I discovered that the windows were not only covered with blinds but also boarded up on the inside so that there was not a single chink. We drove for a long time. In the darkness I could not check my watch, but I think that more than an hour went by. Then the carriage stopped. The driver got in, closed the door behind him and tied a piece of cloth tight over my eyes. "There's no need; I won't peep," I told him in Russian, but once again he took no notice of what I said. He took me by the waist and set me down on the ground, and after that I was led by the hand, but not very far – only eight steps. Rusty hinges squeaked and I suddenly felt cold, as if I had entered a house with thick stone walls.'

'Now as much detail as possible,' Karnovich ordered sternly.

'Yes, yes. They made me go down a steep stairway, which was quite short. I counted twelve steps. There were several people there, all men – I caught the smell of tobacco, boots and a male perfume. An English eau de cologne. I can't remember what it's called, but you could ask Lord Banville and Mr Carr; they use the very same one.'

'The Earl of Essex,' said Fandorin. 'The most fashionable fragrance of the season.'

'Mademoiselle, did you see Mika?' Pavel Georgievich asked.

'No, Your Highness.'

'What do you mean?' Georgii Alexandrovich exclaimed. 'They didn't show you my son, but you gave them the bouquet anyway?'

This reproach seemed outrageously unjust to me. As if Mademoiselle could have defied an entire gang of murderers! But then I could sympathise with the feelings of a father too.

'I did not see Mika, but I heard him,' Mademoiselle said quietly.

'I heard his voice. The boy was very close to me. He was sleeping and rambling in his sleep – he kept repeating: "*Laissez-moi, laissez-moi*,[5] I won't ever ever do it again . . .".'

She quickly took out her handkerchief and blew her nose loudly, seeming to take an awfully long time over this simple procedure. The room began dissolving in front of my eyes, and I did not immediately realise that this was caused by my tears.

'Well then,' Mademoiselle continued in a flat voice, as if she had a cold. 'Since it was definitely Michel, I decided the condition had been met and gave them the bag. One of the men said to me in a loud whisper: "It didn't hurt him, the finger was amputated under an injection of opium. If the game is played fairly, there will be no more need for such extreme measures. Tomorrow be at the same place at the same time. Bring the Empress Anna's diamond clasp. Repeat that." I repeated it: "The Empress Anna's diamond clasp." That was all. Then they led me back to the carriage, drove me around for a long time and put me out beside some bridge or other. I caught a cab and drove to the Cathedral of Christ the Saviour, and the carriage was waiting for me there.'

'Have you told us everything?' Georgii Alexandrovich asked after a pause. 'Perhaps you missed out a few small details. Think.'

'No, Your Highness . . . Except perhaps . . .' Mademoiselle screwed up her eyes. 'Michel never used to talk in his sleep. I suspect that yesterday they gave the child a very strong dose of opium and he has still not woken up.'

Pavel Georgievich groaned, and I involuntarily clenched my fists. We had to free Mikhail Georgievich as soon as possible, before that diabolical Lind ruined his health completely.

'The Empress Anna's diamond clasp! This villain has refined taste. And what has the perspicacious Mr Fandorin to say to all of this?' Simeon Alexandrovich enquired sarcastically, addressing the retired deputy for special assignments directly for the first time that I could recall.

---

5 *Let me go, let me go.*

'I shall be ready to present my reasoning following Mademoiselle Declique's trip tomorrow,' Erast Petrovich replied, without even turning his head towards His Highness. And then he added in a low voice, as if he were speaking to himself: 'A whisper? That is interesting. I beg Your Highnesses' permission to withdraw ...' He clicked open the lid of his Breguet. 'It is already nine o'clock, and I have certain pressing business this evening.'

Yes, yes, I remembered. The gathering of the one-handed bandit's gang.

Pretending that I wished to empty an overflowing ashtray, I overtook Fandorin in the corridor.

'Your Honour,' I said, forcing myself to smile beseechingly, 'take me with you. I won't be a burden to you, and I might even come in useful.'

I found this popinjay profoundly repulsive, but such minor inconveniences had no importance just at that moment. I knew that I would not get to sleep that night – I would be hearing the pitiful voice of Mikhail Georgievich tossing and turning in his delirium. It was quite possible that Karnovich was right, and Fandorin's plan was absolute nonsense, but it was certainly better than doing nothing.

Erast Petrovich looked searchingly into my eyes.

'Well now, Ziukin. I realised yesterday that you are no coward. Come with us if you like. I hope you understand what a dangerous business you are getting involved in.'

The Japanese and I waited round the corner while Fandorin went on ahead alone.

Peeping cautiously round, I saw Erast Petrovich, once again dressed as a 'toff', strolling down the middle of the road with that bouncy stride. There was a crescent moon shining in the sky, as sharp and crooked as a Turkish yataghan, and the night-time Khitrovka street was lit up as brightly as if the street lamps were burning.

Fandorin went down to the basement doors, and I heard him ask: 'Code, are you there?'

I could not make out the answer.

'I'm Striy, from the Warsaw mob,' Erast Petrovich declared in a cheerful voice as he approached the sentry, who was invisible from where I was standing. 'Me and Code are close mates, as tight as tight. Are all your lot here? And has Stump rolled up? Sure, I know the scrip, I know it. Just a moment . . .'

There was an abrupt sound like someone chopping a log of firewood with an axe and Masa pushed me forward: time to go.

We hurried across the empty space and ran down the slope. Fandorin was bending over, examining the door in the gates. A tousle-headed young man was sitting beside him with his back to the wall and his eyes rolled up, opening and closing his mouth like a fish that has been lifted out of the water.

'A cunning d-door,' Erast Petrovich said apprehensively. 'You see that wire? It's just like in a good shop – when you walk in, the bell rings. But we are modest unassuming individuals, are we not? We'll just cut the wire with a knife, like so. Why distract people from their conversation? Especially since it appears that Mr Stump has already arrived or, as they like to say in this beau monde, "rolled up".'

I could not understand why Fandorin was so very cheerful. My teeth were chattering in excitement (I hope that it was excitement and not fear), but he was almost rubbing his hands in glee and in general behaving as if we were engaged in some enjoyable, if not entirely decent, form of recreation. I recalled that Endlung had behaved in the same way before he took Pavel Georgievich to some disreputable spot. I have heard that there are people for whom danger is what wine is to a drunkard or opium to the hopeless addict. Evidently the former state counsellor belonged to this class of people. In any case, that would explain a lot about the way he behaved and the things that he did.

Fandorin pushed the door gently, and it opened without a squeak – the hinges must have been well oiled.

I saw a sloping floor illuminated by the crimson reflections of flames. Somewhere down below there was a fire or torches were burning.

We walked down a rather narrow passage for about twenty steps and then Fandorin, who was at the front, flung out his hand. We heard voices echoing hollowly under stone vaults. My eyes grew slightly accustomed to the gloom, and I saw that the passage was formed by two rows of old oak barrels that were half-rotten from age and the damp air.

Erast Petrovich suddenly crouched over and slipped into a gap between the barrels. We followed him.

It turned out that the huge wooden containers were not standing right up against each other, and the gaps between them formed a kind of a maze. We crept soundlessly along this winding path, maintaining our direction from the flickers of light on the ceiling and the sound of voices that became ever more audible, so that I could already make out individual words, although I did not always understand their meaning.

'. . . Tomorrow I'll drill a hole in your bonce if you yap. When I whistle, that's when you can start crowing.'

Erast Petrovich turned into a narrow opening and stopped moving. Peeping over his shoulder I saw a bizarre and sinister scene.

There was a planking table standing in the middle of a rather wide space, surrounded on all sides by rows of dark barrels. Standing around it were several iron tripods with burning torches thrust into them. The flames fluttered and crackled and thin plumes of black smoke rose up to the vaulted ceiling.

There were six men sitting at the table, one at the head and five along the other three sides. I could make out the leader better than the others because he was facing in our direction. I saw a coarse, powerful face with a prominent forehead, sharp folds alongside the mouth and a lower jaw that broadened towards the bottom, but it was not the face that caught my attention, it was the leader's right arm, lying on the table. Instead of a hand it had a three-pronged fork!

Stump – for there could be be no doubt it was he – thrust his incredible hand into a dish standing in front of him, pulled out a piece of meat and dispatched it into his mouth.

'No one's doing no crowing,' said one of the men siting with his back to us. 'Are we dumb clucks or what? But at least give us something to be getting on with. What's the deal? What are we dossing about like this for? I've done enough polishing the seat of my pants. Don't drink any wine, don't deal any cards. We're bored to death.'

The others began fidgeting and muttering, demonstrating their clear agreement with the speaker.

Stump carried on chewing unhurriedly, looking at them with his deep-set eyes drowned in the shadows under his heavy brow – I could only see the sparks glittering in them. He allowed his comrades to make their din for a while, then suddenly swung his hand and struck the dish hard with his fork. There was a crack, and the stout clay vessel split in two. Immediately it all went quiet.

'I'll give you wine and cards,' the leader drawled in a low, quiet voice and spat out his half-chewed scrap of meat to one side. 'The deal here is the once-in-a-lifetime kind, and not in every life either. A big man has put his trust in us. And if any louse here messes it up for me, I'll hook his chitterlings out with this here fork and make him eat them.'

He paused, and from the motionless figures of the bandits I realised that the threat he had just made was no mere figure of speech but a perfectly literal promise. I felt the goose pimples rising all over my body.

'No need to frighten us, Stump,' said the same bandit, obviously the most reckless desperado in the gang. 'You lay it out straight and clear. Why treat us like lousy mongrels? We've hung around on look-out a couple of times and tailed a couple of gulls. What kind of deal is that? We're wolves, not miserable dogs.'

'That's for me to know,' the head bandit snapped. 'And you'll chirp the way I tell you to.' He leaned forward. 'This shindy's the kind it's best for you not to know about, Axe, you'll sleep better for it. And what they called us in for is still to come. We'll show what we can do. And I tell you what, brothers. Once the job's done, we'll cut and run.'

'Out of Khitrovka?' someone asked. 'Or out of town?'

'Eejit! Out of Roossia!' Stump snapped impressively.

'What d'you mean, out of Roossia?' objected the one he had called Axe. 'Where are we gonna live? Turkishland, is it? I don't speak their lingo.'

Stump grinned, baring a mouthful of jagged, chipped teeth.

'That's all right. Axe, with the loot you'll have, the Muslims'll start chatting your lingo. Believe me, brothers, Stump doesn't make idle talk. We'll all get so well greased up from this job, every one of you will stay greased all the way to the grave.'

'But won't this big man of yours spin us off?' the same sceptic asked doubtfully.

'He's not that kind. The most honest top man in the whole wide world. Compared to him our King is a louse.'

'What sort of man is he then? A real eagle, I suppose?'

I noticed that Fandorin tensed up as he waited for the bandit boss's answer.

Stump clearly found the question rather embarrassing. He picked his teeth with his fork as if he was wondering whether to say anything or not. But eventually he decided to answer.

'I won't try to bamboozle you. I don't know. He's the kind of man who's not that easy to get close to. His toffs rolled up with him – real eagles they are, you're no match for them ... This man doesn't speak our lingo. I've seen him once. In a basement like ours, only smaller and with no light. I tell you, he's a serious man and what he says, he means. He sat there in the dark, so I couldn't see his face. Whispered to his interpreter, and he told me everything in our lingo. Our King likes to bawl and shout, but this here is Europe. You can hear a whisper better than a shout.'

Even though this remark came from the lips of an out-and-out criminal, I was struck by its psychological precision. It really is true that the less a person raises his voice, the more he is listened to and the better he is heard. The late sovereign never shouted at anyone. And the procurator of the Holy Synod, the all-powerful Konstantin Petrovich, speaks in a quiet murmur too. Why, take even Fandorin – so very quiet, but when he starts to speak, the members of the royal family hang on every word.

'Oh-ho, that's mighty. And where was your meet with this man?'

Fandorin half-rose to his feet, and I held my breath. Would he really say?

At that very moment there was a deafening crash that rumbled and echoed through the stone vaults of the basement and crumbs of stone fell from the ceiling onto the table.

'Don't move, you blackguards,' said a deafening voice, amplified many times over by a speaking trumpet. 'This is Colonel Karnovich. You are all in our sights. The next bullet is for anyone who even twitches.'

'Mmmmm,' I heard Fandorin groan in a pained voice.

The colonel really had made his appearance at a very bad moment, but on the other hand the arrest of the entire gang, especially of Stump himself, was surely bound to open some door leading to Doctor Lind. Why, good for Karnovich. How cunningly he had pretended that the information he received from me was of no interest!

The bandits all turned round, but I had no chance to get a good look at them because Stump shouted: 'Douse the lights!' and the robbers all scattered, overturning the tripods as they went.

The cellar went dark, but not for very long at all. A second later, long vicious streaks of fire started hurtling through the air from all sides, and the din that ensued was so loud that I was deafened.

Fandorin pulled on my arm, and we both tumbled to the floor.

'Lie still, Ziukin!' he shouted. 'There's nothing to be done now.'

It seemed to me that the firing went on for a long time, occasionally punctuated by howls of pain and Karnovich's commands.

'Korneev, where are you? Take your lads to the right! Miller, ten men to the left! Torches, get those torches here!'

Soon rays of light started probing the basement – running over the barrels, the overturned table, two motionless bodies on the floor. The shooting had stopped as suddenly as it had begun.

'Come out with your hands up!' Karnovich shouted. 'You've got nowhere to go anyway. The building is surrounded. Stump first!'

'That's for you from Stump!'

A tongue of flame spurted out from the far corner and the rays of light instantly darted to that spot. I saw an overturned barrel and above it the silhouette of a head and shoulders.

'They'll kill him, the b-blockheads,' Fandorin hissed in fury.

There was a deafening salvo, and chips of wood went flying off the barrel in all directions, then again and again. No one fired back from the corner any longer.

'We surrender!' someone shouted out of the darkness. 'Don't fire, chief.'

One at a time, three men came out into the open, holding their hands up high. Two of them could barely stay on their feet. Stump was not among them.

Erast Petrovich stood up and walked out of our hiding place. Masa and I followed him.

'Good evening,' Karnovich greeted Fandorin ironically. The colonel was completely surrounded by stalwart young men in civilian dress. 'Fancy meeting you here.'

Without even glancing at the head of the court police,

Fandorin walked across to the overturned barrel from behind which a lifeless arm could be seen projecting. He squatted down on his haunches and then immediately got up again.

A large number of men appeared out of nowhere on every side. Some put handcuffs on the bandits who had surrendered, some darted around between the barrels and for some reason some even felt the floor with their hands. The rays of electric light, dozens of them, glided over everything. There was a harsh smell of gunpowder and smoke. For some reason I glanced at my watch. It was seven minutes to twelve, which meant that only sixteen minutes had elapsed since we entered the basement.

'You have ruined everything, Karnovich,' said Fandorin, halting in front of the colonel. 'Stump is riddled with bullets, and he was the only one who knew where to find Lind. Where the devil did you spring from, damn you? Have you been spying on me?'

Karnovich looked somewhat embarrassed. He squinted sideways at me and gave no answer, but Fandorin understood anyway.

'You, Ziukin?' he said quietly, looking at me, and shook his head. 'How stupid . . .'

'*Kare da!*' squealed Mr Masa, who was standing some distance away from me. '*Uragirimono!*'

As if it were a dream, I saw him gather speed as he came running towards me, jump high in the air and thrust one foot out in front of him. My vision was obviously working much more rapidly than my thoughts, because I managed to get a very good look at the Japanese shoe (small, made of yellow leather, with a patched sole) as it approached my forehead.

And that was the end of 10 May for me.

11 May

Saturday did not exist for me because I spent a night, a day and another night lying in a dead faint.

12 May

I came to instantly, without any preliminary wandering between oblivion and wakefulness, that is, not at all as if I were emerging from ordinary sleep. One moment I was seeing the basement illuminated by those creeping beams of light and the rapidly approaching yellow shoe, then I closed my eyes, and when I opened them I was in a completely different place: daylight, a white ceiling and at one side, at the limit of my vision, two faces – Mademoiselle Declique and Mr Fandorin. At first for a moment I did not think this fact of any great importance. I simply noted that they were sitting there, looking down at me, and I was lying in bed. And then I began feeling the strange numbness in all my body, heard the regular murmur of rain outside the window and started. Why were their shoulders touching like that?

'*Grace à Dieu!*' said Mademoiselle. '*Il a repris connaissance. Vous aviez raison.*'[1]

I looked from her to Fandorin with a feeling that there was something that I ought to ask him.

'What is *uragirimono?*' I then asked, repeating the resounding word that had stuck in my memory. In fact, I thought that I had only just heard it.

'It means t-traitor in Japanese,' Erast Petrovich replied coolly, leaning over me and for some reason pulling down my lower eyelids with his fingers (I was simply mortified at such

---

[1] *Thank God! He has recovered consciousness. You were right.*

172

familiarity). 'I am glad that you are alive, Ziukin. After a blow like that you might never have recovered consciousness. You have a very thick skull – there is not even any concussion. You have been lying unconscious for almost forty hours. Try to sit up.'

Sitting up without any especial effort, I suddenly felt embarrassed because I saw that I was wearing only my undershirt, and it was unbuttoned over my chest. Noticing my unease, Mademoiselle delicately averted her eyes.

Fandorin handed me a glass of water and in the same measured tone of voice told me something that brought me back to reality: 'You, Ziukin, have done serious damage to our cause by telling Karnovich about our plans. A highly promising lead has been lost. Stump has been killed. Four of his gang, including the sentry whom I stunned, have been taken alive, but they are quite useless to us. One was used for snooping around the Hermitage. Another was the driver in the carriage that you attempted to chase. He was the one who lashed you with his whip, remember? But he does not know who was sitting in the carriage – he did not even hear the child cry out. Stump ordered him to get up on the coach box on Nikolo-Yamskaya Street, drive along a set route, and then get back down again at the Andronnikov Monastery. There he gave up his seat to a different driver, who did not look Russian. And that is all. Stump, at least, knew where L-Lind's lair is. But now we have been left empty-handed. So Masa's anger is understandable. Now that it is clear you are alive and almost well, my assistant will finally be released from custody, and a good thing too – without him I am like a man without arms.'

I touched my forehead and felt a substantial bump. Well, serve me right.

'But are there no leads at all then?' I asked, my voice trembling with awareness of the gravity of my mistake.

'Now all we can do is put our trust in Mademoiselle Declique. I am afraid I have run out of ideas. My Lady, tell Afanasii Stepanovich about your journeys to Lind's place yesterday and today.'

'What, have you already been to see him twice?' I asked in amazement and turned towards the grey window, wondering what time it was.

'Yes, today's meeting was early this morning,' Mademoiselle replied. 'Will you permit me to speak French? It will be much quicker.'

And indeed, in five minutes she gave me an account of the events that had occurred during my enforced absence.

The previous day, Saturday, she had once again been summoned from the church by a note. The carriage (not the same one as the day before, but very much like it and also with boarded-up windows) was waiting on the next side street. The driver was the same – bearded, unspeaking, with his hat pulled down low over his eyes. Fifty-four minutes later (on this occasion Fandorin had given Mademoiselle a watch with phosphorescent hands) she was once again blindfolded and soon found herself in the same underground vault. This time they uncovered her eyes for a few moments so that she could take a brief glance at Mikhail Georgievich. The boy was lying with his eyes closed, but he was alive. The governess was forbidden to look around and all she saw was a bare stone wall dimly lit by a candle, and a chest that served His Highness as a bed.

On the morning of that day the whole procedure had been repeated. Doctor Lind had acquired an aigrette of diamonds and sapphires. During the few seconds that Mademoiselle was not blindfolded, she was able to take a closer look at the prisoner. He was still unconscious, had lost a lot of weight and his left hand was bandaged. Mademoiselle had touched his forehead and felt a strong fever.

Mademoiselle's narrative broke off at that point, but she quickly took herself in hand.

'How I wish this was all over,' she said with a self-control that I found quite admirable. 'Michel will not survive very long in conditions like that. He is a strong healthy child, but everything has its limits.'

'Did you see Lind? Even out of the corner of your eye?' I asked hopefully.

'No. The blindfold was removed for no more than ten seconds and I was strictly forbidden to turn round. I only sensed that there were several men standing behind me.'

I felt an empty ache in the pit of my stomach.

'So the search is no further forward at all?'

Mademoiselle and Fandorin exchanged glances in a way that seemed conspiratorial to me, and I felt a stab of almost physical pain. The two of them were together, a couple, and I had been left on the outside, alone.

'We do have something,' Fandorin declared with a mysterious air and, lowering his voice as if he were revealing some highly important secret, added: 'I have taught Emilie to count the creaks made by the wheels.'

For a moment the only thing I understood was that he had called Mademoiselle Declique by her first name! Could their friendship really have gone that far? And only then did I attempt to penetrate the meaning of his words. I failed.

'The creaks made by the wheels?'

'Why yes. Any axle, even if it is perfectly lubricated, produces a creak which, if you listen closely, is a constant repetition of the same set of sounds.'

'So what?'

'One cycle, Ziukin, is a single revolution, a turn of the wheel. You only have to count how many times the wheel has turned in order to know how far the carriage has travelled. The wheels on carriages of the phaeton type preferred by the kidnappers are a standard size – in the metric system, they are a metre and forty centimetres in diameter. Therefore, according to the laws of geometry, the length of the circumference is equal to four metres and eighty centimetres. The rest is simple. Mademoiselle counts and remembers the number of revolutions from one corner to the next. It is easy to tell when the carriage turns a corner, because it leans either to the right or the left. We are not having the carriage followed, in order not to alarm the kidnappers, however, we do see the direction in which Emilie is driven away. After that everything d-depends on her alertness and her memory. And so,' Fandorin continued in the voice of a teacher expounding a problem in geometry, 'if we know the number and direction of revolutions, and also the d-distance between the corners, we can identify the place where they are hiding the child.'

'Well, and have you identified it?' I exclaimed in eager excitement.

'Not so fast, Ziukin, not so f-fast,' Fandorin said with a smile. 'The mute driver deliberately does not follow a direct route, but turns and twists – evidently checking to see if anyone is on his tail. And so Emilie's task is not a simple one. Yesterday she and I walked along the route taken by the carriage, checking her observations against the g-geography.'

'And what did you discover?' I asked, imagining Mademoiselle walking along the street, leaning on the arm of her elegant escort, both of them serious and intent, united by the common cause, and meanwhile I was lying in bed like a useless block of wood.

'Both times, after wandering around the side streets, the carriage came out onto Zubovsky Square. That is also confirmed by Emilie's observations – at that point on the route she heard the sound of a large number of carriages and a murmur of voices.'

'And after that?'

Mademoiselle looked round shamefacedly at Fandorin – this brief trusting glance made my heart ache once again – and said, as if she were making excuses for herself, 'Monsieur Ziukin, yesterday I managed to remember eleven corners, and today thirteen.' She screwed up her eyes and listed them hesitantly: 'Twenty-two, left; forty-one, right; thirty-four, left; eighteen, right; ninety, left; fourteen, right; a hundred and forty-three, right; thirty-seven, right; twenty-five, right; a hundred and fifteen, right (and here, in the middle, at about the fiftieth turn of the wheels, the noise of the square); fifty-two, left; sixty, right; then right again, but I don't remember how far. I tried very hard, but I lost track . . .'

I was astounded.

'Good Lord, how did you manage to remember so many?'

'Do not forget, my friend, that I am a teacher,' she said with a gentle smile, and I blushed, uncertain as to how I should interpret that form of address and whether such familiarity was permissible in our relations.

'But tomorrow it will all happen again, and you will lose track again,' I said, assuming a stern air for the sake of good order. 'The human memory, even the most highly developed, has its limits.'

I found the smile with which Fandorin greeted my remark most annoying. People smile in that way at the babbling of an innocent child.

'Emilie will not have to remember everything from the very beginning. After Zubovksy Square, the carriage followed the same route both times, and the last corner that our scout definitely remembered was the junction of Obolensky Lane and Olsufievsky Lane. We do not know where the carriage went afterwards, but that spot has been identified with absolute certainty. From there to the final point is not very far – about ten or fifteen minutes.'

'In fifteen minutes a carriage could travel a good ten versts in any direction,' I remarked, piqued by Erast Petrovich's arrogance. 'Are you really planning to search such an immense area? Why, it's larger than the whole of Vasilievsky Island!'

He smiled even more insufferably.

'The coronation, Ziukin, is the day after tomorrow. And then we shall have to give Doctor Lind the Orlov and the game will be over. But tomorrow Emilie will set out again in a b-boarded-up carriage to pay the final instalment – some kind of tiara of yellow diamonds and opals.'

I could not repress a groan. The priceless tiara in the form of a garland of flowers. Why, that was the most important treasure of all in Her Majesty's *coffret*!

'Naturally, I have had to give the empress my word of honour that the tiara and all the trinkets that have gone before it will be returned safe and sound,' Fandorin declared with quite incredible self-assurance. 'Oh, and by the way, I believe I have not yet mentioned one rather important circumstance. Since Karnovich disrupted our Khitrovka operation like a bull charging into a china shop, the overall control of operations directed against Lind has been entrusted to me, and the head of the court police and the high police master of Moscow have been forbidden to interfere under penalty of prosecution.'

This was unheard of! An investigation on which, without any exaggeration, the fate of the tsarist dynasty depended had been entrusted to a private individual! It meant that at that moment Erast Petrovich Fandorin was the most important individual in the entire Russian state, and I suddenly saw him in a quite different light.

'Emilie will start her count at the corner of Obolensky Lane and Olsufievsky Lane,' he explained, no longer smiling but with a most serious expression on his face. 'And then Mademoiselle, with her magnificent memory, will certainly not lose count.'

'But, Your Honour, how will Mademoiselle know that she has reached the right corner?'

'That is very simple, Ziukin, since I shall see the carriage that they put her in. Of course, I shall not follow it, but go directly to Olsufievsky Lane. When I see the carriage approaching, I shall ring a bell, and that will be the signal for Emilie.'

'But will that not seem suspicious to the driver? Why would a respectably dressed gentleman like you suddenly ring a bell? Perhaps you could simply arrest this driver and let him tell you where Lind is hiding?'

Fandorin sighed.

'That is probably exactly what High Police Master Lasovsky would do. Lind must undoubtedly have foreseen such a possibility, but for some reason he is not at all afraid of it. I have certain ideas of my own on that matter, but I shall not go into them just now. As for the respectable gentleman, you really do insult me there. I think you have seen how remarkably well I can transform my appearance. And I shall not only ring a bell, Ziukin, I shall shout as well.'

And suddenly he began yelling in a piercing nasal voice with a strong Tartar accent, miming as if he was shaking a bell: 'Any old rags – kopeck a time! Rusty spoons and ladles! Old ripped pants and rags, rusty spoons and ladles! Your junk for my money!'

Mademoiselle laughed for the first time in those difficult days – at least, in my presence.

'Now, Monsieur Ziukin, you rest and Erast and I will take a little stroll about Maiden's Field, Pogodinskaya and Pliushchikha,' she said, painstakingly enunciating the names of the Moscow streets, but the only word that I heard was Erast.

How could he be 'Erast' to her?

'I am perfectly well,' I assured them both, 'and I would like to accompany you.' Fandorin stood up and shook his head.

'Masa will accompany us. I am afraid that he is still angry with you. And the time spent in the lock-up has probably not improved his mood at all.'

Of course, I did not simply lie there, but I had nothing to occupy myself with, for Somov had taken complete possession of all my responsibilities and, to do him justice, he was managing them quite well – at least I did not discover any serious omissions, although I checked on the condition of the rooms and the tableware and the stables, and even the state of the door handles. There was nothing I had to do, apart from ordering the roses in Her Highness's room to be replaced with anemones and having an empty bottle that had rolled under Lieutenant Endlung's bed taken away.

So I had been relieved of my duties, beaten (deservedly, which was the most painful thing) and humiliated in front of

Mademoiselle Declique, but what tormented me most of all was the nightmarish vision of Mikhail Georgievich languishing in a damp dungeon. Shock, coercion, physical torment, the prolonged effects of narcotics – all of these traumas, suffered at such a young age, would be certain to have dire consequences. It was terrifying to think how they might affect the grand duke's character and psychological health. But it was still too early to be worrying about such things. First His Highness had to be freed from the clutches of the cruel Doctor Lind.

And I promised myself that I would forgive Fandorin everything if only he could save the child.

The members of our household returned early in the evening after attending the ceremony of the consecration of the State Banner in the Armoury Palace.

In the corridor Xenia Georgievna took hold of my sleeve and asked quietly: 'Where is Erast Petrovich?'

Her Highness seemed willing to make me her confidant in her *affaire de cœur*[2], but I felt absolutely no desire to assume this ambivalent role.

'Mr Fandorin has gone out with Mademoiselle Declique,' I replied impassively, bowing and remaining bent as if I had forgotten to straighten up so that I would not have to meet the grand princess's gaze.

Xenia Georgievna seemed quite unpleasantly surprised.

'With Emilie? But why?'

'It has to do with the plans to free Mikhail Georgievich,' I said without going into details, wishing to end this conversation as soon as possible.

'Ah, what an egotist I am!' Tears sprang to the grand princess's eyes. 'I am horrid, horrid! Poor Mika! No, I think of him all the time, I was praying for him all night long.' Suddenly she blushed and corrected herself. 'Well, almost all night . . .'

---

[2] *Affair of the heart.*

These words, which could be construed in only one way, finally spoiled my mood completely, and I am afraid that during supper I was insufficiently attentive in my duties.

The meal was a special one, arranged in honour of our English guests on the occasion of the birthday of the Queen of England, who is known in our Family simply as Granny and is genuinely respected and dearly loved. The last time I had seen 'the grandmother of all Europe' was in the spring in Nice, when Queen Victoria held a party for Xenia Georgievna and Prince Olaf. I thought that the Empress of India and ruler of the leading empire in the world seemed very aged but still strong. Our court servants say that after the death of her husband for a long time she maintained a connection with one of her own servants, but looking at this admirable majestic individual it was quite impossible to believe in such a thing. In any case, there is always all sorts of gossip about royalty, but one should never give any credit to rumours until they have been officially confirmed. I, at least, do not encourage gossip about Her Britannic Majesty in my presence.

In arranging a supper in Granny's honour, Georgii Alexandrovich wished to make up at least in part for the lack of attention paid to his English guests as a result of the misfortune that had befallen the Green House. The preparations had been supervised by Somov – all that remained for me to do was to check the table settings and the menu. Everything was impeccable.

The festivities fell flat, although Endlung tried as hard as he could, and even Georgii Alexandrovich behaved as a genuinely hospitable host ought to. But all efforts were in vain. Pavel Georgievich sat there with a glum face and did not even touch his food; he only drank wine. Xenia Georgievna seemed distracted; His Lordship and Mr Carr did not even look at each other and laughed somehow too loudly at the lieutenant's jokes, as if they were deliberately pretending to be carefree and lighthearted.

From time to time there were prolonged pauses, a sure sign of an unsuccessful evening.

It seemed to me that the shade of the unfortunate little prisoner was hovering over the table, although not a word was spoken about him. After all, the Englishmen had not officially been informed about what had happened – that would have meant the inevitable dissemination of the secret across the whole of Europe. As long as the subject was not touched upon, it did not exist. As men of honour, Lord Banville and Mr Carr would keep silent. And if they did say anything, it would only be in private, among their own circle. That, of course, would fuel rumours, but nothing more than that. And I have already spoken about rumours.

I stood behind Georgii Alexandrovich's chair, giving signs to the servants if anything needed to be brought in or taken out. But my thoughts were far away. I was wondering how I could exculpate my unwitting debt of guilt to Mikhail Georgievich and whether there was some other way in which I could help to save him. And also – I will not attempt to dissemble – several times I recalled the trusting even admiring way in which Mademoiselle Declique had looked at Fandorin – *Erast*. I must admit that in picturing myself as Mikhail Georgievich's rescuer, I imagined how she would look at me in the same way – perhaps with even greater admiration. Foolish, of course. Foolish and unworthy.

'Why does it have to be me?' Pavel Georgievich asked, lowering his voice. 'You were the one who promised to take them to the opera today.'

'I can't,' Georgii Alexandrovich replied just as quietly. 'You will go.'

Just for an instant – evidently because my thoughts were occupied by extraneous matters – I imagined that I had begun to understand English, for the conversation at the table was naturally in that language, but then I realised that these remarks had been made in Russian.

Pavel Georgievich spoke in a jolly voice, with his lips stretched out into a smile, but his eyes were as spiteful as could be. His father regarded him with a perfectly benign air, but I noticed that the back of His Highness's neck was turning crimson, and that certainly boded no good.

By this time Xenia Georgievna was no longer at the table – she had withdrawn, citing a slight migraine.

'Is it because *she* has arrived?' Pavel Georgievich asked, still smiling in the same way and looking at the Englishmen. 'Are you going to see her at the Loskutnaya?'

'None of your business, Paulie,' said Georgii Alexandrovich, smacking his lips as he lit up a cigar. 'You're going to the opera.'

'No!' Pavel Georgievich exclaimed so loudly that the Englishmen actually started.

Endlung immediately began jabbering away in English. Georgii Alexandrovich laughed, added a few words and then, covering his son's hand with his own immense fleshy palm in a paternal manner, rumbled: 'Go to the opera or go to Vladivostok. And I'm not joking.'

'I'll go to Vladivostok; I'll go to the devil if you like!' Pavel Georgievich replied in a honeyed voice, and lovingly set his other hand on top of his father's, so that from the outside this family scene must have appeared quite charming. 'But you go to the opera yourself.'

The threat concerning Vladivostok was heard quite often in the Family. Every time Pavel Georgievich was involved in some escapade or provoked his parents' displeasure in one way or another, Georgii Alexandrovich threatened to use his authority as admiral-general to send him to the Pacific Fleet, to serve the fatherland and settle down. So far, however, this had not happened.

After that they spoke exclusively in English, and my thoughts took a completely different direction.

I had an idea.

The point was that the meaning of the spat between Their Highnesses, which would hardly have been understandable even to someone who knew Russian, was absolutely clear to me.

Izabella Felitsianovna Snezhnevskaya had arrived and was staying at the Loskutnaya hotel.

There was someone who would help me!

Madam Snezhnevskaya was the most intelligent woman I had ever met in my life, and in my time I had seen empresses and high-society lionesses and ruling queens.

Izabella Felitsianovna's story is so fantastic and improbable that the like is probably not to be found in the whole of world history. Possibly some Madam Maintenon or Marquise de Pompadour might have achieved greater power at the zenith of their glory, but their position within the royal household could hardly have been more secure and enduring. Madam Snezhnevskaya, being, as I have already said, a most intelligent woman, had made a truly great innovation in court practice: she had started an affair, not with a monarch or a grand duke, who alas are mortal or inconstant, but with the monarchy, which is immortal and eternal. At the age of twenty-eight Izabella Felitsianovna had earned the sobriquet of a 'crown jewel', and in fact she really did look like some precious decoration from the Imperial Diamond Room: petite, delicate, unutterably elegant, with a voice like crystal, golden hair and sapphire eyes. This little dancer, the youngest and most talented in all the ballet companies of St Petersburg, had been noticed by the deceased sovereign. In paying homage to the charms of this nymph, His Majesty discovered something more in Izabella Felitsianovna than the mere enchantment of beauty and freshness – he discovered intelligence, tact and the basic qualities of a faithful ally of the throne.

As a statesman and exemplary family man, the sovereign could not allow himself to become too obsessed with this magical debutante, and he took the wise step (one must presume, not without regret) of entrusting Madam Snezhnevskaya to the care of the tsarevich, who was causing his august parent great concern with his excessive piety and a certain lack of polish. Izabella Felitsianovna bore the parting from His Majesty with courage and took her important state mission most responsibly, so that the heir to the throne soon changed for the better and even committed several follies (admittedly rather modest and not scandalous in nature), which finally reassured his father the tsar.

In appreciation of her services, Madam Snezhnevskaya received a marvellous palazzo on Bolshaya Dvoryanskaya Street, her own choice of parts at the Mariinsky Theatre and – most important of all – a special, in fact exclusive, position at court, which was the envy of many, many others. However, despite all this, she conducted herself modestly, did not abuse her influence and – almost unbelievably – did not acquire any serious enemies. It was known from reliable sources that the lovelorn tsarevich had offered to marry the beauty in secret, but she prudently declined, and when a tender friendship sprang up between the heir to the throne and Princess Alice she withdrew into the shadows, and in a touching scene of farewell with 'dear Nicky' she gave her blessing to that union. This action subsequently paid dividends, since it was genuinely appreciated by the new tsarina – yet another unprecedented phenomenon – and she began giving her former rival clear signs of favour. Especially when Izabella Felitsianovna, following a decent pause for grieving, entrusted her tender heart to Georgii Alexandrovich. To be quite honest, I think that in many ways Madam Snezhnevskaya gained more than she lost by this change. Georgii Alexandrovich is a distinguished man and a generous soul with a far more pleasant character than his nephew.

Oh, Izabella Felitsianovna was wisdom itself. One could tell her about anything. She understood how important the secrets of the royal family were, for she herself was their custodian. Snezhnevskaya would come up with something special, something that would not occur either to the slippery Colonel Karnovich or the redoubtable Kirill Alexandrovich, or even the artful Mr Fandorin himself.

★

Madam Snezhnevskaya had taken an entire wing in the Loskutnaya, which in itself was an adequate demonstration of this amazing woman's status – just then, at the very height of the coronation celebrations, even the most ordinary hotel room cost five times as much as normal, and it was in any case impossible to find one.

There were numerous baskets of flowers standing in the hallway of the deluxe apartment and I heard the muted sounds of a grand piano coming from somewhere in the maze of rooms. I handed the maid a note and the playing stopped almost immediately. A minute later Izabella Felitsianovna herself came out to me. She was wearing a rich-pink dress of light silk that no other blonde could possibly have presumed to wear, but Snezhnevskaya in this attire did not look vulgar, she looked divine – I cannot find any other word for it. Once again I was astounded by her light porcelain beauty, that most precious kind of beauty, encountered so very rarely, which gives a face that should be familiar the power to take one's breath away and strike one dumb.

'Afanasii!' she said with a smile, looking up at me but managing in some miraculous manner to hold herself as if she were standing on a pedestal, not on the ground. 'Hello, my friend. Is it something from Georgie?'

'No,' I replied with a low bow. 'I have secret business of state importance.'

The clever woman did not ask me a single question. She knew that Afanasii Ziukin would not use such a weighty phrase idly. She knitted her brows in concern for an instant and then beckoned me with her little hand.

I followed her through several communicating rooms to the boudoir. Izabella Felitsianovna closed the door, sat down on the bed, gestured for me to take a seat in an armchair and said just two words: 'Tell me.'

I expounded the gist of the problem to her, without keeping anything back. My story took quite a long time, because so many events had occurred during the previous few days, but even so it was shorter than might have been expected, for Snezhnevskaya did not gasp or clutch at her heart, and she did not interrupt me even once – she only picked faster and faster at her collar with her elegant fingers.

'Mikhail Georgievich is in mortal danger, and there is a terrible threat hanging over the entire house of Romanov,' was how I concluded my extensive account, although I could have dispensed with the dramatic style because my listener had understood everything perfectly well anyway.

Izabella Felitsianovna said nothing for a long time, a very long time. Never had I seen an expression of such agitation on her doll-like face, not even when I took the tsarevich's letters away from her on Georgii Alexandrovich's instructions.

Unable to bear such a long pause, I asked: 'Tell me, is there any solution to this?'

She raised her bright-blue eyes and looked at me sadly and – so I thought – with sympathy. But her voice was firm.

'There is. Only one. To sacrifice the lesser for the sake of the greater.'

'"The lesser" – is that His Highness?' I asked and sobbed in a most shameful fashion.

'Yes. And I assure you, Afanasii, that such a decision has already been taken, although no one speaks of it out loud. Knick-knacks from the *coffret* – very well, but no one will give this Doctor Lind the Orlov. Not for anything in the world. This Fandorin of yours is a clever man. The idea of "renting" is brilliant. Stretch things out until the coronation, and after that it won't matter any more.'

'But . . . but that is monstrous!' I could not help exclaiming.

'Yes, from the ordinary human point of view, it is monstrous,' she said and touched me affectionately on the shoulder. 'Neither you nor I would behave like that with our children. Ah yes, you have no children, I believe?' Snezhnevskaya sighed and then in her pure ringing voice she expressed an idea that I myself had pondered more than once. 'To be born into a ruling house is a special destiny. One that brings immense privileges, but also requires the willingness to make immense sacrifices. A disgraceful scandal during the coronation is unacceptable. Under any circumstances whatever. To hand over one of the most important insignia of the empire to criminals is even less acceptable. But to sacrifice the life of one of the eighteen grand dukes is perfectly acceptable. Even Georgie understands that of course. What is a four-year-old boy compared with the fate of an entire dynasty?'

There was a clear hint of bitterness in these last words, but there was also genuine grandeur. The tears that sprang to my eyes did not go on to run down my cheeks. I do not know why, but I felt chastened.

There was a knock at the door, and the English nanny led in a pair of quite delightful twins who looked very much like Georgii Alexandrovich – ruddy-cheeked and strong-necked, with lively brown eyes.

'Good night, Mummy,' they babbled and ran to fling themselves on Izabella Felitsianovna's neck.

It seemed to me that she hugged and kissed them rather more passionately than this everyday ritual required.

When the boys had been led away, Snezhnevskaya locked the door and said to me: 'Afanasii, your eyes are soggy. Stop it immediately or I'll turn weepy myself. It doesn't happen to me very often, but once I start it will be a long time before I stop.'

'I beg your pardon,' I mumbled, fumbling in my pocket for a handkerchief, but my fingers were not responding very well.

Then she came up to me, took a little lacy handkerchief out of her cuff and dabbed my eyelashes – very cautiously, as if she were afraid of spoiling make-up.

Suddenly there was a knock at the door – loud and insistent.

'Izabo! Open up, it's me!'

'Paulie!' exclaimed Snezhnevskaya, throwing up her hands. 'You must not meet. It would put the boy in an awkward position. In here, quickly!

'Just a moment!' she called. 'I'll just put my shoes on.'

Meanwhile she opened the door of a large mirror-fronted wardrobe and shoved me inside, prodding me with her sharp little fist.

The interior of the dark and rather spacious oak wardrobe smelled of lavender and eau de cologne. I turned round cautiously, made myself as comfortable as possible and tried not to think what an embarrassing situation would result if my presence were to be discovered. But a moment later I heard something that made me forget all about my embarrassment.

'I adore you!' Pavel Georgievich exclaimed. 'How very lovely you are, Izabo! I think about you every day!'

'Stop that! Paulie, you are simply insane! I told you, it was a mistake that will never be repeated. And you gave me your word.'

Oh Lord! I clutched at my heart, and the movement set the dresses rustling.

'You swore that we would be like brother and sister!' Izabella Felitsianovna declared, raising her voice – evidently in order to mask the incongruous noises from the wardrobe. 'And anyway your father telephoned. He should be here at any minute.'

'I rather think not!' Pavel Georgievich declared triumphantly. 'He has gone to the opera with the Englishmen. No one will bother us. Izabo, what do you want him for? He's married, but I'm free. He's twenty years older than you!'

'And I'm seven years older than you. That's a lot more for a woman than twenty years is for a man,' Snezhnevskaya replied.

I deduced from the rustling of silk that Pavel Georgievich was trying to put his arms round her and she was resisting his embraces.

'You are like Thumbelina,' he said passionately. 'You will always be my tiny little girl . . .'

She gave a short laugh: 'Oh yes, a little lapdog – a puppy to the end of its days.'

There was another knock at the door, even more insistent than the previous one.

'My lady, Georgii Alexandrovich is here!' the maid's frightened voice announced.

'How can that be?' Pavel Georgievich cried in alarm. 'What about the opera? Well, that's it. Now he really will send me to Vladivostok! Oh Lord, what shall I do?'

'Into the wardrobe,' Izabella Felitsianovna declared decisively. 'Quickly! No, not the left door, the right one!'

Somewhere very close to me a door squeaked and I heard agitated breathing about three paces away, beyond the multiple layers of dresses. Thank God my brain was unable to keep up with events, otherwise I should probably have simply fainted away.

'Well, at last!' I heard Snezhnevskaya exclaim joyfully. 'I had already given up hope! Why promise and then make me wait like this?'

There was the sound of a prolonged kiss and beyond the dresses Pavel Georgievich gnashed his teeth.

'I was supposed to go to the opera, but I escaped. That scoundrel Paulie ... Give him it in the neck, I will ... Here, I had to come here ... I have to ...'

'Not straight away, not straight away ... Let's have a glass of champagne – it's already waiting in the drawing room ...'

'To hell with champagne. I'm all on fire. Bellochka, it's been hell being without you. Oh, if you only knew! But later, later ... Unbutton this damn collar!'

'No, this is insufferable!' a voice in the wardrobe said in a breathless whisper.

'You're crazy ... Your whole family's crazy ... You were saying something about Paulie?'

'The boy's got completely out of hand! That's it. I've decided to send him to the Pacific. You know, I believe he's rather taken a fancy to you. The little whippersnapper. I know I can trust you completely, but bear in mind that he picked up a nasty disease on the voyage—'

The wardrobe swayed and a door slammed.

'He's lying!' Pavel Georgievich howled. 'I'm cured! Ah, the scoundrel!'

'Wha-a-at!' Georgii Alexandrovich roared in a terrible voice. 'How dare you . . . How dare you . . . dare?'

Horrified, I opened my door a crack and saw something I could not possibly have imagined even in the most appalling nightmare: Their Highnesses had grabbed each other's throats, and Pavel Georgievich was kicking at his father's ankles, while Georgii Alexandrovich was twisting his son's ear.

Izabella Felitsianovna tried to come between the two men, but the admiral-general caught the little ballerina a glancing blow with his elbow, and she was sent flying back towards the bed.

'Afanasii!' Snezhnevskaya shouted imperiously. 'They're killing each other!'

I jumped out of the wardrobe, prepared to accept the blows of both parties, but that proved unnecessary because Their Highnesses senior and junior gaped at me wide-eyed, and the battle came to a natural end.

I caught a quick glimpse of my reflection in a pier glass and shuddered. Tousled hair, dishevelled sideburns, and there was something pink clinging to my shoulder – either a slip or a pair of pantaloons. In my state of abject confusion, I grabbed the shameful item and stuffed it into my pocket.

'Will . . . er . . . will there be any instructions?' I babbled.

Their Highnesses exchanged glances, both looking as if a tapestry or bas-relief on the wall had suddenly started talking. But in any case the threat of infanticide or patricide was clearly over, and I was astounded yet again by Izabella Felitsianovna's presence of mind and acuity of wit.

Their Highnesses were apparently struck by the same thought, because they said almost exactly the same thing simultaneously.

'Well, Bella, you are a most amazing woman,' Georgii Alexandrovich boomed.

And Pavel Georgievich chanted in a bewildered tenor: 'Izabo, I shall never understand you . . .'

'Your Highnesses,' I blurted out, realising what a blasphemous misconception the grand dukes were labouring under. 'It's not at all . . . I have not . . .'

Without listening to what I was trying to say, Pavel Geor-gievich turned to Snezhnevskaya and exclaimed in a tone of childish resentment: 'So he – *he* – can, and I can't?'

I was struck completely dumb, with no idea at all of how to resolve this terrible situation.

'Afanasii,' Izabella Felitsianovna said firmly, 'go to the dining room and bring some cognac. And don't forget to slice a lemon.'

I rushed to carry out this instruction with a feeling of quite inexpressible relief and, to be quite honest, I was in no great hurry to get back. When I finally entered the room, carrying a tray, the picture that met my eyes was quite different: the bal-lerina was standing, with Their Highnesses sitting on pouffes on each side of her. I was rather inaptly reminded of a performance of Chinizelli's circus which Mademoiselle and I had attended with Mikhail Georgievich the previous Easter. We had seen roaring lions sitting on low pedestals while a brave slim female lion-tamer strolled around between them, clutching a massive whip in her hand. The similarity was heightened by the fact that the heads of all three of them – Snezhnevskaya standing and the great dukes sitting – were on the same level.

'. . . I love you both,' I heard and halted in the doorway, because this was clearly not the moment to come barging in with the cognac. 'You are both very dear to me – you, Georgie, and you, Paulie. And you love each other too, do you not? Is there anything in the world more precious than loving devotion and affection for one's kin? We are no vulgar bourgeois. Why hate when you can love? Why quarrel when you can be friends? Paulie is not going off to Vladivostok – we would miss him wretchedly, and he would miss us. And we will arrange everything excellently. Paulie, when are you on duty at the Guards company?'

'On Tuesdays and Fridays,' Pavel Georgievich replied, batting his eyelids.

'And you, Georgie, when are the meetings at the ministry and the State Council?'

Georgii Alexandrovich replied with a rather dull-witted (I beg your pardon, but I cannot find any better definition) expression on his face: 'On Mondays and Thursdays. Why?'

'See how convenient it all is!' Snezhnevskaya exclaimed delightedly. 'So everything's arranged! You, Georgie, will come to see me on Tuesday and Friday. And you, Paulie, will come on Monday and Thursday. And we will all love each other very, very much. And we won't quarrel at all, because there is nothing to quarrel about.'

'Do you love him in the same way as you love me?' the admiral-general asked stubbornly.

'Yes, because he is your son. He is so very much like you.'

'But ... what about Afanasii?' Pavel Georgievich asked, looking round at me in bemusement.

Izabella Felitsianovna's eyes glinted, and I suddenly sensed that she did not find this terrible, impossible, monstrous scene in the least bit arduous.

'And Afanasii too.' On my word of honour, she winked at me. But that is impossible – I must have imagined it – or else it was a nervous tic in the corner of her eye. 'But not in the same way. He is not a Romanov, after all, and I have a strange destiny. I can only love the men of that family.'

And this last sentence sounded perfectly serious, as if Snezhnevskaya had just that moment made a remarkable and possibly not very happy discovery.

13 May

I found myself caught in a false and distressing position, and I did not know how to escape from it.

On the one hand, the previous day's clarification at the Loskutnaya had put an end to the tension between the grand dukes, and at breakfast they regarded each other with a sincere goodwill that reminded me more of two good comrades than a father and son, and I could not but be glad of that. On the other hand, when I entered the dining room with the coffee pot, bowed and wished everybody good morning, they both looked at me with an odd expression on their faces, and instead of the usual nod, they also said 'Good morning,' which confused me completely. I believe that I even blushed.

I had to rid myself of this monstrous suspicion somehow, but I had absolutely no idea how to raise such a subject with Their Highnesses.

As I was pouring Georgii Alexandrovich's coffee, he shook his head reproachfully and yet also, I thought, with a certain hint of approval and droned in a low voice: 'Well, I never . . .'

My hand trembled and for the first time in my life I spilled a few drops straight into the saucer.

Pavel Georgievich did not utter a single word of reproach; he simply thanked me for the coffee, and that was even worse.

I stood beside the door, suffering terribly.

Mr Carr was chattering away incessantly, making elegant gestures with his slim white hands. I think he was talking about the opera – at least, I heard '*Khovanshchina*' repeated several times. Lord Banville had not come to breakfast, owing to a migraine.

What I had to do, I thought, was to approach Georgii Alexandrovich and say this: 'The opinion that Your Highness has formed concerning my presumed relationship with a certain individual well known to you has absolutely nothing in common with reality, and the only reason I happened to be in the wardrobe is that the aforementioned individual wished to avoid compromising Pavel Georgievich. And as for the love that this individual declared for my own humble personage, if a feeling so very flattering to me should indeed exist, then it is without the slightest hint of any passion of a non-platonic nature.'

No, that was probably too involved. What if I were to say: 'The reverence in which I hold the members of the royal family and also the affections of their hearts would never, under any circumstances, allow me, even in my wildest fantasies, to imagine that . . .' Just at that moment my glance accidentally met that of Lieutenant Endlung, who assumed an expression of admiration, raising his eyebrows and winking at me, as well as giving me a thumbs up sign under the tablecloth, from which I concluded that Pavel Georgievich had told him everything. It cost me an immense effort of will to maintain an air of imperturbability.

The Lord had truly decided to subject me to grave trials.

As everyone was leaving the table, Xenia Georgievna whispered to me: 'Come to my room.'

Five minutes later I set out for her room with a heavy heart, already knowing that nothing good awaited me there.

The grand princess had already changed into a promenade dress and put on a hat with a veil, behind which her long beautifully moulded eyes glittered resolutely.

'I wish to take a drive in the landau,' she said. 'It is such a bright sunny day today. You will drive, as you used to do when I was a child.'

I bowed, feeling incredibly relieved.

'Which pair of horses would you like to be harnessed?'

'The sorrels, they are friskier.'

'Right away.'

But my feeling of relief proved premature. When I drove up to the porch Xenia Georgievna did not get into the carriage alone, but with Fandorin, who looked a genuine dandy in a grey top hat, grey frock coat and mother-of-pearl tie with a pearl pin. Now it was clear why her Highness had wanted me to occupy the coach box instead of the coachman Savelii.

We drove through the park, along the avenue, and then Xenia Georgievna ordered me to turn towards the Sparrow Hills. The carriage was brand new, with rubber shock absorbers, and driving it was a sheer pleasure – it did not jolt or pitch, and only swayed ever so slightly.

While the horses were trotting between the trees, the quiet conversation behind my back merged into the muted background of sound, but on the Kaluga Highway we had a strong following wind that snatched up every word spoken and carried it to my ears, with the result that, despite myself, I played the part of an eavesdropper, and there was nothing I could do about it.

'... and nothing else matters ...' Those were the first words that the wind brought me (the voice belonged to Her Highness). 'Take me away. It doesn't matter where to. I would go to the end of the world with you. No, truly, do not grimace like that! We can go to America. I have read that there are no titles or class prejudices there. Why don't you say something?'

I lashed the entirely innocent horses and they started trotting a bit faster.

'Class p-prejudices exist even in America, but that is not the problem ...'

'Then what is?'

'Everything. I am forty years old and you are nineteen. That is one. I am, as Karnovich recently put it, "an individual of no definite profession", while you, Xenia, are a grand princess. That is two. I know life only too well, and you do not know it at all. That is three. And the most important thing of all is that I belong

196

only to myself, but you belong to Russia. We could not be happy.'

His habitual manner of numbering off his arguments seemed inappropriate to me in this particular instance, but I had to admit that this time at least Erast Petrovich was speaking like a responsible man. From the ensuing silence I concluded that Her Highness had been sobered by his words of reason.

A minute later she asked quietly: 'Do you not love me?'

And then he spoiled everything!

'I didn't s-say that. You ... you have d-disturbed m-my emotional equilibrium,' Fandorin babbled, stammering more than usual. 'I d-did not think that such a thing could ever happen to me again, b-but it seems that it has ...'

'So you do love me then? You love me?' she persisted. 'If you do, then nothing else matters. If you don't, it matters even less. One word, just one word. Well?'

My heart was wrung by the hope and fear that I heard in Xenia Georgievna's voice, and yet at that moment in time I could not help admiring her resolve and noble candour.

Naturally, the sly seducer replied: 'Yes, I l-love you.'

How could he possibly dare not to love Her Highness!

'At least, I am in love,' Fandorin immediately corrected himself. 'Forgive me for speaking absolutely honestly. You have completely turned my head, but ... I am not sure that it is simply a matter of you ... Perhaps the m-magic of a title played some part in it ... In that case it is shameful ... I am afraid to p-prove unworthy of your love ...'

At this point I found this heroic gentleman rather pitiful. At least, in comparison with Her Highness, who was prepared to abandon everything for the sake of her feelings, and in this case 'everything' signified so much that it was simply breathtaking.

'And also ...' he said in a more restrained, sadder voice, 'I do not agree with you that nothing matters apart from love. There are more important things than love. That is probably the main lesson I have drawn from my life.'

Xenia Georgievna replied in a ringing voice: 'Erast Petrovich, you have been a poor student of life.' And then she shouted to me: 'Afanasii, turn back!'

For the rest of the way they did not say a word to each other.

I was not present at the meeting that preceded Mademoiselle's departure for her next meeting with Lind, since none of the grand dukes were involved and no drinks were served. I was left languishing in the corridor, and now that my fears for Xenia Georgievna were a little less acute, I was able to focus on the most important thing – the fate of the young prisoner. What the all-wise Snezhnevskaya had said about having to sacrifice the lesser for the sake of the greater had seared my heart, but Izabella Felitsianovna did not know anything about Fandorin's plan. There was still hope – everything depended on whether Mademoiselle was able to determine the location of the hiding place.

The meeting did not last long. I caught Mademoiselle in the corridor and she told me in French: 'I just hope I don't lose count. I didn't sleep all last night – I was training my memory. Erast said that the best way to do it is to learn poetry that you do not completely understand. So I learned a passage from your terrible poet Pushkin:

> 'Oh ye at whom have trembled
> Europe's mighty tribes,
> Oh, predatory Gauls (*ce sont nous, les français*)[1]
> You too have fallen in your graves.
> Oh dread! Oh fearsome times!
> Where are you now, beloved son of fortune and Bellona
>   (*il parle de Napoléon*)[2]
> The voice that scorned the truth, and faith and law,
> Dreaming in pride of casting thrones down by the sword,
> Has vanished like a frightful dream when morning comes!'

---

[1] *That is us, the French.*
[2] *He is speaking of Napoleon.*

'After that, memorising the creaks of the wheels will be a sheer pleasure. Just as long as I don't lose count. I must not lose count. Today is our last chance. I am very nervous.'

Yes, I could see that her affected cheerfulness and all this jolly banter was merely a screen for profound anxiety.

I wanted to say that I was I was very much afraid for her. After all, Fandorin had said that Doctor Lind did not leave witnesses. It would be nothing to him to kill the intermediary when she was no longer needed. If those in higher spheres were willing to abandon Mikhail Georgievich to his fate, then who would be concerned about the death of a mere governess?

'I should not have run after that carriage. It was an unforgivable mistake,' I finally said in Russian. 'You see, now you will have to carry the can for me.'

It was not what I wanted to say – it came out wrongly – and there was that phrase 'carry the can', which a foreigner was unlikely to know. But even so Mademoiselle understood me perfectly well.

'Do not be so afraid, Athanas,' she said with a smile, calling me by my given name for the first time. On her lips it acquired an unfamiliar Caucasian ring. 'Lind will not kill me today. I still have to bring him the Orlov tomorrow.'

I am ashamed to admit it, but at that moment I felt a sense of relief as I recalled how confidently Snezhnevskaya had declared that the Orlov would not be handed over to the kidnappers under any circumstances. It was a base unworthy feeling, and I blanched at the realisation that in that moment I had betrayed poor little Mikhail Georgievich, who had already been abandoned by everyone else. In my opinion, the very worst of sins is to abuse those most precious of human feelings, love and trust.

And then I felt even more ashamed, because I remembered that Mr Masa had called me that Japanese word. *Ura . . . girimono*?

I really had behaved irresponsibly on that occasion. And as a decent human being I was obliged to apologise.

Having wished the governess success in her difficult and

dangerous mission, I went to find the Japanese servant.

I knocked at the door and heard an unintelligible sound which, upon reflection, I decided to regard as permission to enter.

Mr Masa was sitting on the floor in nothing but his underwear, that is in the same attire in which I had once seen him jumping against the wall. There was a sheet of paper lying in front of him, and Fandorin's valet was painstakingly tracing out complicated patterns on it with a brush.

'What you want?' he asked, squinting at me with his narrow, spiteful little eyes.

I was rather taken aback by his rude tone of voice, but I had to finish what I had begun. My late father always used to say that true dignity lay not in the way one was treated by others, but in the way one acted oneself.

'Mr Masa,' I said, bowing, 'I have come to tell you, firstly, that I harbour no claims on you for the blow that you gave me, for my own offence was fully deserving of such treatment. And, secondly, that I am truly sorry that I was unwittingly responsible for the failure of Mr Fandorin's plan. Please forgive me.'

The Japanese bowed formally to me in reply, without getting up off the floor.

'And I ask you forgive me,' he said, 'but cannot forgive you. Your humbre servant.'

And he bowed again.

Well, have it your own way, I thought. I had done my duty. I said goodbye and left the room.

I needed to occupy myself with something until Mademoiselle's return, so that the time would not drag so very slowly. I walked round the rooms, and in the drawing room my eye was caught by a carpet on the wall hung with weapons from the Caucasus and Turkey. I stood on a chair, took down a dagger with silver knurling decoration and ran my finger along it. The scabbard was clean, with not a single speck of dust. I wondered if Somov was meticulous enough to pay the same attention to the blade as he did to the scabbard.

I slowly drew the blade out, breathed on it and held it up to the light. Just as I had thought – smears. And what if one of the guests were to examine it, out of simple curiosity? That would be awkward. Somov had a long way to go before he would be a genuine butler after all, I decided with a certain feeling of inner satisfaction.

I heard strange flapping footsteps and saw Mr Masa, still in his Japanese underwear and with no shoes on his feet. Good Lord, the liberties that he took! Wandering round the house in that state!

I suppose I must have looked very angry, and the naked dagger in my hand probably looked most ominous. In any case, the Japanese was clearly frightened.

He ran up to me, seized hold of my arm and began jabbering so fast that I could not make out more than half of what he said: 'Now I see you trury sorry. You genuine samurai, accept your aporogies. No need hara-kiri.'

All I understood was that for some reason he wished to temper his wrath with mercy and was no longer angry with me. Well then, so much the better.

I did not complete my round of the rooms. The footman Lipps sought me out in the pantry, where I was checking whether the napkins had been well ironed, and told me I was wanted immediately in Pavel Georgievich's room on the first floor.

Lieutenant Endlung was also sitting in the room. He glanced at me with a mysterious air as he smoked a long Turkish chibouk.

'Sit down, Afanasii, sit down,' His Highness said to me, which was already unusual in itself.

I cautiously lowered myself onto the edge of a chair, anticipating nothing good from this conversation.

Pavel Georgievich looked excited and determined, but the subject that he broached was not at all what I had been dreading.

'Filya has been telling me for a long time, Afanasii, that you are not at all as simple as you seem,' the grand duke began, with a nod towards Endlung, 'but I would not believe him. Now I see that it is true.'

I was on the point of trying to explain myself, but His Highness gestured abruptly as if to say 'Be quiet' and then continued.

'And that is why we have discussed things and decided to enlist your support. You must not think that I am some heartless good-for-nothing, and I have just been sitting around doing nothing all this time or making the rounds of the restaurants. No, Afanasii, all that is nothing but a facade, in actual fact Filya and I have been thinking of only one thing – how to help poor Mika. The police are all well and good, but we're not entirely useless either. We have to do something, otherwise those state know-it-alls will finally get the criminals to starve my brother to death or just simply kill him. That glass bauble means more to them!'

This was the plain truth. I thought exactly the same but, to be quite honest, I was not expecting any sensible proposals from the dashing sailors, and I merely inclined my head respectfully.

'Endlung has a theory of his own,' Pavel Georgievich went on excitedly. 'Tell him, Filya.'

'Gladly,' the lieutenant responded, blowing out a cloud of smoke. 'Judge for yourself, Afanasii Stepanovich. It couldn't possibly be simpler. What do we know about this Doctor Lind?'

I waited for Endlung to answer his own question. He raised one finger and continued: 'Only one thing. That he is a misogynist. He simply has to be a misogynist! Any normal man fond of the tootsies, like you and me –' I could not help wincing at that remark '– would never stoop to such abominations. That's true, surely?'

Somehow I was not really convinced of the lieutenant's powers of analysis. However, Endlung surprised me.

'And who is it that cannot stand women?' he asked with a triumphant air.

'Yes, indeed, who?' Pavel Georgievich echoed.

His Highness and his friend exchanged glances.

'Come on now, Afanasii, think.'

I thought a little more.

'Well, there are many women who cannot bear their sisters.'

'Ah, Afanasii, what a slowcoach you are, really. We're talking about Doctor Lind, not women.'

Endlung said emphatically: 'Buggers.'

For a moment I did not understand what he meant, but then I realised that he was employing the French word *bougre*, which means men who are referred to in decent society as homosexuals. In any case, the lieutenant immediately explained his idea by using a different term that is not accepted at all in good society, and which I therefore shall not repeat.

'And suddenly everything is clear!' Endlung exclaimed. 'Lind is a bugger, and his entire gang are all queers – buggers and pansies.'

'What?' I asked.

'Pansies, also known as girlies, little nieces, snivellers, passive queers. Naturally, in a gang like that, they'll all stick up for each other! And it's no accident that Lind chose Moscow for his atrocities. Thanks to Uncle Sam, this place is a real Mecca for queers now. You know what the people say: "What a queer place Moscow is these days!"'

I had heard this phrase alluding to the specific partialities of Simeon Alexandrovich before and I considered it my duty to say to Endlung: 'Surely, Mr Gentleman of the Bedchamber, you do not think that the governor general of Moscow could be involved in the abduction of his own nephew?'

'Of course not!' Pavel Georgievich exclaimed. 'But crowds of all sorts of riff-raff hang around Uncle Sam. For instance, take our own dear guests, Carr and Banville. Let us concede that His Lordship is more or less known to us, although the acquaintance is only recent. But who is this Mr Carr? And why did Banville ask Papa to invite him here?'

'Oh come now, Your Highness, such a great event – the coronation.'

'And what if it was for a completely different reason?' Endlung asked, with a sweeping gesture of his pipe. 'What if he's not really a lord at all? And of course that slicker Carr is especially suspicious. Remember, they arrived at the Hermitage on the very day of the kidnapping. They're always wandering about, ferreting things out. I'm absolutely certain that one or the other of them is connected with Doctor Lind, or perhaps even both of them are.'

'Carr, beyond a shadow of a doubt, it's Carr,' the grand duke declared confidently. 'Banville is a man from high society, after all. There's no way to fake those manners and that way of talking.'

'And just who, Paulie, told you Doctor Lind is not a man from high society?' the lieutenant objected.

They were both right, and in general it all sounded very far from stupid. This was something I had not expected.

'Should you not inform Colonel Karnovich of your suspicions?' I suggested.

'No, no,' said Pavel Georgievich, shaking his head. 'He or that blockhead Lasovsky will only ruin everything again. And in any case they both have plenty to worry about with the coronation tomorrow.'

'Mr Fandorin, then?' I asked reluctantly.

Endlung and His Highness looked at each other.

'You know, Afanasii,' the grand duke said slowly, 'Fandorin is a clever chap, of course, but he seems to be preparing some cunning kind of operation. So let him get on with it.'

'We'll manage on our own,' the lieutenant snapped. 'And we'll see whose operation is more cunning. But we need someone to help us. Tell me, Ziukin, are you with us or not?'

I agreed immediately, without even the slightest hesitation. I found the idea of doing something useful again, and without Mr Fandorin being involved, immensely inspiring.

'What do we have to do?' I asked.

'First, tail them,' Endlung announced briskly. 'Both of them. Paulie can't do it – he's too conspicuous and also he has heaps of responsibilities. The royal family has an all-night vigil today, and in general he's going to be like a little pug dog on a tight lead. That's why we've brought you in. So I'm going to follow

Carr and you, Ziukin, are going to follow Banville.'

I noted that he had kept the most promising suspect for himself, but I did not object – it was Endlung not I who had come up with the idea.

'Ah, how I envy you!' His Highness exclaimed ruefully.

In accordance with our agreement, I installed myself with the *Moscow Gazette* on the bench beside the stairs, from where I had a view of His Lordship's door. Endlung sat down to lay out a game of patience in the small drawing room, because he could see Mr Carr's room from there.

In anticipation of our surveillance work I had changed my livery for a good suit of dark-grey English wool, a present from the grand princess the previous year. Endlung had also changed into civilian clothes – a sandy-coloured two-piece suit and dandified shoes with white gaiters.

To while away the time, I read the text of the solemn announcement to the people of the next day's coronation:

His most Serene, Sovereign and Great Highness, the Emperor Nikolai Alexandrovich, having ascended the ancestral throne of the Russian Empire and the Kingdom of Poland and Grand Dukedom of Finland incorporated therein, has deigned, in the fashion of those devout sovereigns, his ancestors, to decree as follows:

The most sacred coronation of His Imperial Majesty and his anointment from the spiritual world shall take place, with the help of Almighty God, on the fourteenth day of this month of May.

His Imperial Majesty has decreed that his consort, Her Majesty the Empress Alexandra Feodorovna, shall also be privy to these most sacred proceedings. This triumphant festivity is hereby proclaimed to all loyal subjects so that on this long-awaited day they might redouble their prayers to the King of Kings to illumine His Majesty's kingdom with all the power of His grace and strengthen it in peace and quietude, to His own most sacred glory and the unshakeable prosperity of the state.

The sublime dignity of these majestic words filled my heart with a calm certitude. Reading official documents had always had a most salutary effect on me, and especially now, when the inviolability of the edifice of the Russian monarchy had suddenly come under threat.

I also studied with pleasure the composition of the company of heralds that was reading out this message every day on the Senate Square of the Kremlin: 'An adjutant general with the rank of full general, two adjutant generals of adjutant-general rank, two high masters of coronation ceremonies, two heralds, four masters of ceremony, two Senate secretaries, two divisions in mounted formation – one of Her Majesty the Empress Maria Feodorovna's cavalry guards and the other of the mounted life-guards, with kettledrums and full choruses of trumpets, each division to have two trumpeters with trumpets decorated with cloth of gold displaying the state crest and twelve lead mounts in richly decorated horsecloths.' How beautiful! Such music in every word, in the sound of every rank and title!

The previous year, on the initiative of the new empress, who wished to be more Russian than the Russians themselves, a genuine revolution had almost taken place in the names of court rankings when a project was conceived to replace all the German titles with old ones from Muscovy. According to Endlung the unrest among the servants at court had been reminiscent of the picture *The Last Day of Pompeii* by the artist Briullov, but, thank God, it had come to nothing. When the High House Marshal Prince Alten-Coburg-Svyatopolk-Bobruisky learned that under the new (or rather, old) order he would simply be called a butler, there was a great scandal, and the project was consigned to oblivion.

Through a hole I had made in a page of the newspaper, I saw Mr Freyby approaching along the corridor and pretended to be absorbed in reading, but even so the Englishman stopped and greeted me.

The butler's company usually had a calming effect on me, but on this occasion his appearance was most inopportune, for the door of Lord Banville's room might open at any moment.

'Good news?' Freyby asked, nodding at the newspaper and fishing his dictionary out of his pocket. '*Khoroshii . . . novost?*'

I did not have my dictionary with me – it was in my livery – and so I limited myself to a simple nod.

After looking me over carefully, the Englishman pronounced a phrase of four words: 'You look better today.' Then he rustled the pages of his lexicon again and translated it into Russian: '*Ty . . . smotret . . . luchshe . . . sevodnya.*'

I started and looked up at his ruddy features. Why would he advise me to *look better*? How did he know about our plan? What did he know in general?

The butler smiled benignly, bowed and proceeded on his way.

Five minutes later Mr Carr came out into the corridor, looking rather strange: despite the clear warm weather, he was wrapped in a long cloak reaching right down to his heels; his broad hat with a drooping brim was pulled down almost as far as his nose; and I also noticed that his shoes had heels that were high and extremely thin. On pressing my eye right up against the hole in the page, I saw that the English gentleman was even more thickly painted and rouged than usual.

Stepping gracefully, Mr Carr walked through to the exit. Then Endlung strode past me, whistling light-heartedly. He looked round and winked, and I remained at my post. But I did not have to wait for long. Literally half a minute later His Lordship's door squeaked and Banville followed them out, walking on tiptoe. He was also wearing a cloak, but not such a long one as Mr Carr's.

There was something mysterious going on. I waited for as brief a moment as possible, put on my bowler hat and joined this strange procession, bringing up the rear. On that day the emperor and empress had moved from the Alexandriisky Palace to the Kremlin, and so all the police agents had disappeared from the park, which was most opportune as to any observer our man-oeuvres would certainly have seemed suspicious. I could not signal to Endlung because I was afraid of startling Lord Banville, and the lieutenant himself did not look round. However, he was strolling along casually, and I soon realised that His Lordship was not interested in Endlung at all, but in Mr Carr.

Outside the gates the latter took a cab and drove off in the direction of Kaluga Square. As he was getting into the carriage, the flap of his cloak fell open and something bright and pearly, like the hem of a brocade or satin dress, glinted in the light of the setting sun.

Endlung walked a bit further along the pavement, tapping his cane, stopped a cab coming towards him and, after exchanging a few words with the cabby, drove off in the same direction. But Banville was unlucky – there were no more cabs on the street. The Briton ran out into the roadway, looking after the carriages as they drove away. I concealed myself in the bushes, just to be on the safe side.

Five minutes went by, or perhaps even ten, before His Lordship managed to get a cab. Banville obviously knew, or had guessed, where Mr Carr had gone to, because he shouted something very brief to the driver, and the carriage rattled off over the cobblestones.

Now it was my turn to feel nervous. But I did not wait for an empty cab to come along – I stopped a little man driving a water wagon, offered him two roubles and took a seat beside a barrel at the front. The man lashed his dray horse with his whip; it shook its tangled mane, snorted and set off along the broad street at a pace every bit as good as a cabman's mare. No doubt in my respectable attire I must have looked very strange on that rough wooden cart, but at the time that was of absolutely no import-ance whatever – the important thing was to keep Lord Banville in my field of vision.

We drove across Krimsky Most Street, already familiar to me, and turned into a side street. Leaving the Cathedral of Christ the Saviour behind on our right, we found ourselves on a rich and beautiful street lined with nothing but palaces and mansions on both sides. Carriages were drawing up one after another outside the brightly illuminated front entrance of one of the houses. Banville also got out there and paid his driver. He walked past a haughty doorman covered in gold braid and went in through a pair of tall doors decorated with mouldings. I was left standing on the pavement as the water carter went rumbling on his way with my two roubles.

As far as I could tell, there was a masquerade about to begin in the mansion because everyone who arrived was wearing a mask. On looking more closely at the guests, I discovered that they were divided into two types: men in ordinary frock coats and suits, and individuals of indeterminate sex, like Mr Carr, swathed in extremely long cloaks. Many people arrived in pairs, arm in arm, and I guessed what kind of gathering was taking place.

Someone took hold of my elbow from behind. I looked round – it was Endlung.

'This is the Elysium,' he whispered, and his eyes sparkled. 'A privileged club for Moscow queers. Mine's in there as well.'

'Mr Carr?' I asked.

The lieutenant nodded and twitched the curled ends of his wheat-coloured moustache thoughtfully.

'It's not that simple just to walk in. We need make-up. Eureka!' He slapped me on the shoulder. 'Follow me, Ziukin! The Variety Theatre is only five minutes from here; I have lots of lady friends there.'

He took me by the arm and led me across the rapidly darkening street.

'Did you see that some of them have cloaks that reach right down to the ground? Those are the pansies – they're wearing women's dresses under their cloaks. There's no way you would make a pansy, Ziukin; you'll have to be the auntie. So be it, I shall perform a heroic feat for the sake of the royal family and dress up as a pansy.'

'Who am I going to be?' I asked, thinking that I must have misheard.

'The auntie. That's what the pansies' patrons are called.'

We turned into the stage entrance of the theatre. The attendant bowed low to Endlung and even doffed his peaked cap, for which he received a coin from the lieutenant.

'Quick, quick,' said the decisive gentleman of the bedchamber, urging me on as he ran up a steep and non-too-clean staircase. 'Now, where would be best? Ah, Zizi's dressing room would do. It's five to nine now, almost time for the interval.'

In the empty dressing room he took a seat in front of the mirror as if he belonged there, examined his own face critically and said with a sigh: 'I shall have to shave the damn moustache off. The Russian navy hasn't made such sacrifices since the Black Sea fleet was scuttled. Right, you English buggers, you'll answer to me for this . . .'

With a steadfast hand he picked up a pair of scissors from a small table and snipped off first one side of his moustache and then the other. Such willing self-sacrifice demonstrated yet again that I had underestimated Lieutenant Endlung, and that Georgii Alexandrovich had been quite right about him.

When the courageous sailor had lathered up the remaining stubble and opened a razor, two rather pretty but quite incredibly over-painted young ladies came in, wearing dresses with spangles and necklines that were much too low.

'Filya!' one of them, light-haired and slim, exclaimed, and threw herself on Endlung from behind, giving him a loud kiss on the neck.

'Filiusha!' the other one, a plump brunette, squealed just as joyfully, and kissed the lathered lieutenant on the cheek.

'Zizi, Lola, careful!' he shouted at the young ladies. 'I'll cut myself.'

Then there was a positive hail of questions and comments, so that I could no longer tell which of the girls had said what: 'Why are you shaving off your moustache? You'll look a real freak without it! Hey, you'll blunt my Zolingen with that stubble of yours! Are we going anywhere after the show? And where's

Paulie? Who's this with you? Phoo, he's terribly stuffy, doesn't look like much fun.'

'Who's not much fun – Afanasii?' Endlung interceded for me. 'If you only knew ... He can give me a hundred points start. The moustache? That's for a bet. Afanasii and I are going to a masquerade. Come on, girls, turn me into a lovably plump little lady, and make him something a bit more, you know, showy. What's this?'

He took a thick ginger beard off a hook on the wall and answered his own question.

'Aha, from *Nero*. Little Lola's simply delightful in that role. Turn this way, brother Ziukin ...'

The actresses set to work merrily, without stopping talking for a single moment. And five minutes later there was a most unsavoury-looking gentleman glaring out at me from the mirror, with a thick red beard and tangled eyebrows of the same colour, thick hair cut in a fringe and a monocle into the bargain.

Endlung's transformation took more time, but he became completely unrecognisable. After adjusting the folds of his sumptuous dress, which was completely covered in ruffles, the lieutenant put on a half-mask, stretched out his thickly painted lips into a smile and was suddenly transformed into a well-padded floozy. I noticed for the first time that he had coquettish little dimples in his cheeks.

'Very chic!' Endlung said approvingly. 'Girls, you are absolute kittens! We'll win this bet. Forward, Afanasii, time is precious!'

As we approached the entrance flooded with electric light, I also put on a half-mask. I was very much afraid that they would not let us into the club, but obviously we looked entirely *comme il faut*, and the doorman opened the doors for us with a respectful bow.

We entered a richly appointed hallway, where Endlung threw off the cloak he had put on over his ethereal dress. There was a wide white stairway leading up, and the flight of steps ended at a huge mirror in a bronze frame, with two couples like us standing in front of it, preening themselves.

I was about to walk on by, but Endlung nudged me with his elbow, and I realised that it would have looked suspicious. For the sake of appearances, we loitered in front of the mirror, but I deliberately screwed up my eyes in order not to see the caricature created by Lola and Zizi's deft hands. The lieutenant, however, regarded his reflection with quite evident enjoyment: he adjusted his little curls, extended his leg and stretched out his foot. Thank God, they had chosen him a dress with no *décolleté* and covered shoulders.

The spacious hall was furnished with luxurious good taste in the very latest Venetian style – with gold and silver panels on the walls, cosy little alcoves and large grottoes created using tropical plants in tubs. There was a buffet with various wines and hors d'œuvres in the corner, and a bright-blue grand piano on a high platform. I had never seen one like that before. On all sides there was the sound of muted voices and laughter, and the smell of perfume and expensive tobacco.

At first glance it looked like a perfectly ordinary high-society rout. On closer observation, however, one was struck by the excessively ruddy cheeks and dark eyebrows of some of the beaux, and the ladies looked very strange altogether: far too broad in the shoulder, with prominent Adam's apples, and one actually had a slim moustache. Endlung also noticed her, and a shadow flitted across his animated face – apparently he had sacrificed his moustache in vain. Then again, there were some creatures with nothing at all to indicate that they were not men. For instance, one in the costume of Columbine, who seemed vaguely familiar to me, could probably have rivalled the slim waist and suppleness of Miss Zizi herself.

Endlung and I walked arm-in-arm between the palm trees, trying to spot Banville and Carr. Almost immediately a gentleman wearing a steward's ribbon in a bow on his chest came dashing up to us, pressed his hands to his heart and chanted reproachfully: 'A breach, a breach of the rules. Those who arrive together must amuse themselves separately. You'll have plenty of time for spooning later, my darlings.'

He winked at me in a most brazen fashion and pinched Endlung gently on the cheek, for which the lieutenant immediately slapped him on the forehead with his fan.

'A frisky one,' the steward said to the gentleman of the bedchamber. 'Permit me to introduce you to the Count of Monte Cristo.'

He led a red-lipped old man in a black curly wig over to Endlung.

'And you, Ginger, will discover ecstasy in the company of a delightful nymph.'

I assumed that in this circle it was the custom to address everyone familiarly, and replied in the same tone: 'Thank you, my considerate friend, but I would prefer—'

However, a brash nymph in a Greek tunic with a gilded harp clasped under her arm was already hanging on my elbow.

She immediately began talking some nonsense or other in an extremely unnatural falsetto, continually pursing her lips up into a tight heart shape.

I dragged the companion who had been imposed on me across the hall and suddenly saw Mr Carr. He was wearing a velvet mask, but I recognised him immediately from his blindingly bright yellow hair. The fortunate Englishman was sitting all alone by the wall, drinking champagne and gazing around. I saw that the lieutenant and his old man had occupied the next table. My eyes met Endlung's, and he turned his head emphatically to one side.

I followed the direction of his glance. Lord Banville was standing behind a column nearby, although he was more difficult to identify than Mr Carr, because his mask covered his face right down to the chin. However, I recognised the familiar trousers with scarlet trimming.

I seated myself on a couch and the nymph gladly plumped

down beside me, pressing her thigh against my leg.

'Are you tired?' she whispered. 'And you look like such a strong boy. What a sweet wart you have. Just like a raisin.'

She touched my cheek with her finger. I barely managed to stop myself from slapping the impudent woman, that is man, on the hand.

'Lovely beard, so silky soft,' the nymph cooed. 'Are you always such a surly bugaboo?'

Without taking my eyes off Banville, I muttered: 'Yes, always.'

'The way you looked at me just now stung like a whiplash.'

'I'll give you a lashing all right, if you don't keep your hands to yourself,' I snarled, deciding not to beat about the bush.

'On my botty?' she squealed with a quiver and pressed her entire body against me.

'I'll give you a drubbing you'll remember for a long time,' I said and shoved her away.

'A long, long time?' my tormentor babbled and heaved a deep sigh. 'How lovely you are! Charming! Charming!'

The steward trotted over to a very tall slim gentleman wearing a scarlet silk mask beneath which a well-tended imperial beard could be seen. I spotted the austere dispassionate face of Foma Anikeevich behind the new arrival and immediately guessed who this was. The governor general's butler looked as if he was accompanying his master to a perfectly ordinary rout. Foma Anikeevich had not put on a mask, and he was carrying a long velvet cloak over his arm – he had deliberately not left it in the cloakroom so that the guests would not be confused concerning his status. A subtle man, no two ways about it.

'Where shall I seat you, divine Filador?' I heard the steward ask in honeyed tones.

The governor general glanced round the hall from his height of almost two metres and set off resolutely towards the spot where Mr Carr was sitting alone. He sat down beside the Englishman, kissed him on the cheek and whispered something in his ear, tickling him with his moustache. Carr smiled, his eyes sparkled and he leaned his head over to one side.

I saw Banville withdraw deeper into the shadows.

A Columbine appeared quite close to him, the same one who had recently impressed me with her unaffected gracefulness. She stood by the wall, looking at His Highness and wringing her slim hands. This was a familiar gesture, and now I knew who it was – Prince Glinsky, Simeon Alexandrovich's adjutant.

Meanwhile a performance began on the stage. Two pansies started singing a duet – a romance by Mr Poigin: 'Oh, do not go; stay here with me.'

They sang most skilfully, with genuine feeling, and I was quite absorbed despite myself, but at the words 'My fiery caresses will kindle and consume you' the nymph suddenly laid her head on my shoulder and her fingers slid inside my shirt, as if unintentionally, which reduced me to a state of genuine horror. Overcome by panic, I looked round at Endlung. He was laughing wildly and lashing his wrinkled beau across the hands with his fan. The lieutenant was apparently faring no better than I was. The singers were rewarded with tumultuous applause, in which my admirer joined, relieving me temporarily of her importunate advances.

The steward walked up on to the stage and announced: 'At the request of our dear Filador, there will now be a performance of the belly dance that everyone has come to love so well. The dancer is the incomparable Madam Desirée, who travelled to Alexandria especially in order to master this ancient and high art! Please welcome her!'

To the sound of applause a well-padded middle-aged gentleman walked up onto the stage, wearing turquoise stockings, a short cape and a skirt studded with sequins, so that his stomach – round and unnaturally white (I assume because it had recently been shaved) – was left exposed.

The accompanist started playing a Persian melody from the opera *Odalisque* and 'Madam Desirée' began shaking her hips and thighs, which set her substantial belly quivering in waves.

I found this sight extremely unappetising, but it threw the audience into a frenzy. There were shouts from all sides: 'Bravo! You charmer!'

And at this point my nymph cast all restraint aside – I was only just in time to catch her hand as it descended onto my knee.

'You're so unapproachable, I adore you,' she whispered in my ear.

Simeon Alexandrovich suddenly pulled his companion sharply towards him and pressed his lips against Mr Carr's in a prolonged kiss. I involuntarily glanced at Foma Anikeevich, who was standing behind the grand duke's chair with an imperturbable expression on his face, and thought: how much self-control and willpower he must have to bear his cross with such dignity. If Foma Anikeevich knew that I was here in the hall, he would probably die of shame. Thank God, I thought, that it is impossible to recognise me in this ginger beard.

And then something happened.

Lord Banville ran out from behind his column, shouting something unintelligible. He covered the distance to the table in several bounds, grabbed Mr Carr by the shoulders and dragged him to one side, lisping something in his foreign language. Simeon Alexandrovich jumped to his feet, took hold of Mr Carr's dress and pulled him back. I also got up, realising that an appalling scandal highly dangerous to the monarchy was unfolding before my very eyes, but what happened next exceeded even my very worst fears. Banville let go of Mr Carr and gave His Highness a resounding slap across the face! The music broke off, the belly dancer squatted down on her haunches in fright, and it went very, very quiet. The only thing to be heard was Lord Banville's agitated breathing.

This was unprecedented! A physical insult inflicted on a member of the royal family! And by a foreigner. I believe I groaned, and rather loudly too. But a moment later I realised that there was no member of the royal family present, and there could not be. The slap had been received by Mr Filador, the man in the scarlet mask.

Simeon Alexandrovich's eyebrows curved together in an expression of perplexity – apparently His Highness had never found himself in a situation like this before. The governor general spontaneously put one hand to his bruised cheek and took a step back. His Lordship, however, no longer displaying the slightest sign of agitation, slowly pulled a white glove off one of his hands. Oh God! This really would be beyond repair – there would be a challenge to a duel, and a public one. Banville would name himself, and then His Highness would no longer be able to maintain his anonymity.

Foma Anikeevich moved forward, but he was forestalled by Columbine. She ran up to His Lordship and delivered a rapid sequence of slaps – one, two, three, four – to the Briton's face. They were even louder than the one that Simeon Alexandrovich had received. Banville's head swung from side to side.

'I am Prince Glinsky!' the adjutant declared in French, tearing off his mask. He looked very fine at that moment – not a woman and not a youth, but some special kind of being, like the arch-angels in old Italian paintings. 'You, sir, have violated the con-stitution of our club, and for that I demand satisfaction from you!'

Banville also removed his mask, and I seemed to see him properly for the first time. Fire in his eyes, cruel folds running down from the sides of his nose, bloodless lips and two patches of scarlet on his cheeks. I had never seen a face more terrible. How could I possibly have regarded this vampire as a harmless eccentric?

'I am Donald Neville Lambert, the eleventh Viscount Banville. And you, Prince, will receive complete satisfaction from me. And I from you.'

Foma Anikeevich threw the velvet cloak across the grand duke's shoulders and delicately tugged on his elbow. Ah, how superb! He had maintained complete presence of mind even in such a desperate situation. The governor general could not be present, even in a mask, at a challenge to a duel. It was not merely a scandal but a criminal offence, and it was the authorities' sacred responsibility to suppress such activities.

His Highness and Foma Anikeevich hastily withdrew. Mr Carr darted after them, holding on his half-mask.

The steward waved to the accompanist, who started fingering the piano keys again, and I did not hear how His Lordship's conversation with the prince ended. They went out almost immediately, accompanied by two other gentlemen, one of whom was wearing a smoking jacket and the other a woman's dress with gloves that reached up to his elbows.

I found the young adjutant's action truly admirable. How about that for a pansy! To sacrifice his career and reputation, to put his very life at stake – and all to save the superior whom he loved and who had treated him in a manner that was far from charitable.

The nymph immediately jumped to her feet. 'Yes, yes, let's go,' she whispered, grasping me firmly by the elbow. 'I'm all on fire.'

Believing that it would not be difficult to rid myself of this outrageous creature outside in the street, I started walking towards the exit, but the nymph tugged me in the opposite direction.

'No, silly. Not that way. Downstairs here, in the basement, they have excellent rooms! You promised to give me a drubbing that I would remember for a long time . . .'

My patience finally snapped at that.

'Sir, release my arm,' I said in a cool voice. 'I am in a hurry.'

'"Sir!"' the nymph gasped, as if I had sworn at her in the foullest of language. And then she shrieked, 'Gentlemen! He called me "sir"! He is not one of us, gentlemen!'

She pulled away from me in disgust.

Someone at one side said: 'And I see that beard looks false too!'

A sturdy-looking gentleman in a light-blue morning coat tugged on Nero's beard, and it slipped sideways in a most treacherous fashion.

'Right, you villain, you odious spy, you'll pay for this!' the sturdy gentleman said with a ferocious grin, and I barely managed to dodge the weighty fist that he swung at me.

'Hands off!' Endlung roared, dashing up to my assailant and giving him a jab to the jaw in accordance with the rules of English boxing.

This blow sent the gentleman in the light-blue morning coat tumbling to the floor, but then others came dashing towards us from every direction.

'Gentlemen, they are Guardians,' someone shouted. 'There's a whole gang of them here. Beat them!'

Punches and kicks showered down on me from all sides, and one, which landed in my stomach, winded me. I doubled over, was knocked off my feet and not allowed to get up again.

I think Endlung put up a desperate resistance, but the odds were simply too great. We were soon standing side by side, each restrained by a dozen pairs of hands.

There were faces radiating hate everywhere.

'They're Guardians! Squares! Bastards! Oprichniks! Kill them, gentlemen, just as they kill us.'

Another hail of blows descended on me. There was a salty taste in my mouth and one of my teeth was wobbly.

'Put them in the torture chamber. Let them rot there!' someone shouted. 'To teach the others a lesson!'

This ominous suggestion met with approval from the others.

We were bundled out into the corridor and dragged down a narrow stairway. I was kept busy dodging kicks, but Endlung swore, using a range of maritime terms, and fought for every single step. Finally we were carried along a dimly lit passage without a single window and tossed into a dark room. I struck the floor painfully with my back and an iron door slammed shut behind us.

When my eyes had adapted slightly to the gloom I saw a small grey rectangle in the top corner of the opposite wall. Holding onto the wall, I went across to it. It was a small window, but I could not reach it – it was too high.

Turning towards the spot where I calculated they must have thrown Endlung, I asked: 'Have these gentlemen lost their minds? What are squares? Guardians?'

The invisible lieutenant groaned in the darkness and spat. '***,' he said with profound feeling, using words that I will not repeat. 'They've broken a crown on my tooth. Squares are non-homosexual men, which includes you and me. And the Guardians, Ziukin, are a secret society that protects the honour of the dynasty and ancient Russian houses against dishonour and disgrace. Surely you must have heard of them? The year before last they forced that...oh, what is his name...the composer...damn, I can't remember...they forced him to take poison for pansifying ***.' Endlung mentioned the name of one of the youthful grand dukes, which I shall most certainly not repeat. 'And last year they threw that old bugger Kvitovsky into the Neva for pestering young lawyers. Those are the Guardians that they took us for. We're lucky that they didn't tear us to pieces on the spot. So we're going to die of hunger and thirst in this cellar. What a fine day, Monday the thirteenth.'

The lieutenant started squirming about on the floor, evidently making himself more comfortable, and remarked philosophically: 'And a fortune-teller in Nagasaki told me I would die in a sea battle. I'll never believe any predictions of the future again.'

14 May

When I woke up, I was barely able to straighten my arms and legs. Sleeping on a stone floor, even one covered with a carpet, was a harsh and cold experience. It had taken a long time for my nerves to settle down the night before. I had walked along the walls, tried picking at the lock with a tiepin, until I could feel that my strength was almost exhausted. I had lain down, thinking that I would never fall asleep and envying Endlung, who was snoring away serenely in the darkness. But eventually even I was overcome by slumber. I cannot say that it was refreshing – I awoke feeling completely shattered – but the lieutenant was still sleeping as sweetly as ever, with his head cradled on one elbow, and the thick-skinned fellow could clearly not give a damn for anything in the world.

I was able to examine the pose in which my companion in misfortune was sleeping because our prison cell was no longer pitch black: there was a feeble grey light entering the cell through the small window. I got up and limped closer. The window turned out to be barred and I was not able to see anything through it. It obviously opened into a niche that was a lot lower than street level. But there could be no doubt that the niche did look out towards the street – I could hear the muted clattering of wheels, horses neighing and a police constable's whistle. All of which meant that the morning was well advanced. I took my watch out of my pocket. It was almost nine o'clock. What were they thinking about our absence in the Hermitage? Ah yes, their

Highnesses would be too busy to be concerned about us – it was coronation day. And then afterwards, when Pavel Georgievich told them about our mission, it would not make any difference. After all, Banville and Carr were not to blame for what had happened to us. Were we really going to die in this stone cell?

I looked around. A high, gloomy ceiling. Bare walls, absolutely empty. But suddenly I noticed that the walls were not bare at all – there were strange objects hanging on them. I walked closer and shuddered in horror. For the first time in my life I realised that cold sweat was not just a figure of speech but a genuine natural phenomenon: I automatically raised a hand to my fore-head, and it was sticky, wet and cold.

Hanging on the walls in a strict geometrical arrangement were rusty chains with shackles, enormous spiked whips, seven-tailed lashes and other instruments intended for infernal torture.

We really had been confined in a torture chamber!

I do not normally think of myself as a coward, but I was unable to contain a howl of genuine horror.

Endlung lifted his head up off his elbow, blinking sleepily and looking around. Yawning, he said: 'Good morning, Afanasii Stepanovich. Only don't tell me that it isn't good. I can see that for myself from that twisted expression on your face.'

I pointed a trembling finger at the instruments of torture. The lieutenant froze just as he was, with his mouth open in an unfinished yawn. He whistled, got lightly to his feet and took the shackles down off the wall, then the terrible whip. He turned them over this way and that in his hands and shook his head.

'Oh, the jokers. Take a look at this . . .'

I timidly took hold of the whip and saw that it was not leather at all. It was light and soft, made of silk. The shackles proved to be dummies too – the iron hoops for wrists and ankles were lined with thick quilted material.

'What are these for?' I asked, bewildered.

'We must assume that this chamber is intended for

sadomasochistic fun and games,' Endlung explained with the air of a connoisseur. 'All people can be divided into two categories . . .' He raised one finger didactically. 'Those who like to make others suffer, and those who like to be made to suffer. The first group are called sadists, and the second masochists, I don't remember why. You, for instance, are definitely a masochist. I read somewhere that it is mostly masochists who go into service. And I am probably a sadist, because I really hate it when people batter me in the face, like yesterday. The best marriages and friendships are formed between a sadist and a masochist – each provides what the other needs. To put it simply, I hurt and abuse you in every way I can, and you lap it up like honey. Understand?'

No, I did not understand this at all, but I remembered the mysterious words spoken by my nymph the previous day and suspected that there might just be a grain of truth in Endlung's strange theory.

I felt better about the whips and the chains, but I had enough reasons to feel distressed even without them.

Firstly, there was my own fate. Were they really going to leave us here to die of hunger and thirst?

We went over to the outside wall and the lieutenant stood on my shoulders and shouted out of the window in a stentorian voice for a long time, but we clearly could not be heard from the street. Then we started hammering on the door. It was covered with felt on the inside, and our blows sounded muted. We could not hear a single sound from the outside.

Secondly, I was depressed by the stupidity of the situation in which we found ourselves. Yesterday Mademoiselle Declique was supposed to have identified Lind's location; today Fandorin would carry out his operation to rescue Mikhail Georgievich; and I was sitting here like a mouse in a trap, all thanks to my own stupidity.

And thirdly, I was very hungry. After all, we had not eaten supper the day before.

I sighed involuntarily.

'You, Ziukin, are a fine fellow,' Endlung said in a voice hoarse from shouting. 'That's what I've always said about people like you – still waters run deep. A man for the lovely ladies, a smart comrade and no sniveller. Why the hell are you a menial servant? Join us on the *Retvizan* as a senior quartermaster. Our lads will give you a hearty welcome – I should think so, grand ducal butler. We'd bring all the other ships down a peg or two. Really, I mean it. You could transfer from court service to the navy – that can be arranged. You'd be accepted as an equal in the mess. Just how much longer can you carrying on pouring coffee into other people's cups? We'd have great fun, by God we would. I remember you have no trouble with the ship rolling and pitching. Ah, Ziukin, you haven't been to Alexandria!' The lieutenant rolled his eyes up and back. '*Himmeldonnerwetter*, the brothels they have there! You'd be sure to like it, with your taste for petite ladies – they serve up little dolls that you can sit on the palm of your hand, but they still have the full set of tackle. I tell you, a tiny little waist like that, but up here they're like this, and like that!' He demonstrated with rounded gestures. 'I myself have always adored well-built women, but I can understand you too – the petite ones have their own special attraction. Tell me about Snezhnevskaya, as one comrade to another.' Endlung put his hand on my shoulder and looked into my eyes. 'What has that Polish girl got that that gives them all such a thrill? Is it true what they say, that at moments of passion she makes special sounds that drive men insane, the same way the sirens' song affected Odysseus' companions? Come on!' He nudged me with his elbow and winked at me. 'Paulie says he didn't hear any special kind of chanting during their only date, but Paulie's still a pup – he probably wasn't able to arouse genuine passion in that little Polish piece of yours – and you're a man of experience. Come on, tell me. What is it to you? We're not going to get out of here alive anyway. I'd really like to know what kind of sounds they are.' And the lieutenant broke into song: 'I hear the sounds of a Polish girl, the heavenly sounds of the beautiful Pole.'

Of course I did not know anything about any passionate sounds supposedly produced by Izabella Felitsianovna, and even if I had, I would not have revealed what I knew about such matters. I tried to indicate this by assuming the appropriate expression.

Endlung sighed in disappointment.

'So it's a lie? Or are you just being cagey? All right, don't tell me if you don't want to, although that's not the way good comrades behave. Sailors don't play cagey like that. You know, when you don't see dry land for months at a time, it's good to sit in the mess, telling each other all sorts of stories . . .'

There was a mighty rumbling of bells from somewhere far away, as if it was coming from the very bowels of the earth.

'Half past nine,' I said excitedly, interrupting the lieutenant. 'It has begun!'

'I'm so unlucky,' Endlung complained bitterly. 'I'm never going to see a tsar crowned, even though I am a gentleman of the bedchamber. I was still in the Corps at the last coronation, and I won't live until the next one – the tsar's younger than I am. I really wanted to see it! I even have a ticket for a good spot put away. Right opposite the porch of the cathedral. I expect they're coming out of the Cathedral of the Assumption right now, aren't they?'

'No,' I answered, 'they'll be coming out of the cathedral later. I know the entire ceremony off by heart. Would you like me to tell you about it?'

'I should say so!' the lieutenant exclaimed, pulling his legs up under him, Turkish style.

'Well then,' I began, trying to recall the schedule of the coronation. 'At the present moment Sergii, the Metropolitan of Moscow, is addressing His Majesty and explaining to him the heavy burden of serving as the tsar, and also the great mystery of anointment. In fact he has probably already finished. In the place of honour, by the royal gates, among the gold-embroidered court uniforms and pearl-trimmed ceremonial dresses, there are simple white peasant shirts and modest crimson *kokoshnik* head-dresses – these are the descendants of the heroic Ivan Susanin, saviour of the Romanov dynasty, who have been brought here from the province of Kostroma. And now the emperor and empress proceed along the scarlet carpet towards the thrones, set high up facing the altar, and a special throne has been installed for Her Majesty the dowager empress. Today the emperor is wearing his Preobrazhensky Regiment uniform with a red sash over his shoulder. The empress is wearing silver-white brocade and a necklace of pink pearls, and her train is carried by four pages of the bedchamber. The tsar's throne is an ancient piece of work, made for Tsar Alexei Mikhailovich, and it is known as the Diamond Throne because there are eight hundred and seventy diamonds embedded in it, as well as rubies and pearls. The foremost dignitaries of the empire hold the state regalia on velvet cushions: a sword, a crown, a shield and a sceptre surmounted by the illustrious Orlov diamond.' I sighed, closed my eyes and saw the sacred stone there in front of me, as large as life. 'It is absolutely clear, as transparent as a teardrop, with a very slight greenish-blue tinge, like seawater in sunlight. Weighing almost two hundred carats and shaped like half an egg, only larger, there is no more beautiful diamond in the entire world.'

Endlung listened as if he were spellbound. I must confess that I also got carried away and went on for a long time describing to my appreciative listener the entire great ceremony, occasionally checking my watch in order not to get ahead of events. And just at the very moment when I said 'And now the emperor and empress have come out onto the porch and are performing the low triple bow to the ground before the entire people; and now there will be an artillery salute,' there really was a rumble of thunder in the distance, and it lasted for several minutes for, according to the ceremonial, the cannon had to fire one hundred and one times.

'How wonderfully you described it all,' Endlung said with feeling. 'As if I had seen it all with my own eyes. I just didn't understand about the lacquered box and the man turning the handle.'

'I don't understand that too well myself,' I admitted.' However, I have seen with my own eyes the announcement in the *Court Gazette* that the coronation will be recorded using the very latest cinematographic apparatus, for which a special handler has been hired. He will turn the handle, and that will produce something like moving pictures.'

'What will they think of next?' said the lieutenant, squinting wistfully at the grey window. 'Well, now they've stopped their clattering, I can hear the gurgling in my belly.'

I remarked guardedly: 'Yes, indeed. I feel really hungry. Are we really going to die of hunger?'

'Oh, come on, Ziukin,' my fellow prisoner protested. 'We won't die of hunger; we'll die of thirst. A man can live two or even three weeks without food. Without water we won't even last three days.'

My throat was indeed feeling dry, and meanwhile it was getting rather stuffy in our little cell. Endlung had taken off his woman's dress a long time ago, leaving himself in nothing but his drawers and a close-fitting undershirt with blue and white stripes – what is known as a singlet. Now he even took off his singlet, and I saw a tattoo on his powerful shoulder – an entirely natural representation of a man's privates with varicoloured dragonfly wings.

'They drew that for me in a Singapore brothel,' the lieutenant explained when he noticed my embarrassed glance. 'I was still a warrant officer at the time. I did it for a bet, to show off. Now I can never marry a respectable woman. It looks as though I'm going to die a bachelor.'

This last sentence, however, was spoken without the slightest trace of regret.

I spent the entire second half of the day walking around the cell, with the torments of hunger, thirst and inactivity becoming worse and worse all the time. From time to time I tried shouting out of the window or banging on the door, but with no result.

In his gratitude for my description of the coronation, Endlung entertained me with endless stories of shipwrecks and uninhabited islands where sailors of various nationalities had died slow deaths without food or water. It had been dark for a long time when he started a heart-rending story about a French officer who was forced to eat his companion in misfortune, the ship's quarter-master.

'And what do you think?' the half-naked gentleman of the bedchamber said brightly. 'Afterwards Lieutenant Du Bellet testified in court that the quartermaster's meat was wonderfully tender, with a fine layer of fat, and tasted like young pork. The court acquitted the lieutenant, of course, taking into account the extreme circumstances and also the fact that Du Bellet was the only son of an aged mother.'

At that point the instructive tale was broken off because the door of the cell suddenly opened without a sound, and we both blinked in the bright light of a torch. The blurred shadow that appeared in the doorway spoke in the voice of Foma Anikeevich: 'I beg your pardon, Afanasii Stepanovich. Yesterday, of course, I recognised you under the ginger beard, but it never even entered my head that things could end so badly. Just now at the reception in the Faceted Chamber I happened to hear two habitués of this establishment whispering to each other and laughing as they recalled the lesson they had given to two "Guardians", and I wondered if they could be talking about you.' He came into the dungeon and asked solicitously: 'How have you managed here, gentlemen, with no water, food or light?'

'Badly, very badly!' Endlung exclaimed and threw himself on our rescuer's neck. I suspect that such impetuousness demonstrated by a sweaty gentleman wearing nothing but his drawers can hardly have been much to Foma Anikeevich's liking.

'This is our court's gentleman of the bedchamber, Filipp Nikolaevich Endlung,' I said. 'And this is Foma Anikeevich Savostianov, butler to His Highness the governor general of Moscow.' Then, with the necessary formalities concluded, I quickly asked about the most important thing: 'What has happened to Mikhail Georgievich? Has he been freed?'

Foma Anikeevich shrugged. 'I know nothing about that. We have our own misfortune. Prince Glinsky has shot himself. A terrible disaster.'

'How do you mean, shot himself?' I asked, astonished. 'Did he not fight a duel with Lord Banville?'

'As I said, he shot himself. He was found in the Petrovsko-Razumovsky Park with a gunshot wound in the heart.'

'So the little cornet was unlucky,' said Endlung, starting to pull on his dress. 'The Englishman didn't miss. He was a grand lad, even if he was a queer.'

15 May

'... and also the assistant pantry man broke the dish for game from the Sèvres service. I have already ordered him to be fined half a month's pay; anything further is at your discretion. And then there is Her Highness's maid Petrishcheva. The footman Kriuchkov reported that she had been seen in the bushes with Mr Fandorin's valet in a quite unambiguous position. I did not take any measures, since I do not know how you usually deal with behaviour of that sort ...'

'The first time, a reprimand,' I said, looking up from the plate to explain to Somov. 'The second time, out on her ear. If she has served the time, severance pay. We're very strict with that sort of thing.'

It was just getting light outside, and the lamp was lit in the kitchen. I ate some reheated soup with great gusto and then applied myself to some cutlets. More than twenty-four hours without a single bite to eat is certainly no joke.

After Foma Anikeevich released Endlung and me from our incarceration, the lieutenant's path and mine had parted. He went to the Variety Theatre to change his clothes. He had invited me too, saying that the girls slept in rooms at the theatre. They would give us food and drink, and show us a bit of affection.

But I had more important business to deal with.

And, moreover, this business did not include household concerns, so I listened to my assistant rather inattentively.

'How did the coronation go?' I asked, trying to work out if

Somov might know something about the previous day's operation. He ought not to, but he was far from stupid; in fact he seemed quite shrewd to me. But in any case he did not ask a single question about the reasons for my absence. Perhaps I could simply ask casually whether Mikhail Georgievich had been brought back from Ilyinsk?

'Absolutely magnificent. But –' Somov lowered his voice '– some of our people are saying there were bad omens . . .'

That put me on my guard. Bad omens on such a day, that is no trivial matter. A coronation is an exceptional event, every minor detail is significant. Among the court servants there are fortune-tellers who will lay out cards for the entire course of the ceremonies, hour by hour, in order to determine how the reign will proceed and when during its course convulsions can be expected. This we can call superstition, but there are other signs that cannot simply be dismissed. For instance, during the coronation of Alexander the Liberator a bottle of champagne suddenly burst for no reason at all on a table at the evening reception – it was like a bomb exploding. At that time, 1856, bombers had still not been heard of, and so no one knew how to interpret the incident. Its significance only became clear much later, after a quarter of a century. And at the last coronation the sovereign placed the crown on his head before he was supposed to, and our people whispered that his reign would not be a long one. And it was not.

'First of all,' Somov began, with a glance at the door, 'when the hairdresser was arranging Her Majesty's crown on her coiffure, he was so excited that he pushed too hard on one hairpin, and the empress cried out. He pricked her so badly that there was blood. And then, when the procession had already begun, the chain of His Majesty's Order of St Andrew broke, and it fell on the ground! Only our people know about the hairpin, but many people noticed the incident with the order.'

Yes, that is not good, I thought. However, it could have been worse. The main thing was that the crowning of the tsar had taken place, and Doctor Lind had not disrupted this supremely solemn festivity after all.

'What about the Englishmen?' I enquired vaguely, unsure whether anyone at the Hermitage knew anything about the duel.

'Lord Banville has left. Yesterday at noon. He did not even attend the coronation. He simply left a note for His Highness and moved out. He looked very pale and angry, as if he was offended about something or unwell. But he left extremely generous gratuities for all the senior personnel. For you, Afanasii Stepanovich, a gold guinea.'

'Change it into roubles and share it equally between Lipps and the two coachmen, from me. They have all worked very well,' I said, deciding that I did not want any gratuity from that murderer. 'And what of Mr Carr?'

'He is still here. His Lordship even left his butler with Mr Carr – he left alone.'

'And is Mademoiselle Declique missing her pupil very badly?' I asked with feigned nonchalance, finally broaching the most important subject.

There were quiet footsteps in the corridor. I looked round and saw Fandorin. He was wearing a Hungarian housecoat with decorative cording; he had a net on his hair and felt slippers on his feet. A smooth creature, stepping gently through the half-light with a glitter in his eyes – a real tomcat.

'The night d-doorman informed me that you had returned. But where is Endlung?' he asked, without a greeting of any kind.

From the question about Endlung I assumed that Pavel Georgievich had told Fandorin about our expedition. Despite the intense dislike that this man provoked in me, I was impatient to talk to him.

'You may go, Kornei Selifanovich,' I said to my assistant, and the intelligent man left immediately. 'The gentleman of the bedchamber is all right,' I replied curtly, and in order to prevent any further disagreeable questions, I added: 'Unfortunately, it was simply a waste of our time.'

'Things are not going so well here either,' said Fandorin, taking a seat. 'You d-disappeared yesterday evening, before Emilie had come back. She managed her assignment perfectly and we determined the precise location of Lind's secret hideaway. It turned out that he is hiding the child in the tomb of the Princess Bakhmetova, which stands close to the wall of the Novodevichy Convent. The princess took her own life because of an unhappy love a hundred years ago and they would not allow her to be buried inside the convent, so her disconsolate parents built a sort of mausoleum for her. The Bakhmetov line has since become extinct, so the tomb is dilapidated and the lock on the door is rusty. However, that is merely a facade. Mademoiselle tells me that every time she was led into the cold interior with her eyes blindfolded, she heard the sound of well-oiled hinges. We have not been able to obtain an accurate architectural plan of the chapel; all we know is that the tomb itself is located underground in the v-vault.'

Erast Petrovich began drawing on the table with his finger.

'We made ready yesterday at dawn. This (he put down the breadbin) is the monastery. Here (he positioned the salt cellar beside it) we have the tomb. There is wasteland all around, and there is a pond here. (He splashed a little tea onto the oilcloth.) In short, there is no way to approach unnoticed. We have positioned men in disguise around the spot at a considerable distance but not made any attempt to go inside.'

'Why not?' I asked.

'The point is, Ziukin, that since the Time of Troubles all the ground around the Novodevichy Convent has been riddled with underground passages. It was besieged by the Poles and then the False Dmitry, and later the Streltsy dug under it to free the Tsarina Sophia from captivity. I am sure that Lind, being the highly prudent and cautious individual that he is, chose this spot for a good reason. There must be a line of retreat – that is always his tactic. And so I decided to take a different approach.'

He knitted his brows and sighed.

'The delivery of the stone was set for five o'clock yesterday, since the coronation was due to conclude at two. Immediately after the ceremony the Orlov was removed from the sceptre—'

'Permission was given for the exchange?' I exclaimed. 'So she was wrong, and they decided to save Mikhail Georgievich after all!'

'Who is *she*?' Fandorin asked, but he could see from my face that there would be no answer, and he continued: 'I was entrusted with the Orlov on one condition. I gave a guarantee that Lind would not keep the stone under any circumstances. Not under *any* circumstances,' he repeated significantly.

I nodded. 'That is, if a choice has to be made between the life of His Highness and the diamond . . .'

'Precisely so.'

'But how can we be sure that the doctor will not manage to keep the Orlov? How will Mademoiselle Declique be able to stop him? And then, you said yourself that there are underground passages . . .'

'I set one condition for Lind, which Emilie communicated to him the day before yesterday. Since we are not dealing with any ordinary jewel here but a holy relic, the d-diamond cannot be entrusted to a weak woman. The governess was to be accompanied by an escort. One man, unarmed, so that Lind need not fear an attack . . .'

'And who was this escort?'

'I was,' Fandorin said ruefully. 'It was good idea, don't you think?'

'And what happened?'

'It didn't work. I disguised myself as an old stooped footman but clearly not carefully enough. Emilie and I waited for more than an hour in the cathedral. No one approached us. And yet the day before yesterday, when she was alone, there were no difficulties: another note, a closed carriage in one of the side streets nearby and so on. Yesterday we waited until a quarter past six and came back with nothing for our pains.'

'Surely Lind could not have abandoned the exchange?' I asked in a dismal voice.

'Indeed not. There was a letter waiting for us at the Hermitage, delivered in the same manner as before, by the postman but without any stamp. Here, read it, especially since it concerns you directly.'

I cautiously took the sheet of paper, which gave off a faint aroma of scent.

'The Earl of Essex?' I asked.

'In person. B-but read it, read it.'

'I have decided to make the Romanov dynasty a generous gift on the occasion of the coronation . . .' I read the first sentence in French and everything began swimming in front of my eyes. Could it really be?

But no, my joy was premature. I batted my eyelids to disperse the haze and read the note through to the end:

I have decided to make the Romanov dynasty a generous gift on the occasion of the coronation. A gift that is worth a million, for that is the sum agreed as one day's payment for the Orlov, which I have kindly loaned to the Russian monarchy. And so you may keep the stone for one more day, entirely without charge. After all, it would be impolite of me, to say the least, to cast a shadow over your day of celebration.

We will complete our little transaction tomorrow. The governess must be in the cathedral at seven o'clock in the evening. I understand your reluctance to entrust such a valuable treasure to this woman, and I have no objections to a single escort. However, it must be someone I know, that is Monsieur Doggy Sideburns.

Yours sincerely,
Doctor Lind

My heart began beating faster and faster.

'So this is why you are telling me all this?'

'Yes,' said Fandorin, looking into my eyes. 'Afanasii Stepanovich, I need to ask you to take part in this dangerous business. You are not a police agent or a member of the armed services; you are not obliged to risk your life to p-protect the interests of the state, but circumstances have determined that without your help—'

'I agree,' I said, interrupting him.

At that moment I did not feel afraid at all. I was thinking of only one thing: Emilie and I would be together. I think it was the first time that I had thought of Mademoiselle by her first name.

There was a brief pause, and then Erast Petrovich got to his feet.

'Then get some rest, you look tired. Be in the d-drawing room at ten o'clock. I'll give you and Emilie a briefing.'

The late sun had warmed the velvet curtains, and there was a distinct smell of dust in the shaded drawing room. Velvet is always a problem – it is in the nature of the material: if it is left hanging for years without being washed regularly, as it had been here in the Hermitage, you simply cannot completely get rid of the dust that has eaten into it. I made a mental note to have the curtains changed that very day. Provided, of course, that I came back from the operation alive.

The success of the proposed undertaking appeared highly doubtful to me. At this last meeting – I had to assume that it was indeed the very last – only those directly involved in the operation were present: Mademoiselle and I, Mr Fandorin and the two colonels, Karnovich and Lasovsky, who were as meek as lambs and as quiet as mice, and listened to Erast Petrovich with emphatic respect, which may have been genuine or false, I do not know.

The plan of the area between the Novodevichy Convent and the Novodevichy Embankment that was laid out on the table had been carefully drawn, not like that morning's demonstration on the oilcloth. Cross-hatched circles marked the positions of the secret sentries who surrounded the wasteland on all sides: the senior agent (Fandorin gave his name – Kuzyakin) in a hollow in an old oak tree on the corner of Vselensky Square; six 'attendants' in the dormitory of the children's clinic that had windows over-looking the pond; eleven 'monks' on the wall of the convent; seven 'boatmen' and 'buoy keepers' on the river; one man dis-guised as a female street trader on the turn-off from Pog-odinskaya Street; three ' beggars' at the gates of the convent; two 'fishermen' by the pond, the closest of all. The total number of agents in the first ring of the cordon was thirty-one.

'The exchange must take place as follows,' Fandorin explained after he had indicated the positions of the sentry posts. 'The two of you will be led to the chapel and taken inside. You will demand that your blindfolds be removed. The doctor's own jeweller is bound to be there. You will give him the Orlov to examine and then take it back. Then Mademoiselle Declique will go down into the vault and collect the boy. When the boy is brought out to you, you hand over the stone. At that point, Ziukin, your mission is over.'

I could hardly believe my ears. I was already familiar with Mr Fandorin's adventurous disposition, but I had not expected such irresponsibility, even from him. The most astounding thing was that the head of the court police and the high police master of Moscow had listened to this insane plan with a perfectly serious air and did not utter a single word of protest!

'What nonsense!' I declared with a trenchancy that was quite uncharacteristic of me (but entirely justified by the circumstances). 'I shall be alone, unarmed, and Mademoiselle's presence will not help me. They will simply take the diamond away from me once they are satisfied that it is genuine. And they will not even think of returning Mikhail Georgievich. They will simply escape through some underground passage and kill all three of us. A fine operation that will be! Wouldn't it be better to wait until Mademoiselle Declique and I have been taken inside, and then storm the tomb?'

'No, it would not,' Fandorin replied curtly.

And Karnovich explained: 'If the place is stormed, His

Highness will certainly be killed. And so will the two of you.'

I said nothing and glanced at Emilie. I must admit that she looked much calmer than I was and she was gazing at Fandorin as if she trusted him completely, which was particularly painful to see.

'Erast Petrovich,' she said quietly, 'Doctor Lind is very cunning. What if Monsieur Ziukin and I are taken to a different place today, somewhere completely new? If that is the case, then your *embuscade*[I] will be in vain.'

I turned to the sagacious Fandorin, for the question had, as they say, hit the bullseye.

'That is not out of the question,' he admitted. 'But I have taken certain m-measures to deal with it. And your concerns, Ziukin – that they will take the stone and not return the boy – are also perfectly reasonable. It will all depend entirely on you. And so now I come to the m-most important thing of all.'

And so saying, he went across to a small wooden chest standing on a table beside the window, opened it and, using both hands, lifted out a smooth, shiny golden sphere the size of a small Crimean melon.

'Here is your guarantee,' said Erast Petrovich, setting the sphere down in front of me.

'What is it?' I asked, leaning over it.

The mirror surface of the sphere showed me a comically extended reflection of my own face.

'A bomb, Afanasii Stepanovich. Of appalling destructive power. There is a small button on the inside. Pressing it releases the detonator, and after that the slightest jolt – for instance dropping the sphere on a stone floor – is sufficient to cause an explosion that would completely obliterate you, Lind and his men, and the entire chapel. The Orlov, as it happens, would survive, because it is indestructible and afterwards we would c-certainly find it among the rubble ... You will have to explain all this to the

---

[I] *Ambush.*

doctor. Tell him that at the slightest sign of foul play you will drop the sphere. This is the only argument that will have any effect on Lind. It is our little surprise, so to speak.'

'But the bomb is not genuine?'

'I assure you that it is entirely g-genuine. The charge consists of an explosive mixture invented by chemists at the Imperial Mining and Artillery Laboratory. The Commission of the Central Artillery Department has not approved the mixture for use because the risk of accidental explosion is too great. If they try to search you when you are getting into the carriage, you will say that the sphere is a case for the Orlov and you will not allow them to open it under any circumstances. Say that the journey is cancelled if they do not agree. But then, if it is the same mute coachman who comes for you, any discussion is unlikely.'

Erast Petrovich picked up the sphere and prised open a barely visible lid with his nail.

'The Orlov really is inside, in the upper section of the sphere. When you take out the stone to hand it over for inspection, you press here and so activate the mechanism. Under no cir-cumstances do this in the carriage, or else the jolting might produce an explosion. And after you have pressed the button you will tell Lind or his men what kind of toy this is.'

I glanced inside the sphere. The priceless relic of the House of Romanov was lying in a rounded niche, glinting with a dull bluish light. At close quarters the miraculous stone seemed to me like a cut-crystal door handle, similar to those that adorned the chest of drawers in the grand duchess's dressing room. To be quite honest, I was far more impressed by the red metal button that was almost invisible against the background of scarlet velvet.

I wiped the sweat off my forehead and looked at Emilie. If things went badly, or if I simply made a blunder, we would die together, and the fragments of our bodies would be intermingled. She nodded to me calmly, as if to say: It is all right. I trust you and everything is certain to turn out well.

'But then what?' I asked. 'Lind will not want to be blown up, that is clear enough, so he will not break the rules of the game. He will give us Mikhail Georgievich and then escape through some cunning secret passage. And the Orlov will be lost forever!'

'That must not happen, no matter what!' said Karnovich, joining in the conversation for the first time. 'Remember, Mr Fandorin, you have guaranteed the stone's safety with your own life.'

Fandorin smiled at me as if he had not heard the colonel.

'In that eventuality, Ziukin, I have another surprise in store for the doctor.'

However the smile, which was really quite inappropriate in the situation, rapidly disappeared, to be replaced by an expression of uncertainty or perhaps even embarrassment.

'Emilie, Afanasii Stepanovich ... the risk to which you are exposing yourselves is undoubtedly v-very great. Lind is a man of paradoxical intelligence; his actions and reactions are frequently unpredictable. A plan is all very well, but anything at all could happen. And after all, Emilie, you are a lady and not even a Russian subject ...'

'Never mind the risk, that is all right,' Mademoiselle said with sublime dignity. 'But we – Mr Ziukin and I – will be easier in our minds if we know what other surprise you have in mind.'

Fandorin carefully closed the gold lid and the blue radiance glimmering above the table disappeared.

'It is best if you do not know that. It must be a surprise for you two as well. Otherwise the plan may go awry.'

A strange business. When we found ourselves alone together, sealed off from the world in the dark carriage, neither of us said a word for a long time. I listened to Mademoiselle's regular breathing, and as time passed and my eyes grew accustomed to the gloom, I could make out her vague silhouette. I wanted to hear her voice, to say something encouraging to her but, as usual, I simply could not find the right words. The metal sphere was lying on my knees, and although the detonator was not yet activated, I gripped the infernal device firmly with both hands.

My fears that I would have problems with Doctor Lind's intermediary concerning the strangely rounded bulky bundle had proved unfounded. The first stage of the operation had gone smoothly – as the common folk say, without a hitch.

Mademoiselle and I had been standing in the cathedral for less than five minutes when a boy who looked like one of the ordinary little beggars who are always jostling on the porch there handed me a note – I even had to give the little villain five kopecks of my own money. Our shoulders pressed together as we unfolded the sheet of paper (once again I caught a whiff of the scent The Earl of Essex) and read the single short line: 'L'église d'Ilya Prorok'.[2] I did not know where that was, but Mademoiselle, who had had an opportunity to study all the surrounding streets and side streets in close detail, confidently showed me the way.

A few minutes later we were outside a small church, and there was a black carriage with curtained windows waiting in front of the next building. It looked very much like the one that I had seen a week earlier, although I could not vouch for it being the same one. A tall man with a hat pulled down very low jumped down off the coach box. All I could see of his face was a thick black beard. Without saying a word, he opened the door and pushed Mademoiselle inside.

I showed him my bundle and pronounced the phrase that I had prepared in a severe tone of voice: 'This is the object of the exchange. It must not be touched.'

I do not know if he understood me, but he did not touch the bundle. He squatted down and very rapidly ran his hands over my entire body, touching even the most intimate places without the slightest sign of embarrassment.

'If you do not mind, sir . . .' I protested, but the search was already over.

Without speaking, the bearded man pushed me in the back, I

---

[2] *The Church of the Prophet Elijah.*

got into the carriage and the door slammed. I heard the squeak of a bolt. The carriage swayed, and we set off.

I expect that at least half an hour must have passed before we struck up a conversation. It was Mademoiselle who began it, because I had still not thought of a way to start.

'Strange,' she said when the carriage swayed on a corner and our shoulders touched. 'It is strange that he did not caress me today.'

'What?' I asked, amazed.

'How do you say – *perquisitionner*?'

'Ah, to frisk, to search.'

'Yes, thank you. Strange that he did not search me. He usually does, to see if it is possible to hide a little pistol in the pantaloons.'

I took the liberty of leaning down to her ear and whispering: 'We have a better weapon than that.'

'Careful!' Mademoiselle gasped. 'I'm afraid!'

A woman is always a woman, even the very bravest!

'It's all right,' I reassured her. 'The detonator has not been activated yet; there is nothing to be afraid of.'

'I keep thinking about Monsieur Fandorin's second surprise,' Mademoiselle suddenly said in French. 'Could it possibly be that the bomb will go off in any case, blowing us and Doctor Lind and His Highness to pieces, and then afterwards, as Monsieur Fandorin said, they will find the stone among the rubble? The most important thing for the tsar is to keep the Orlov and avoid any publicity. And for Monsieur Fandorin, the main thing is to take his revenge on Doctor Lind. What do you think, Athanas?'

To be quite honest, her suspicions seemed quite plausible to me, but after a moment's thought I found an appropriate objection.

'In that case they would have given us a fake instead of the genuine stone. Then they would not have to search for anything in the rubble.'

'And what makes you sure that it is the genuine Orlov in the sphere?' she asked nervously. 'We are not jewellers, after all.

242

When you press the button, there will be an explosion, and that will be the promised surprise that you and I were not supposed to know about under any circumstances.'

I turned cold inside. This conjecture seemed only too logical.

'Then that is our destiny,' I said, crossing myself. 'If you have guessed right, then the decision was taken by a higher power, and I shall carry it out to the letter. But you do not have to go into the chapel. When we get there, I shall tell the driver that there is no need for you to be present; I shall collect Mikhail Georgievich myself.'

Mademoiselle squeezed my hand.

'Thank you, Athanas. You have restored my faith in human dignity. No. No, I shall go with you. I feel ashamed that I could have suspected Erast of being disloyal. For him, no precious stone, not even such a special one, could possibly be more important than the life of a child. And our lives too,' she concluded in a quiet voice.

The second half of her brief emotional declaration somewhat spoiled the pleasant impression of the first, but nonetheless I was touched. I wanted to respond to her grip on my fingers, but that would probably have been too great a liberty. And so we rode on, with her hand still touching mine.

Unlike Mademoiselle, I was not entirely convinced of Mr Fandorin's nobility. I thought it quite probable that the earthly existence of Afanasii Ziukin would come to an end in the very near future, and not in a quiet, humdrum fashion, as the entire logic of my life would have dictated, but amidst unseemly uproar and clamour. Emilie's company rendered this thought less repulsive, which was undoubtedly an expression of a quality that I cannot stand in other people and have always tried to suppress in myself – cowardly selfishness.

Meanwhile, it was becoming harder and harder to breathe in the sealed carriage. There were drops of sweat running down my face and inside my collar. This was unpleasantly ticklish, but I could not wipe them away with my handkerchief – to do that,

I would have had to take my hand away. Mademoiselle was also breathing rapidly.

Suddenly a thought occurred to me, so simple and terrible that the sweat started flowing even more abundantly. I tried to insert my hand into the bundle and open the lid of the sphere quietly without frightening Mademoiselle, but even so there was an audible click.

'What was that?' Mademoiselle asked with a start. 'What was that sound?'

'Lind's plan is simpler and more cunning than Fandorin imagines,' I said, gasping for air. 'I suspect that the doctor has ordered us to be driven in this closed coffin until we suffocate, so that he can take the Orlov without any trouble. But it won't work – I am activating the detonator. As long as I remain conscious, I shall hold the bomb steady with both hands. But when I am exhausted, the sphere will fall ...'

'*Vous êtes fou!*' Mademoiselle exclaimed, pulling her hand away and seizing hold of my elbow. '*Vous êtes fou! N'y pensez pas. Je compte les détours, nous sommes presque là.*'[3]

'Too late, I have already pressed the button,' I said, and took a firm grip of the sphere with both hands.

And then a minute later the carriage really did stop.

'Well then, may God help us,' Emilie whispered and crossed herself, only not in the Orthodox manner, but in the Catholic way, from left to right.

The door opened, and I screwed my eyes up against the bright light. Nobody blindfolded me, and I saw the peeling walls of a small chapel and also, a little distance away, perhaps a hundred paces, the towers of an old convent. As I stepped onto the foot-plate, I stole a glance around me. There were fishermen sitting by the pond and on the edge of the nearby square a knotty old oak stood, covered in fresh greenery, presumably with senior

---

[3] *You're insane! Do not even think of it! I am counting the turns of the wheels. We are almost there!*

police agent Kuzyakin concealed somewhere amongst it. I felt a little bit calmer, although the failure to blindfold us probably signified that Lind did not intend to let us go alive. Mademoiselle looked over my shoulder and also started gazing around – ah, yes, this was the first time she had been here without a blindfold. All right, Doctor, I thought. If we are to die, we'll take you with us, and I pressed the bundle tight against my chest.

The driver, standing to one side of the open door of the carriage, seized me by the elbow and pulled as if to say: Get out. I grimaced at the strength of those steely fingers.

The rusty door with the heavy padlock barely even creaked as it swung open to admit us. I walked into the gloomy interior, which was more spacious than it appeared from the outside, and saw several male figures. Before I could get a clear look at them, the door closed behind us, but the light did not disappear; it merely changed from grey to yellow because there were several oil lamps hanging on the walls.

There were four men. The one who caught my attention was a lean grey-haired gentleman with a toothless non-Russian face and steel-rimmed spectacles. Could this be Doctor Lind himself? Standing one on each side of him were two tall broad-shouldered men whose faces were drowned in the shadows – bodyguards, I presumed. The fourth man was the coachman, who had followed us in and leaned back against the closed door as if to cut off our retreat.

One of the bodyguards gestured to the coachman, clearly indicating that he should leave.

The coachman nodded, but he did not move.

The bodyguard pointed angrily to the door.

'*Taubstummer Dickkopf!*'[4] the great brute swore.

So that was why the driver had behaved so strangely with us! And now it was clear why Lind had not been afraid that the bearded man might be taken by the police.

---

4 *Deaf-mute blockhead!*

The other bodyguard replied, also in German: 'Ah, to hell with it. Let him stay there. He's probably as curious as we are to see what happens.'

Then the grey-haired gentleman stretched his hand out towards the bundle, and I realised that the truly important business had begun.

'Did you bring it? Show me,' he said in a dull voice, speaking French.

I dropped the shawl in which the sphere was wrapped onto the floor and opened the lid. The stone glittered from its velvet niche with a gentle muted light.

Enunciating every word slowly and clearly, I explained about the surprise and the conditions of exchange. Thank God, my voice did not tremble even once. The most important thing was for Lind to believe me. If it came to the crunch, I would not play the coward.

He heard me out without interrupting and nodded as if I were talking about something that went without saying. He clicked his fingers impatiently. 'All right, all right. Give it to me. I'll check it.'

And he took a small magnifying glass bound in copper out of his pocket.

So he was not Lind but the jeweller, just as Fandorin had predicted. I prised the stone out with two fingers and it seemed to fit snugly into the palm of my hand, as if had been created to match its size. With my other hand I held the bomb carefully against my chest.

The jeweller took the diamond and walked over to one of the lamps. The bodyguards, or whoever they really were, surrounded him and drew in their breath loudly when the facets of the Orlov sparkled with unbearable brilliance.

I glanced round at Mademoiselle. She was standing still but with her fingers locked together. Raising her eyebrows, she indicated the sphere with her glance, and I nodded reassuringly as if to say: Don't worry, I won't drop it.

The light of the oil lamp was not enough for the jeweller. He took out a little electric torch too and pushed a switch. A thin, bright ray of light touched the diamond, and I screwed up my eyes. Sparks seemed to scatter from the surface of the stone.

'Alles in Ordnung,'[5] the jeweller said dispassionately in perfect German and put the magnifying glass in his pocket.

'Give me back the stone,' I demanded.

When he did not do as I said, I held the open sphere out in front of me with both hands.

The jeweller shrugged and put the diamond back in its niche.

Heartened by this success, I raised my voice: 'Where is His Highness? Under the terms of the agreement, you must now give him back immediately!'

The lipless man pointed to the stone floor, and for the first time I noticed a square black trapdoor with a metal ring for a handle.

'Who needs your boy? Take him before he croaks.'

On the lips of this respectable-looking gentleman the crude word 'croaks', used about a little child, sounded so unexpected and terrible that I shuddered. My God, what kind of people were they!

Mademoiselle drew in a noisy breath and dashed to the trap-door, grabbed the ring and pulled with all her might. The door lifted a little, and then fell back into the gap with a resounding metallic clang. None of the thugs moved to help the lady. Emilie looked at me in despair, but I could not help her – to do that I would have had to put down the sphere.

'Aufmachen!'[6] I shouted menacingly, lifting the bomb higher.

With clear reluctance, one of the bandits moved Mademoiselle aside and easily lifted the cover up with one hand.

The gap that was revealed was not black, as I had expected, but filled with a trembling light. Obviously there was an oil lamp

---

5 *All is in order.*
6 *Open it!*

in the vault too. A smell of dampness and mould came up through the opening.

Poor Mikhail Georgievich! How could they have kept him in that hole all these days!

Gathering up the hem of her skirt, Mademoiselle started to go down. One of the thugs followed her. I could feel my pulse pounding rapidly in my temples.

I heard the sound of voices coming from below and then a piercing shout from Emilie: 'Mon bébé, mon pauvre petit. Tas de salauds!'[7]

'Is His Highness dead?' I roared, ready to throw the bomb on the floor and damn the consequences.

'No, he's alive!' I heard. 'But very poorly!'

I cannot express the relief that I felt at those words. Of course His Highness was chilled to the bone, wounded and drugged with opium, but the important thing was that he was alive.

The jeweller held out his hand. 'Give me the stone. Your companion will bring the boy out now.'

'Let her bring him out first,' I muttered, suddenly realising that I had no idea of what to do next. There had been nothing about that in Fandorin's instructions. Should I give him the stone or not?

Suddenly the bodyguard who was still in the room leapt towards me with astounding agility and pressed his palms tight over my hands, which were holding the bomb. The jolt was only very slight and the detonating mechanism was not set off, but the diamond tumbled out of its niche and clattered across the floor. The jeweller grabbed it and put it in his pocket.

It was pointless trying to struggle with the great brute, and the coachman with the black beard also came up from behind – I had already had occasion to know of his great strength. Oh Lord, now I had ruined everything.

'Now this is surprise number two,' the deaf mute whispered

---

7 My baby, my poor little one. You scum!

in my ear, and in the same second he punched the thug on the forehead. The blow did not seem very strong to me, but the German's eyes rolled up, he opened his hands and sank down on to the floor.

'Hold it tight,' the coachman said in Fandorin's voice.

In a single bound he reached the jeweller and put one hand over his mouth, at the same time holding a stiletto to his chin from below.

'*Taisez-vous! Un mot, et vous êtes mort!*[8] Ziukin, switch off the bomb, we won't be needing it any more.'

The speed at which events were moving had left me numb, so I was not at all surprised by the coachman's transformation into Fandorin; in fact, I was more impressed by the fact that Erast Petrovich had completely stopped stammering.

I obediently gripped the depressed button with my fingernails and pulled. It popped out with a gentle click.

'Shout to say that you have the stone and the child can be released,' Fandorin said quietly in French.

The jeweller batted his eyelids with unnatural speed. He could not nod because the gesture would have impaled his head on the blade of the stiletto.

Fandorin removed his hand from the jeweller's mouth but kept the dagger in its vertical position.

His prisoner worked his sunken mouth and licked his lips, then threw his head back as if he wanted to look at something on the ceiling and suddenly shouted loudly: '*Alarme! Fuiez-vous!*'[9]

He was about to shout something else, but the narrow strip of steel slid in between his throat and his chin right up to the hilt and he wheezed. I gasped out loud.

Before the dead man had even collapsed to the floor, a head appeared out of the hatch – I think it belonged to the bandit who had gone down with Mademoiselle.

---

[8] *Quiet! One word and you're dead!*
[9] *Alarm! Run!*

Fandorin leapt to the opening and kicked him hard in the face. There was the dull sound of a body collapsing heavily and Erast Petrovich jumped down without waiting even for a second.

'Oh, Lord!' I blurted out. 'Oh, my Lord God.'

I heard a loud crash from below and voices shouting in German and French.

Crossing myself with the golden sphere, I ran to the opening and looked down.

It was a genuine roughhouse: a huge brute clutching a knife in one raised hand had pinned Fandorin to the floor, and another bodyguard was lying motionless further away. Erast Petrovich was clutching his opponent's wrist with one hand to hold back the knife, and trying to reach his throat with the other. But he simply could not reach it. It seemed that the former state counsellor needed to be rescued.

I flung the sphere, aiming at the back of the giant's head, and I was right on target. There was a squelching sound as it hit home. The blow would undoubtedly have smashed any ordinary man's skull, but this one merely swayed forward. That, however, was enough for Fandorin to reach his throat. I did not see exactly what Erast Petrovich's fingers did, but I heard a sickening crunch, and the huge brute slumped over sideways.

I quickly went down into the vault. Fandorin had already jumped to his feet and was gazing around.

We were in a square room with corners drowned in dark shadow. At the centre of the vault there was a moss-covered gravestone, on which an oil lamp was burning.

'Where is she?' I asked, flustered. 'Where is His Highness? Where is Lind?'

There was a trunk standing by one wall with a heap of rags on it, and I realised that must be where Mikhail Georgievich had been kept. However, Fandorin dashed in the opposite direction.

I heard the clatter of rapidly receding footsteps – it sounded as if there were three or four people running.

Fandorin grabbed the lamp and lifted it up high, and we saw

250

the entrance to a passage in the wall. It was blocked by a metal grille.

The darkness was illuminated by a sudden flash; there was a spiteful whistling sound and a dull echo.

'Get behind the projection!' Fandorin shouted to me as he jumped to one side.

'Emilie, are you alive?' I called as loudly as I possibly could.

The darkness replied in Mademoiselle's muted voice: 'There are three of them! And Lind's here! He's—'

The voice broke off with a shriek. I dashed to the metal grille and began shaking it, but it was locked shut.

Erast Petrovich pulled me back by my sleeve – and just in time. They started shooting again out of the passageway. One of the metal bars exploded into a shower of sparks and an invisible rod of iron struck the wall, scattering fragments of stone onto the floor.

I heard men's voices in the distance and someone – a woman or a child – groaned in a high-pitched voice.

'Lind!' Erast shouted loudly, speaking in French. 'This is Fandorin! I have the stone! The exchange is still in force. I'll give you the Orlov for the woman and the child!'

We held our breath. It was quiet – no voices, no steps. Had Lind heard?

Fandorin raised a hand in which a small black revolver had appeared out of nowhere and fired at the lock – once, twice, three times.

Sparks showered into the air again, but the lock did not fly open.

16 May

I sat by the river gazing dully at the long rafts of rough brown logs floating past, trying to understand whether it was I who had gone insane or the world around me.

Afanasii Ziukin declared an outlaw? Being hunted by the police and gendarmes?

Then perhaps Afanasii Ziukin was not really me at all but someone else.

But no, the entire might of the of the empire's forces of law and order had been mobilised precisely to find us – Mr Fandorin and myself. And the reason for that was not some monstrous misunderstanding but our own criminal behaviour. Yes indeed, *our* behaviour, because I had become Fandorin's accomplice willingly.

I needed to assess everything clearly from the very beginning, to recall every last detail of the events of the previous night.

When we finally managed to break open the lock and enter the passage, any attempt to overtake Lind was already pointless. But in our extreme agitation we did not realise this immediately. Fandorin ran ahead, lighting the way with a lantern he had taken from a table, and I ran after him, hunching over in order not to bang my head against the low ceiling. The swaying beam of light picked tangles of cobwebs out of the darkness, exposed shards of some kind under our feet, lit up the clay walls with a damp gleam.

After about twenty paces the passage divided in two. Erast Petrovich squatted on the ground for a moment, shone his lantern down and confidently turned to the right. Thirty seconds later the tunnel divided again. After studying the tracks clearly visible in the thick layer of dust, we went to the left. Another seven or eight forks were negotiated with the same ease, and then the oil in the lantern ran out, and we were left in total darkness.

'Wonderful,' Fandorin muttered angrily. 'Absolutely wonderful. Now not only can't we pursue Lind, we can't even find the way back either. Who would ever have believed there was such a maze down here? They must have been digging it for three hundred years, if not longer: the monks during the Time of Troubles and the rebel Streltsy, and the Old Believers hiding their ancient books and church silver from the Patriarch Nikon; and since there are stone galleries, there must have been quarries here at some time . . . All right, Ziukin. Let's go wherever our path leads.'

Making our way in total darkness was slow and difficult. I fell several times when I stumbled over obstacles on the floor. The first time I fell some live creature darted out from under me with a squeal and I grabbed at my heart. I have one shameful and unmanly weakness – I cannot stand rats and mice. I am instinctively repulsed by those creeping, darting, thieving vermin. On the next occasion I caught my foot on something shaped like a root, and when I felt it with my hand, it proved to be a human ribcage. When I stretched my length on the ground for the third time, I heard something jingle underneath me. I clutched at my pocket – and the Orlov was not there.

I shouted out in horror: 'I've dropped the stone.'

Fandorin struck a match, and I saw a broken crock containing irregular round objects that glinted dully in the light. I picked one up – it was a silver coin, very old. But I had no interest at all in coins just then. I wondered if I could possibly have dropped

253

the diamond earlier, during one of my other falls. In that case finding it would be very far from easy.

Thank God, with his third match Fandorin spotted the diamond, half-buried in the dust, and he kept it. After what had happened, I did not dare to object. I tipped two handfuls of coins from the treasure trove into my pockets and we wandered on.

I do not know how many hours it lasted. Sometimes we sat down on the ground to draw breath. This was the second night in succession I had spent underground and, Lord help me, I would be hard pressed to say which of them I liked less.

We could not even look to see what time it was, because our matches were soon soaked by the damp air and refused to strike. When I stumbled over those familiar bones for the second time, it became clear that we were wandering in circles.

Then Fandorin said: 'You know, Ziukin, this will not do. Do you want rats to run over your naked ribs?'

I shuddered.

'Well, nor do I. So we must stop simply strolling about, hoping for things to work out somehow or other. We need a system. From now on we follow a strict alternation: one turn to the right, one turn to the left. Forward!'

But even after the introduction of the 'system' we walked for a very long time, until eventually we saw a feeble light glimmering in the distance. I was the first to go dashing towards it. The passage narrowed and shrank until we had to crawl on all fours, but that was all right, because the light kept growing brighter and brighter. At the very end I grabbed hold of a cold, rough root, and it suddenly tore itself out of my hand with an angry hiss. A snake! I gasped and jerked away, banging the back of my head against the stone ceiling. I saw yellow spots on the narrow head of the black band as it rippled away from me – a harmless grass snake – but my heart was still pounding insanely.

The burrow had led us out to the edge of the water on a riverbank. I saw a dark barge wreathed in morning mist, the roofs of warehouses on the far side of the river and the semicircular arches of a railway bridge in the distance.

'We haven't really travelled very far,' said Fandorin, straightening up and dusting off his soiled coachman's coat. I saw that he had already rid himself of the long black beard and I thought he had left the hat with the broad brim back in the vault. I followed the direction of his glance. Just a few hundred paces away the domes of the Novodevichy Convent were glinting gently in the first rays of sunlight.

'Evidently the nuns used this passage as a secret way to reach the river,' Fandorin surmised. 'I wonder what for.'

I could not have cared less.

'And there's the bell tower,' I said, pointing. 'Quickly, let's go. Mr Karnovich and Mr Lasovsky must be tired of looking for us. Or if not for us, for the Orlov. Won't they be delighted!'

I smiled. At that moment the sense of open space, the light and the freshness of the morning filled me with the same feeling of life's completeness that Lazarus must have felt when he rose from the dead.

'Do you really want to give the Orlov back to Karnovich?' Fandorin asked incredulously.

For a moment I thought I must have misheard, but then I realised that, like myself, Mr Fandorin was delighted by the successful outcome of our appalling night and was therefore in the mood for a joke. Well, there are circumstances in which even Ziukin is not averse to a joke, even if his companion is not the most pleasant.

'No, I want to take the stone to Doctor Lind,' I replied with a restrained smile intended to indicate that I had appreciated his joke and was replying in kind.

'Well, that is just it,' Erast Petrovich said, nodding seriously. 'You understand that if we give the stone to the authorities, we shall never see it again. And then the boy and Emilie are doomed.'

Now I realised that he was not joking at all.

'Do you really intend to enter into an independent bargain with Doctor Lind?' I asked, just to make certain.

'Yes. What else can we do?'

Neither of us spoke as we stared at each other in mutual perplexity. My mood of exaltation vanished without a trace. A terrible presentiment turned my mouth dry.

Fandorin looked me over from head to foot, as if seeing me for the first time and asked in a curious tone of voice: 'Just a m-moment, Ziukin, don't you love little Mika?'

'Very much,' I said, surprised at such a question.

'And then . . . you are rather partial to Emilie, I believe?'

I was feeling very tired; we were both smeared with dust and clay; the air smelled of grass and the river; and all of this gave me the feeling that the ordinary conventions did not apply. That was the only reason why I answered this outrageously immodest question: 'I am not indifferent to Mademoiselle Declique's fate.'

'So, the stake in this game is the lives of t-two people. People whom you . . . well, let us say, to whose fate you are "not indifferent". And you are prepared to sacrifice those people for a piece of polished carbon?'

'There are things that are more important than love,' I said in a quiet voice and suddenly remembered that Fandorin had said the same thing to Xenia Georgievna quite recently.

I found this memory disturbing and felt it necessary to clarify my meaning: 'For example, honour. Fidelity. The prestige of the monarchy. National holy relics.'

I felt rather foolish explaining such things, but what else was there for me to do?

Fandorin paused before he spoke: 'You, Ziukin, have a choice. Do you see the police cordon around the chapel? Either you go across to it and tell them that Fandorin has absconded, t-taking the Orlov with him, or we try to save Emilie and the child together. Decide.'

So saying he took the black beard and shaggy wig out of his pocket – apparently he had kept them after all – and put on this hirsute disguise, transforming himself into a simple shaggy peasant of the kind who move into the large cities in search of work.

I do not know why I stayed with him. Upon my word of honour, I do not know. I did not say a word, but I did not move from the spot.

'Well, are we off to hard labour in the same fetters?' Fandorin asked with quite inappropriate merriment, holding out his hand.

His handshake was firm, mine was feeble.

'Sit here for a while and don't make yourself obvious. I'll go and reconnoitre.'

He strode off in the direction of the convent and I knelt down beside the water. It was pure and transparent. I first drank my fill and then, when the ripples had dispersed, I contemplated the reflection of my face. Nothing in it seemed to have changed: a moustache, sideburns, a prominent forehead with a receding hairline. And yet it was not the face of Housemaster Ziukin, butler of the Green House and faithful servant of the throne, but that of a state criminal.

Erast Petrovich's return roused me from my melancholy torpor but did nothing to improve my mood.

Apparently the police and soldiers had cordoned off not only the chapel but the entire convent. The search had already been going on for many hours in the underground labyrinth. The police constable with whom Fandorin spoke told him that all the police stations had been sent verbal portraits of two highly dangerous criminals who had committed some unknown crime that must be truly heinous. All routes out of Moscow were completely sealed off and it was only a matter of time before the two villains were caught. One of them was a lean youthful-looking man with dark hair and a slim moustache, special features, grey hair at the temples and a characteristic stammer. The other – and here Fandorin described my own modest person but in far greater detail. And so I learned that my nose was of the divided cartilage type, my wart was not merely on my neck but in its third left segment, and my eyes were of a marshy yellow hue with an almond-shaped outline.

'How did you manage to get the constable to talk?' I asked in amazement. 'And did he not find your stammer suspicious?'

'Getting a stranger to talk requires knowledge of psychology and physiognomical analysis,' Erast Petrovich explained with a haughty air. 'And as for the stammer, as you may have observed, when I assume a different identity, I change my voice and my way of speaking and all the other characteristics of speech. It is no longer me, or at least not entirely me. The stammer is the result of a concussion suffered very long ago by Fandorin, not by the grave little peasant who spoke so respectfully to the police constable.'

I gestured impatiently.

'All your psychology is worth nothing in the present circumstances. We cannot save anyone. We need someone to save us. The police have our descriptions. We ought to give ourselves up. If we explain what happened, they will forgive us.'

Fandorin shrugged with outrageous flippancy. 'Never mind those descriptions. We shall change our appearance. Dye your hair blond, dress you up as a civil servant, shave off your moustache and sideburns—'

'Not for anything in the world!' I exclaimed. 'I have had them for more than twenty years!'

'As you wish, but with your *favoris de chien*, as Lind puts it, you really are easy to identify. You are condemning yourself to remain inside, confined within four walls, while I shall move around the city quite freely.'

This threat did not frighten me in the least, and in any case I was already thinking about something else.

'I can imagine how puzzled Their Highnesses are by my strange disappearance,' I murmured dejectedly.

'They are more likely indignant,' Fandorin corrected me. 'Viewed from the outside, the situation seems quite unambiguous. Naturally, everyone has decided that you and I conspired with Lind and have been working with him from the very beginning. Or else that we decided to take the opportunity to steal the Orlov. That is why the police are so very interested in us.'

I groaned. Why, of course, that was exactly how our behaviour appeared!

Fandorin also hung his head. Evidently he had finally realised the position in which we now found ourselves as a result of his inclination to irresponsible adventures. But no, it turned out to be something quite different that was saddening him.

'Ah, Ziukin, what a magnificent operation, and it failed! Taking the place of the coachman was so simple, almost a stroke of genius. From what Emilie told me, I guessed that the driver was a deaf mute. That, plus the hat pulled so low over his eyes and the thick black beard, made the task easier. The police have the coachman now, but he will be no use to them. Not only is he mute, he is like a wild beast. That is why Lind was not afraid of exposing him to the danger of arrest. Everything should have gone so smoothly! We would have saved the boy and captured Lind.' He gestured in annoyance and frustration. 'Well, if we hadn't taken him alive, we would have dropped him on the spot. It would be no loss to the human race. I ought to have gone down as well. Who could have imagined that the jeweller would not be afraid of a dagger? That was why everything went wrong. How devoted they are to Lind. What is his hold on them? No, it is simply quite incredible!' Erast Petrovich jumped to his feet in agitation. 'That damned Belgian was thinking about Lind, not himself. That is no mere bandit's honour, it is absolutely genuine selfless love!'

'How do you know that the jeweller was Belgian?'

'What?' he asked absent-mindedly. 'Ah, from his accent. Belgian, from Antwerp. Absolutely no doubt about it. But that is not important. Something else, however, is. What d-do you make of what Emilie said? You remember, she shouted: "And Lind's here. He's—" What was to come next? I have the feeling that she was about to mention a name that we know or else some distinctive or unusual characteristic. If it was a name, then whose? If it was a characteristic, then what? "He is a hunchback"? "He is Chinese"? "He is a woman"?' Fandorin narrowed his eyes. 'As for being Chinese or a woman, I don't know – anything is possible – but Lind is no hunchback. I know that for certain – I would have noticed . . . Never mind, we shall find out soon enough.'

These last words were spoken with such calm conviction that I felt a stirring of hope.

'And so, Ziukin, let us d-discuss and assess the plusses and minuses of our situation.' Erast Petrovich sat down on the sand beside me, picked up several small stones and drew a line across the sand. 'The boy is still in Lind's hands. That is bad.' One stone, a black one, was set down on the left of the line. 'Emilie has become a hostage too. That is also bad.' A second black stone was added to the first.

'And what is good?' I burst out. 'Add to this that all the police and secret police in the empire are hunting for you and me and not Doctor Lind. That His Highness is seriously ill as a result of the ordeals he has suffered, perhaps even at death's door. That Lind, as you said yourself, does not leave witnesses alive!'

Fandorin nodded in agreement and put down three more stones on the same side.

'And now let us look at things from the other side. It is good that you and I have the Orlov and are willing, as a last resort, to make an exchange. That is one. It is good that Lind has lost m-most of his gang. Almost all of them, in fact. Four on the day of the kidnapping, then all of Stump's gang, and another five yesterday. Emilie shouted, "There are three of them." So Lind has only two men left, and to start with he had almost twenty. That is two. Finally, yesterday I managed to tell Lind my name and specify the terms of a possible exchange. That is three.'

Looking at the five black stones and the three white ones, I did not feel my spirits suddenly rise.

'But what is the point? We do not even know where to look

for him now. And even if we did, our hands are tied. We can't even take a step in Moscow without being arrested.'

'You have advanced two theses, one of which is unsound and the other incorrect,' Erast Petrovich objected with a professorial air. 'Your last thesis, that our movements are restricted, is incorrect. As I have already had the honour of informing you, it is not at all difficult to change our appearance. Lind is the one whose movements are restricted. He has a burden on his hands – two prisoners, a sick child and a woman of extremely resolute character. The doctor will not dare to kill them because he has studied me enough to know that I will not allow myself to be deceived. That, by the way, is one more plus for us.' He put down a fourth white stone. 'And as for your first thesis, it is basically unsound, for a very simple reason: you and I are not going to look for Lind. The oats do not go to the horse. Lind will find us himself.'

Oh how exasperating I found that imperturbable manner, that didactic tone! But I tried to control myself.

'Permit me to enquire why on earth Lind will seek us out. And, most importantly, how?'

'Now instead of two theses you have asked two questions.' Fandorin chuckled with insufferable self-assurance. 'Let me answer the first one. We and the doctor are in a classic bargaining situation. There are goods and there is a buyer. The goods that I require and Lind has are as follows: firstly, little Mika; secondly, Emilie; thirdly, Doctor Lind's own skin. Now for my goods, the ones that my trading partner covets. Firstly, a two-hundred-carat diamond, without which the doctor's entire Moscow escapade will end as a shameful failure, and Lind is not used to that. And secondly, my life. I assure you that the doctor has as many counts to settle with me as I have with him. And so he and I will strike an excellent bargain.'

As he said this, Erast Petrovich looked as if he were not talking about a battle with the most dangerous criminal in the world but some amusing adventure or a game of whist. I have never liked people who show off, especially in serious matters, and Fandorin's bravado seemed out of place to me.

'Now for your second question,' he continued, taking no notice of the frown on my face. 'How will Lind seek us out? Well, that is very simple. This evening you and I will look through the advertisements and personal announcements in all the Moscow newspapers. We are certain to find something interesting. You don't believe me? I am prepared to wager on it, although I do not usually gamble.'

'A wager?' I asked spitefully, finally losing patience with his bragging. 'By all means. If you lose, we shall go and give ourselves up to the police today.'

He laughed light-heartedly. 'And if I win, you will shave off your celebrated sideburns and moustache. Shall we shake on it?'

The bargain was sealed with a handshake.

'We have to pay a visit to the Hermitage,' said Fandorin, growing more serious. 'To collect Masa. He will be very useful to us. And also to pick up a few essentials. M-money, for example. I did not bring my wallet with me on this operation. I foresaw that the meeting with Lind was certain to involve jumping, brandishing fists, running and all kinds of similar activities, and any superfluous weight, even the slightest, is a hindrance to that. There you have one more proof of the old truth that money is never a superfluous burden. How much do you have with you?'

I put my hand into my pocket and discovered that in one of my numerous tumbles during the night I had dropped my purse. If I was not mistaken, it had contained eight roubles and some small change. I took out a handful of tarnished silver coins and gazed at them ruefully.

'Is that all that you have?' Erast Petrovich asked, taking one of the irregular round objects and twirling it in his fingers. 'A Peter the Great *altyn*. We are not likely to be able to buy anything with that. Any antique shop would be glad to take your t-treasure, but it is too risky for us to appear in crowds with our present appearance. So, this is a strange situation: we have a diamond that is worth goodness knows how many millions but we can't even buy a piece of bread. That makes a visit to the Hermitage all the more necessary.'

'But how is that possible?' I asked, raising my head above the grass growing on the riverbank. There was a line of soldiers and police standing right round the pond and the open field. 'Everything here is cordoned off. And even if we broke out of the cordon, there is no way that we can walk right across the city in broad daylight!'

'It's easy to see that you know nothing of the geography of the old c-capital, Ziukin. What do you think that is?' Fandorin jerked his chin towards the river.

'What do you mean? The Moscow River.'

'And what do you see every day from the windows of the Hermitage? That wet, g-greenish thing flowing slowly towards the Kremlin? We shall have to commit yet another crime, although not as serious as the theft of the Orlov.'

He walked over to a flimsy little boat moored to the bank, looked it over and nodded.

'It will do. Of course there are no oars, but I think that p-plank over there will suit perfectly well. Get in, Ziukin. They won't think of looking for us on the river, and we don't have very far to sail. I feel sorry for the boat's owner. The loss will probably be more ruinous for him than the loss of the Orlov would be for the Romanovs. Right then, let's have your treasure trove.'

He delved into my pocket unceremoniously, clawed out the coins, put them beside the small stake to which the boat was moored and sprinkled a little sand over them.

'Well, why are you just standing there? Get in. And be careful or this battleship will capsize.'

I got in, soaking my shoes in the water that had accumulated in the bottom of the boat. Fandorin pushed off with the plank, and we drifted out very, very slowly. He worked away desperately with his clumsy oar, delving alternately on the left and the right, but despite these Sisyphean labours our bark barely moved at all.

Ten minutes later, when we had still not even reached the middle of the river, I enquired: 'But just how far do we have to sail to reach the Neskuchny Park?'

'I th-think about . . . three v-versts,' Fandorin replied with an effort, bright red from his exertions.

I could not resist a sarcastic comment: 'At this speed we should probably get there by tomorrow morning. The current is slow here.'

'We don't need the current,' Erast Petrovich mumbled.

He started brandishing his plank even more vigorously, and the bow of our boat struck a log. A steam tug was passing by, towing a string of logs after it. Fandorin tied the mooring rope to a trimmed branch, dropped the plank in the bottom of the boat and stretched blissfully.

'That's it, Ziukin. We can take half an hour's rest, and we'll be at our destination.'

Grassy fields and market gardens drifted by slowly on the left; then came the white walls of the Novodevichy Convent, the sight of which I was thoroughly sick by now. On the right there was a tall wooded bank. I saw a white church with a round dome, elegant arbours, a grotto.

'You see before you Vorobyovsky Park, laid out in the English manner in imitation of a n-natural forest,' Fandorin told me in the voice of a true guide. 'Note the hanging bridge across that ravine. I saw a bridge exactly like it in the Himalayas, only it was woven out of shafts of bamboo. Of course, the drop below it was not twenty *sazhens*, it was a gulf of two versts. But then, for anyone who falls, the difference is immaterial . . . And what have we here?'

He leaned down and took a simple fishing rod out from under the bench. He examined it with interest, then turned his head this way and that and picked a green caterpillar off the side of the boat with an exclamation of joy.

'Right, now, Ziukin, here's to luck!'

He tossed the line into the water and almost immediately

pulled out a silver carp the size of an open hand.

'How about that, eh?' Erast Petrovich exclaimed, thrusting his trembling prey under my nose. 'Did you see that? It took l-less than a minute! A very good sign! That's the way we'll hook Lind!'

A perfect little boy! A boastful irresponsible boy. He put the wet fish in his pocket and it began moving as if his coat were alive.

A familiar bridge appeared ahead of us, the same one that could be seen from the windows of the Hermitage. Soon I spotted the green roof of the palace itself beyond the crowns of the trees.

Fandorin cast off from the log. When the rafts had drifted past us, we set a course for the right bank, and a quarter of an hour later we were at the railings of the Neskuchny Park.

This time I surmounted the obstacle without the slightest difficulty, thanks to the experience I had accumulated. We made our way into the thickets, but Fandorin was wary of approaching the Hermitage.

'They certainly won't be looking for us here,' he declared, stretching out on the grass. 'But it would still be best t-to wait until dark. Are you hungry?'

'Yes, very. Do you have some provisions with you?' I asked hopefully because, I must confess, my stomach had been aching from hunger for a long time.

'Yes, this.' He took his catch out of his pocket. 'Have you never tried raw fish? In Japan everybody eats it.'

Naturally I declined such an incredible meal, and watched with some revulsion as Erast Petrovich gulped down the cold slippery carp, daintily extracting the fine bones and sucking them clean.

After completing this barbarous meal, he wiped his fingers on a handkerchief, took out a box of matches and then extracted a cigar from an inside pocket. He shook the matchbox and announced delightedly: 'They have dried out. You don't smoke, do you?'

He stretched contentedly and put one hand under his head.

'What a picnic we are having, eh? Wonderful. Real heaven.'

'Heaven?' I half-sat up at that, I felt so indignant. 'The world is falling apart before our very eyes, and you call it "heaven"? The very foundations of the monarchy are trembling; an innocent child has been tormented by fiends; the most worthy of women is being subjected, perhaps, at this very moment to . . .' I did not finish the sentence because not all things can be said aloud. 'Chaos, that is what it is. There is nothing in the world more terrible than chaos, because from chaos comes insanity, the destruction of standards and rules . . .'

I was overcome by a fit of coughing before I had fully expressed my thoughts, but Fandorin understood me and stopped smiling.

'Do you know where your mistake lies, Afanasii Stepanovich?' he said in a tired voice, closing his eyes. 'You believe that the world exists according to certain rules, that it possesses m-meaning and order. But I realised a long time ago that life is nothing but chaos. It possesses no order whatever, and no rules either.'

'And yet you yourself give the impression of a man with firm rules,' I said, unable to resist the jibe as I looked at his neat parting, which had remained immaculate despite all our alarming adventures.

'Yes, I do have rules. But they are my own rules, invented by myself for myself and not for the whole world. Let the world suit itself, and I shall suit myself. Insofar as that is possible. One's own rules, Afanasii Stepanovich, are not the expression of a desire to arrange the whole of creation but an attempt to organise, to at least some degree, the space that lies in immediate proximity to oneself. And I do not manage even a trifle like that very well . . . All right, Ziukin. I think I'll have a sleep.'

He turned over on to one side, cradled his head on one elbow and fell asleep immediately. What an incredible man!

I cannot say what I found more painful: my hunger, my anger or the awareness of my own helplessness. And yet I do know – it was the fear. Fear for the life of Mikhail Georgievich, for Emilie, for myself.

Yes, yes, for myself. And it was the very worst of all the varieties of fear known to me. I was desperately afraid, not of pain or even of death, but of disgrace. All my life the thing of which I had been most afraid was to find myself in a position of disgrace and thereby sacrifice the sense of my own dignity. What would I have left if I were deprived of my dignity? Who would I be then? A lonely ageing man of no account with a lumpy forehead, a bulbous nose and 'doggy sideburns' who had wasted his life on something meaningless.

I had discovered the recipe for maintaining dignity a long time before, in my youth. The magical formula proved to be simple and brief: make every possible effort to avoid surprises. This meant that I had to foresee and make provision for everything in advance. To be forearmed, to perform my duties conscientiously and not to go chasing after chimerical illusions. That was how I had lived. And what was the outcome? Afanasii Ziukin was a thief and a deceiver, a scoundrel and a state criminal. At least, that was what the people whose opinion I valued thought of me.

The sun passed its highest point in the sky and began gradually declining towards the west. I grew weary of wandering around the small glade and sat down. An intangible breeze rustled the fresh foliage; a bumblebee buzzed with a bass note among the dandelions; lacy clouds slid slowly across the azure sky.

I won't get to sleep anyway, I thought, leaning back against the trunk of an elm.

'Wake up, Ziukin. It's time to go.'

I opened my eyes. The clouds were moving as unhurriedly as before, but now they were pink instead of white, while the sky had darkened. The sun had already set, which meant that I had slept until about nine o'clock at least.

'Stop batting your eyes like that,' Fandorin said cheerfully. 'We're going to storm the Hermitage.'

Erast Petrovich took off his long-skirted driver's coat, and was left wearing a sateen waistcoat and a light-blue shirt – he was almost invisible against the thickening twilight.

We walked quickly through the empty park to the palace. When I saw the brightly lit windows of the Hermitage, I was overcome by an unutterable melancholy. The house was like a white ocean-going yacht sailing calmly and confidently through the gloom, but I, who so recently had stood on its trim deck, had fallen overboard and was floundering among the dark waves, and I did not even dare to cry for help.

Fandorin interrupted my mournful thoughts: 'Whose window is that – the third from the left on the ground floor? You're not looking in the right place. The one that is open but with no light in it?'

'That is Mr Freyby's room.'

'Will you be able to climb in? All right, forward!'

We ran across the lawn, pressed ourselves against the wall and crept up to the dark open window. Erast Petrovich formed his hands into a stirrup and hoisted me up so adroitly that I was easily able to climb over the window sill. Fandorin followed me.

'Stay here for a while. I'll be b-back soon,' he said

'But what if Mr Freyby comes in?' I asked in panic. 'How shall I explain my presence to him?'

Fandorin looked around and picked up a bottle with brown liquid splashing about in it off the table. I thought it must be the notorious whisky with which the English butler had once regaled me.

'Here, take this. Hit him on the head, tie him up and put a gag in his mouth – that napkin over there. There's nothing to be done about it, Ziukin, this is an emergency. You can apologise to him later. The last thing we need now is for the Englishman to shout and raise the alarm. And stop shaking like that; I'll be back soon.'

And indeed he did return in no more than five minutes. He was holding a travelling bag in one hand.

'I have all the most essential items here. They have searched my room but not touched anything. But Masa is not there. I'll go to look for him.'

I was left alone again, but not for long – the door soon opened again.

This time, however, it was not Erast Petrovich but Mr Freyby. He reached out his hand, turned a small lever on the oil lamp, and the room was suddenly bright. I blinked in confusion.

Grasping the bottle firmly, I took an uncertain step forward. The poor butler, he was not to blame for anything.

'Good evening,' Freyby said politely in Russian, glancing curiously at the bottle, then he added something in English: 'I didn't realise that you liked my whisky *that* much.' He took the dictionary out of his pocket and with impressive dexterity – he had clearly developed the knack – rustled the pages and said: '*Ya . . . ne byl . . . soznavat . . . chto vi . . . lyubit . . . moi viski . . . tak . . . mnogo.*'

This threw me into a state of total embarrassment. To hit someone over the head when he has started a conversation with you, that was absolutely unthinkable.

The Englishman looked at my confused expression, chuckled good-naturedly, slapped me on the shoulder and pointed at the bottle: 'A present. *Podarok.*'

The butler noticed that I was holding the travelling bag in my other hand.

'Going travelling? Coo-choo-choo?' he asked, imitating the sound of a steam locomotive, and I realised that Freyby thought I was setting out on a journey and had decided to take the bottle of drink with me because I had taken such a liking to it.

'Yes, yes,' I muttered in Russian. 'Voyage. Tenk yoo.'

Then I slipped out through the door into the corridor as quickly as I could. God only knew what Freyby thought about Russian butlers now. But this was no moment to be concerned about national prestige.

In the next room, Mr Carr's, a bell jingled to summon a servant.

I barely had time to conceal myself behind a drape before the junior footman Lipps came trotting along the corridor. Oh, well done, Lipps. That meant there was firm order in the house. I was not on the spot, but everything was still working like clockwork.

'What can I do for you, sir?' Lipps asked as he opened the door.

Mr Carr said something in Russian in a lazy voice. I made out 'ink', spoken with a quite incredible accent, and the footman left at the same praiseworthy trot. I backed into the adjoining corridor that led to my room; I had decided to hide in there for the rest of my wait. I took a few short steps, clutching the travelling bag and the bottle tight against my chest, and then my back suddenly encountered something soft. I looked round. Oh Lord, Somov.

'Hello, Afanasii Stepanovich,' my assistant babbled. 'Good evening. I have been moved into your room ...'

I gulped and said nothing.

'They said that you had run off ... that you and Mr Fandorin would soon be found and arrested. They have already taken the gentleman's Japanese servant. They say you are criminals,' he concluded in a whisper.

'I know,' I said quickly. 'But it is not true, Kornei Selifanovich. You have not had much time to get to know me, but I swear to you that what I am doing is for the sake of Mikhail Georgievich.'

Somov looked at me without saying anything, and from the expression on his face I could not tell what he was thinking. Would he shout or not? That was the only thing that concerned me at that moment. Just in case, I took a firm grip on the neck of the bottle with my fingers.

'Yes, I really have had very little time to get to know you well, but you can tell a great butler straight away,' Somov said in a quiet voice. 'Permit me to take the liberty of saying that I admire you, Afanasii Stepanovich, and have always dreamed of being like you. And . . . and if you require my help, simply let me know. I will do anything.'

I felt a sudden tightness in my throat and was afraid that if I tried to speak, I might burst into tears.

'Thank you,' I said eventually. 'Thank you for deciding not to give me away.'

'How can I give you away when I have not even seen you?' he asked with a shrug, then turned and walked away.

As a result of this entirely remarkable conversation, I lowered my guard a little and turned the corner without bothering to look first and see if there was anyone in the corridor. But there was Her Highness's maid, Liza Petrishcheva, turning this way and that in front of the mirror.

'Ah!' squealed Liza, the foolish empty-headed girl who had been caught in the embraces of Fandorin's valet.

'Sh-sh-sh!' I said to her. 'Quiet, Petrishcheva. Do not shout.'

She nodded in fright, then suddenly swung round and darted away, howling: 'Help! Murder! He's he-e-e-ere!'

I dashed in the opposite direction, towards the exit, but heard the sound of excited men's voices coming from there. Which way could I go?

Up to the first floor, there was nowhere else.

I dashed up the stairs in the twinkling of an eye and saw a white figure in the dimly lit passage. Xenia Georgievna!

I froze on the spot.

'Where is he?' Her Highness asked hastily. 'Where is Erast Petrovich?'

I heard the tramping of many feet downstairs.

'Ziukin's here! Find him!' I heard an authoritative bass voice say.

The grand princess grabbed hold of my arm. 'To my room!'

We slammed the door and thirty seconds later several people ran by along the corridor.

'Search the rooms!' the same bass voice commanded.

Suddenly there were shouts from downstairs and someone howled: 'Stop! Stop, you filthy swine!'

There was a shot and then another.

Xenia Georgievna squealed and swayed on her feet, and I was obliged to grab hold of her arms. Her face was as white as chalk, and her dilated pupils had turned her eyes completely black.

There was the sound of breaking glass on the ground floor.

Her Highness pushed me away sharply and dashed to the window sill. I followed her. Down below we saw a dark figure that had obviously just jumped from a window.

It was Fandorin – I recognised the waistcoat.

The next second another two figures in civilian clothes leapt out of the same window and grabbed Erast Petrovich by the arms. Xenia Georgievna gave a piercing screech.

However, Fandorin demonstrated a quite remarkable flexibility. Without freeing his hands, he twisted round like a spring and struck one of his opponents in the groin with his knee, and then dealt with the other in exactly the same manner. Both police agents doubled over, and Erast Petrovich flitted across the lawn like a shadow and disappeared into the bushes.

'Thank God!' Her Highness whispered. 'He is safe!'

People began running around outside the house, some in uniforms, some in civilian clothes. Some went dashing down the drive towards the gates, others rushed off in pursuit of the fugitive. But there were not very many pursuers, perhaps about ten. How could they catch the fleet-footed Mr Fandorin in the wide spaces of the dark park?

I had no need to feel concerned for Erast Petrovich, but what was going to happen to me?

There was a loud knock at the door.

'Your Imperial Highness! There is a criminal in the house! Are you all right?'

Xenia Georgievna gestured for me to hide in the wardrobe. She opened the door of the room and said in a discontented voice: 'I have a terrible migraine, and you are shouting and clattering. Catch your criminal but do not bother me again!'

'Your Highness, at least lock yourself in.'

'Very well.'

I heard the sound of a key turning in a lock and came out into the centre of the room.

'I know,' Xenia Georgievna said in a feverish whisper, clasping my shoulders in a tremulous embrace. 'It is all lies. He could not have committed a robbery. And you, Afanasii Stepanovich, are not capable of such a thing either. I have guessed everything. You want to rescue Mika. I do not ask you to tell me exactly what you plan to do. Just tell me, am I right?'

And she really did not ask me any more questions. She went down on her knees in front of an icon and started bowing low to the floor. I had never seen Her Highness display such piety before, not even when she was a child. She seemed to be whispering something as well, probably a prayer, but I could not make out the words.

Xenia Georgievna prayed for an unbearably long time. I believe it must have been at least half an hour. And I stood there, waiting. All I did was put the bottle of whisky into the travelling bag. Quite clearly, I could not leave it in the grand princess's room, could I?

Her Highness did not rise from her knees until everything was quiet in the house and the pursuers had returned, talking loudly among themselves. She walked over to the secretaire, touched something inside it that made a jingling sound and then called me over to her. 'Take this, Afanasii. You will need money. I do not have any, you know that. But here is a pair of opal earrings and a diamond brooch. They are my own, not the family's. These things can be sold. They are probably worth a lot.'

I tried to protest, but she would not listen to me. To avoid being drawn into a long argument, for which this was quite the wrong time, I took the jewels, promising myself firmly that I would return them to Her Highness safe and sound.

Then Xenia Georgievna took a long silk sash from a Chinese dressing gown out of the wardrobe.

'Tie this to the window catch and climb down. It will not reach all the way to the ground – you will have to jump – but you are brave; you will not be afraid. May the Lord preserve you.'

She made the sign of the cross over me and then suddenly kissed me on the cheek. I was quite overcome. And it must have been my state of disorientation that made me ask: 'Is there anything you would like me to tell Mr Fandorin?'

'That I love him,' Her Highness replied briefly and pushed me towards the window.

I reached the ground without injuring myself in any way, and also negotiated the park without any adventures. I halted at the railings beyond which lay Bolshaya Kaluga Street, almost empty at this hour of the evening. After waiting until there were no passers-by anywhere in sight, I clambered over to the other side very nimbly. I had definitely made great progress in the art of climbing fences.

However, what I ought to do now was not clear. I still had no money so I could not even hire a cab. And where would I actually go?

I halted indecisively.

There was a newspaper boy wandering along the street. Still a little child, about nine years old. He was shouting with all his might, although there didn't seem to be anyone there to buy his goods.

'The latest *Half-Kopeck News*. Get your *Half-Kopeck News*. The newspaper for private ads! An admirer for some, a bride for others! An apartment for some, a good job for others!'

I started, recalling my wager with Fandorin. I rummaged in my pockets, hoping to find a copper half-kopeck or one-kopeck piece. There was something round and flat behind the lining. An old silver coin, a Peter the Great *altyn*.

Well, never mind. He probably would not notice in the dark.

I called the newspaper seller, tugged a folded paper out of his bag and tossed the silver coin into his mug – it jangled every bit as well as copper. The boy plodded on his way as if nothing at all had happened, bawling out his crude doggerel.

I walked over to a street lamp and unfolded the grey paper.

And I saw it – right there in the centre of the front page, with letters a full *vershok* in height:

My eagle! My diamond‚precious love! I forgive you.
I love you. I am waiting for your message.
Your Linda
Write to the Central Post Office,
to the bearer of treasury note No. 137078859.

That was it! No doubt at all about it! And how cunningly it had been composed. No one who did not know about the diamond and the exchange would have the slightest idea!

But would Fandorin see this paper? How could I inform him? Where should I seek him now? What terrible luck!

'Well then?' a familiar voice asked out of the darkness. 'That's genuine love for you. This passionate declaration has been published in all the evening papers.'

I swung round, astonished at such a fortunate encounter.

'Why do you look so surprised, Ziukin? After all, it was clear that if you managed to escape from the house, you would climb over the railings. I just d-did not know exactly where. I had to engage four newspaper boys to walk up and down the railings and shout about private advertisements at the tops of their voices. That's it, Ziukin. You have lost the wager. So much for your remarkable drooping moustache and sideburns.'

17 May

Staring out at me from the mirror was a puffy thick-lipped face with the beginnings of a double chin and unnaturally white cheeks. Deprived of its sumptuous drooping moustache and combed sideburns, my face seemed to have emerged out of some cloud or bank of fog to appear before me naked, exposed and defenceless. I was quite shaken by the sight of it – it was like seeing myself for the first time. I had read in some novel that as a man passes through life he gradually creates his own self-portrait, applying a pattern of wrinkles, folds, hollows and protuberances to the smooth canvas of the persona that he inherited at birth. Everyone knows that wrinkles can be intelligent or stupid, genial or spiteful, cheerful or sad. And the effect of this drawing, traced by the hand of life itself, is to make some people more beautiful with the passing years, and some more ugly.

When the initial shock had passed and I looked at the self-portrait a little more closely, I realised that I could not say with any certainty whether I was pleased with the work. I supposed I was pleased with the pleated line of the lips – it testified to experience of life and a quite definite firmness of character. However, the broad lower jaw hinted at moroseness, and the flabby cheeks provoked thoughts of a predisposition to failure. The most astounding thing of all was that the removal of the covering of hair had altered my appearance far more than the ginger beard I had recently worn. I had suddenly ceased to be a grand-ducal butler and become a lump of clay, which could now be moulded into a man of any background or rank.

However, Fandorin, having studied my new face with the air of a connoisseur of painting, seemed to be of a different opinion. Setting aside the razor, he muttered as if to himself: 'You are hard to disguise. The gravity is still there, the prim fold on the forehead has not disappeared either, or the alignment of the head ... Hmm, Ziukin, you are not at all like me, not in the least, except that we are about the same height ... But never mind. Lind knows that I am a master of self-transformation. Such obvious dissimilarity might actually make his men quite certain that you are me. Who shall be we dress you up as? I think we should make you a civil servant, sixth or seventh class. You don't look at all right for any rank lower than that. You stay here; I'll g-go to the military and civil uniform shop on Sretenka Street. I'll look out something for myself at the same time. Here in Russia the easiest way to hide a man is behind a uniform.'

The previous evening Erast Petrovich had found an announcement of an apartment for rent in the same *Half-Kopeck News* where Doctor Lind had placed his notice:

For rent, for the coronation, a seven-room apartment
with furniture, tableware and telephone.
Close to the Clear Ponds. 5000 roubles.
Use of servants possible for additional charge.
Arkhangelsky Lane, the house of state counsellor's
widow Sukhorukova. Enquire at porter's lodge.

The number of rooms appeared excessive to me, and the price – bearing in mind the coronation celebrations were almost over – was quite staggering, but Fandorin would not listen to me. 'On the other hand, it is close to the post office,' he said. And before the evening was out we were installed in a fine gentleman's apartment located on the ground floor of a new stone house.

The porter was so pleased to receive payment in advance that he did not even ask to see our passports.

After taking tea in a sumptuously but rather tastelessly furnished dining room, we discussed our plan of further action. Actually, our discussion was more like a monologue by Fandorin, and for the most part I listened. I suspected that for Erast Petrovich a so-called discussion was simply a matter of him thinking aloud, and any requests for my opinion or advice ought be regarded as no more than figures of speech.

It is true, though, that I began the conversation. Lind's initiative and the acquisition of a roof over our heads had had a most heartening effect on me, and my former despondency had vanished without trace.

'The business does not seem so very complicated to me,' I declared. 'We will send a letter with a statement of the terms of exchange, and occupy an observation post close to the window where they hand out the poste restante correspondence. When the bearer of the treasury note turns up, we shall follow him inconspicuously, and he will lead us to Lind's new hideout. You said yourself that the doctor has only two helpers left, so we shall manage things ourselves, without the police.'

The plan seemed very extremely practical to me, but Fandorin looked at me as if I were blathering some kind of wild nonsense.

'You underestimate Lind. The trick with the bearer of the note has a completely different meaning. The doctor of course expects me to trail his messenger. Lind must already know that I am playing my own game and the authorities are no longer helping me but on the contrary trying to hunt me down. Anything that is known to the entire municipal police is no longer a secret. So Lind thinks that I am acting alone. If I wait at the post office trying to spot the doctor's courier, someone else will spot me. The hunter caught in his own trap.'

'What are we to do?' I asked, perplexed.

'Fall into the trap. There is no other way. I have a trump card that Lind does not even suspect exists. And that trump card is you.'

I squared my shoulders because, I must admit, it was pleasing to hear something like that from the smug Fandorin.

'Lind does not know that I have a helper. I shall disguise you very cunningly, not so that you will look like Fandorin, but so that you will look like a *disguised* Fandorin. You and I are almost the same height, and that is the most important thing. You are substantially more corpulent, but that can be concealed by means of loose-fitting garments. Anyone who spends too long hanging around that little window will arouse Lind's suspicions of it being me in disguise.'

'But at the same time it will not be hard to recognise Lind's man, for surely he will "hang around", as you put it, somewhere close by.'

'Not necessarily, by any means. Lind's men might work in rotation. We know that the doctor has at least two helpers left. They are almost as interesting to me as Lind himself. Who are they? What do they look like? What do we know about them?'

I shrugged.

'Nothing.'

'Unfortunately, that is actually the case. When I jumped down into the underground vault at the tomb, I had no time to see anything. As you no doubt recall, that bulky gentleman whose carotid artery I was obliged to crush threw himself on me straightaway. While I was busy with him, Lind was able to withdraw and maintain his complete anonymity. What was it that Emilie tried to tell us about him? "He's ..." He's what?'

Fandorin frowned discontentedly.

'There is no point in trying to guess. There is only one thing that we can say about his helpers. One of them is Russian, or at least has lived in Russia for many years and speaks the language absolutely fluently.'

'What makes you think that?'

'The text of the notice, Ziukin. Do you think that a foreigner would have written about a "diamond-precious love"?'

He stood up and started walking round the room. He took a set of jade beads out of his pocket and started clicking the small green spheres. I did not know where these beads had come from – probably out of the travelling bag. That was undoubtedly the source of the white shirt with the fold-down collar and the light-cream jacket. And the bottle of whisky, Mr Freyby's present, had migrated from the travelling bag to the sideboard.

'Tomorrow, or rather, t-today, Lind and I shall fight our decisive battle. He and I both understand this. A tie is not possible. Such is the peculiar nature of our barter: both parties are determined to take everything, and without trading anything for it. What would a tie signify in our case? You and I save the hostages but lose the Orlov.' Fandorin nodded towards the travelling bag, where he had concealed the stone the previous day. 'Lind remains alive, and so do I. And that does not suit either him or me. No, Ziukin, there will be no tie.'

'But what if Mademoiselle and Mikhail Georgievich are already dead?' I asked, giving voice to my greatest fear.

'No, they are alive,' Fandorin declared confidently. 'Lind knows quite well that I am no fool. I will not hand over the stone until I am convinced that the hostages are alive.' He clicked his beads once again and put them away in his pocket. 'So this is what we shall do. You, in the role of the false Fandorin, keep an eye on the window. Lind's men keep an eye on you. The real Fandorin keeps an eye on them. All very simple really, is it not?'

His self-assurance inspired me with hope, but infuriated me at the same time. That was the very moment at which the agonising doubt that had been tormenting me since the previous evening was finally resolved. I would not tell him what Xenia Georgievna had said. Mr Fandorin already had too high an opinion of himself without that.

He sat down at the table and, after a moment's thought, jotted down a few lines in French. I looked over his shoulder.

For me, unlike you, people are more important than precious
stones. You will get your diamond. At four a.m. bring the boy
and the woman to the open ground where the Petersburg Chaussée
turns towards the Petrovsky Palace. We shall conduct the
exchange there. I shall be alone. It does not matter to me how
many people you have with you.

                                                        Fandorin

'Why precisely there, and why at such a strange time?' I asked.

'Lind will like it: the dead hour before dawn, a deserted spot.
In essence it makes no difference whatsoever, but things will be
decided all the sooner . . . Go to bed, Ziukin. Tomorrow will be
an interesting day for us. And I shall go and post the letter in the
box at the Central Post Office. Correspondence that arrives in
the morning is handed out beginning from three in the afternoon. That is when you will take up your position. But first we
shall transform you beyond all recognition.'

I cringed at those words. And, as it turned out, I was right to
do so.

The Moscow Central Post Office seemed a poor place to me, no
comparison at all with the post office in St Petersburg. It was
dark and cramped with no facilities whatever for the customers.
In my view a city of a million people ought to acquire a somewhat
more presentable central post office. For my purposes, however,
the squalidness of this state institution actually proved most
opportune. The congestion and poor lighting made my aimless
wandering around the hall less obvious. Fandorin had dressed
me up as a collegiate counsellor of the Ministry of Agriculture
and State Lands, and so I looked very impressive. Why would
such a staid gentleman with clean-shaven chops spend so
many hours at a stretch sauntering around between the battered
counters? Several times I halted as if by chance in front of a
chipped mirror in order to observe the people coming in less

conspicuously. And, why not admit it? I also wanted to get a better look at myself.

I fancied that the appearance of an individual of the sixth rank suited me very well indeed. It was as if I had been born with those velvet buttonholes decorated with gold braid and the Order of St Vladimir hanging round my neck. (The order had come out of that same travelling bag.) Nobody stared at me in amazement or disbelief – I was a perfectly regular official. Except perhaps for the attendant in the poste restante window, who from time to time cast attentive glances in my direction. And quite naturally too – I had been marching past him since three o'clock in the afternoon. And business hours at the post office during the coronation celebrations had been extended right up to nine, owing to the large volume of mailings, so I was stepping out for quite a long time.

But never mind the attendant at the window. The worst thing of all was that time was going to waste. None of the people who approached the little window presented treasury bills. No one loitered nearby for a suspiciously long time. I did not even notice something that Fandorin had warned me about: someone who left the hall and returned repeatedly.

As the end of the day approached, despair began to take a grip of me. Could Lind really have worked out our plan? Had everything gone wrong?

But at five minutes to nine, when the post office was already preparing to close, a portly sailor with a grey moustache wearing a dark-blue pea jacket and a cap with no cockade came striding in briskly through the doors. He was clearly a retired boatswain or pilot. Without bothering to look round, he walked straight across to the little window with the poste restante sign and rumbled in a voice rendered hoarse by drink: 'There's supposed to be a little letter here for me. For the bearer of a banknote with the number . . .' He rummaged in his pocket for a while and took out a note, held it out as far as possible from his long-sighted eyes and read: 'One three seven zero seven eight eight five nine. Got anything?'

I moved closer without making a sound, vainly struggling to control the trembling in my knees.

The post office attendant gaped at the sailor. 'There hasn't been any such letter,' he said eventually after a lengthy pause. 'Nothing of the kind has come in today.'

It hasn't come in? I groaned inwardly. There where on earth had it got to? It looked as if I had just spent the best part of six hours hanging about here in vain!

The boatswain started grumbling too: 'Oh that's good, getting an old man running round the place, and all for nothing. Aaagh!'

He wiggled his thick eyebrows angrily, rubbed his sleeve over his luxurious moustache and walked towards the door.

Only one thing was clear – I had to follow him. There was no reason to stay in the post office any longer, and the working day was already over.

I slipped out into the street and followed the old man, maintaining a substantial distance. However, the sailor never looked round even once. He kept his hands in his pockets and walked as if he were in no hurry, waddling along but at the same time moving remarkably fast. I was barely able to keep up with him.

Absorbed in the chase, I did not remember at first that the plan had allocated a quite different role to me – that of decoy. I had to check to see if there was anyone following me. Obeying the instructions I had been given, I took out of my waistcoat pocket a fob watch in which Fandorin had installed a little round mirror, and pretended to be studying the dial.

There he was! Walking twenty paces behind me, a suspicious-looking character: tall, stooped, wearing a wide-peaked cap, with his coat collar raised. He clearly had his eyes fixed on me. Just to make sure, I turned the watch slightly to examine the far side of the street and discovered another man who looked equally suspicious – the same kind of burly thug, demonstrating the same kind of unambiguous interest in my person. Had they taken the bait?

Two of them at once! And perhaps Doctor Lind himself was not far away?

Could Fandorin see all this? I had played the role of the bait faithfully; now it was up to him.

The boatswain turned into a side street. I followed him. The other two followed me. There was no doubt at all left: those two charmers were the doctor's helpers!

Suddenly the sailor turned into a narrow entrance. I slowed down, struck by an understandable concern. If those two followed me, and Fandorin had fallen behind or gone off somewhere else altogether, it was very probable that I would not get out of this dark crevice alive. And now the old man did not seem as simple as he had at the beginning. Ought I really to walk straight into a trap?

Unable to stop myself, I looked round quite openly. Apart from the two bandits the side street was completely deserted. One pretended to read the sign of a grocery shop; the other turned away with a bored air. And there was no sign of Erast Petrovich!

There was nothing else for it – I walked through the narrow entranceway then into a courtyard, then another archway, and another, and another. It was already dusk out in the street, and in here it was dark in any case, but I could still have made out the boatswain's silhouette. The only problem was that the old man had disappeared, simply vanished into thin air! He could not possibly have got through this sequence of passages so quickly, not unless he had broken into a run, but in that case I would have heard the echoes of his steps. Or had he turned off at the first courtyard?

I froze.

Then suddenly, from out of the darkness on one side, I heard Fandorin's voice: 'Don't just hang about like that, Ziukin. Walk without hurrying and stay in the light, so that they can see you.'

No longer understanding anything that was going on, I obediently walked on. Where had Fandorin come from? And where had the boatswain got to? Had Erast Petrovich really had enough time to stun him and hide him away?

I heard steps clattering behind me, echoing under the low vaulted ceiling. They started clattering faster and moving closer. Apparently my pursuers had decided to overtake me. Then I heard a dry click that made the hairs on the back of my neck stand on end. I had heard more than my share of clicks like that, when I was loading revolvers and cocking firing hammers for Pavel Georgievich – His Highness loves to fire his guns at the shooting range.

I turned round, expecting a roar and a flash, but there was no shot after all.

I saw two silhouettes, and then a third, against the background of a bright rectangle. The third one detached itself from the wall and threw out one foot with indescribable speed, and one of my pursuers doubled over. The other pursuer swung round smartly, and I quite clearly glimpsed the barrel of a pistol, but the fast-moving shadow swung one hand through the air – upwards, at an oblique angle – and a tongue of flame shot up towards the stone vault, while the man who had fired the gun went flying back against the wall, slid down it to the ground and sat there without moving.

'Ziukin, come here!'

I ran across muttering: 'Purge us of all defilement and save our souls.' I could not say myself what had come over me – it must have been the shock.

Erast Petrovich leaned down over the seated man and struck a match, and it was not Erast Petrovich at all, but my acquaintance the boatswain with the grey moustache. I started blinking very rapidly.

'Curses,' said the boatswain. 'I miscalculated the blow. And all because it's so damn dark in here. The nasal septum has fractured and the bone has entered the brain. Killed outright. Well then, what about the other one?'

He moved across to the first bandit, who was struggling to get up off the ground.

'Excellent, this one's fresh as a cucumber. Give me some light on him, Afanasii Stepanovich.'

I struck a match. The feeble flame lit up a pair of vacant eyes and lips gasping for air.

The boatswain, who was, after all, none other than Fandorin himself, squatted down on his haunches and slapped the stunned man resoundingly across the cheeks.

'Where is Lind?'

No reply. Nothing but heavy breathing.

'*Où est Lind? Wo ist Lind?* Where is Lind?' Erast Petrovich repeated, pausing between the different languages.

The eyes of the man lying on the ground were no longer vacant but animate with a fierce spite. His lips came together, twitched, stretched out, and a gob of spittle went flying into Fandorin's face.

'*Du, Scheissdreck! Küss mich auf—*'[1]

The hoarse screeching broke off as Fandorin jabbed the bandit in the throat with the edge of his open hand. The spiteful glow in the man's eyes faded and the back of his head struck the ground with a dull thud.

'You killed him!' I exclaimed in horror. 'Why?'

'He wouldn't have told us anything anyway, and we have v-very little time left.'

Erast Petrovich wiped the spittle off his cheek and pulled off the dead man's jacket. He dropped something small and white onto his chest – I could not really see it properly.

'Quick, Ziukin! Get that uniform off. Leave it here. Put this on.'

He pulled off his grey moustache and eyebrows and threw the

---

[1] *You, shit! Kiss me on—*

boatswain's pea jacket on the ground, leaving himself in a short frock coat with narrow shoulder straps. He attached a cockade to his cap, and I suddenly realised that it was a police cap, not a navy one.

'You don't have a sabre,' I remarked. 'A police officer has to have a sabre.'

'I'll get a sabre, don't worry. In a little while,' said Fandorin, grabbing me by the arm and pulling me after him. 'Quick, Ziukin, quick!'

It was a shame simply to fling a good-quality uniform on the ground, and so I hung it on the handle of a gate – it would come in useful for someone.

Erast Petrovich looked round as he ran.

'The order!'

I took the Order of St Vladimir off my neck and put it in my pocket.

'Where are we going in such a hurry?' I shouted, dashing after him.

There was no answer.

We ran out of the side street back on to Myasnitskaya Street, but turned into a gateway just before the post office. It led into a narrow stone courtyard with only a few service doors in the walls. Fandorin dragged me into a corner behind some large rubbish containers stuffed to the brim with brown wrapping paper and scraps of string. Then he took out his watch.

'Ten minutes past nine. We dealt with that quickly. He probably hasn't come out yet?'

'Who is *he*?' I asked, breathing hard. 'Lind?'

Fandorin stuck his hand straight into a rubbish container and extracted a long narrow bundle. Inside it there was a sword belt and a police sabre.

'Our acquaintance from the poste restante. He's the one, didn't you realise?'

'He is Doctor Lind?' I said, astounded.

'No, he is Lind's man. It all turned out to be very simple, much

287

simpler than I expected. And it explains the mystery of the letters. Now we know how they reached the Hermitage without a stamp. A post office counter attendant working for Lind – let us call this individual the Postman for brevity's sake – simply put them into the sack with the post for the Kaluzhskaya district.

'And the letter we sent today also fell straight into his hands. He noticed you cruising up and down near the window and informed Lind, who sent his men. They waited patiently for you outside in the street. Or rather they waited for Fandorin, since they thought it was me.'

'But . . . But how did you manage to guess all this?'

He smiled smugly. 'I was sitting in the tea room opposite the post office, waiting for you to come out and follow the man who collected the letter. Time went by, and you still didn't come out. It seemed strange to me for Lind to act so slowly. After all, he is no less interested in this encounter than I am. Of all the people going into the post office, no one stayed inside for long, and I didn't spot anyone suspicious. Things began to get interesting with the arrival of the two gentlemen known to you, who appeared at about a quarter to four. They actually arrived together and then separated. One took a seat in my tea room, two tables away from me, after asking in German for a place at the window. He kept his eyes fixed on the doors of the post office and never looked around him at all. The second went into the building for a moment and then came back out to join the first. That meant you had been discovered, but for some reason Lind's people were not showing any interest in the contents of the letter. I thought about that for a long time and eventually formed a hypothesis. Just before the post office closed I set out to test it. You saw the way the Postman gaped at me when I claimed to be the bearer of the treasury bill? It was a total surprise to him, since there could not be any bearer – he knew that quite definitely. The Postman could not control his facial expression and gave himself away. We must assume that he is the doctor's Russian assistant who drew up the playful announcement for the newspaper. The Postman is the one who can lead us back to Lind.'

'But what if he was alarmed by the appearance of the mysterious boatswain and has already gone running to warn the doctor?'

'Tell me, Ziukin, have you ever had occasion to receive letters via the poste restante? No? It shows. The post office keeps the letter or package for three days free of charge and then starts charging a daily penalty.'

I thought hard but failed to discover any connection between this circumstance and the apprehension that I had expressed.

'Well, what of it?'

'This,' Erast Petrovich said with a patient sigh. 'Wherever payments are taken there is financial accounting. Our friend cannot leave until he has cashed up and handed over the takings – it would look far too suspicious. That door over there is the service entrance. In about five minutes, or ten at the most, the Postman will come out of it and set off very quickly straight to Lind, and we shall follow along. I hope very much that the doctor has no more helpers left. I am really sick of them.'

'Why did you kill that German?' I asked, remembering the incident. 'Just because he spat at you? He was stunned, helpless!'

Fandorin was surprised. 'I see, Ziukin, that you think I am a worse monster than Lind. Why should I want to kill him? Not to mention the fact that he is a valuable witness. I only put him to sleep, and not for long, about four hours. I expect that will be long enough for the police to find our two friends. An interesting discovery, is it not – a corpse and beside it a man with a revolver in his pocket. And I also left my visiting card with a note: "This is one of Lind's men."'

I recalled the white thing that Fandorin had dropped onto the bandit's chest.

'Perhaps Karnovich and Lasovsky will be able to shake something out of him. Although it is not very likely. There are no traitors among Lind's helpers. But at least the police will start to question whether you and I are thieves, and that in itself is no bad thing.'

This final consideration sounded most reasonable, and I was about to tell Fandorin so, but he placed his hand over my mouth in an outrageously cavalier fashion.

'Quiet!'

A narrow door swung open violently and the familiar counter attendant came out almost at a run, now wearing a peaked uniform cap and carrying a file under his arm. Taking short strides, he strutted past the rubbish containers and headed out through the gateway.

'He's in a hurry,' Erast Petrovich whispered. 'That's very good. It means he was not able to telephone or has nowhere to phone to. I wonder how he informed Lind about your arrival? By note? That would mean that the doctor's lair is somewhere quite close. All right. Time to go.'

We walked out quickly into the street. I started looking around, trying to spot a free cab – after all, if the Postman was in a hurry, he was sure to take a carriage. But no, the hurrying figure in the black post office uniform crossed the boulevard and disappeared into a narrow little street. So Erast Petrovich had guessed right, and Lind was somewhere not far away.

Without stopping, Fandorin told me: 'Drop back about ten *sazhens* behind me and keep your distance. But d-do not run!'

It was easy for him to say 'Do not run!' Erast Petrovich himself has a miraculous way of striding along rapidly but without any visible signs of haste, and so I was obliged to move in the manner of a wounded hare: I walked for about twenty steps, and then ran for a brief stretch, walked and ran, walked and ran. Otherwise I would have fallen behind. It was already completely dark, which was most opportune since otherwise I fear that my strange man-oeuvres would have attracted the attention of the occasional passer-by. The Postman wound his way through the side streets for a little while and suddenly stopped in front of a small detached wooden house with a door that opened straight onto the pavement. There was light at one of the curtained windows – someone was at home – but the Postman did not ring the door-bell; he opened the door with a key and slipped inside.

'What are we going to do?' I asked, catching up with Fandorin.

He took hold of my elbow and led me away from the little house.

'I don't know. Let's t-try to work that out.' By the light of a street lamp, I saw the smooth forehead below the lacquered peak of the police cap gather into wrinkles. 'There are several possibilities. The first: Doctor Lind and the hostages are here. Then we need to keep watch on the windows and wait. If they try to leave, then we strike. The second possibility: only Lind is here and Emilie and the boy are somewhere else. We still have to wait until the doctor comes out and follow him until he leads us to the hostages. The third possibility: neither Lind nor the p-prisoners are here, only the postman and his family. After all, there was someone in the house, was there not? In that case, someone has to come to the Postman from Lind. There is hardly likely to be a telephone connection in this little house. So once again we need to wait. We can see who comes, and then act according to the circumstances. So, there are three alternatives, and in every case we have to wait. Let's m-make ourselves com-fortable – the wait might drag on for a while.' Erast Petrovich looked around. 'I tell you what, Ziukin, get a cabby from the boulevard. Don't tell him where he's going. Just say that you're hiring him for a long time, and he'll be generously paid. And meanwhile I'll look for a comfortable spot.'

When I drove back to the corner in a cab a quarter of an hour later, Fandorin emerged from the dense shadows to meet us. Straightening his sword belt, he said in a stern commanding voice: 'Badge number 345? You'll be with us all night long. Secret business. You'll be paid twenty-five roubles for your work. Drive into that entranceway and wait. And no sleeping now, Vologda. Understand?'

'I understand, what's so hard to understand?' the cabby replied briskly. He was a young peasant with a clever snub-nosed face. I didn't understand how Fandorin guessed from his appearance that he was from Vologda, but the cabby certainly did stretch his vowels to the limit.

'Let's go, Afanasii Petrovich. I've found a most comfortable spot.'

Opposite the little wooden house was a more impressive detached property surrounded by a trellis fence. Erast Petrovich bounded over the fence in an instant and beckoned for me to follow his example. Compared with the railings at the Neskuchny Park it was simple.

'Well, not bad, is it?' Fandorin asked proudly, pointing to the other side of the street.

The view of the Postman's house from there really was ideal, but our observation point could only have been called 'most comfortable' by a masochistic (I believe I have remembered the word correctly) habitué of the chamber at the Elysium club. Right behind the fence there were thick prickly bushes that immediately started catching at my clothes and scratching my forehead. I groaned as I tried to free my elbow. Would I really have to sit here all night?

'Never mind,' Fandorin whispered cheerfully. 'The Chinese say: "The noble man does not strive for comfort." Let's watch the windows.'

We started watching the windows.

To tell the truth, I failed to spot anything remarkable – just a vague shadow that flitted across the curtains a couple of times. In all the other houses the windows had gone dark a long time ago, while the inhabitants of our house seemed to have no intention of going to sleep at all – but that was the only thing that might have seemed suspicious.

'And what if there is a fourth?' I asked after about two hours.

'A fourth what?'

'Alternative.'

'Which is what?'

'What if you were mistaken and the post office employee has nothing to do with Lind?'

'Out of the question,' Fandorin hissed rather too angrily. 'He definitely does. And he is bound to lead us to the d-doctor himself.'

Oh, to taste the honey that your lips drink, I thought, recalling the old folk saying, but I said nothing.

Another half-hour went by. I started thinking that probably for the first time in my life I had lost track of the days. Was today Friday or Saturday, the seventeenth or the eighteenth? It was not really all that important, but for some reason the question gave me no peace. Finally I could stand it no longer, and I asked in a whisper: 'Is today the seventeenth?'

Fandorin took out his Breguet, and the phosphorescent hands flashed in the darkness.

'It has been the eighteenth for five minutes.'

18 May

The previous day had been warm, and so had the evening, but after several hours of sitting still I was chilled right through. My teeth had started to chatter, my legs had gone numb, and any hope that our nocturnal vigil would produce some useful result had almost completely evaporated. But Fandorin remained completely unruffled – indeed, he had not stirred a muscle the whole time, which made me suspect that he was sleeping with his eyes open. And what irritated me most of all was the calm, I would even say *complacent*, expression on his face, as if he were sitting there listening to some kind of enchanting music or the song of birds of paradise.

Suddenly, just when I was seriously considering the idea of rebellion, Erast Petrovich, without any visible change in his demeanour, whispered: 'Attention.'

I started and looked carefully but failed to see any change. The windows in the house opposite us were still lit up. There was not a single sign of movement, not a single sound.

I glanced at my companion again and saw that he had not yet emerged from his sleep, swoon, reverie or whatever – his general strange state of trance.

'They are about to come out,' he said quietly.

'Why do you think that?'

'I have fused into a single reality with the house and allowed the house to enter into myself so that I can feel it b-breathing,' Erast Petrovich said with a completely serious air. 'It is an oriental t-technique. It would take too long to explain. But a minute ago the house began creaking and swaying. It is preparing to expel people from within itself.'

It was hard for me to tell if Fandorin was joking or was simply raving. I rather inclined towards the latter option, because it was not funny enough to be a joke.

'Mr Fandorin, are you asleep?' I enquired, and at that very moment the windows suddenly went dark.

Half a minute later the door opened and two people came out.

'There is no one left in the house; it is empty n-now,' Fandorin pronounced slowly, then suddenly grabbed hold of my elbow and whispered rapidly. 'It's Lind, Lind, Lind!'

I jerked my head round with a start and saw that Erast Petrovich had completely changed: his face was tense, his eyes were narrowed in an expression of intense concentration.

Could it really be Lind after all?

One of the two who had come out was the Postman – I recognised his build and the peaked cap. The other man was average in height, wearing a long operatic cloak like an almaviva thrown over his shoulders and a Calabrian hat with a sagging brim that hung very low.

'Number two,' Fandorin whispered, squeezing my elbow in a grip that was extremely painful.

'Eh? What?' I muttered in confusion.

'Alternative number two. Lind is here, but the hostages are somewhere else.'

'But are you certain it really is Lind?'

'No doubt about it. Those precise, economical and yet elegant movements. That way of wearing the hat. And finally that walk. It is he.'

My voice trembled as I asked: 'Are we going to take him now?'

'You have forgotten everything, Ziukin. We would detain Lind if he had come out with the hostages, according to alternative number one. But this is number two. We follow the doctor; he leads us to the boy and Emilie.'

'But what if—'

Erast Petrovich put his hand over my mouth again, in the same way as he had done before so recently. The man in the long cloak had looked round, although we were talking in whispers and he could not possibly have heard us.

I pushed Fandorin's hand away angrily and asked my question anyway: 'But what if they are not going to the hostages?'

'The time is five minutes past three,' he replied, apropos of nothing at all.

'I didn't ask you the time,' I said, angered by his evasiveness. 'You are always making me out—'

'Have you really forgotten,' Fandorin interrupted, 'that we made an appointment with the doctor at four in the morning? If Lind wishes to be punctual, he needs to collect the prisoners as quickly as possible in order to get to the waste g-ground by the Petrovsky Palace on time.'

The fact that Erast Petrovich had started stammering again suggested that he was feeling a little less tense. And for some reason I also stopped trembling and feeling angry.

The moment Lind (if it was indeed he) and the Postman turned the corner, we skipped back over the fence. I thought in passing that since I had met Mr Fandorin I had climbed more walls and fences than at any other time in my life, even when was I was a child.

'Get into the carriage and follow me with caution,' Erast Petrovich instructed me as he walked along. 'Get out at every corner and look round it. I shall signal to you to drive on or to wait.'

And in precisely that unhurried manner we reached the boulevard, where Fandorin suddenly beckoned for us to drive up to him.

'They have taken a cab and are going to Sretenka Street,' he said as he sat down beside me. 'Come on now, Vologda. Follow them, only don't get too close.'

For quite a long time we drove along a succession of boulevards, sometimes moving downhill at a spanking pace and then slowing to drive up an incline. Although it was the middle of the night, the streets were not empty. There were small groups of people walking along, making lively conversation, and several times we were overtaken by other carriages. In St Petersburg they like to poke fun at the old capital city for supposedly taking to its bed with the dusk, but apparently this was far from true. You would never see so many people out walking on Nevsky Prospect at three o'clock in the morning.

We kept driving straight ahead, and turned only once, at the statue of Pushkin, onto a large street that I immediately recognised as Tverskaya. From here to the Petrovsky Palace it was three or four versts straight along the same route that the imperial procession had followed during the ceremonial entry into the old capital, only in the opposite direction.

On Tverskaya Street there were even more people and carriages, and they were all moving in the same direction as we were. This seemed very strange to me, but I was thinking about something else.

'They are not stopping anywhere!' I eventually exclaimed, unable to contain myself. 'I think they are going straight to the meeting place!'

Fandorin did not answer. In the dim light of the gas lamps his face looked pale and lifeless.

'Perhaps Lind still has some accomplices after all, and the hostages will be delivered directly to the rendezvous?' he speculated after a long pause, but his voice somehow lacked its habitual self-confidence.

'What if they have already been ...' I could not bring myself to finish the dreadful thought.

Erast Petrovich spoke slowly, in a quiet voice, but his reply sent shivers running down my spine: 'Then at least we still have Lind.'

After the Triumphal Gates and the Alexander Railway Station, the separate groups of people fused into a single continuous stream that spread across the roadway as well as the pavements and our horse was forced to slow to a walk. But Lind's carriage was not moving any faster – I could still see the two hats beyond the lowered leather hood ahead of us: the doctor's floppy head-gear and the Postman's peaked cap.

'Good Lord, it's the eighteenth today!' I exclaimed, almost jumping off the seat when I remembered the significance of the date. 'Mr Fandorin, there cannot be any meeting on the waste ground! With so many problems on my mind, I completely forgot about the programme of events for the coronation! On Saturday the eighteenth of May there are to be public revels on the open ground opposite the Petrovsky Palace, with free food and drink and the distribution of souvenirs. There must be a hundred thousand people on that waste ground now!'

'Damn!' Fandorin swore nervously. 'I didn't take that into account either. But then I didn't think that there would be any meeting. I just wrote down the first thing that came into my head. What an unforgivable blunder!'

On every side we could hear excited voices – some not entirely sober – and jolly laughter. For the most part the crowd consisted of simple people, which was only natural – free honey cakes and sweet spiced drinks were hardly likely to attract a more respectable public, who if they did come to take a look out of curiosity would go into the grandstands, where entrance was by ticket only. They said that at the last coronation as many as three hundred thousand people had gathered for the public festivities, and this time probably even more would come. Well, here they were. People must have been making their way there all night long.

'Tell me, Mister Policeman, is it true what they say, that they're going to give everyone a pewter mug and fill it right up to the brim with vodka?' our driver asked, turning his round animated face towards us. He had obviously been infected by the mood of the festive crowd.

'Halt,' Erast Petrovich ordered.

I saw that Lind's cab had stopped, although there was still a long way to go before the turn to the Petrovsky Palace.

'They're getting out!' I exclaimed.

Fandorin handed the cabby a banknote and we set off at a sprint, pushing through the slow-moving crowd.

Although there was a half-moon peering through the clouds, it was quite dark, and so we decided to move a little closer, to a distance of about ten paces. There were bonfires blazing in the open field on the left of the road and on the right, behind the bushes, and so the two silhouettes, one taller and the other slightly shorter, were clearly visible.

'We must not lose sight of them,' I kept repeating to myself over and over, like an incantation.

During those minutes of pursuit I seemed to forget all about His Highness and Mademoiselle Declique. Some ancient and powerful instinct that had nothing to do with pity and was stronger than fear set my heart pounding rapidly but steadily. I had never understood the attraction of the hunt, but now it suddenly occurred to me that the hounds must feel something like this when the pack is unleashed to run down the wolf.

We were forcing our way through a genuine crush now, almost like Nevsky Prospect at the height of the day. From time to time we had to put our elbows to work. A hulking factory hand pushed in front of us and blocked our view. I managed somehow to squeeze through under his elbow and gasped in horror. Lind and the Postman had disappeared!

I looked round despairingly at Fandorin. He drew himself up to his full height and, I think, even stood on tiptoe as he gazed around.

'What can we do?' I shouted. 'My God, what can we do?'

'You go right; I'll go left,' he said.

I dashed to the edge of the road. There were people sitting on the grass in large and small groups. Others were wandering aimlessly among the trees, and in the distance a choir was singing out of tune. Lind was not on my side. I rushed back to the road and collided with Erast Petrovich, who was forcing his way through towards me.

'We've let them get away . . .' I wailed.

It was all over. I covered my face with my hands in order not to see the crowd, the bonfires, the dark dove-grey sky.

Fandorin shook me impatiently by the shoulder. 'Don't give up, Ziukin. Here's the wasteland where the meeting was set. We'll walk around, keep looking and wait for the dawn. Lind won't go anywhere. He needs us as much as we need him.'

He was right, and I tried to take myself in hand and focus my mind.

'The stone,' I said, suddenly feeling anxious. 'You haven't lost the stone, have you?'

If we could just get them back alive, and then come what may. That was all I could think of at that moment.

'No, it is here,' said Fandorin, slapping himself on the chest.

We were being bumped and jostled from all sides, and he took firm hold of my arm.

'You look to the right, Ziukin, and I shall look to the left. We'll walk slowly. If you see the men we are looking for, do not shout, simply nudge me in the side.'

I had never walked arm-in-arm with a man before. Or indeed with a woman, with the exception of one brief affair a very long time before, when I was still very green and stupid. I will not recall it here – the story is really not worth the effort.

The nights are short in May. There was already a strip of pink along the horizon in the east, and the twilight was beginning to brighten. It was obvious that many people had camped here the evening before, and it was becoming more and more crowded around the campfires. Occasionally I could feel empty bottles under my feet. And the crowds kept on coming along the main road from Moscow.

On the left, beyond the barriers and lines of police, there was a wide open field covered with specially built fairground booths and pavilions with walls of freshly cut timber. That was probably where the tsar's gifts to the people were being kept. I cringed at the thought of the pandemonium that would break out here in a few hours time, when this sea of people, their patience exhausted by hours of waiting, went flooding past the barriers.

We wandered from the barriers to the palace and back – once, twice, three times. It was already light, and every time it was harder to force our way through the ever-denser mass of bodies. I continually turned my head to and fro, surveying the half of the area that had been assigned to me, and I struggled with all my strength against a rising tide of despair.

Somewhere in the distance a bugle sounded a clamorous reveille, and I remembered that the Khodynsk army camps were not far away.

I suppose it must be seven o'clock, I thought, trying to recall exactly when reveille was. And at that very second I suddenly saw the familiar Calabrian hat with the civil servant's cap beside it.

'There they are!' I howled, tugging on Fandorin's sleeve with all my might. 'Thank God!'

The Postman looked round, saw me and shouted: 'Ziukin!'

His companion glanced round for a moment – just long enough for me to catch a glimpse of his spectacles and beard – and then they plunged into the very thickest part of the crowd, where it was jostling right up against the barriers.

'After them!' cried Erast Petrovich, giving me a furious shove.

There was a stout merchant in front of us and he simply would not make way. Without the slightest hesitation, Fandorin grabbed his collar with one hand and the hem of his long frock coat with the other, and threw him aside. We went dashing through the crowd, with Erast Petrovich leading the way. He carved through the throng like an admiralty launch slicing through the waves, leaving rolling breakers on each side. From time to time he jumped incredibly high into the air – obviously to avoid losing sight of Lind again.

'They're forcing their way through towards the Khodynsk Field!' Erast Petrovch shouted to me. 'That's quite excellent! There's no crowd there but a lot of police!'

We'll catch them now, any moment now, I realised, and suddenly felt my strength increase tenfold. I drew level with Fandorin and barked: 'Make way there!'

Closer to the barriers the most prudent and patient of the spectators were standing absolutely chock-a-block, and our rate of progress slowed.

'Move aside!' I roared. 'Police!'

'Ha, there's a cunning one!'

Someone punched me so hard in the side that everything went black and I gasped for breath.

Erast Petrovich took out his police whistle and blew it. The crowd reeled back and parted at the harsh sound, and we advanced a few more steps with relative ease, but then coarse caftans, pea jackets and peasant shirts closed back together again.

Lind and the Postman were very close now. I saw them duck under a barrier into the open space right in front of the police cordon. Aha, now they were caught!

I saw the hat lean across to the cap and whisper something into it.

The Postman turned back, waved his arms in the air and bellowed: 'Good Orthodox people! Look! On that side they're pouring in from the Vaganka! They've broken through! They'll get all the mugs! Forward, lads!'

A single roar was vented from a thousand throats. 'Hah, the cunning swine! We've been here all night, and they want to grab the lot! Like hell they will!'

I was suddenly swept forward by a force so irresistible that my feet were lifted off the ground. Everything around me started moving, and everyone scrabbled with their elbows, trying to force a way through to the tents and pavilions.

I heard whistles trilling and shots fired into the air ahead of me. Then someone roared through a megaphone: 'Go back! Go back! You'll all be crushed!'

A chorus of voices replied cheerfully: 'Don't you worry, yer 'onour! Press on, lads!'

A woman shrieked desperately.

Somehow I managed to find the ground with my feet and move along with the crowd. Fandorin was no longer there beside me – he had been swept away somewhere to one side. I almost stumbled when I stepped on something soft and did not immediately realise that it was a person. I caught a glimpse of a trampled soldier's white tunic under my feet, but it was impossible to help the fallen man as my hands were pinned tight against my sides.

Then bodies began falling more and more often, and I could only think of one thing: God forbid that I might lose my footing – there was no way I would ever get up again. To my left there was someone running along over the people's shoulders and heads, with his black tarred boots twinkling. Suddenly he swayed, flung up his arms and went crashing down.

I was being carried straight towards the sharp corner of a planking pavilion covered in fresh splinters. I tried to veer a little to one side, but it was hopeless.

'Take him!' voices shouted from my right. 'Take the little one!'

They were passing a boy of about eight from one pair of raised hands to another. He was gazing around in terror and sniffing with his bloody nose.

I was flung against the wall and my cheek dragged across the splinters, making the tears spurt from my eyes. I struck my temple against a carved window frame and as I started slipping down I had just enough time to think: It's over. Now they will crush me.

Someone gripped me under the armpits and jerked me back onto my feet. Fandorin. I was already so stunned that his appearance did not surprise me in the least.

'Brace your hands against the wall!' he shouted. 'Otherwise they'll crush you!'

He swung his arm and smashed out the patterned shutter with a single blow of his fist. Then he picked me up by my sides and thrust me up with incredible strength so that I flew over the window sill rather than climbed it, and landed with a crash on a floor that smelled of fresh wood shavings. There were neat pyramids of coronation mugs standing all around me. Erast Petrovich hauled himself up and also climbed into the pavilion. One of his eyebrows was split, his uniform was tattered, his sabre had come halfway out of its scabbard.

Were we really safe now?

I looked out of the window and saw that the field was jammed solid with people out of their minds. Screaming, groaning, crunching sounds, laughter – all of these were mingled together in the hubbub. There had to be a million of them! Clouds of dust swirled and shimmered in the air, transforming it into a thick fatty broth.

Someone had climbed into the next pavilion and began throwing mugs and sacks of presents out of the window. A brawl immediately started up beside the wall there.

'Oh Lord, save Thy people,' I blurted out, and my hand reached up of its own accord to make the sign of the cross.

'What are you up to?' someone shouted up at us. 'Toss out the mugs! Is there any drink?'

The pavilion creaked and wood dust sprinkled down from the ceiling. I cried out in horror as I saw our frail refuge falling to pieces. Something struck me on the back of my head, and it was a relief when I lost consciousness.

I do not know who dragged me out from under the debris and then carried me to a safe place, or why they did it. In all probability I was once again indebted to Fandorin for saving me, although I do not find that a pleasant thought.

However it happened, I came round on a wooden grandstand

at the edge of the Khodynsk Field. The sun was already high in the sky. I lifted my head, then immediately dropped it again, hitting it hard against the rough surface of the bench. I then managed to sit up after a fashion and felt my pounding head with my hands. It did not feel as if it was really mine. Although there was a substantial lump on the top of it, otherwise I seemed to be more or less unhurt. Fandorin was nowhere to be seen. I was in a strange drowsy state and could not get rid of the metallic ringing sound in my ears.

The first thing I did was survey the vast field. I saw booths and pavilions twisted awry and tight lines of soldiers moving slowly across the grass. And everywhere, almost completely covering the ground, there were bodies: many were motionless, but some were still moving. It was distressing to watch, this feeble stirring. There was a buzzing in my temples and my eyes were blinded by the bright sun. I tucked my head into my crossed arms and either fell asleep or fainted. I do not know how long I sat there, leaning against the skirting of the grandstand, but the next time I woke up it was long after midday and the field was empty. There were no soldiers and no bodies.

My head was no longer hurting so badly, but I felt very thirsty.

I sat there, wondering feebly if I ought to go somewhere or if it would be better to stay where I was. I stayed, and it was the right thing to do, because soon Erast Petrovich appeared. He was still wearing his police uniform, but his boots were absolutely filthy and his white gloves black with soil.

'Are you back with us?' he asked in a gloomy voice. 'My God, Ziukin, what a disaster. The only time I ever saw the like was at Plevna. Thousands killed and mutilated. This is the worst of all Lind's atrocities. He has taken an army of slaves with him into the grave like some ancient king.'

'So Lind was crushed too?' I asked without any great interest, still unable to shake off my lethargic drowsiness.

'I cannot see how he could possibly have survived in such a crush. However, let us go and check. The soldiers and police

have just finished laying out the mangled bodies for identification – over there, along the side of the road. The line of the
dead is almost a verst long. But how can we identify him? We
don't even know what he looks like. Except perhaps for the
cloak . . . Let's go, Ziukin, let's go.'

I limped along after him.

The line of dead bodies stretched along the main highway,
running as far as the eye could see in both directions. There were
cabs and carts driving out from Moscow as the order had been
given to transport the dead to the Vagankovskoe Cemetery, but
they had not started moving them yet.

There were high-ranking officials striding about everywhere
with sombre faces: military officers, police officers, civilians, each
one accompanied by his own retinue. Oh, you will all get it in
the neck for allowing the coronation to be wrecked, I thought,
but more in sympathy than condemnation. It was Lind who had
started the slaughter, but it was the men in charge who would
have to pay.

I had a strange feeling as I slowly walked along the side of the
road – as if I were some kind of high noble reviewing a parade
of the dead. Many of the corpses grinned at me, their white teeth
exposed in their flattened faces. From the beginning I felt as if I
were frozen, and then I completely turned to stone, which was
probably all for the best. I only stopped once, beside that boy
whom they had tried to pass out of the crowd. Evidently they
had failed. I stared with apathetic curiosity at the transparent
blueness of his wide staring eyes and hobbled on. There
were quite a number of people staring into the dead faces like
Fandorin and myself – some looking for relatives, some simply
curious.

'Look at this, look here,' I heard a voice say. 'What a rich man
he was, eh?'

A crowd of idlers had gathered round one dead body, and
there was a police constable on guard. It was just another dead
body – skinny, with straw-coloured hair and a crushed nose – but

there were about a dozen purses and several watches on chains laid out on its chest.

'A pickpocket,' a lively old man explained to me and clicked his tongue regretfully. 'That old buzzard fate didn't spare him either. And he was expecting such a rich haul.'

Ahead of me someone started howling – they must have recognised a dear one – and I hurried on to get past as quickly as possible.

I strode on rapidly for about another twenty paces, and then my stupor seemed to vanish as if by magic. That black frock coat was familiar!

Yes, it was definitely him. The Postman!

Fandorin also saw him and walked over quickly. He squatted down.

The face of the doctor's helper was entirely undamaged apart from the imprint of the sole of someone's boot on one cheek. I was struck very powerfully by the expression of surprise on the frozen features. What had he found so astonishing in the final moment of his criminal life? What had he seen that was so incredible? The gaping abyss of hell?

Erast Petrovich straightened up abruptly and declared in a hoarse voice: 'Lind is alive!'

Seeing my eyebrows shoot up in bewilderment, he bent down, parted the corpse's blood-soaked clothes and unbuttoned its shirt to expose the pale hairy chest. There was a neat black triangular wound just below the left nipple.

'There, you see it,' Fandorin said in a quiet voice. 'A familiar sign. That is Lind's stiletto. The doctor remains true to himself – he leaves no witnesses.' Erast Petrovich straightened up and looked in the direction of Moscow. 'Let's go, Ziukin. There's nothing more we can do here. Quickly!'

He strode off rapidly, almost running, in the direction of the Petrovsky Palace.

'Where are you going?' I shouted, chasing after him.

'Where else but the Postman's house? Lind might still be there.

After all, he doesn't know that we discovered his hideaway.'

We could not walk all the way into Moscow, and all the cabs had been commandeered by the police to transport the dead, after the wounded had been taken to the hospitals in the morning. The carriages were setting off one after the other in the direction of the Tverskaya Gate, each bearing a doleful cargo.

High Police Master Lasovsky walked past, surrounded by a group of blue uniforms. I hastily turned my face away, only realising afterwards that in my present condition it would have been almost impossible to recognise me, not to mention the fact that just at that moment Afanasii Ziukin was probably the very last thing on the colonel's mind. The kidnapping of Mikhail Georgievich, even the disappearance of the Orlov, paled into insignificance in comparison with the tragedy that had just taken place. Fate had not inflicted such a blow on a new monarch in Russia since at least 1825. Good Lord. What an international scandal! And what a monstrous omen for the reign just begun!

The high police master's face was pale and miserable. Naturally, for he would be held responsible in the first instance. Mere resignation would not be enough. The person in charge of arranging the coronation festivities was the governor general of Moscow, but how could you bring the uncle of His Imperial Majesty to trial? But someone at the top of the local authorities had to be tried. Why had they not foreseen that there would be so many people? Why had they set up such a weak cordon?

Fandorin drew himself erect and saluted the police chief smartly, but Lasovsky did not even glance in our direction.

'Excellent,' Erast Petrovich said to me in a low voice. 'There's our cab.'

A short distance away I saw the high police master's famous carriage, harnessed to a pair of black trotters. The coachman Sychov, frequently mentioned by the Moscow newspapers in connection with the indefatigable police chief's daily outings in search of drunken yard keepers and negligent constables, was solemnly ensconced on the coach box.

Erast Petrovich drew his sword and dashed towards the carriage, jangling his spurs smartly.

'An urgent dispatch!' he shouted at the coachman and jumped straight into the carriage at a run. 'Come on, Sychov, wake up! An order from the high police master!' He turned back to me and saluted. 'Your Excellency, I implore you, quickly now!'

The coachman glanced at the brusque officer and looked at me. I was wearing the simple jacket taken from the German bandit, but Sychov did not seem particularly surprised. On an insane day like this, God only knew who the high police master's two in hand might be ordered to carry.

'Open your eyes wider, stare hard,' Fandorin whispered as he took a seat facing me. 'You're an important individual. They don't drive just anybody around in this carriage.'

I drew myself erect and, as befits a genuinely important individual, directed my gaze a little to the side and up, gathering my forehead into stately wrinkles. Thank God I had seen enough ministers and generals in my time.

'Drive on, Sychov, drive on!' Erast Petrovich barked, prodding the driver in his cotton-wadded back.

The coachman hastily shook his reins, the wonderful horses set off at a trot, and the carriage swayed gently on its soft springs.

Every now and then Sychov bellowed: 'Mind yourselves, there!'

The bleached white trunks of the roadside poplars flashed by. The bleak queue of carts covered with sackcloth fell further and further behind. People on the pavements turned round to gaze in hope and fear – or at least it seemed to me that they did – and policemen saluted.

Erast Petrovich ordered the coachman to stop at the Alexander Railway Station. We got out, Erast Petrovich dropped his visiting card on the leather seat and waved for Sychov to drive back to where he had come from.

We got into a cab and drove off at a spanking pace towards Myasnitskaya Street.

'What's happening up there on the Khodynka, Your Honour?' the cabby asked, turning towards us. 'They're saying as the Yids poured dope into the official wine, so the people was drugged, and nigh on a hundred thousand Orthodox folk was crushed. Is that true or not?'

'It's a lie,' Erast Petrovich replied curtly. 'Drive on, drive on!'

We flew into the familiar side street with a rumble and a clatter. Fandorin jumped down and beckoned the yard keeper with an imperious gesture.

'Who lives at that address?' he asked, pointing to the Postman's house.

'Post Office Attendant Mr Ivan Zakharovich Tereshchenko,' the yard keeper replied, saluting with his broom held rigidly to attention.

'Retired army man?' Erast Petrovich enquired sternly.

'Yes, sir, Your Honour! Private First Class of the Prince Heinrich of Prussia Sixth Dragoons Regiment Fyodor Svishch!'

'Very well, Svishch. This gentleman and I have come to carry out the arrest of this Tereshchenko. You have a whistle. Go round to the back of the house from the courtyard and keep your eyes on the windows. If he tries to get out, whistle for all you're worth. Is that clear?'

'Yes, sir, Your Honour!'

'And wait!' Fandorin shouted after the former private, first class, who was already dashing off to carry out his orders. 'Do you have a crowbar? Bring it here and then take up your post.'

We ourselves took up a position on the porch where we could not be seen from the windows.

Erast Petrovich rang the bell and then knocked on the door.

'Tereshchenko! Mr Tereshchenko! Open up, this is the local inspector of police! In connection with today's events!'

He put his ear to the door.

'Break it open, Ziukin.'

I had never held such a crude instrument as an iron crowbar in my hands before, never mind used it to break in a door. It turned out to be far from simple. I struck the lock once, twice, three times. The door shuddered but it did not open. Then I stuck the flat sharp end into the crack, leaned against it and tried to lever the lock apart, but that did not work either.

'Right. Damn you and your crowbar, Ziukin!'

Erast Petrovich moved me aside. Grabbing the porch railings he launched himself into the air and smashed both of his feet into the door, which went crashing inwards and hung crookedly on one hinge.

We quickly ran through all the rooms with Fandorin clutching a little black revolver at the ready. No one. Scattered items of clothing, false beards, a ginger wig, a few canes, cloaks and hats, crumpled banknotes on the floor.

'We're too late!' Erast Petrovich sighed. 'Just a little bit too late!'

I groaned in disappointment, but he looked round the small drawing room carefully and then suddenly said in a quiet stealthy voice: 'Ah, but this is interesting.'

There was an open casket standing on a small table beside the window. Fandorin took out a long object that glittered in his fingers, giving off yellow sparks.

'What is that?' I asked in amazement.

'I presume it is the celebrated coronet,' he replied, keenly examining the diadem, which was encrusted with priceless yellow diamonds and opals. 'And here is the Empress Anna's clasp, and the Empress Elisaveta's neckband, and the small d-diamond bouquet with a spinel, and the, what's it called ... aigrette. I promised Her Imperial Majesty that her jewels from the coffret would be returned safe and sound, and that is what has happened.'

I dashed across to the casket and froze in awe. What a stroke of luck! All of these fabulous jewels glowing with the sacred aura of the history of the imperial house, safely returned to the throne! This alone was enough to justify Fandorin's entire wild adventure and totally restore my own good name. The only possible greater happiness would be the rescue of Mikhail Georgievich and Mademoiselle Declique.

But of course Fandorin was delighted by this miraculous discovery for a completely different reason.

'Lind was here only very recently and evidently intends to return. That is one. He really does have no one left to help him. He is quite alone. That is two. And finally we have an excellent chance of catching him. That is three.'

I thought for a moment and worked out the logic for myself: 'If he was not planning to return, he would not have left the casket behind, right? And if he still had any helpers, he would have left them to guard the treasure. What are we going to do?'

'First of all, mend the front d-door.'

We dashed back into the entrance hall. The blow from Fandorin's feet had torn one hinge out bodily, but that was not the only problem. Far worse was the fact that a crowd of onlookers had gathered and they were staring avidly at the windows and the gaping hole.

'Damnation!' Erast Petrovich groaned. 'We raised such a racket that the entire street has come running to look, and in ten minutes the entire b-block will be here! Soon the real police will turn up and spoil everything for us. No, we won't see Lind here again. But at least we have to check to see if any clues have been left behind.'

He went back inside and started picking up the clothes scattered on the floors of the rooms, paying special attention to a narrow shoe covered in dust. Its partner was nowhere nearby.

Meanwhile I went out into the cramped corridor and, for lack of anything better to do, glanced into the small untidy kitchen with a tiled stove in the corner. I found nothing remarkable in the kitchen apart from a very large number of cockroaches, and I was about to leave it when my eyes fell on a trapdoor set into the floor. It must be a cellar, I thought, and suddenly felt as if I had been nudged by some mysterious force. Simply in order to kill time while Fandorin was carrying out his search, I leaned down and lifted up the door. The dark opening exuded that special mouldy smell of dampness and earth, the smell that cellars where beetroot, carrots and potatoes are kept ought to have.

Just as I was just about to close the door, I heard a sound that made me turn cold and then set me trembling. It was a groan, weak but quite unmistakable!

'Mr Fandorin!' I shouted at the top of my voice. 'Come here!'

And I took the paraffin lamp off the kitchen table with trembling hands, lit it with a match and went down into the darkness and the cold. When I was only halfway down the steps, I saw her.

Mademoiselle Declique was lying huddled up against the wall on some grey sacks. She was wearing nothing but her shift – my eyes were drawn to a slim ankle with a bruise around the bone, and I hastily averted my eyes – but this was no time for respecting the proprieties.

I set the lamp down on a barrel (to judge from the smell, it must have contained pickled cabbage) and dashed over to where she lay. Her head was thrown back and her eyes were closed. I saw that one of Emilie's hands was handcuffed to an iron ring set into the wall. Mademoiselle's poor face was covered with bruises and blotches of dried blood. Her undershirt had slipped down off one white shoulder, and I saw a huge bruise above her collarbone.

'Ziukin, are you down there?' Fandorin's voice called from somewhere above me.

I did not reply because I had rushed to examine the other corners of the cellar. But His Highness was not there.

I went back to Mademoiselle and cautiously raised her head.

'Can you hear me?' I asked.

Fandorin jumped down onto the floor and stood behind me.

Mademoiselle opened her eyes, then screwed them up against the light of the lamp and smiled. '*Athanas, comme tu es marrant sans les favoris. Je t'ai vu dans mes rêves. Je rêve toujours . . .*'[1]

---

[1] *Athanas, how funny you are without your sideburns. I dreamed about you. I am still dreaming.*

313

She was clearly not well, otherwise she would never have spoken to me in such a familiar manner.

My heart was breaking with pity for her. But Fandorin was less sentimental.

He moved me aside and slapped the prisoner on the cheek.

'*Emilie, où est le prince?*'[2]

'*Je ne sais pas . . .*'[3] she whispered and her eyes closed again.

'What, have you not guessed who Lind is?' Emilie said, looking at Fandorin incredulously. 'And I was certain that with your great intellect you had solved everything. Ah, it seems so simple to me now! Truly, we were all blind.'

Erast Petrovich looked embarrassed, and I must admit that the solution seemed very far from simple to me.

The conversation was taking place in French, since after everything that Mademoiselle had suffered it would simply have been too cruel to torment her with Russian grammar. I had noticed before that when Fandorin spoke foreign languages he did not stammer at all, but I had not had any time to ponder this surprising phenomenon. It seemed that his ailment – for I considered stammering to be a psychological ailment – was in some way linked to expressing himself in Russian. Could this stumbling over the sounds of his native tongue perhaps be an expression of secret hostility to Russia and all things Russian? That would not have surprised me in the least.

We had arrived at our rented apartment half an hour before. Fandorin was holding the casket, but I had an even more precious burden: I was carrying Emilie, muffled up in Doctor Lind's cloak. Mademoiselle's body was smooth and very hot – I could feel that even through the material. That must have been why I started feeling feverish myself, and I could not recover my breath for a long time, although Mademoiselle was not at all heavy.

---

[2] *Emilie, where is the prince?*

[3] *I do not know . . .*

We decided to put our dear guest in one of the bedrooms. I laid the poor woman on the bed, quickly covered her with a blanket and wiped the drops of sweat off my forehead.

Fandorin sat down beside her and said: 'Emilie, we cannot call a doctor for you. Monsieur Ziukin and I are, so to speak, outside the law at present. If you will permit me, I will examine and treat your wounds and contusions myself, I do have certain skills in that area. You must not feel shy with me.'

And now, why this? I thought, outraged. What incredible impudence!

But Mademoiselle did not find Fandorin's suggestion impudent at all. 'This is no time for me to be shy,' she said, smiling feebly. 'I shall be very grateful to you for your help. I hurt all over. As you can see, the kidnappers did not treat me very gallantly.'

'Afanasii Stepanovich, heat some water,' Fandorin ordered briskly in Russian. 'And I saw some alcohol and embrocation in the bathroom.'

The famous surgeon Pirogov in person! Nonetheless I did as he said, and also brought some clean napkins, mercurochrome and adhesive plaster that I found in one of the drawers in the bathroom.

Before the examination began, Mademoiselle cast a timid glance in my direction. I hastily turned away, and I am afraid that I blushed.

I heard the rustle of light fabric. Fandorin said anxiously: 'Good Lord, you're bruised all over. Does this hurt?'

'No, not much.'

'And this?'

'Yes!'

'I think the rib is cracked. I'll strap it with the plaster for the time being. How about here, under the collarbone?'

'It hurts when you press.'

There was a mirror not far away on the wall. I realised that if I took two sly steps to the right I would be able to see what was happening on the bed, but I immediately felt ashamed of this unworthy thought and moved to the left instead.

'Turn over,' Erast Petrovich ordered. 'I'll feel your vertebrae.'

'Yes, yes, it hurts there. On the coccyx.'

I gritted my teeth. This was becoming genuinely unbearable! I regretted not having gone out into the corridor.

'Someone kicked you,' Fandorin stated. 'It's a very sensitive spot, but we'll put a compress on it, like that. And here too. Never mind, it will hurt for a few days and then get better.'

I heard water splashing, and Mademoiselle groaned quietly a few times.

'It is all over, Athanas. You can revolve now,' I heard her say in Russian and immediately turned round. Emilie was lying on her back, covered up to her chest with the blanket. She had a neat piece of white plaster on her left eyebrow, one corner of her mouth was red from mercurochrome, and I could see the edge of a napkin under her open collar.

I could not look Mademoiselle in the eye and glanced sideways at Fandorin, who was washing his hands in a basin with a self-composed air, like a genuine doctor. I bit my lip at the thought that those strong slim fingers had touched Emilie's skin, and in places that it was impossible even to think about without feeling giddy. But the most surprising thing was that Mademoiselle did not seem embarrassed at all and was looking at Fandorin with a grateful smile.

'Thank you, Erast.'

Erast!

'Thank you. I feel a lot better now.' She laughed quietly. 'Alas, I have no more secrets from you now. As a respectable man you are obliged to marry me.'

This risqué joke made even Fandorin blush. And you can imagine how I felt.

In order to steer the conversation away from the indecent and painful direction that it had taken, I asked dryly: 'Nevertheless, Mademoiselle Declique, where is His Highness?'

'I do not know. We were separated as soon as we left the

underground passage and kept in different places ever since then. The boy was unconscious, and I was very faint myself. They hit me quite hard on the head when I tried to shout.'

'Yes, yes,' Erast Petrovich said eagerly. 'What were you trying to tell us? You shouted: "Lind's here. He's . . ." But not another word after that.'

'Yes, he put his hand over my mouth and punched me in the face. I recognised him despite the mask.'

'You recognised him!' Erast Petrovich and I exclaimed in a single voice.

And then Mademoiselle raised her eyebrows in surprise and asked the question that embarrassed Fandorin so greatly.

'What, have you not guessed who Lind is?' Emilie said, looking at Fandorin incredulously. 'And I was certain that with your great intellect you had solved everything. Ah, it seems so simple to me now! Truly, we were all blind.'

Fandorin and I glanced at each other, and I could tell from his furtive expression that he wished to ascertain whether I had been more quick-witted than he had. Unfortunately I had not. But I would have paid dearly to make it so.

'Oh, good Lord. Why it's Banville,' she said, shaking her head in amazement at our slow-wittedness. 'Or at least the person we knew as Lord Banville. I recognised his voice back there in the vault. When someone called down: "Alarm! Run!" Lind forgot his usual caution and shouted in English: "Take the kid and the slut! Run for it!" It was Banville!'

'Banville?' Erast Petrovich repeated, perplexed. 'But how is that possible? Surely he is a friend of Georgii Alexandrovich? They have known each other for a long time!'

'Not so very long,' I put in, trying to gather my thoughts. 'His Highness only made Banville's acquaintance this spring, in Nice.'

'I was not aware of that,' Fandorin said hastily, as if he were trying to offer excuses. 'Yes indeed, how simple . . .' He changed from French to Russian and said: 'Even Homer sometimes nods.

But my own lack of insight in this case is absolutely unforgivable. Why, of course!'

He jumped up and started striding around the room, almost running in fact, and gesticulating fitfully. I had never seen him in such an agitated state. The words spurted from his lips, tumbling over each other.

'The doctor began putting his plan into action in Nice. He must have gone there deliberately to seek out his future victim – so many Russian grand dukes go to the Côte d'Azur in spring! And it was already known that the coronation would be in May! Win the trust of members of the imperial family, become a friend, obtain an invitation to the c-celebrations, and everything else was just a matter of precise technical preparation!'

'And another thing!' I put in. 'A hatred of women. You said yourself that Lind cannot bear to have women around him. Now it is clear why. So Endlung was right!'

'Endlung?' Erast Petrovich echoed in a hollow voice and rubbed his forehead furiously, as if he wished to rub right through it to his brain. 'Yes, yes indeed. And I attached no importance to his idiotic theory – precisely because it was that blockhead who thought of it. A genuine case of "Out of the mouths of fools . . ." Ah, Ziukin, snobbism is a truly terrible sin . . . Banville! It was Banville! And that fragrance, The Earl of Essex . . . How cleverly he gave himself freedom of movement by pretending to leave so suddenly! And the duel that came at just the right moment! And a shot straight to Glinsky's heart – I recognise Lind's diabolical accuracy in that! An excellent disguise: an eccentric British homosexual. The conceptual breadth and fine detailed planning, the incredible boldness and ruthlessness – these are definitely Lind's signature! And I have failed to catch him again . . .'

'But there is still Mr Carr,' I reminded him. 'He is Lind's man too, surely?'

Erast Petrovich gestured hopelessly.

'I assure you that Carr has nothing to do with all this. Otherwise Lind would not have left him behind. The doctor brought along his affected cutie to make his camouflage more convincing, and probably in order to combine work and pleasure. Lind is well known for his sybaritic habits. Dammit, the most upsetting thing is that Endlung was right! A gang of homosexuals, united not only by financial interests but by other ties as well. So that is the source of their great loyalty and self-sacrifice!'

Mademoiselle wrinkled up her forehead, listening attentively to Fandorin's lamentations, and I think that she understood everything, or almost everything.

'Oh yes, Lind really does hate women,' she said with a bitter laugh. 'I know that very well from my own experience. All the time I was a prisoner I was only given one piece of bread and two mugs of water. It was a good thing that barrel was there beside me, with that terrible cabbage of yours. I was kept on a chain, with no clothes. And yesterday evening Banville, I mean Lind, came down into the cellar as angry as a thousand devils and started kicking me without saying a word! I think he must have had some bad news. The pain was bad, but the fear was worse.' Emilie shuddered and pulled the blanket right up to her chin. 'He is not a man; he is pure evil. The doctor beat me without saying a single word and flew into such a rage that if the owner of the house had not been there he would probably have beaten me to death. The owner is quite a tall man with a gloomy face. He was the only one who did not hurt me. He gave me the bread and water.'

Mademoiselle gingerly touched the plaster on her forehead.

'You saw what Lind did to me, Erast! The scum! And there was no reason for it!'

'He was angry when he found out that he had lost two of his helpers,' I explained. 'Mr Fandorin killed one of them and handed the other over to the police.'

'What a pity you did not kill both of them, Erast,' she said, sniffing and wiping a tear of anger off her eyelashes. 'Those Germans were absolute swine. Which of them did you kill, the lop-eared one or the one with freckles?'

'The one with freckles,' Erast Petrovich replied.

And I had not seen either of them properly – there was no time and it was dark in that passage.

'Never mind,' I observed. 'At least now the doctor has been left entirely alone.'

Fandorin pursed his lips sceptically. 'Hardly. There is still someone guarding the boy. If the poor boy is still alive . . .'

'Oh, the little one is alive, I am sure of it!' Mademoiselle exclaimed. 'At least, he was still alive yesterday evening. When the owner of the house dragged that raging lunatic Banville off me, I heard him growl: "If not for the stone, I'd send him both heads – the kid's and the slut's." I think he meant you, Erast.'

'Thank God!' I blurted out.

I turned towards the icon of St Nicholas hanging in the corner and crossed myself. Mikhail Georgievich was alive, there was still hope.

However, there was another question that was still tormenting me. It was not the kind of question that one asks, and if one does ask, one has no right to expect a reply. Nonetheless, I decided that I would. 'Tell me, did they . . . did they . . . abuse you?'

To make things quite clear, I spoke these words in French.

Thanks be to God, Emilie was not offended. On the contrary, she smiled sadly. 'Yes, Athanas, they did abuse me, as you might have noticed from my bumps and bruises. The only comfort is that it was not the kind of abuse that you obviously have in mind. Those gentlemen would probably have preferred to kill themselves rather than enter into physical relations with a woman.'

This bold direct answer embarrassed me and I averted my eyes. If there was one thing about Mademoiselle Declique that I did not like, it was the unfeminine exactitude with which she expressed herself.

'Well then, let us sum up,' Fandorin declared, hooking his fingers together. 'We have rescued Emilie from the clutches of Doctor Lind. That is one. We now know what the doctor looks like. That is two. We have recovered the empress's jewels. That is three. Half of the job has been done. The rest is simple.' He heaved a sigh, and I realised that he was using the word 'simple' ironically. 'Rescue the boy. Eliminate Lind.'

'Yes, yes!' Mademoiselle exclaimed, lifting herself abruptly off the pillow. 'Kill that foul beast!' She looked at me with a plaintive expression and said in a feeble voice: 'Athanas, you cannot imagine how hungry I am . . .'

Ah, what a stupid, insensitive blockhead! Fandorin was only interested in Lind, but I ought to have known better!

I went dashing towards the door, but Erast Petrovich grabbed hold of the flap of my jacket.

'Where are you off to, Ziukin?'

'Where? To the dining room. There is cheese and biscuits in the sideboard, and pâté and ham in the icebox.'

'No ham. A g-glass of sweet tea with rum and a piece of black bread. She must not have anything more yet.'

He was right. After fasting the stomach should not be burdened with heavy food. But I put in four spoons of sugar, cut a substantial slice of bread and splashed in a good helping of whisky from Mr Freyby's bottle.

Mademoiselle drank the tea with a smile on her split lips, and the colour returned to her pale cheeks.

My heart was wrung with an inexpressible pity. If I could have got my hands on that vile Doctor Lind, who had kicked and beaten a helpless woman, I would have put my hands round his neck and no power on earth could have forced my fingers apart.

'You need to get some sleep, Emilie,' Fandorin said, getting to his feet. 'We will decide in the morning how to proceed from here. Afanasii Petrovich,' he said, switching into Russian, 'will you agree to spend the night here, on the couch? In case Emilie might need something?'

Need he have asked! I wanted so much to be alone with her. Just to be there, not to talk. Or, if there was a chance, to speak of the feelings that filled my heart. But where would I find the words?

Fandorin left the room. Emilie looked at me with a smile, and I sat there, a pitiful awkward creature, licking my lips, clearing my throat, clasping and unclasping my fingers. Finally I gathered the courage to speak.

'I . . . I missed you very badly, Mademoiselle Declique.'

'You may call me Emilie,' she said in a quiet voice.

'Very well. That will really not be excessive familiarity, because after all that you have been through – that is, that you and I have been through – I dare to hope that you and I . . .' I hesitated and blushed painfully. 'That you and I . . .'

'Yes?' she said with an affectionate nod. 'Tell me. Tell me.'

'That you and I can think of ourselves not just as colleagues, but as friends.'

'Friends?'

I thought I heard a note of disappointment in her voice.

'Well, of course I am not so presumptuous as to expect a particularly close or intimate friendship.' I corrected myself quickly so that she would not think I was exploiting the situation in order to inveigle myself into her confidence. 'We have simply become good companions. And I am very glad of it . . . There.'

I did not say any more, because I thought there had in any case already been a highly significant shift in our relationship: the right to address each other by our first names had been legitimised, and in addition I had offered her my friendship, and my offer seemed to have been received favourably.

And yet Emilie was looking at me as if she had been expecting something else.

'You regard me as a friend, a companion?' she asked after a long pause, as if she were making quite sure.

'Yes, as a dear friend,' I confirmed, casting my reserve aside.

Then Mademoiselle sighed, closed her eyes and said in a quiet voice: 'I'm sorry, Athanas. I am very tired. I am going to sleep.'

I could not tell when she fell asleep. Her breast carried on rising and falling evenly, her long eyelashes fluttered slightly, and occasionally a shadow ran across her face like a small cloud passing over the smooth surface of bright azure waters.

I spent the whole night alternating between brief periods of shallow sleep and periods of wakefulness. Emilie only had to stir or sigh and I immediately opened my eyes, wondering if I should bring her some water, tuck her in or adjust her pillow. I was not at all distressed by these frequent awakenings; on the contrary, I found them pleasant, even delightful. It was a long, long time since I had felt such peace.

19 May

I served a genuine breakfast: with chinaware and silverware on a
starched tablecloth. Without a chef of course it is impossible to
prepare anything proper, but even so there was an omelette and
cheeses and smoked meats.

Emilie was looking much better today and she ate with a great
appetite. Her eyes flashed with life and her voice was strong and
cheerful. Women possess an astounding ability to recover from
the most grievous of ailments if the conditions of their life suddenly change for the better. I had had the opportunity to witness
such transformations on many occasions. It is also true that
members of the weaker sex are affected most positively by the
company of men and male attention, and in this sense we treated
Mademoiselle like a genuine queen.

Fandorin came to breakfast in morning tails and a white tie,
clearly demonstrating that the liberties that he had been obliged
to take the previous day had in no way diminished his respect for
our guest. I appreciated his gesture. To tell the truth, the tenor
of my own thoughts was similar, only, unlike Erast Petrovich, I
did not have any clothes into which I could change and had to
make do with shaving my exposed features properly.

While we were drinking coffee – I was also at the table because
I was not present as a butler but as a private individual – Erast
Petrovich spoke about our business. The conversation was con-
ducted in French.

'I did not sleep very much last night, but I did do a lot of thinking. The reason for my unforgivable error seems clear to me now. I had not expected such audacity from Doctor Lind. In all his previous operations he has behaved with extreme caution. But evidently this time the prize was too great and Lind decided to occupy the most advantageous position possible. Being inside the Hermitage, he was able to observe all our preparations. And another source of information for him was Mr Carr, so artfully offered up to Simeon Alexandrovich. The drama of passions and jealousies was probably no more than a performance. The governor general confided in his English darling, who then told everything he had heard to the false Lord Banville.'

'Perhaps the doctor's audacity is explained by the fact that he has decided to retire forever once he has his colossal trophy?' Emilie suggested. 'How much money does a man need, after all?'

Fandorin twisted down the corner of his mouth.

'I do not know what this man likes more, money or sheer villainy. He is no ordinary moneygrubber, he is a true poet of evil, a virtuoso engineer of cunning and cruelty. I am sure that the doctor derives pleasure from the erection of his brain-teasing constructions, and this time he has truly excelled himself by raising up a veritable Eiffel Tower. We have undercut this complicated structure, and it has collapsed, but its fragments appear to have caused substantial damage to the edifice of the Russian monarchy.'

I sighed heavily, thinking that the previous day's catastrophe could indeed lead to quite unforeseeable consequences. If only there was no uprising as a result. And it was frightening to think what the émigré newspapers and the press of hostile nations would write.

'I did not fully understand the allegory of the collapsed tower, but it seems to me, Erast, that you have precisely defined the most important feature of Lind's character,' Emilie said, nodding in agreement. 'He is truly a poet of evil. And of hate. This man is full of hate, he literally exudes it. If only you had heard how he pronounces your name! I am certain that settling accounts with you means just as much to him as this ill-fated diamond. By the way, did I understand the meaning of the doctor's curses correctly? You still have the stone?'

'Would you like to take a look at it?'

Fandorin took a folded handkerchief out of his pocket and extracted the diamond from it. The bluish facets drew in the rays of the morning sun and glittered with bright rainbow sparks.

'So much light,' Mademoiselle said thoughtfully, screwing her eyes up slightly against the unbearable radiance. 'I know what light that is. Over the centuries the stone has extinguished many lives, and they are all still shining there, inside it. I would wager that in the last few days the Orlov has begun to sparkle more brightly than ever, after absorbing new nourishment.'

She glanced at me, or rather at the top of my head, and said: 'Forgive me, Athanas. Yesterday I was too concerned with myself and I did not even ask what happened to you. Where did you get that purple lump on your head?'

'Ah yes, you know nothing about it!' I exclaimed. 'That is why you did not understand the Eiffel Tower.'

And I told her about the previous day's carnage at the Khodynsk Field, concluding my narrative with the words: 'Lind is not merely ruthless but also preternaturally cunning. Thousands of people were killed, but he survived unscathed.'

'No, no, this is more than just cunning,' said Mademoiselle, throwing up her hands, and the bedspread slipped off her shoulder.

The three of us would certainly have looked very strange to an outsider: Fandorin in a white tie, I in a torn jacket and Mademoiselle wrapped in a silk bedspread – we had no other clothing there for Emilie.

'I think Doctor Lind is one of those people who likes to kill two hares with one stone,' Mademoiselle continued. 'When we were running through that appalling underground passage, he said something to his men in German after you shouted about the exchange: "I have four matters to deal with in Moscow: the diamond, Fandorin, Prince Simeon and that Judas, Carr." From this I conclude, Erast, that your assumption about Lind play-acting jealousy is false. He was genuinely affronted by his lover's betrayal. And as for yesterday's catastrophe, most probably it was meant to serve a different purpose – to settle scores with the governor general of Moscow. If Lind had simply wanted to get away, he would have invented something less complicated and less risky. After all, he could have been trampled underfoot in the crush himself.'

'You are a very intelligent woman, Mademoiselle,' Erast Petrovich said in a serious voice. 'And so you think that the life of our lover of dyed carnations is in danger?'

'Undoubtedly. Lind is one of those people who never retreat or forgive. His failure will only further incite the hate that is seething and boiling inside him. You know, I formed the impression that those men attached some special, almost mystical significance to homosexuality. Lind's cut-throats did not simply fear or respect their leader; it seemed to me that they were in love with him – if that word is appropriate here. Lind is like a sultan in a harem, only instead of odalisques he is surrounded by thieves and murderers. I think you were right about Mr Carr – for Lind he was something like a lapdog or a greyhound, an occasion for mixing work and pleasure. I am certain the doctor will not forgive him for being unfaithful.'

'Then we have to save Carr.' Fandorin put his crumpled napkin down on the table and stood up. 'Emilie, we shall send you to the Hermitage, and you will warn the Englishman of the danger.'

'Are you suggesting I should appear in the palace wrapped in this rag?' Mademoiselle exclaimed indignantly. 'Not for the world! I would rather go back to the cellar!'

Erast Petrovich rubbed his chin, perplexed.

'Indeed. You are right. I had not thought of that. Ziukin, do you know anything about women's dresses, hats, shoes and all the rest of it?'

'Very little indeed,' I admitted.

'And I know even less. But there is nothing to be done. Let us give Emilie a chance to perform her morning toilette, while we make a visit to the shops on Myasnitskaya Street. We shall buy something there. Emilie, will you trust our taste?'

Mademoiselle pressed one hand to her heart.

'My dear gentlemen, I trust you in everything.'

We stopped at the Myasnitsky Gate and hesitantly surveyed the frontages of the ready-made-clothing shops.

'How do you like that one there?' Fandorin asked, pointing to a gleaming shop window bearing a sign – THE LATEST PARIS FASHIONS.

'I have heard Her Imperial Highness say that this season the fashion is for everything from London. And also let us not forget that Mademoiselle Declique does not have those things that a respectable lady cannot manage without.'

'In what s-sense?' Fandorin asked, staring at me dull-wittedly and I had to express my meaning more directly: 'Underclothes, stockings, pantaloons.'

'Yes, yes, indeed. I tell you what, Ziukin. I can see that you are a man well-informed about such matters. You give the orders.'

The first difficulties arose in the shoe shop. Looking at the piles of boxes, I suddenly realised that I had absolutely no idea what size we needed. But here Fandorin's keen powers of observation proved most helpful. He showed the salesman his open palm and said: 'That length plus one and a half inches. I think that will be just right.'

'And what style would you like?' the salesman asked, squirming obsequiously. 'We have prunellas on a three-quarter heel – the very latest chic. Or perhaps you would like satin lace-ups, Turkish sateen slippers, Russian leather bottines from Kimry, chaussurettes from Albin Picquot?'

We looked at each other.

'Give us the ones that are the latest chic,' Fandorin decided boldly and paid nineteen roubles and fifty kopecks.

We moved on, carrying a lilac-coloured box. The sight of this elegant cardboard construction reminded me of another container that I had not seen since the previous day.

'Where is the casket?' I asked, suddenly anxious. 'What if thieves should break in? You know Moscow is full of riff-raff.'

'Do not be c-concerned, Ziukin. I have hidden the casket where even the detective department of the police will not find it,' he reassured me.

We bought a dress and hat rather easily in the shop BEAU BRUMMEL. GOODS FROM LONDON. We were both rather taken by a dress of light straw-coloured barège with gold thread and a cape. Fandorin paid out a hundred and thirty-five roubles for it and upon my soul, it was well worth the money. The hat of lace tulle (my choice) cost twenty-five roubles. Erast Petrovich considered the paper violets on the crown excessive, but in my opinion they matched Emilie's eyes perfectly.

We had a hard time of it in the lady's underwear shop. We were delayed here for a long time because we were unable to give a proper answer to a single question that the saleswoman asked. Fandorin looked embarrassed and I wished the earth would open up and swallow me, especially when the shameless girl started enquiring about the size of the bust. It was in this shop that I overheard a conversation that completely spoiled my mood, so that I took no further part in discussing the purchases and relied entirely on Erast Petrovich.

Two ladies were talking to each other – in low voices, but I could hear everything quite clearly.

'... and the sovereign shed a tear and said: "This is a sign from above that I should not rule. I shall set aside the crown and go into a monastery, to spend the rest of my days praying for the souls of those who have been killed,"' said one of the women, a plump and self-important individual but, judging by her appearance, not from the very highest society. 'My Serge heard that with his own ears because yesterday he was His Majesty's duty orderly.'

'Such nobility of soul!' exclaimed her companion, a somewhat younger and simpler lady, gazing respectfully at the plump woman. 'But what about Simeon Alexandrovich? Is it true what they say, that he was the one who persuaded the tsar and tsarina to go to that ill-fated ball?'

I cautiously stole closer, pretending to be absorbed in studying some lacy bloomers with frills and ribbons.

'Absolutely true,' said the first woman, lowering her voice. 'Serge heard His Highness say: "It's nothing important. The hoi polloi have trampled each other in the rush to get hold of something for nothing. Stop playing the baby, Nicky, and get on with ruling."'

The fat lady seemed unlikely to have enough imagination to invent something like that. How like Simeon Alexandrovich it was to repeat word for word the phrase that was spoken to Alexander the Blessed by the killer of his father!

'Ah, Filippa Karlovna, but why did they have to go to the French ambassador's ball on such an evening?'

Filippa Karlovna sighed dolefully. 'What can I tell you Polinka? I can only repeat what Serge said: "When God wants to punish someone, He takes away their reason." You see, Count Montebello had ordered a hundred thousand roses to be brought from France especially for the ball. If the ball had been postponed, the roses would have withered. And so Their Majesties came to the rout but as a token of mourning they did not dance. And now there are rumours among the common folk that the tsar and his German woman danced with delight at knowing they had killed so many Orthodox souls. It's terrible, simply terrible!'

Oh Lord, I thought, what inexcusable frivolity! To set the whole of Russia against oneself for the sake of some roses! The Khodynsk Field tragedy could still have been explained by some unfortunate confluence of circumstances; an exemplary trial of the organisers of the revels could have been arranged – anything at all, as long as the authority of the supreme ruler was maintained. But now universal hatred would be directed not only against the governor general of Moscow, but also against the tsar and tsarina, and everybody would say roses are more important to them than people.

We walked back along the street, carrying numerous boxes and bundles. I do not know what Fandorin was thinking about, but he had an air of concentration – probably he was making plans for further action. With an effort I also forced myself to start thinking in practical terms: how could we find the fugitive Lord Banville and Mikhail Georgievich?

Suddenly I stopped dead in my tracks. 'And Freyby?' I exclaimed.

'What about Freyby?'

'We have forgotten all about him, but he is one of Lind's men too, that is obvious! And the doctor left him in the Hermitage for a good reason – to act as his spy! Why, of course!' I groaned, appalled at the belatedness of my realisation. 'Freyby behaved strangely from the beginning. On the very first day he said that there must be a spy in the house. He deliberately led us astray so that suspicion would not fall on him! And there is something else. I completely forgot to tell you. When Lieutenant Endlung and I set out to follow Banville and Carr, Freyby said to me: "Look more carefully today." I was struck by it at the time – as if he knew what I was going out to do!'

'"Look more carefully today"? That is what he said?' Fandorin asked in surprise.

'Yes, with the help of his dictionary.'

We were obliged to interrupt our conversation because we were already approaching the house.

Mademoiselle greeted us still wearing the same bedspread, but with her hair neatly brushed and smelling fragrant.

'Oh, presents!' she exclaimed, surveying our baggage with delight. 'Quick, quick!'

And she set about untying the ribbons and string right there in the hallway.

'*Mon Dieu, qu'est-ce que c'est?*'[1] Emilie muttered as she extracted the pantaloons chosen by Erast Petrovich from their pink packaging. '*Quelle horreur! Pour qui me prenez vous?*'[2]

Fandorin was a pitiful sight. His face fell completely when Mademoiselle declared that the pink corset with the lilac lacing was absolutely vulgar, only *coquettes* wore things like that and it exceeded her modest proportions by at least three sizes.

I was indignant. This man could not be trusted to do anything! I had only been distracted for a minute, and he had spoiled everything. The silk stockings were the only purchase he had made that received approval.

But there was a shock in store for me too. When she took the wonderful hat with violets that I liked so much out of its box, Mademoiselle first raised her eyebrows in surprise and then laughed. She ran across to the mirror and turned her head this way and that.

'*Un vrai épouvanteil!*'[3] was her pitiless judgement.

The remarkable dress of barège and the silk shoes, the latest Parisian chic, were judged no less harshly. 'I see, gentlemen, that in the most important things of all you are not to be trusted,' Emilie concluded with a sigh. 'But at least I can get to the Hermitage, and then change my clothes.'

Before he put Mademoiselle in the cab, Erast Petrovich gave her his final instructions.

'Tell them that Ziukin and I rescued you from captivity and we are continuing our search for Lind. Do not give away our address. You do not know that we have the Orlov and the other jewels. Rest and recover your strength. And one other thing.' He whispered although the coachman could not possibly have

---

[1] *My God, what is it?*
[2] *How horrible! Who do you take me for?*
[3] *A real scarecrow!*

understood French: 'As far as we can tell, Freyby is one of Lind's men. Keep an eye on him and take special care. But not a word about this to Karnovich, or the colonel might spoil everything in his eagerness. Definitely do tell him about Banville. Let the police join in the search, it will make Lind's life more difficult. Well that is all. Goodbye. If something urgent comes up, telephone. You know the number.'

He shook her hand. Ah, gloves, I thought. We had completely forgotten to buy her gloves!

'Goodbye, my friends,' Emilie said, fluttering her long eye-lashes and switching her gaze from Fandorin to me. 'I am eternally in your debt. You freed me from that dreadful cellar, where I was choking to death on the smell of rotten potatoes.' Her grey eyes glinted mischievously. 'It was very romantic, just like a novel about chivalrous knights. Although I have never heard of knights rescuing a beautiful lady from an enchanted castle with a yard keeper's crowbar before.'

She waved to us in farewell and the carriage set off towards the Myasnitsky Gate.

We gazed after her for a long time, until the cab disappeared round a bend. I glanced sideways at Fandorin. He looked thoughtful, even rather bewildered. Could this lady's man possibly have developed special feelings for Emilie?

'What next?' I asked in an emphatically cool voice.

Fandorin's face suddenly turned gloomy and determined, but he did not answer me straight away, only after a very lengthy pause indeed.

'Right, Ziukin, the women and the wagons are in a safe place. And we are b-back on the warpath. Doctor Lind is strolling around at liberty, and that means our mission has not been completed.'

'The most important thing is to save His Highness,' I reminded him. 'I hope that the desire for vengeance will not lead you to disregard Mikhail Georgievich's fate.'

He was embarrassed, it was quite obvious. That meant my reminder had been timely.

'Yes, yes, of course. But in any case we first need to reach our irrepressible doctor. How are we going to do it?'

'Through Freyby?' I said with a shrug. 'The butler must have some way to contact Lind.'

'I keep thinking about Mr Freyby,' said Erast Petrovich, climbing the steps and opening the door. 'Something there doesn't add up. If he really is Lind's man, then why would he warn us about a spy? And why would he tell you to keep a sharp eye on his master? There's something wrong here. Can you recall the exact words that he spoke?'

'I remember them very well. *"Vy . . . smotret' . . . luchshe . . . sevodnya."* He fished every word out of his dictionary.'

'Hmm. And what was it in English? "You . . . watch out today"?'

'No, that wasn't it.' I wrinkled up my forehead and tried to delve into my memory. 'It was something that began with "b".'

'With "b"? Better?'

'Yes, that was it!'

'Well then, let us try to reconstitute the English phrase. *Vy* is "you", *smotret'* is "see" or "look", then comes "better", and *sevodnya* is "today". "You see better today" makes no sense. So it must be "You look better today."'

'Yes, that's right! The very words!' I exclaimed in delight.

Erast Petrovich shrugged.

'Then I'm afraid that I must disappoint you, Ziukin. That is by no means a recommendation to keep a closer eye on Lind, but an expression that means, "You *are looking* better today."'

'Is that all?' I asked, disappointed.

'I'm afraid so. You and Mr Freyby have fallen victim to literal translation.'

Fandorin seemed proud of his little victory. Naturally. The previous day's embarrassment over Banville had left his glorious reputation as an analytical genius badly tarnished.

'You should never place too much confidence in dictionaries.

But he gave you very good advice about the spy. I should have thought about that from the very beginning. There was definitely someone in the Hermitage spying for Lind. The doctor knew everything: the times of arrivals, the daily routine, even where you went for a walk and who was in the company. Banville, Carr and Freyby arrived too late. They simply could not have found out all those things in time.'

'Then who is the spy?'

'Let us think.' Erast Petrovich sat down on a couch in the drawing room and crossed one leg over the other. 'Wait . . . Why, of course!' He slapped himself on the knee. 'Did you hear the Postman call out "Ziukin" yesterday at the Khodynka?'

'Of course I did.'

'But how did he know that you were Ziukin? Were you acquainted with him?'

'No, but he saw me at the post office, and naturally he remembered me.'

'Who did he see at the post office?' asked Erast Petrovich, jumping to his feet. 'An official of the Ministry of Agriculture and State Lands. The Postman was supposed to think you were Fandorin in disguise, but somehow or other he realised who you were, although he had never seen you before. Just what is the source of such incredible astuteness?'

'Well, obviously Lind explained it to him later,' I suggested.

'Very well, that is also possible. But how did the doctor know that you were involved in the operation? The letter in which I arranged the meeting was written in my name, without any mention of you. Did you tell anyone that you were now assisting me in this risky business?'

I hesitated for a moment, and then decided there was no point in being secretive in such important matters.

'When we were in the Hermitage I told two people about our plans. But when I explain how it happened, you will understand I had no other—'

'Who?' Erast Petrovich asked quickly. 'The names!'

'Her Highness—'

'You saw Xenia?' he interrupted excitedly. 'What did she say?'

I replied coolly: 'Nothing. She hid me, and that was enough.'

'And who was the other person?' Fandorin asked with a sigh.

'My Moscow assistant, Somov. He proved to be an honourable man. Not only did he not give me away, he even promised to help...'

I related the content of my conversation with Somov, trying to recall everything in precise detail.

'Well then, Somov is our spy,' Erast Petrovich said with a shrug. 'That is as clear as day. He was based at the Hermitage before you arrived from St Petersburg. He had a thorough knowledge of the house and the disposition of the rooms. He must have made a careful study of the park and identified the spot for the ambush. It was easy to guess that after an exhausting journey the child would be taken out for a walk. And apart from Somov no one could have informed Lind that you were working for me.'

I said nothing. There were no objections I could raise against what Fandorin had said, but I had already formed an opinion of Somov that I was reluctant to abandon.

'I see you are doubtful. Very well, let us make certain. You told me that Somov had moved into your room? That means he has a telephone there. Telephone him. Say we are in a desperate situation and need his help.'

'And then what?'

'And then g-give the phone to me.'

I told the lady operator the number, Erast Petrovich pressed the second earpiece to his ear and we waited. For a very long time there was nothing but the ringing tone, and I had already decided that Kornei Selifanovich must be busy dealing with household matters in some distant corner of the palace, but after about three minutes there was a click and Somov's breathless voice.

'Hermitage. What can I do for you?'

'Listen and do not say a word,' I said. 'Do you recognise me?'

'Yes,' he replied after a pause.

'Are you still prepared to help us?'

'Yes.' This time there was not the slightest delay.

'We have to meet.'

'I . . . I can't just now. You can't imagine what's going on here. Mr Carr has been found dead! Just now! I walked in and he was lying in his room with a knife stuck in his chest. A kitchen knife, for filleting white fish. The police have turned the entire house upside down and they're scouring the garden!'

'Ask how long ago he was killed,' Erast Petrovich whispered.

'How long ago was he killed?' I asked.

'What? How should I know? Wait, I do know! I heard the gentlemen from the court police say that the body was still very warm.'

'That Lind is no man, he's a devil!' I whispered with my hand over the receiver. 'He carries on settling scores, no matter what!'

'Ask if Emilie has got back.'

'Tell me, Kornei Selifanovich, has Mademoiselle Declique shown up yet?'

'Mademoiselle? Why, has she been found?' Somov's voice trembled. 'Do you know something about her?'

There had to be some reason why he was so agitated, there had to be. I immediately recalled how he had pestered Emilie with his French lessons. Perhaps Fandorin was not so far wrong in suspecting him!

'Surely Banville would not have dared to go back into the Hermitage?' I asked Erast Petrovich. 'That's simply incredible!'

'Of course it's incredible,' he remarked coolly. 'Carr was stabbed by Somov. He certainly knows all about kitchen knives.'

'I can't hear anything!' said the voice in the receiver. 'Afanasii Stepanovich, where are you? How can I find you?'

Fandorin took the mouthpiece from me.

'This is Fandorin here. Hello, Somov. I would like to see you. If you value the life of His Highness, leave the house immediately by the back entrance, walk through the park and in thirty minutes, no later, be at the Donskoi Cemetery, by the wall opposite the entrance. Delay may be fatal.'

And he hung up, without waiting for a reply.

'Why such a rush?' I asked.

'I do not want him to meet Emilie, who will reach the Hermitage at any moment now. We don't want Somov to get the idea of eliminating a dangerous witness. You heard how agitated he was. If the audacity with which Somov killed Carr is anything to go by, your estimable assistant was planning to make a run for it in any case.'

I shook my head, far from convinced that it was Somov who had killed Carr.

'Right, Afanasii Stepanovich,' said Fandorin, putting his little revolver in his pocket. Then he took another pistol of rather more impressive proportions out of his travelling bag and stuck it into his belt. 'This is where our p-paths part. I shall meet Somov and have a good talk with him.'

'What does "a good talk" mean?'

'I shall tell him that he has been discovered and offer him a choice: to serve hard labour for life or to help catch Lind.'

'And what if you are mistaken, and he is not guilty of anything?'

'I shall understand that from the way he behaves. But Somov is the spy, I am certain of it.'

I followed Erast Petrovich round the room, observing his preparations. Everything was happening too fast. I had no time to gather my thoughts.

'But why do we have to separate?'

'Because if Somov is Lind's man, it is highly likely that at this very moment he is telephoning his boss, and the welcome awaiting me at the cemetery will be somewhat hotter than I was counting on. Although of course they have no time at all to prepare. But it's a convenient spot, isolated.'

'All the more reason why I must go with you!'

'No, Ziukin. You must stay here and guard this.'

Erast Petrovich put his hand in his pocket and pulled out the diamond, wrapped in his handkerchief. I held out my hand reverently and felt the strange warmth radiating from the sacred stone.

Fandorin swung round on his heels and went out into the corridor. I stayed close behind. In the kitchen doorway Erast Petrovich squatted down on his haunches, hooked up one of the floorboards, and a moment later he was holding the familiar casket.

'There you are, Ziukin, now I d-do not owe the House of Romanov anything. You can be regarded as a plenipotentiary representative of the royal family, surely?' He smiled briefly. 'The important thing is, never leave the telephone. I shall definitely call you.'

'Where from?'

'I do not know yet. From some hotel, restaurant or post office.'

In the doorway Fandorin turned and looked back at me. His glance seemed strange, as if there was something he could not bring himself to tell me, or he was hesitating over what to do next. I did not like this at all; in fact, to tell the truth, I was frightened that he might have changed his mind and intended to take the jewels with him.

I took a step back, tightening my grip on the casket, and said: 'You'll be late. It's a long way. What if Somov doesn't wait for you?'

'He will,' Fandorin replied absent-mindedly, clearly thinking about something else. Could that possibly be pity in his eyes? 'Listen, Afanasii Stepanovich . . .'

'What?' I asked cautiously, sensing that he was about to tell me something very important.

'No . . . never mind. Wait for my call.'

He turned and left.

What an abominable way to behave!

★

339

I made myself as comfortable as possible beside the telephone.

Judging that Fandorin could not call me during the next hour in any case, I took some money (Erast Petrovich had left an entire wad of banknotes on the table), went to Myasnitskaya Street and bought fresh cod, some remarkable Moscow ham and newspapers. I took the casket with me, pressing it close to me with my elbow and keeping a keen lookout to spot any thieves who might be loitering nearby. The Orlov was hanging round my neck, in a bag specially made out of a woollen sock.

Weary of all the shocks it had endured, my heart had also been tempered and toughened by them. Only a few days earlier I would scarcely have been able to sit there so calmly, drinking tea, eating and looking through the newspapers. As the common folk would say, a few of my corners had been knocked off.

The Moscow newspapers did not exactly pass over the Khodynsk Field disaster in silence – how could they, when the entire city was filled with wailing and weeping? But they wrote evasively, laying the greatest emphasis on the charitable actions of members of the imperial family. A certain fitting delicacy and concern for the authority of the dynasty could be discerned in that.

For example, the *Moscow Gazette* gave a highly detailed description of a visit to the Staro-Ekaterinskaya Hospital by the dowager empress, during which Her Majesty gave each of the victims a bottle of Madeira. The emperor and empress had given instructions for the funerals to be paid for by the treasury and families who had lost their breadwinner were awarded compensation. This was indeed a most noble gesture, but it seemed to me that the newspaper was excessively admiring of Their Majesties' generosity, making no comment on the reason for the royal benefaction. The people of Moscow were unlikely to find the tone of the article to their taste. And I was totally dismayed by the *Moscow Illustrated Newspaper*, which could think of nothing better than to reproduce the artistically designed menu for the forthcoming supper for three thousand in the Faceted Palace:

LUCULLAN BOUILLON

ASSORTED PIES

COLD HAZEL GROUSE À LA SUVOROV

CHICKENS ROASTED ON THE SPIT

SALAD

WHOLE ASPARAGUS

ICE CREAM

DESSERT

That is to say, I could see perfectly well that, owing to the sad events, the menu that had been drawn up was modest in the extreme, with no extravagances at all. Only a single salad? No sturgeon, no stuffed pheasants or even black caviar! A truly spartan meal. The highly placed individuals who had been invited to the supper would appreciate the significance of this. But why print such a thing in a newspaper that had many readers for whom 'dog's delight' sausage was a treat?

On sober consideration, what I detected in all of this was not concern for the prestige of the authorities but rather the diametrical opposite. Obviously, Simeon Alexandrovich and the high police master had forbidden the newspapers to write openly about what had happened, and so the editors were doing their best, each in his own way, to inflame the resentment of the common people.

Feeling very upset, I put the newspapers aside and gazed out of the window. This occupation, which appears so pointless at first glance, is excellent for calming agitated nerves, especially on a clear May evening, when the shadows are so soft and golden, the trees are still growing accustomed to their newly acquired foliage and the sky is clear and serene.

I spent a rather long time in quiet contemplation free of all thoughts. And when the outlines of the houses were completely blurred and then effaced by the twilight, and the street lamps came on, the telephone rang.

'Listen carefully and d-do not interrupt,' I heard Fandorin's voice say. 'Do you know the Vorobyovsky Hills?'

'Yes, they're not far from—'

'There's a decorative p-park there. We saw it from the boat, remember? Do you remember the bridge suspended on cables over the ravine? I told you I had seen one almost exactly like it in the Himalayas?'

'Yes, I remember, but why are you telling me all this?'

'Be there tomorrow morning. At six. Bring the stone and the casket.'

'Why? What has ha—'

'Yes, and one more thing,' he said, interrupting me unceremoniously. 'Do not be surprised as I shall be dressed as a monk. I might well be late, but you, Ziukin, be there on time. Do you understand all that?'

'Yes, that is no. I don't understand a single—'

I heard the disconnect signal and slammed the receiver down in extreme indignation. How dare he talk to me in that fashion? He had not explained anything; he had not told me anything! How had his meeting with Somov gone? Where was Fandorin now? Why was he not coming back here? And, most importantly, why did I have to take the jewels to such a strange place?

I suddenly recalled the strange expression with which he had looked at me when we parted. What was it he had wanted to tell me as he left, but had not been able to bring himself to say?

He had said: 'This is where our paths part.' What if our paths had parted not only in the literal but also the figurative sense? Oh Lord, and I had no one to ask for advice!

I sat there, looking at the silent telephone and thinking intently.

Karnovich? Out of the question.

Lasovsky? I could assume that he had been removed from his post, and even if he had not been removed . . .

Endlung? Of course. He was a fine chap. But he would be no help in a such a puzzling business.

Emilie! She was the one who could help me.

342

I had to telephone the Hermitage, I realised, and ask for Mademoiselle Declique in a disguised voice, preferably a female one . . . And at that very moment the telephone came to life and began ringing desperately. God be praised! So Fandorin was not quite such an ignorant fellow as I had supposed. We had simply been cut off.

I deliberately spoke first, so that he would not have a chance to shock me with some new trick in his usual manner.

'Before I do as you demand, be so good as to explain,' I said hurriedly, 'what happened with Somov? And why disguise yourself as a monk? Could you not find any other costume? This is sacrilege!'

'*Mon Dieu*, what are you saying, Athanas?' Mademoiselle's voice said and I choked, but only for a moment.

It was simply wonderful that she had phoned me herself!

'Who were you talking to?' Emilie asked, changing into French.

'Fandorin,' I mumbled.

'What monk? What has Somov got to do with anything? I'm ringing from his room, your old room, that is. Somov has gone missing; no one knows where he is. But that is not important. Carr has been killed!'

'Yes, yes, I know.'

'You know? How?' She sounded amazed. 'All the grand dukes are here, and Colonel Karnovich. He has been interrogating Freyby for several hours. The poor colonel has completely lost his head. He took almost no notice of my arrival – all he said to me was: "You can tell me later; it's not important just now." I try to tell him about Lord Banville, but he does not believe me! He tells me I am mentally disturbed because of all the shocks. Can you believe it? He imagines that Freyby is Doctor Lind! I want to ask you and Erast for advice. Perhaps I should try once again? Explain to Karnovich that Freyby is only a minor figure? Or perhaps tell him that you have found the empress's stolen jewels?

Then all these gentlemen will calm down and start listening to me. What should I do?'

'Emilie, I am in need of advice myself,' I confessed. 'Never mind about Mr Freyby. I don't think he is guilty of anything, but let Karnovich carry on questioning him. At least that will keep him busy. Don't tell anyone about the jewels. I have a different idea . . .'

I hesitated, because the idea had only just occurred to me and it had not been properly formulated yet. I picked the telephone book up off the table and opened it at the letter 'p'. Was the Vorobyovsky Park listed?

As I leafed through the pages, I said what I would not have been able to say if Emilie had been standing there in front of me: 'I am so glad to hear your voice. I was feeling completely lost and alone, but now I feel much better. I hope I am not speaking too boldly?'

'Good Lord, Athanas, sometimes your formality makes you quite insufferable!' she exclaimed. 'Are you never going to say the words that I long to hear? Simply and clearly, with no quibbling or evasion?'

I guessed immediately which words she wanted to hear, and my throat went dry.

'I don't entirely understand,' I croaked, nonplussed by her directness. 'I think I have already said far more than might be considered acceptable, bearing in mind—'

'There you go humming and hawing again,' Mademoiselle interrupted me. 'All right, damn you. I'll shake your declaration out of you when we meet. But in the meantime tell me your idea. Only be quick. Someone could come in at any moment.'

I told her about Fandorin's strange demands.

Emilie listened without saying a word.

'I intend to act differently,' I said. 'Let us meet and I shall give you the casket and the Orlov. At dawn I shall go to the meeting place and demand an explanation from Fandorin. If his answers satisfy me and I realise that he really does need the stone for this

344

business, I shall telephone you from the office in the Vorobyovsky Park. There is an apparatus there, I have just checked. Be ready. From the Hermitage to the Vorobyovsky Park is a fifteen-minute ride in a cab. Fandorin will not lose much time as a result of these precautions.'

I heard her breathing in the earpiece, and that quiet music warmed my heart.

'No,' Emilie said after a long pause. 'I do not like your idea at all, Athanas. Firstly, I am not sure that I will be able to leave the Hermitage unnoticed today. Secondly, I am afraid that we will cause problems for Erast. I trust him. And you should trust him too. He is a truly noble man. More than that, he is an exceptional man. I have never met anyone else like him in my life. If you want the little prince to be rescued, go to the meeting with Erast and do exactly as he says.'

Her verdict shocked me, and in the most unpleasant way. She had even spoken like Fandorin: 'Firstly ... Secondly ...' How clever this man was at making people adore him!

I asked in a trembling voice: 'You trust him that far?'

'Yes. Implicitly,' she snapped, and suddenly laughed. 'Naturally, apart from dresses and corsets.'

What an incredible woman – joking at such a moment! But she was immediately serious again.

'I implore you, Athanas, do everything that he says.' She hesitated. 'And also ... be careful. For my sake.'

'For your sake?' I asked stupidly, which of course I should not have done, because no self-respecting lady could possibly have expressed herself more clearly.

But Mademoiselle repeated: 'Yes, for my sake. If anything happens to Mr Fandorin, even though he is a genuine hero and an exceptional man, I can survive.' She hesitated again. 'But if anything happens to you, I am afraid ...'

She did not finish the sentence, and there was no need for her to.

Totally and completely unsettled, I babbled in a pathetic voice:

'Thank you, Mademoiselle Declique. I shall make sure to contact you tomorrow morning.'

Then I quickly hung up.

Oh Lord, had I imagined it? And had I understood the meaning of her words correctly?

Need I say that I did not sleep a wink all night long until the dawn?

20 May

In accordance with my invariable habit, I reached the meeting place earlier than the appointed time.

At twenty minutes to six I arrived in a cab at the main avenue of the Vorobyovsky Park, which was entirely deserted at that early hour. As I walked along a sandy path, I glanced absent-mindedly to the left, where the city lay shrouded in blue-grey shadows, and screwed my eyes up against the bright sunlight. The view was very beautiful, and the morning freshness of the air set my head spinning, but my state of mind was not conducive to poetic ecstasy. My heart alternately stood still and pounded furiously. I pressed the casket firmly against myself with my right hand, and beneath my undershirt the two-hundred-carat diamond swayed very slightly against my chest. A strange thought came to me: how much was I, Afanasii Ziukin, worth just at that moment? To the Romanov dynasty I was worth a great deal, immeasurably more than Ziukin without the casket and the Orlov dangling in a woollen sock on a ribbon. But to myself I was worth exactly as much as I had been a week or a year earlier. And for Emilie too my value had probably not changed a jot because of all these diamonds, rubies and sapphires.

This realisation lent me strength. I no longer felt like a pitiful unworthy vessel chosen by the mere whim of fate as a temporary shrine for priceless treasures, but the defender and saviour of the dynasty.

As I approached the bushes behind which the hanging bridge

should be located, I glanced at my watch again. A quarter to six.

A few more steps, and the ravine came into sight, the dew on its steep grassy slopes glinting with a cold metallic gleam. From down below came the murmur of a stream, invisible under the light swirling mist. But my glance only slid over the fissure in passing and immediately turned to the narrow bridge. It turned out that Fandorin had arrived even earlier and was waiting for me.

With a wave of his hand he moved quickly towards me, striding confidently along the gently swaying ribbon of wood. Neither the baggy monk's habit nor the black hood with the mantle falling to his shoulders could conceal the grace of his erect figure. We were separated by a distance of no more than twenty paces. The sun was shining from behind his back, and this suddenly made it look as if the black silhouette with its glowing halo was descending towards me directly from the heavens along a slim ray of gold.

Shielding my eyes with one hand, I took hold of the cable that served as a handrail with the other and stepped onto the bridge, which swayed elastically beneath my feet.

After that everything happened very quickly. So quickly that I did not even have the time to take another step.

On the opposite side of the ravine a slim black figure dashed towards the bridge. I saw that one of its hands was longer than the other and glinted brightly in the sun. The barrel of a revolver!

'Look out!' I shouted, and Fandorin swung round with lightning speed, poking a hand clutching a small revolver out of the sleeve of his habit.

Erast Petrovich swayed, evidently blinded by the rays of the sun, but fired at the same moment. Following an interval so very brief that it was almost impossible to hear, Lind's weapon also roared.

They both hit the target.

The slim figure on the far side of the ravine tumbled over onto its back, but Fandorin was also thrown back and to one side. He clutched the cable with one hand and for a brief moment stayed on his feet – I caught a glimpse of a white face bisected by a thin strip of moustache before it disappeared behind the crêpe curtain of the mantle. Then Erast Petrovich swayed, tumbled over the cable and plunged down.

The bridge jerked to the left and the right as if it was drunk, and I was obliged to clutch the cable with both hands. The casket slipped out from under my elbow, struck a plank, then a rock and split apart, and Her Majesty's jewels fell into the grass, shooting out a glimmering spray of coloured light.

The double echo of the shots rumbled along the ravine and then dissolved. It became very quiet again. There were birds singing and somewhere in the distance a factory whistle hooted to announce the start of a shift. Then I heard a rapid regular knocking, like the rattling of a tea glass in its metal holder on a train as it hurtles along at top speed.

It took me some time to realise that it was my teeth chattering.

The body on the far side of the ravine lay motionless.

The other, its form widened by the spreadeagled black habit, lay below me, at the very edge of the stream. The mist that had lined the bottom of the ravine only a minute earlier was thinner now, and I could see that one of the body's hands was dangling lifelessly into the water. There could be no hope that Fandorin was alive after such a fall – the crunch of the impact with the ground had been far too fearsome.

I had not liked this man. Perhaps I had even hated him. At least I had wanted him to disappear from our lives once and for all. But I had not wished his death.

His trade was risk – he constantly toyed with danger – but somehow I had not thought that he could be killed. He had seemed immortal to me.

I do know how long I stood there, clutching the cable and looking down. Perhaps for a moment, perhaps for an hour.

I was brought back to my senses by a spot of sunlight that leapt out of the grass straight into my eye. I started, gazed in incomprehension at the source of the light and saw the yellow star-shaped diamonds of the tiara. I stepped off the bridge onto the ground in order to gather up the scattered treasures but then did not do it. They were safe enough where they were.

Whatever he may have been like, Fandorin had not deserved this, to be left lying like carrion on the wet gravel. I crossed myself and began making my way down. I slipped twice but did not fall.

I stood over the dead man not knowing what to do. Suddenly, making up my mind, I leaned down, took hold of his shoulders and began to turn him over onto his back. I do not know why. It was simply unbearable to see how he, always so elegant and so full of life, lay there with his broken body arched grotesquely while the rapid water stirred his lifeless hand.

Fandorin proved a lot lighter than I had expected and I turned him over with no great difficulty. I hesitated briefly, then threw the bundled-up mantle back off the face and . . .

No, here I must break off. Because I do not know how to describe my feelings at that moment, when I saw the black moustache pasted onto the face and the trickle of scarlet blood flowing from the dead Mademoiselle Declique's mouth. Probably I did not feel anything at all. Obviously I must have suffered a kind of *paralysie émotionelle*[1] – I do not know how to say it in Russian. I did not feel anything, I did not understand anything; for some reason I simply kept trying to wipe the blood off Emilie's pale lips, but the blood kept flowing and it was impossible to stop.

'Is she dead?' someone shouted down to me.

Not surprised at all, I slowly raised my head.

Fandorin was making his way down the opposite slope of the ravine, clutching his shoulder.

His face seemed unnaturally white to me, and there were drops of red seeping between his fingers.

★

---

[1] *Emotional paralysis.*

Fandorin spoke and I listened. I was feeling rather unsteady, and because of that for most of the time I looked down at the ground, to make sure that it did not completely disappear from under my feet.

'I guessed yesterday morning, as we were seeing her off to the Hermitage. Do you remember that she joked about knights with a yard keeper's crowbar? That was careless. How could a prisoner who was chained in the cellar see you and me breaking in the door with the yard keeper's crowbar? She was unlikely even to have heard the noise. Only someone who was peeping from behind a curtain could have observed what we were doing.'

Erast Petrovich grimaced as he bathed his wounded shoulder with water from the stream.

'Can't tell if the bone was hit ... I don't think so. At least it was small calibre. But such accuracy! Against the sun, without aiming! An incredible woman ... And so, after her strange words about the crowbar, the scales fell from my eyes, so to speak. I wondered exactly why the bandits had kept Emilie in her negligee? After all, sexual harassment by this band of misogynists was out of the question; indeed, from what she said they must have found the very sight of the female body repulsive. And now recall the items of men's clothing scattered about in the house. It's all very simple, Afanasii Stepanovich. You and I caught Lind by surprise and, instead of running, he (if you don't mind, I shall speak about the doctor as a male, as I am accustomed to doing) made a bold move. He threw off his male clothing, hastily pulled on a woman's shift from Mademoiselle Declique's wardrobe, went down into the cellar and chained himself to the wall. Lind had very little time. He was not even able to hide the casket.'

Slowly and cautiously, an inch at a time, I transferred my glance to the recumbent body. I wanted to take another look at the lifeless face, but I did not get that far – my eye was caught by a dark bruise showing from under the open collar of the habit. It was an old bruise, one I had seen in the apartment on

Arkhangelsky Lane. And then the dense shroud of fog enveloping my brain suddenly quivered and thinned.

'But what about the bruises and contusions?' I shouted. 'She didn't beat herself! No. Everything you say is lies! There has been a terrible mistake!'

Fandorin grabbed my elbow with a vice-like hand and shook me.

'Calm down. The bruises and contusions were from Khodynsk Field. He was seriously battered there as well. After all, he was caught in just as bad a crush as we were.'

Yes. Yes. Fandorin was right. The shroud of fog enveloped me once again in its protective mantle, and I was able to carry on listening.

'I have had enough time to reconstruct the entire plan of Lind's Moscow operation.' Erast Petrovich ripped a handkerchief apart with his teeth, bound up his wound crudely and wiped large beads of sweat off his forehead. 'The doctor made his preparations unhurriedly, well in advance. After all, everyone already knew when the coronation would be last year. The idea was brilliant – to blackmail the entire imperial house. Lind calculated that fear of a worldwide scandal would drive the Romanovs to make any sacrifice. The doctor chose an excellent position for managing his operation – inside the very family against whom he intended to strike. Who would ever suspect the excellent governess of such an outrage? With his extensive connections, it was not hard for Lind to forge references. He gathered together an entire t-team. In addition to his usual helpers, he engaged the Warsaw bandits and they put him in touch with the Khitrovka gang. Oh, this man was a truly remarkable strategist!'

Fandorin looked thoughtfully at the woman lying at his feet. 'It is strange that I cannot say "she" and "she was" about Lind...'

I finally managed to force myself to look at Emilie's dead face. It was calm and mysterious, and a bloated black fly had settled on the tip of her snub nose. I squatted down and drove the vile insect away.

'But, after all, the most important secret of the doctor's power was precisely femininity. It was a very strange gang, Ziukin, a gang of extortionists and murderers ruled by love. All of Lind's men were in love with him – with her, each in his own way. "Mademoiselle Declique's" true genius was that this woman was able to find the key to any man's heart, even a heart absolutely unequipped for love.'

I sensed his gaze on me, but I did not look up. There were already two flies circling above Emilie's face; they had to be driven away.

'Do you know what Somov told me b-before he died, Ziukin?'

'Is he dead too?' I asked indifferently.

Just at that moment I noticed an entire colony of ants climbing up Emilie's sleeve, so I had plenty to keep me busy.

'Yes, I checked him very simply. I turned my back to him. And of course he immediately attempted to take advantage of my apparent g-gullibility. There was a short struggle, which ended with your assistant impaling himself on his own knife. Even as he wheezed his last, he was still struggling to reach for my throat. I am not easily frightened but by God the sight of such a frenzy sent cold shivers running down my spine. I shouted at him: "What, what did you all find in her?" And do you know what answer he gave me, Ziukin? "Love." That was the final word he spoke. Oh, she knew how to inspire love. I believe you too felt the influence of Doctor Lind's charms, did you not? I'm afraid that you were too scrupulous altogether. As far as I can tell, Somov fared better than you did. I found this on him.'

He took a small silk bag out of his pocket and extracted a lock of chestnut hair from it. I recognised the hair immediately as Emilie's. So that was the kind of French lessons they had. But there was no time for me to feel upset. The cursed flies had performed an outflanking manoeuvre and I caught one, the most persistent, on Mademoiselle's ear.

'Now it is clear why Doctor Lind had no women friends and was regarded as a m-misogynist. Homosexuality has nothing to do with it. Emilie cunningly led us astray by laying a false trail. We must assume that Lord Banville left the empire long ago, after making the poor boy Glinsky pay for the loss of his lover. Ah the exquisite Mr Carr, the innocuous fancier of blue carnations and green forget-me-nots! He was killed to make us even more sure that Lind was Lord Banville. While you and I played the idiot and chose pantaloons and stockings for the doctor, Mademoiselle must have searched the apartment, failed to find the casket or the Orlov and decided to make another move in her complicated game by telephoning Somov at the Hermitage and ordering him to do away with Carr. The operation was entering its final stage. Lind had to get back the jewels and take possession of the diamond.'

'No!' I exclaimed, overcome by a sudden horror. 'No, there's something wrong here! You are mistaken after all!'

He gaped at me in amazement, and I, choking on my sobs, told him about my last telephone conversation with Emilie.

'If . . . if she was Doctor Lind, then why did she refuse? I . . . myself offered to give her the casket and the diamond! She would not take them! She said she trusted you and I must not get in your way.'

But this did not unsettle Fandorin at all. 'Naturally,' he said, nodding. 'The loot on its own was not enough for the doctor. He – dammit, I mean *she* – wanted my head as well. Once she had found out the time and place of the meeting from you, she had the opportunity to conclude her Moscow operation at a single stroke. In a most triumphant manner, redressing all the failures and settling all accounts in full.'

Erast Petrovich hesitated. He looked as if he was feeling guilty and intended to beg my pardon.

I was not mistaken – he did indeed start to apologise: 'Afanasii Stepanovich, I have treated you cruelly. I used you without explaining anything to you or taking you into my confidence. But I could not tell you the truth. You were captivated by Emilie and would never have believed me. Yesterday evening I deliberately spoke abruptly to you on the telephone and did not g-give you any information. I needed to provoke your s-suspicion. I knew that, assailed by doubts, you would turn for advice to the only person you trusted, Mademoiselle Declique. And you would tell her everything. I also chose the monk's clothes deliberately. Lind, with his – O Lord, with *her* – uncanny quick-wittedness, was bound to realise what a convenient costume it would be for her.

'The hood, the black mantle and the habit make it possible to mask both the figure and the face. I told Lind the plan of action myself, through you. Mademoiselle was well aware of your habit of arriving everywhere ahead of time. She reached the bridge at twenty minutes past five and waited. I had warned you that I might be late, and so she had no doubt that you would be the first to arrive. She would have time to take the jewels from you and prepare to meet me. But I took up a position in the bushes at half past four. I could have shot Lind sooner, before you arrived, without exposing myself to any risk, but God only knows what you would have imagined afterwards. You would never have believed that Mademoiselle Declique was guilty unless she proved it to you herself. Which she did in quite excellent fashion. Of course that has cost me a bullet hole in my shoulder, and if the sun had not been shining in her eyes the outcome of the duel would have been even sadder for me ...'

I was not thinking about anything at that moment, simply listening.

Fandorin looked from me to the dead woman and narrowed his cold blue eyes. 'What I do not know is what she intended to do with you,' he said pensively. 'Simply kill you? Or perhaps win you over to her side? What do you think? Could she have done that? Would a quarter of an hour have been enough for you to forget everything else for the sake of love?'

Something stirred inside me at those words. Not quite resentment, not quite anger – a bad kind of feeling, but faint, very faint.

And at the same time I remembered that there was something that I simply, absolutely had to ask.

Ah yes.

'What about Mikhail Georgievich? Where is he?'

A shadow flitted across Fandorin's face – pale and tired but still very handsome.

'Do you still have to ask? The boy was killed, I think on that day when you tried to save him by chasing after the carriage. Lind decided that he would take no more risks and chose Mademoiselle Declique – that is himself – as the intermediary instead of you. Or perhaps that is how it was planned from the very beginning. Our Emilie played her role quite brilliantly. To make everything completely credible she even led us to the vault, from which it was so convenient to escape through an underground passage. She would have got away with everything if not for my little surprise with the coachman.'

'But on that day His Highness was still alive!'

'What makes you think so? It was Lind, that is Emilie, who shouted up to us that the child was alive. The little mite had already been lying dead for days somewhere, at the bottom of a river or in an unmarked grave. And the most revolting thing is that before they killed the child, they cut off his finger while he was still alive.'

It was impossible to believe such things. 'How can you know that? You weren't there, were you?'

Erast Petrovich frowned.

'But I saw the finger. It was clear from the droplets of dried blood that it had not been amputated from a dead body. That is why I continued to believe for so long that the child might be ill and drugged but was still alive.'

I looked at Emilie again, this time I looked long and hard. That is Doctor Lind, I told myself, the one who tortured and killed Mikhail Georgievich. But Lind was Lind, and Emilie was Emilie. There had not been any connection between them.

'Ziukin! Afanasii Stepanovich, wake up!'

I slowly turned towards Fandorin, not understanding what else he wanted from me.

Erast Petrovich was grimacing in pain as he pulled on his frock coat.

'I shall have to disappear. I have eliminated Lind, saved the Orlov and recovered Her Majesty's jewels, but I was not able to save the grand duke. The emperor has no more use for me, and the Moscow authorities have cherished their animosity towards me for a long time. I shall go abroad; there is nothing more for me to do here. Only . . .'

He waved his hand through the air as if he wished to say something but could not make up his mind.

'I wish to ask to ask you a favour. Please tell Xenia Georgievna . . . that I have thought a lot about our argument . . . and I am no longer so convinced that I was right . . . And give her this.' He handed me a sheet of paper. 'It is an address in Paris through which she can contact me. Will you give it to her?'

'Yes,' I said in a wooden voice, putting the paper away in my pocket.

'Well, g-goodbye.'

The grass rustled as Fandorin scrambled up the slope. I did not watch him go.

He swore once – he must have jolted his wounded shoulder – but even so I did not look round.

I realised that I would have to collect up the scattered jewels: the tiara, the diamond clasp, the collar, the small bouquet, the fountain aigrette. But, most important of all, what was I to do with Mademoiselle Declique? Of course I could walk up to the park office and bring some attendants – they would carry the body up the slope. But I couldn't leave Emilie here alone, for the ants to crawl over her and the flies to settle on her face.

On the other hand, even though she was not heavy (after all, I had already carried her in my arms), would I be able to carry her up such a steep slope on my own?

I supposed it was worth trying.

'... most profound gratitude to Divine Providence for having preserved this sacred symbol of the tsar's power for Russia.'

His Majesty's voice trembled and the sovereign paused in order to control a sudden surge of emotion. The empress made the sign of the cross, and the tsar immediately followed her example and also bowed to the icon hanging in the corner.

No one else present crossed themselves. Nor did I.

The royal audience had been granted to me in the large drawing room of the Hermitage. Despite the solemn significance of the event, only those privy to the circumstances of the drama that had been played out were present: members of the royal family, Colonel Karnovich and Lieutenant Endlung.

Everyone was wearing mourning armbands as on that day it had been announced that His Highness Mikhail Georgievich had died in a suburban palace from a sudden attack of measles. Since it was known that all the younger Georgieviches were suffering from this dangerous illness, the news seemed credible, although of course certain dark fantastic rumours had already begun to spread. However, the truth was far too unlikely for anyone to believe.

Xenia Georgievna and Pavel Georgievich stood there with their eyes wet with tears, but Georgii Alexandrovich kept himself in hand. Kirill Alexandrovich looked impassive. One could only assume that from his point of view a most wretched story had concluded in a fashion that was not the most catastrophic possible. From time to time Simeon Alexandrovich dabbed his red eyes with a scented handkerchief, however I suspect that he was not sighing for the little prince so much as for a certain Englishman with straw-yellow hair.

Having regained control of his voice, His Majesty continued: 'However, it would be unjust to thank the Almighty without rewarding the individual whom the Lord chose as His own good instrument, our faithful House Master Afanasii Ziukin. Our eternal gratitude to you, our precious Afanasii Stepanovich, for your fidelity to duty and devotion to the tsarist house.'

'Yes, dear Afanasii, we are most pleased indeed at you,' Her Imperial Majesty echoed, smiling at me and as usual confusing the difficult Russian words.

I noticed that despite the period of mourning the small diamond bouquet was glimmering radiantly on the tsarina's breast.

'Approach, Afanasii Stepanovich,' the sovereign said in a solemn voice. 'I wish you to be aware that the Romanovs know how to value and reward selfless service.'

I took three steps forward, inclined my head respectfully and fixed my eyes on His Majesty's gleaming lacquered boots.

'For the first time in the history of the tsarist house and in contravention of an ancient rule, we are elevating you to the high rank of master of the chamber and appointing you to manage the entire staff of court servants,' the tsar declared.

I bowed even lower. Only yesterday such incredible advancement would have set my head spinning and I would have thought myself the very happiest of mortals, but now my numbed feelings did not respond at all to the joyful news.

And the outpouring of imperial grace and favour was not yet over.

'In exchange for the contents of a certain casket, which, thanks to you, have been returned to the tsarina –' I thought I detected a crafty note in the emperor's voice at this point '– we confer on you a diamond snuffbox with our monogram and a gratuity from our personal fund of ten thousand roubles.'

I bowed again. 'I thank you most humbly, Your Imperial Majesty.'

That completed the ceremony and I backed away behind the members of the royal family. Endlung gave me a secret wink and pulled a respectful face as if to say: such an important individual will not wish to know me now. I tried to smile at him, but I could not.

But the sovereign was already addressing the members of the

Green House. 'Poor little Mika,' he said and knitted his brows mournfully. 'A bright angel fiendishly done to death by heinous criminals. We grieve together with you, Uncle Georgie. But while not forgetting kindred feeling for one moment, let us also remember that we are not simple members of society but members of the imperial house, and for us the authority of the monarchy stands above all other things. I will say words now that might possibly seem monstrous to you, but nonetheless I am obliged to say them. Mika died and now he dwells in heaven. We were not able to save him. But the honour and reputation of the Romanovs has been saved. This appalling event has not become public, and that is the most important thing. I am certain, Uncle Georgie, that this thought will help you to cope with your grief as a father. Despite all the shocks and disturbances, the coronation was completed without disruption ... Almost without disruption,' the sovereign added and frowned, obviously recalling the trouble at Khodynsk Field. This qualification rather spoiled the impression of a little speech imbued with true majesty.

Georgii Alexandrovich weakened the effect still further when he said in a low voice: 'We'll see what you say about paternal feelings, Nicky, when you have children of your own ...'

Xenia Georgievna came up to me in the corridor, put her arms round me without saying anything, rested her head on my shoulder and let her tears flow. I stood quite still, only stroking Her Highness's hair cautiously.

Eventually the grand princess straightened up, looked up at me and asked in surprise: 'Afanasii, why aren't you crying? Good Lord, what has happened to your face?'

I did not understand what she meant and turned my head to glance in the mirror hanging on the opposite wall.

It was a perfectly normal face, except that it was rather stiff.

'Did you tell him what I said?' Xenia Georgievna whispered, sobbing. 'Did you say that I love him?'

'Yes,' I replied after hesitating for a moment. I had not immediately realised what she meant.

'And what did he say?' Her Highness's eyes, wet with tears, gazed at me with hope and fear. 'Did he send me anything?'

I shook my head. 'No, only this.' I took the opal earrings and diamond brooch out of my pocket. 'He said he did not want them.'

Xenia Georgievna squeezed her eyes shut for a moment but no longer. After all, Her Highness had been taught self-control since she was a child. And now there were no more tears running down her delicate cheeks.

'Thank you, Afanasii,' she said in a quiet voice.

Her Highness's voice sounded as weary as if she were not nineteen but at least forty.

I went out onto the veranda. I was suddenly having difficulty breathing. Clouds had settled over Moscow earlier in the evening. There was clearly going to be a thunderstorm that night.

I had a strange feeling. Fate and monarchal favour had showered fabulous gifts on me and elevated me to a height of which I had never even dreamed, but I felt as if I had lost everything I possessed, and lost it forever. The wind rustled across the treetops in the Neskuchny Park, setting the leaves trembling, and for some reason I suddenly remembered Endlung's suggestion that I should join the navy. I imagined the clear horizon, the foaming crests of the waves, the fresh breath of the sea breeze. Sheer nonsense, of course.

Mr Freyby came out through the glass doors. He had not had an easy time of it during the last few days either. He had been left alone without any masters. He had been held under serious suspicion, subjected to hours of interrogation, and now, together with the luggage, he would take back to England a lead coffin containing the body of Mr Carr.

However, none of these ordeals had left any mark at all on the English butler. He looked as phlegmatic and benign as ever.

He gave me an affable nod and stood beside me, leaning on

the railings. He lit his pipe. This was company that suited me perfectly, since with Mr Freyby it was entirely possible to remain silent without the slightest feeling of awkwardness.

A line of carriages drew up at the entrance. Everyone would start going home now.

Their Majesties began walking down from the porch, accompanied by members of the imperial family. On the final step the sovereign stumbled and almost fell. Kirill Alexandrovich just managed to grab his nephew in time.

Beside his tall stately uncles, His Majesty looked entirely unimpressive, like a Scottish pony among a herd of thoroughbred racehorses. Of all the Romanovs, for some reason the Lord had chosen this one to lay on his feeble shoulders the heavy burden of responsibility for the fate of the monarchy.

The regal couple climbed into their carriage. The grand dukes saluted and Xenia Georgievna sank into a curtsey. Her Highness looked proud and haughty, as befits a princess.

For the sake of the imperial audience I had decked myself out in the green livery with gold braid. For the last time, as it turned out. Something was weighing down the side pocket. I absent-mindedly stuck my hand in and felt a book. Ah yes, the Russian–English lexicon, a present from Mr Freyby.

I wondered what the perspicacious Englishman thought of the Russian tsar.

I leafed though the pages and put together a question: 'Vot yu sink ebaut nyu tsar?'

Mr Freyby watched the gilded landau with footmen of the chamber on the monkey boards as it drove away. He shook his head and said: 'The last of the Romanovs, I'm afraid.'

He also took out a dictionary – English–Russian – and muttered to himself: 'The article is out ... "Last" is *posledny*. Right ... "of" is *iz* ...' And with unassailable confidence he declared, clearly enunciating each word: '*Posledny – iz – Romanov.*'